Kierkegaard in the Pulpit: Sermons Inspired by His Writings, adds over twenty-five more sermons to Marshall's already published collection in *Kierkegaard for the Church*. They cover all of the major themes in Christianity—from repentance in the Parable of the Prodigal Son, to joy in the Christmas story—showing that Kierkegaard's severe understanding of the Christian faith can indeed be preached in its full splendor to the ordinary congregation. All these sermons were preached at his church in Seattle. Included also is a preface on the atonement, essays on Judaism, judgment, Postmodernism, criticism and the Mary and Martha story, and the parable on the Lilies and the Birds.

Ronald F. Marshall is the author of the acclaimed *Kierkegaard for the Church: Essays and Sermons* (Wipf & Stock, 2013). He has been the pastor at First Lutheran Church of West Seattle since 1979, where he and his wife, Jane L. Harty, live. They have three grown children: Susannah, Ruth, and Anders.

Praise for *Kierkegaard for the Church*

"I greatly appreciate the way in which Marshall's treatment of Kierkegaard's understanding of Christianity exculpates his teaching from . . . a subjectivist reductionism . . . . Marshall has mined out of Kierkegaard voluminous authorship many assertions of orthodox Christianity, particularly those that bear on Christology, the way of salvation, and obedient discipleship."
—**Carl E. Braaten,** Professor Emeritus, Lutheran School of Theology in Chicago

"Marshall's gathering of his scattered published essays creates a high water mark in Kierkegaard research."
—**Robert L. Perkins,** General Editor, *International Kierkegaard Commentary*, 26 vols.

"My copy of this book, with all of its markings, is now a family treasure to be left to my daughter, Silvie, to be read when she gets older. I've made notes in it . . . to help her focus on . . . what I believe are the foundational, 'light bulb' parts of Christianity . . . . And it's full of them—which are the guts of Luther, Kierkegaard and Pastor Marshall!"
—**Rollie Storbakken,** Member of First Lutheran Church of West Seattle & retired iron worker

"In *The Nature and Destiny of Man*, Reinhold Niebuhr drew on Kierkegaard for his devastating analysis of diverse forms of pride. Marshall presents Kierkegaard offering perhaps an even more copious critique of human selfishness and arrogance."
—**Paul R. Sponheim,** Professor Emeritus, Luther Seminary, Saint Paul, Minnesota

"Marshall's book brings into clear focus much appreciated structure and commentary to Kierkegaard's writings. It is dense with ideas and thought, and can rightly be described as a distillation. It reads very slowly like native Kierkegaard, but you never wind up getting lost or wondering what happened. For me this book will go in my library right next to Hofstadler's Pulitzer Prize winning, *Gödel, Escher, Bach: An Eternal Golden Braid* —for re-reading about every six years."
—**Ben Johnson**, member of St. Andrew's Lutheran Church, Bellevue, Washington

"Marshall . . . takes Kierkegaard's criticisms of the Danish church and emphasis on individual engagement with the religion into pragmatic sermons and essays on the philosopher's role in churches today."
—**Washington State Magazine**

"Marshall, writing on Kierkegaard's feisty, prophetic spirit in *Kierkegaard for the Church*, asks how his words about Christianity change the way we learn and practice the Christian faith today."
--**Curtis L. Thompson,** Professor of Religion, Thiel College, Greenville, Pennsylvania

洞月亮

CAVE MOON PRESS
YAKIMA 中 WASHINGTON

2016

Kierkegaard in the Pulpit:

Sermons Inspired by His Writings

Ronald F. Marshall

月亮
CAVE MOON PRESS
YAKIMA 中 WASHINGTON

Kierkegaard in the Pulpit:
Sermons Inspired by His Writings

Copyright © 2016 by Ronald F. Marshall
Copyright © 2014 "The Hotel Kierkegaard" p. 393—Heather Hudson
Copyright © 2003 "In the House of Martha and Mary" p. 351—Eileen Kennedy

Reider Thomte photograph p. 352, courtesy of Concordia College Archives, Moorhead, Minnesota

All rights reserved. This book or any portion thereof may not be reproduced or used in any manner whatsoever without the express written permission of the publisher except for the use of brief quotations in a book review.

Printed in the United States of America

First Printing, 2016

ISBN: 978-0-6927-4984-5

Library of Congress Control Number: 2016917142

Dedicated to

First Lutheran Church of West Seattle
(est. 1918)

In Memoriam

Martin Luther
(1483-1546)

"*O, Luther is still the master of us all.*"
(JP 2:2465)

"*[Christ's] kingdom is based on speaking; therefore He must suffer every kind of interruption and much of it, so that there is an eternal quarreling in words and preaching.*"
(LW 20:203)

Contents

Figures	xiii
Epigram	
Kierkegaard's Wild Birds	xiv
Kierkegaard's Writings	
Abbreviation Index	xv
Acknowledgements	xviii
Preface: Preaching the Atonement	xx
Introduction: The Bottleneck	xxxvi
Chapter 1: On Judging Others	1
Chapter 2: Sermons	23
Sermon 1: Take the Test	27
Sermon 2: Endure	39
Sermon 3: Don't Doubt	51
Sermon 4: Fight Depression	63
Sermon 5: Be Doers of the Word	75
Sermon 6: Serve	86
Sermon 7: Hate Yourself	97
Sermon 8: Hate Yourself–Again	108
Sermon 9: Thank God Rightly	119
Sermon 10: Trust in the Serpent	131
Sermon 11: Don't Be Surprised	142
Sermon 12: Pray for Servants	154
Sermon 13: Rejoice in the Remnant	165
Sermon 14: Stand Firm	177
Sermon 15: Come to Your Senses	183
Sermon 16: Stick to the Bible	195
Sermon 17: Labor for Love	202
Sermon 18: Rejoice at Christmas	209

Sermon 19: Welcome Saint Stephen at Christmas	216
Sermon 20: Do Your Duty	222
Sermon 21: Prepare Yourselves	228
Sermon 22: Glorify the Cross	240
Sermon 23: Rejoice in Christ's Victory	247
Sermon 24: Follow Saint Philip	254
Sermon 25: Overthrow the World!	265
Sermon 26: Fear the Fires of Hell	272
Sermon 27: Long for Christ's Return	283
Appendix One: On Judaism	290
Appendix Two: On *Kierkegaard for the Church*	314
Appendix Three: On Postmodernism	318
Appendix Four: On Mary & Martha	331
Appendix Five: On Daphne Hampson	352
Appendix Six: On the Lilies and the Birds	366
Conclusion: Old Christianity	380
Postscript: The Hotel Kierkegaard	388
About the Author	395
Index	397

Figures

Jaroslav Pelikan Letter	li
Pegasus Coin	29
Human Skulls	221
Christ in Limbo	253
Luther at Sixty-three	313
Hipster Jesus	323
The Lamentation of Christ	330
Icon of Mary and Martha	351
In the House of Martha and Mary	351
Daphne Hampson	352
Reidar Thomte	352
The Flagellation of Christ	386
The Hotel Kierkegaard	393

Epigram

Kierkegaard's Wild Birds

"The point in the whole thing is this: there is a zenith of Christianity in ethical rigorousness and this must at least be heard. But no more. It must be left to everyone's conscience to decide whether he is capable of building the tower so high. But heard it must be. But the trouble is simply that practically all Christendom and all the clergy, too, live not only in secular prudence at best but also in such a way that they brazenly boast about it and as a consequence must interpret the life of Christ to be fanaticism. This is why the other must be heard, heard if possible as a voice in the clouds, heard as the flight of wild birds over the heads of the tame ones." (JP 6:6445)[1]

---

[1] Like unto this wildness, note the mythological "divine night [with its] mysteries of the forest, the madness of the underworld, the lunacy of the moon, the weird road, the wildness of the deer and the whale, the descent, the dive of the genius away from rationality, [and] the ecstasy of art." Robert Bly, "The City & the Forest," in Daniel Deardorff, *The Other Within: The Genius of Deformity in Myth, Culture & Psyche* (East Montpelier, Vermont: Heaven & Earth Publishing, 2009) p. xiii.

Abbreviations

Kierkegaard's Writings

BA: *The Book on Adler*, trans. Howard V. Hong and Edna H. Hong. Princeton: Princeton University Press, 1998.

CA: *The Concept of Anxiety*, trans. Reidar Thomte in collaboration with Albert B. Anderson. Princeton: Princeton University Press, 1978.

CD: *Christian Discourses*, trans. Howard V. Hong and Edna H. Hong. Princeton: Princeton University Press, 1997.

COR: *The Corsair Affair*, trans. Howard V. Hong and Edna H. Hong. Princeton: Princeton University Press, 1982.

CUP: *Concluding Unscientific Postscript*, two volumes, trans. Howard V. Hong and Edna H. Hong. Princeton: Princeton University Press, 1992.

EO: *Either/Or*, two volumes, trans. Howard V. Hong and Edna H. Hong. Princeton: Princeton University Press, 1987.

EUD: *Eighteen Upbuilding Discourses*, trans. Howard V. Hong and Edna H. Hong. Princeton: Princeton University Press, 1990.

FSE: *For Self-Examination* and *Judge For Yourself!*, trans. Howard V. Hong and Edna H. Hong. Princeton: Princeton University Press, 1990.

FT: *Fear and Trembling* and *Repetition*, trans. Howard V. Hong and Edna H. Hong. Princeton: Princeton University Press, 1983.

JFY: *Judge For Yourself!* and *For Self-Examination*, trans. Howard V. Hong and Edna H. Hong. Princeton: Princeton University Press, 1990.

JP: *Soren Kierkegaard's Journals and Papers*, 7 vols., ed. trans. Howard V. Hong and Edna H. Hong, assisted by Gregor Malantschuk. Bloomington and London: Indiana University Press, 1, 1967; 2, 1970; 3 and 4, 1975; 5-7, 1978.

PC: *Practice in Christianity*, trans. Howard V. Hong and Edna H. Hong. Princeton: Princeton University Press, 1991.

PF: *Philosophical Fragments*, trans. Howard V. Hong and Edna H. Hong. Princeton: Princeton University Press, 1985.

PV: *The Point of View*, trans. Howard V. Hong and Edna H. Hong. Princeton: Princeton University Press, 1995.

R: *Repetition* and *Fear and Trembling*, trans. Howard V. Hong and Edna H. Hong. Princeton: Princeton University Press, 1983.

SUD: *The Sickness unto Death*, trans. Howard V. Hong and Edna H. Hong. Princeton: Princeton University Press, 1980.

TA: *Two Ages*, trans. Howard V. Hong and Edna H. Hong. Princeton: Princeton University Press, 1978.

TDIO: *Two Discourses on Imagined Occasions*, trans. Howard V. Hong and Edna H. Hong. Princeton: Princeton University Press, 1993.

TM: *The Moment and Late Writings*, trans. Howard V. Hong and Edna H. Hong. Princeton: Princeton University Press, 1998.

UDVS: *Upbuilding Discourses in Various Spirits*, trans. Howard V. Hong and Edna H. Hong. Princeton: Princeton University Press, 1993.

WA: *Without Authority*, trans. Howard V. Hong and Edna H. Hong. Princeton: Princeton University Press, 1997.

WL: *Works of Love*, trans. Howard V. Hong and Edna H. Hong. Princeton: Princeton University Press, 1995.

OTHER WRITINGS

BC: *The Book of Concord* (1580), ed. T. Tappert, Philadelphia: Fortress, 1959.

IKC: *International Kierkegaard Commentary*, 24 volumes, ed. Robert L. Perkins, Macon, Georgia, 1984–2010.

LHP: *Sermons of Martin Luther: The House Postils*, 3 vols., ed. E. F. A. Klug, Grand Rapids: Baker Books, 1996.

KJV: *The Bible: Authorized King James Version with Apocrypha*, ed. Robert Carroll, Stephen Prickett. Oxford: Oxford University Press, 1998, 2008.

LW: *Luther's Works*, American Edition, 55 vols., ed. Jaroslav Pelikan (1-30), Helmut T. Lehmann (31-54) and the Index by Joel W. Lundeen (55), Saint Louis and Philadelphia: Concordia and Fortress, 1955–1986. And ed. Christopher Boyd Brown (58–60, 67–69, 75–77), Saint Louis: Concordia, 2009–2015.

RSV: *The New Oxford Annotated Bible With the Apocrypha: Revised Standard Version, Containing the Second Edition of the New Testament*, ed. Herbert G. May and Bruce M. Metzger. New York: Oxford University. 1973.

SML: *Sermons of Martin Luther* (1906–1909), 8 vols., ed. John N. Lenker. Grand Rapids: Baker Book House, 1988.

Acknowledgements

The following sections of this book were previously published. Grateful acknowledgement is given to the original publishers for permission to republish these essays and sermons in this single volume. Changes have been made throughout to these chapters—some more than others. Their original titles, noting where and when they were first published, are listed below:

Chapter One: "Judging One Another," *Lutheran Commentator* 7 (March/April 1994): 6, and "Judging Rightly," *The Messenger: Newsletter of First Lutheran Church of West Seattle*, November 1998.

Sermon 1: "Take the Test," *Lutheran Forum Online*, posted June 2, 2009.

Sermon 14: "Stand Firm," *Lutheran Forum Online*, posted November 25, 2010.

Sermon 16: "Stick to the Bible," *Word Alone Online*, posted March 3, 2011.

Sermon 19: "Welcome Saint Stephen at Christmas," *Logia Online (Blogia)*, posted December 20, 2011.

Appendix One: "Luther's Alleged Anti-Semitism," *Logia: Journal of Lutheran Theology*, 21 (Reformation 2012): 5–8.

Appendix Two: "Helping Out My Daughter," *The Messenger: Newsletter of First Lutheran Church of West Seattle*, February 2014.

I would also like to thank my church, First Lutheran Church of West Seattle, for allowing me time to work on this book. I dedicate it to them—where all the sermons were first preached. Thanks also to Sonja Clemente for helping prepare portions of this book for publication.

Acknowledgements

I also thank Jane L. Harty, Jeff Sagmoen, and Philip M. Nesvig, for proof-reading the entire manuscript and helping me out of many a jam. Thanks as well to Bruce Kirmmse for his critique of appendix six on the lilies and the birds.

Thanks as well go to Doug Johnson of *Cave Moon Press* for his generous and exquisite help in bringing this book to publication and for his inspired cover design. A special thanks to Jon and Alice Nelson for their financial help with the dissemination of this book.

Thanks to my wife, Jane L. Harty, who discussed with me many of these sermons after they were preached. Thanks as well go to Eileen Kennedy and Heather Hudson for their beautiful artwork. Thanks also to Ben Johnson and Dale Korsmo for keeping my computer up and runing during the writing and production of this book.

Finally I would like to thank God for inspiring me and strengthening me in the writing of this book. I like Kierkegaard's prayer, in this regard, on tracing everything back to God—the author of all good gifts (Jas 1:17):

> O, my God, I am almost tempted to admire myself for what I have done—but God be praised that you help me to trace everything back to you in adoration, I who never can thank you sufficiently for the good that has been done for me, far more than I ever expected, could have expected, dared to expect. (JP 6:6671)

Preface

Preaching the Atonement

All of the sermons in this book preach the atonement of Christ because Søren Kierkegaard (1813–1855) believed in its importance.[1] Even though he was not an ordained minister, he completed his pastoral education and preached a few times at the Friday Eucharist in Copenhagen during his short life of forty-two years. And if the sermons in this book are to be inspired by his writings, then his convictions must control them.

But this will not be easy because Kierkegaard cared deeply about preachers and their sermons—thinking that neither of them were much to write home about. That was because both were without the passion that earnestness and conviction required,[2] and they also failed to lead to good

---

1   Kierkegaard thought that all of his writings "pointed definitively to 'Discourses at the Communion on Fridays' (JP 6:6407) which dwell on the atonement of Christ." Søren Kierkegaard, *Discourses at the Communion on Fridays*, trans. Sylvia Walsh (Bloomington & Indianapolis: Indiana University Press, 2011) 4, 25–30. For a biographical sketch of Kierkegaard, see Ronald F. Marshall, *Kierkegaard for the Church: Essays and Sermons* (Eugene, Oregon: Wipf & Stock, 2013), Appendix 1, Part 1, "A Dangerous Man."

2   EUD 69; BA 107; JP 3:3129, 3:3619, 6:6531. On this lack of passion, Kierkegaard tells a scathing little parable about dry old tea leaves: "Charming religiousness—just as authentic as tea made from a piece of paper which once lay in a drawer together with another piece of paper in which a few dried tea leaves had been kept, leaves which had already

works as required by the Gospel itself.³ But most of all, they were not very good because they neglected the atonement—or the crucifixion of Christ Jesus—which is at the heart of Christianity (CD 289, JFY 147).⁴ For Kierkegaard fervently believed that Jesus was the one stricken, smitten by God and afflicted in Isaiah 53:4–5⁵—as the New Testament says he was.⁶

---

been used three times . . . . [And] if one wanted to point out the difference, it is that with respect to tea men would say: Thank you for this, but if you have stronger tea I would be grateful for it. But with respect to Christianity man's interest is precisely in getting it as thin as possible; he is not grateful for getting it stronger but shields himself against this" (JP 4:4722–23).

3   JP 2:1883, 3:2334, 3:3525, 5:5634, 6:6717.

4   See also JP 1:983, 2:1909, 2:2139. For a fuller discussion of Kierkegaard's view on the atonement, see Ronald F. Marshall, *Kierkegaard for the Church*, 9–20, 212, 218. There I make three points: [1] Kierkegaard's view depends on Luther's catechism, [2] the point of Kierkegaard's view on the atonement is to show how divine wrath is overcome, and [3] his view does not obstruct, but rather reinforces the believer's ethical striving.

5   On a similar passage in Genesis 22, see "Sacrifice of Isaac," *The Christian Century* (June 15, 2014): 47: "Christian interpreters from the patristic period (if not earlier, see Hebrews 11:17) had interpreted the story typologically. Melito of Sardis, for example wrote: 'For as a ram [Christ] was bound . . . and he carried the wood upon his shoulders. And he was led up to be slain like Isaac by his Father. But Christ suffered, whereas Isaac did not [die]' (Fragment 9–11)."

6   See Acts 8:32–35, 1 Pt 2:24, Mt 8:17. The New Testament also teaches that this sacrifice was necessary [δει] in order for God to forgive us (Mt 16:21; Lk 24:26; Jn 12:34; Acts 17:3). Kierkegaard may have been encouraged by Martin Luther in this regard. See his Commentary on Isaiah 53 (1544): "Christ does not die in order to be reduced to ashes, but to fill the whole earth with righteousness, salvation, and life, and to reestablish the kingdom of heaven. He did not die in order to perish, but to give his life for our sins, to be . . . an expiation for our sins. The will of God was that he be victim, reconciliation, ransom, redemption, price of our sins. For the wrath of God could not be appeased or put off except by so great a victim, namely the Son of God who could not sin.

This substitutionary view of Christ's death on the cross is at the center of all of the sermons in this book[7]—even though it has been balked at from the beginning by many from within the church.[8]

Charles Hefling has recently added his voice to this relentless cascade of criticism against the atonement. He opposes, argues against, and finally rejects what Kierkegaard believed to be true—namely that

> God is just.[9] Justice, divine or human, requires that wrongdoers, whose wrongdoing makes them liable to punishment, should be

---

There was no other sacrifice by which God could be appeased, other than this victim who gave his life." Quoted in Marc Linehard, *Luther: Witness to Jesus Christ* (1973), trans. Edwin H. Robertson (Minneapolis: Augsburg, 1982) 363.

7 See Sylvia Walsh, "Kierkegaard's Theology," *The Oxford Handbook of Kierkegaard*, ed. John Lippitt and George Pattison (Oxford: Oxford University Press, 2013) 299: "Among the several theories of atonement in the Christian tradition, a variant of the Latin or legal theory of Anselm is clearly dominant in Kierkegaard's theology."

8 On this persistent assault, see Adonis Vidu, *Atonement, Law, and Justice: The Cross in Historical and Cultural Context* (Grand Rapids, Michigan: Baker Academic, 2014), and Inna Jane Ray, *Atonement Muddle: An Historical Analysis and Clarification of a Salvation Theory* (Berkeley, California, 1997, 2013). Note also the more benign assault in the 2014 student brochure for Lutheran Campus Ministry at the University of Washington in Seattle, Washington: "We believe that God came to the world in the form of Jesus Christ so that we could learn how to better follow God, so that we might . . . know we are loved and so that God might have a better understanding of what it is to be human." What is missing from this credo is Acts 2:23: "Jesus [was] delivered up [to death on a cross] according to the definite plan and foreknowledge of God." This sacrifice of Jesus Christ to God the Father (Eph 5:2; Heb 9:14) is the indispensable "means," as Luther put it in his *Large Catechism* (1529), by which "redemption was accomplished" (BC 414).

9 See Is 61:8; Ez 18:25; Rom 3:5; 1 Jn 1:9.

punished.¹⁰ Humans, one and all, are sinners.¹¹ As such they incur a penalty, which in justice ought to be paid and which has, in fact, been paid—not, however, by those who owe it and deserve to pay it, but by Jesus.¹² The verdict never changed.¹³ Sinners are guilty. But because he died, the sentence has been suspended for everyone else. Instead of punishing, God pardons.¹⁴ That is the good news.¹⁵

Hefling cannot abide by this view because he says it is incoherent.¹⁶ And he draws three conclusions from this view.

---

10 See Lv 26:14–17; Rom 2:5.
11 See Is 53:6; Rom 3:23.
12 See Rom 8:4.
13 See Eph 2:3.
14 See Rom 5:9.
15 Charles Hefling, "Why the Cross?" *The Christian Century* (March 20, 2013): 24–27. Even though Hefling opposes this view, he knows that there is "much to be said for [it]. For one thing, it supplies a comprehensible link between Christ's suffering and a beneficial result, forgiveness. . . . For another thing, it gives God all the credit, . . . it is altogether an amazing, gracious gift. And for yet another and perhaps the most important thing, [it] is not just conceivable but imaginable . . . .[Its] speech is framed not in cool theological abstractions, . . . but in vivid, moving affect-laden narrative images . . . . [Its] appeal is emotional, imaginative, existential . . . . I can picture Christ taking my place, enduring the pains I ought to have felt, and my imagination of how deeply he suffered, brings home to me how great the penalty is that I have been spared." Even so, "it does not follow that the criterion of credibility for a claim is whether it packs a visceral punch . . . . The standard account of atonement, for all its affective effectiveness, might be like that—convincing, but only until you start to think about it [and then] upon examination its implications [become] intellectually bogus or morally repulsive."
16 See also Adam Gopnik, "Bigger Than Phil: When Did Faith Start to

The first is that Christ's vicarious suffering for sinners makes no sense because guilt "in the relevant sense is not the sort of thing that can be siphoned out of one person and into another. Nor is it any better to argue that punishing the innocent, though admittedly wrong as a rule, can in exceptional cases be just, provided it serves to 'send a message' that dramatizes the heinousness of disobedience in order to deter those who might be inclined to disobey. There is a name for that: terrorism."

Next he says that this view is too impersonal—giving rewards and punishments out to those who have not personally earned or deserved them. Indeed, we "disappear like ants," Kierkegaard would say, because in redemption what matters most happens high above us in "divine combat of divine passion with itself" (JP 1:532).[17] And third, there is no positive good

---

Fade?" *The New Yorker* (February 17 and 24, 2014): 111: "Some people of great sensibility and intelligence [like] Elizabeth Bishop, William Empson, and Wallace Stevens, . . . recoil at the idea of a universe set up as a game of blood sacrifice and eternal torture, or even with the promise of eternal bliss not easily distinguishable from eternal boredom. They find a universe of matter, pleasure, and community-made morality the only kind of life possible, and the only kind worth living."

17 Kierkegaard, however, does not see this to be a weakness. In this combat God overturns his wrath against sinners because of the suffering and death of his only begotten Son, Jesus Christ. And so in paganism, "man propitiates his gods, and religion becomes a form of commercialism and, indeed, of bribery. In Christianity, however, God propitiates his wrath by his own action . . . . It was not man, to whom God was hostile, who took the initiative to make God friendly, nor was it Jesus Christ, the eternal Son, who took the initiative to turn his Father's wrath against us into love. The idea that the kind Son changed the mind of his unkind Father by offering himself in place of sinful man is no part of the gospel message—it is a sub-Christian, indeed an anti-Christian idea, for it denies the unity of will in the Father and the Son and so in reality falls back into polytheism, asking us to believe in two different gods. But the Bible rules this out absolutely by insisting that it was God himself who took the initiative in quenching his own

in this view of redemption, since it is based on the cancellation of a debt, which is nothing but "a double negative" that simply takes "away the taking away." Forgiveness, however, is more than that—it is about changing "both the forgiver and the forgiven"—something which a double negative cannot do.

In response to this attack, we could see Kierkegaard bolstering the atonement by what he wrote in his journal. There Kierkegaard begins epistemologically, noting how an anguished conscience is required for any proper understanding of the atonement. This is one of his central points regarding the atonement, and so he passionately writes:

> Remove the anguished conscience, and you may as well lock the churches and convert them into dance halls. The anguished conscience understands Christianity. In the same way an animal understands when you lay a stone and a piece of bread before it and the animal is hungry: the animal understands that one is for eating and the other is not. The anguished conscience understands Christianity. If we first have to prove the necessity of being hungry before we eat—well, then eating becomes finicky. But you say, "I still cannot grasp the Atonement." Here I must ask in which understanding—in the understanding of the anguished conscience or in the understanding of indifferent and objective speculation. How could anyone

wrath against those who, despite their ill-dessert, he loved and had chosen to save." J. I. Packer and Mark Dever, *In My Place Condemned He Stood: Celebrating the Glory of the Atonement* (Wheaton, Illinois: Crossways Books, 2007) 36. See also *Kierkegaard for the Church*, 13n46 on Hosea 11:8.

> sitting placidly and objectively in his study and speculating ever be able to understand the necessity of an atonement, since an atonement is necessary only in the understanding of anguished conscience. If a man had the power to live without needing to eat, how could he understand the necessity of eating—something the hungry man easily understands. It is the same in the life of the spirit. A man can acquire the indifference which renders the Atonement superfluous—yes, the natural man is actually in this situation, but how could someone in this situation be able to understand the Atonement? .... [Therefore] man must be taught by a revelation concerning how deeply he lies in sin.
>
> (JP 3:2461)

In this passage Kierkegaard makes three points that stand against Hefling's criticism. The first one has to do with the special way in which an anguished conscience can grasp the atonement. Such a person has a deep yearning to be rescued from the dread of damnation—and therefore "feels a need" for the atonement, as Kierkegaard would say (JP 4:4016). "On the whole [then] one cannot truly speak of Christianity without perpetual self-accusation" (JP 1:108).[18] For "becoming a Christian is a life-and-death battle, a protracted life-and-death struggle, full of the most dreadful episodes (which dying to the world, corresponding to dying, naturally must be)" (JP

---

18 On this battle against the self, Kierkegaard adds: "When Christianity entered the world, the depravity against which it had to battle most directly was in the sphere of carnal lusts and cravings, wild unbridled passions, [and] the animality in man" (JP 6:6911).

6:6681).[19] But if no such calamity is plausible, then a rescue of this sort is out of the question and the atoning death of Jesus comes off as pointless—for the "situation is certainly different if it is a matter of an eternal perdition, of being saved from it by another who suffers the punishment of death for me" (JP 2:1936).[20] Even so, "most people do not have the need to have [such a] need developed" (JP 5:6016). With the majority, then, the atonement goes begging. And that is because of the loss of the presupposition of the anguished conscience—without which the sacrificial death of Jesus Christ makes no sense. So to fail to find the Atonement understandable, comes from

---

19 Dwelling on sin in this manner is frowned upon by many American Christians today. But when that happens, there is a terrible cost to pay, for grace is then "eviscerated in [these sermons when we] fail to acknowledge notions of human depravity and separation from a transcendent God." Marsha G. Witten, *All Is Forgiven: The Secular Message in American Protestantism* (Princeton, New Jersey: Princeton University Press, 1994) 140. See also Matt Jenson, *The Gravity of Sin* (London and New York: T & T Clark, 2006) 2: "[To] speak of humanity as sinful [is] something which has been all too often sidelined in contemporary theological anthropology." Note, however, his softening conclusion: "We may not say less than that sin catapults one into the wrong orbit—oneself—and represents [a] kind of stultifying, isolating, self-aggrandizing *and* self-diminishing posture. While we are wary of adopting a gendered account of sin due to its descriptive poverty and extra-biblical grammar, we must listen carefully to feminist accounts of the ways in which pride-based harmartiologies have served to lock women into structures of oppression and even insinuate slothful postures among women. In other words, the way we speak about sin can quickly become itself sinful in its underwriting and prescribing of certain forms of sin" (186–87).

20 Kierkegaard adds this about how disturbing hell is: "To believe that there is a hell, that others go to hell—and then get married, beget children, live in a parsonage, think about getting a bigger parish, etc.—that is frightful egotism. But the [New Testament] is not like that. Anyone who believes that there is a hell, that others go to hell, is *eo ipso* a missionary, that is the least he can do" (JP 6:6851).

ignoring its necessary presupposition.

Next Kierkegaard notes that we do not *naturally* possess this necessary presupposition. Therefore the Christian cannot settle in with what comes naturally—snatching "at finite consolations closer at hand," as Kierkegaard says (JP 5:5896). No, "human nature cannot carry Christianity; it always reverses the relationship, evades the demand, avoids what Christianity really is . . . . This means that Christianity, instead of being in the divine egoity, is adroitly shifted into human egotism" (JP 3:3779). Therefore Kierkegaard insists that we must "die to being human in the ordinary sense," for Christianity is "heterogeneous with what is naturally understood to be man" (JP 6:6616, 6932). And so a Christians pastor must not be a "mild and kind-hearted and nice man. No, the best thing would be for him to make preliminary studies in a penitentiary—but even this is hardly adequate" (JP 4:4983).

And Kierkegaard's last point in this above quoted passage is that we will need to be shown by God himself just how bad off we are if we ever are going to see the need for the atonement. For "in the Atonement it is precisely the consciousness of sin that leads us closer to God," according to Kierkegaard—and so sin's every assault is designed to "only lead us closer to God" (JP 4:4011). The "basic evil of the age [then] is that . . . it secularizes and finitizes every higher endeavor—that is, it denies that a higher endeavor truly exists" (JP 6:6859). For indeed, man "is a fallen spirit" (JP 6:6881). We are trapped in our "body of sin, [which is] the whole apparatus of the prison [we] have had to bear" (JP 6:6898). Because of the devastation sin brings into our lives,[21] it "must be struggled against with all the combative power one has" (JP 6:6468). Otherwise we will be like the fool who

---

21 See Ecc 9:18.

substitutes the artistic for decisive Christianity; for Christian dignity he substitutes the most beautiful and spellbinding edition of human distinction; he substitutes the most refined prudential concerns and considerations for Christian venturesomeness, the most tasteful worldly culture for Christian heterogeneity with the world, a rare, uniquely refined enjoyment of this world and this life for renunciation and self-denial. (JP 6:6844)

As a consequence, the atonement ends up sounding meaningless. But when Kierkegaard exposes Hefling's waywardness, his criticisms all fall flat.

They are also deflated because they presuppose that the atonement gets us off the hook altogether. But Kierkegaard questions this in a couple of ways. First he argues that even though Jesus suffers in our place, we still have to suffer in this life. For atonement does not mean that God "simply . . . waives every punishment but that the sufferer now suffers his punishment in an entirely different way because he knows that he is reconciled with God." And so it is "a crass misunderstanding to think that atonement should exempt one from punishment." What instead is the case is that "the spiritual consolation in the forgiveness of sins [and atonement] is that the sinner gains the confident courage to dare to believe that God is gracious toward him, although he still suffers his punishment. But this is a genuine transubstantiation with regard to punishment" (JP 3:3637). Indeed it is. And it is needed because Christ's suffering calls us to join in with him at our level. Without it, Christianity becomes inherently unbalanced:

> Thus from generation to generation Christianity in the Church has been transformed egotistically into something more and more according to man's interest: the Atonement makes imitation into a nothing, or we completely cheat our way out of imitation. Then Christendom more and more develops a bad conscience, and the thought that to relate oneself to God should mean suffering becomes completely foreign; and the very opposite—success and prosperity—becomes the sign of being related to God—and then Christianity is abolished.
>
> (JP 2:1911)

But this is not as it should be—for out of thanksgiving to God for the atonement, we must not allow the "boundlessness of [the] Atonement [to stifle] the childlike which simply and in a childlike way wants to do what it can as well as possible, [but] always with God's permission, please note," he adds (JP 2:1469). And this should happen even though we also know that at "the moment of death," when we "stand before God," all our striving and suffering with Christ "will be sheer paltriness."[22] But still we do not flee from suffering because the Christian holds that it would be absolutely "detestable... to want to use grace... to avoid all striving" (JP 2:1909).

And secondly we need to strive to live righteous lives even though Christ has died for us. And this is because "out

---

22 Kierkegaard adds to this devaluation of striving: "Christ's Atonement... transforms the little I do almost into a jest; whether I reform the whole world or as a hired man care for my job, it is one and the same, for Christ's Atonement is infinitely everything" (JP 2:2139).

of joy over the reconciliation comes an honest striving.... Consequently, faith first of all. It is not by a good life, good works, and the like that one achieves faith. No, it is faith which works that one does truly good works" (JP 1:983). So if imitation, striving to follow Christ, and suffering with Jesus, are completely excluded, then "grace is taken in vain. [For imitation] there must be, but not in such a way that one becomes self-important" (JP 2:1877). Because this suffering to which the Christian is called is so arduous, the benefits of the atonement are necessary to aid and abet that very suffering, imitation, and following of Christ. "The fact that satisfaction was not made would continually torment [the Christian] and disturb his bliss" (JP 2:1423):

> [For when] this infinite grace was proclaimed to him, he was also told: Now begins a new life ...Now he is supposed to begin. Introduce now the requirement of the ideal—and remember it was a completely new life he should begin—[but] in that very moment he is unable to lift a finger.... Consequently, the moment he shuts the door of grace, as it were, and goes out full of holy resolve to begin a new life, alas, blissfully stirred by the thought that now all is forgiven and he will never get into that situation again—that very same minute, that very same second, he is on the way to new guilt—in the form of "the best he can do." In that same moment he must return again and knock on the door of grace. He must say: O, infinite grace, have mercy on me for being here again so soon and having to plead for grace, for now

> I understand that in order to have peace and rest, in order not to perish in hopeless despair, in order to be able to breathe and in order to be able to exist at all, I need grace not only for the past but grace for the future . . . . Here, alas, is the difficulty. Measured by the criterion of "imitation," the first step in my future will again make me in need of the Atoner—indeed, I cannot even make a beginning because I am stifled by anxiety. (JP 2:1919)

So even the struggling and suffering and striving to be like Christ cannot be done without the grace that is there in the atonement of Christ.

God does not save sinners through Christ in order to send us out on our own to live righteous lives all by ourselves. Saying so would falsify the New Testament and misrepresent Kierkegaard's discourses—falsely charging him with leaving out the atonement (JP 5:5991). No, Kierkegaard believed that we need God both for redemption and for imitation—for "at no time can we do without God" (CD 64).[23] Therefore "he who trusts in the atonement is greater than the most profound penitent." And that is because repentance "always entraps itself, for if it is to be the highest, the ultimate in a man, the saving factor, then it enters into a dialectic once more—whether it now is deep enough" (JP 3:3078). For indeed, if constant reference is not made to the atonement—clinging to the very cross of Christ (CD 284)[24]—then doubts run rampant for "it takes the

---

23 And so Annie Sherwood Hawks (1835–1918) rightly has us sing: "I need thee every hour, In joy or pain; Come quickly and abide, Or life is vain." *American Lutheran Hymnal* (Columbus, Ohio: The Lutheran Book Concern, 1930), Hymn 629.

24 See also JFY 134. On this clinging to the cross of Christ, see the re-

Atonement to bring [the sinner] to a halt" (JP 4:4013). Even so, Christians are not awash in peacefulness and restfulness (UDVS 218). Struggles are not completely eradicated:

> [For] men want . . . . to have an easy life. But believing in the Atonement is illustrated symbolically[25] by the Jews when they were attacked by serpents in the wilderness and Moses raised up the sign of the cross.[26] Believing in the Atonement means: bitten by serpents, while the bites pain and tempt men to think only of this and of the possibility of getting the serpents killed—then to believe. Not everyone bitten by the serpents can make up his mind or find the grace to believe the Atonement.
>
> (JP 4:4366)

---

view of Fleming Rutledge's *The Crucifixion* (2015): "Rutledge stresses that God has done and is doing [on the cross of Christ] something that we cannot do for ourselves." Anthony B. Robinson, "Crux of the Matter," *The Christian Century* (October 14, 2015) 45.

25 See John 3:14.
26 See Numbers 21:4–9.

Introduction

The Bottleneck

This book is written for those who want to see what sermons inspired by the writings of Kierkegaard would look like. It is especially for those who think this cannot be done for the ordinary congregation because what Kierkegaard wrote is too difficult to translate into a Sunday sermon in such[1] a congregation.

---

1   Some may think these sermons would find their best home in a university congregation or campus ministry. But, as counter-intuitive as it may seem, they would probably actually fare the worst there. This is because Kierkegaard would agree with Luther that "nowhere is youth more grossly corrupted and misled [than in the universities]. That they fall into fornication, gluttony, and other open wickedness is the least of their corruption; [the worst being] that they are instructed in false, heathenish art and ungodly, human doctrine.... No one can bemoan that enough, for through it the most devout and clever lads are miserably ruined in the universities.... [There they] absorb poisons of which they can never rid themselves; they hold evil to be good [Is 5:20].... All this is what accounts for the fact that the sun of the gospel is darkened and obscured by human teaching.... Since the beginning of the world even the devil himself could not have invented anything more powerful to suppress faith and the gospel than the universities." Martin Luther, "The Misuse of the Mass" (1521) LW 36:224–25. See also his famous treatise, "To the Christian Nobility" (1520) LW 44:207: "I greatly fear that the universities, unless they teach the Holy Scriptures

Kierkegaard, after all, thought that Christianity was more[2] about intensity than extensity (JP 3:2994). And he thought those two impulses oppose each other thereby creating a "bottleneck" within Christianity itself (JP 2:2056). He thought that for Christians the Crucifixion, which has to do with intensity, opposed Pentecost, which has to do with extensity and the spreading of the message to as many people as possible. At the cross Jesus was abandoned and alone, but at Pentecost, crowds of people joined in from all over the world. Intensity

---

diligently and impress them on the young students, are wide gates to hell." So universities would not be naturally receptive to these sermons but more likely hostile to them for going against their favored way of life. For an equally bleak assessment of American universities, see George M. Marsden, *The Soul of the American University: From Protestant Establishment to Established Nonbelief* (New York: Oxford University Press, 1994) 432: "In the interest of social harmony, the tendency has been to exclude from academic life all but the blandest religious views." See also in this regard, Stanley Hauerwas, *The State of the University: Academic Knowledges and the Knowledge of God* (Oxford: Blackwell Publishing, 2007) 32, 29, 7: "I obviously think that the university as we know it is in deep trouble . . . [and that it] cannot fulfill its task to teach 'universal knowledge' without the church's assistance . . . . [So given] for example, the Gospel imperative that we are to forgive enemies; what difference might that make for the practice of the law? Given that we believe that all creation glorifies God, how should we think about the attempt to reduce creation to 'nature' in the name of mechanistic explanations? These are not questions I think should or could only be asked at universities shaped by the church, but hopefully such questions should be on the agenda of any university that deserves the name university." Note also the new *cogito* of the universities: "I am talked about, therefore I am" (21n20).

2 But this does not mean Kierkegaard opposed world missions: "[We] have completely forgotten that to be a Christian means essentially to be a missionary. Christianity in repose is *eo ipso* not Christianity. As soon as anything of that sort appears, it means: become a missionary. Christianity in repose, stagnant Christianity, creates an obstruction, and this formidable obstruction is the sickness of Christendom" (JP 3:2731).

has to do with the few,[3] but extensity has to do with the many.[4] So the conflict between the two is easy to see—and therein lies the bottleneck.

This conflict between intensity and extensity makes Christianity difficult (JP 2:2056)—and this difficulty is not foreign and imposed from outside, but endemic to Christianity itself. For Christianity fosters the combination of the difficult (intensity) with the easy (extensity)—it combines kindness (extensity) with severity (intensity).[5] But our tendency as sinners is to skip the difficult part—in order to avoid the bottleneck and sail away smoothly. Against this misrepresentation, Kierkegaard worked to reestablish severity in our Christian speech and behavior.[6] He called that tough element the dialectical part of Christianity (JP 3:2873). But when it finally is reestablished, it clogs up Christianity. And this clogging, or bottleneck, is what makes preaching Christianity, in Kierkegaard's way, so difficult to do. For indeed,

---

3 See Mt 7:14: "The gate is narrow and the way is hard that leads to life, and those who find it are few" (RSV).
4 See 1 Tm 2:4: "God desires men to be saved" (RSV).
5 See Romans 11:22.
6 But even this noble undertaking is not carefree: "The tragedy is that we have brought Christianity down to our level and imagine that it is up to us to discuss whether or not we want rigorousness, while we go around thinking we still have Christianity if we do not want it so rigorous. But then I surely am mad to want to have it rigorous. Eulenspiegel [a famous peasant clown in northern Germany in the fourteenth or fifteenth century] never did find the tree he wanted for his hanging (he had bargained for permission to choose the tree himself)—so it is with rigorousness" (JP 6:6614) (JP 5, p. 469n62). Even so, Kierkegaard goes on to explain: "I had to introduce rigorousness—and introduced it simply to provide movement into Christianity's clemency. This is my understanding of Christianity and my task. If I had understood only its frightful rigorousness—I would have kept silent" (JP 6:6590).

extensity spreads and sprawls with great complacency—it generally spreads to such a degree that intensity is not permitted to slip in at all with even as much as a little bit of a dot.
(JP 6:6907)

In this book I want to show that it is possible to preach with both intensity and extensity—in spite of the complacency of extensity.

This book is also for readers of my book, *Kierkegaard for the Church*,[7] who want more than the seven sermons included there. This larger collection also has the advantage of taking up many more Christian themes than the first set of seven sermons did. This larger sampling is important because it shows that the inherent difficulties in Kierkegaard's Christian views do not restrict what can be preached on. People think that this is a problem because of Kierkegaard's blistering attack on the finite—refusing to "profit temporally by proclaiming—Christianity, which is renunciation of things temporal" (JP 6:6843). For indeed Christianity is difficult precisely because it insists upon "becoming a Christian in earnest—actually dying to the world in this life—in this life actually renouncing flesh and blood, a successful career, honor, reputation, etc." (JP 6:6475). This is a breathtaking project that looks impossible to proclaim from the pulpits of ordinary churches. It appears to be too tough to preach.[8] For indeed,

---

7   See Ronald F. Marshall, *Kierkegaard for the Church: Essays and Sermons* (Eugene, Oregon: Wipf and Stock, 2013), Foreword by Carl E. Braaten, and an Epilogue by Robert L. Perkins. For a review of this book, see Appendix Two below.

8   Nevertheless, "sometimes (often) the happy ending is heaven, and the getting there is a really difficult but formative part of sanctification. And sometimes what God wants in the interim is for us to find our happiness, holiness, and identity in Him, rather than our perfect jobs, perfect 2.5 kids (or 6.5 kids in the case of our church), and perfect

Christianity is the predominance of the outlook of eternity over everything temporal; Christianity grips a man in such a way that because of the eternal he forgets everything of this earth,[9] considers everything of this earth to be "loss,"[10] exposes himself even to suffering all possible persecution for the sake of the eternal.[11] (JP 6:6958)

This predominance is difficult to bear in worldly affairs. That is because Christianity is "a service of the spirit," which runs contrary to "an animal definition of man" (JP 6:6917).[12] That animal definition has a chokehold on us.[13] Therefore radical

---

testimonies." Kevin DeYoung & Ted Kluck, *Why We Love the Church: In Praise of Institutions and Organized Religion* (Chicago: Moody Publishers, 2009) 193.

9 See Col 3:2: "Set your minds on things that are above, not on things that are on earth" (RSV); and also 2 Cor 4:18: "[We] look not to the things that are seen but to the things that are unseen; for the things that are seen are transient, but the things that are unseen are eternal" (RSV).

10 See Phil 3:8: "Indeed I count everything as loss because of the surpassing worth of knowing Christ Jesus my Lord. For his sake I have suffered the loss of all things, and count them as refuse, in order that I may gain Christ" (RSV).

11 See Acts 5:41: "[They] left . . . rejoicing that they were counted worthy to suffer dishonor for the name [of Jesus]" (RSV).

12 Therefore every "striving which does not apply one-fourth, one-third, two-thirds, etc. of its power to systematically *working against* itself is essentially secular striving.... Reduplication means to work against oneself while working; it is like the pressure on the plow-handles, which determines the depth of the furrow—whereas working which does not work against itself is merely a superficial smoothing over" (JP 6:6593).

13 So does childhood, Kierkegaard notes: "Christ's contemporaries.... first of all entertained earthly expectations—and then everything was turned upside down and becoming a Christian in spirit and in truth became an earnest matter. So also when a child is brought up in Chris-

measures are needed if anyone is ever to be born of the spirit[14] and taken into the realm of the eternal. Kierkegaard's help with this is extreme, to say the least:

> It was incendiarism, . . . setting fire to men by evocatively introducing a passion which made them heterogeneous with what is naturally understood to be man,[15] heterogeneous with the whole of existence . . . . Therefore the passion introduced was: to love God, and its negative expression: to hate oneself[16] . . . . [Sometimes] one uses . . . featherbeds, blankets, . . . and the like to smother [this] fire [by getting] busily involved in . . . massive popularization . . . under the name of spreading Christianity . . [As a result] Christianity [becomes] reassurance, reassurance about eternity in order that we may all the better be able to rejoice and enjoy this life[17] . . . . [But] while man by nature wishes for

tianity from childhood. The child appropriates Christianity as a worldly gospel—and then at a later age the man experiences the terror [Acts 14:22; Jn 16:33] if he is to have the spiritual impact of Christianity" (JP 6:6798).
14 Kierkegaard was suspicious, however, of appealing to the Holy Spirit to bail us out: "But the whole thing about the Holy Spirit is rubbish," he writes, "an escapism by means of which one evades the tasks—whereas I have so much respect for the Holy Spirit that I have not dared to speak of him because I understand that as soon as I begin doing so I must present the existential even more strongly" (JP 6:6792).
15 See Jn 15:19: "If you were of the world, the world would love its own; but because you are not of the world, but I chose you out of the world, therefore the world hates you" (RSV).
16 See John 12:25: "He who loves his life loses it, and he who hates his life in this world will keep it for eternal life" (RSV).
17 And when this happens, "Christianity has [then] been degraded to the lowest possible paganism" (JP 6:6881).

what can give him pleasure in life, the religious
person on active duty needs a proper dose of
disgust with life in order to be fit for his task;[18]
disgust with life, taken properly (for the way it
is used is crucial),[19] is the best safeguard against
getting involved in stupid nonsense.

(JP 6:6932)

Kierkegaard justifies his account of Christianity by rooting this

---

18 Kierkegaard also construes this disgust as the weight of eternity inserted into temporality: "There must be weight—just as . . . the clock's works need a heavy weight in order to run properly, and the ship needs ballast. Christianity would furnish . . . this regulating weight, by making it every individual's life-meaning that whether he becomes eternally saved is decided for him in this life. Consequently Christianity puts eternity at stake. Into the middle of these finite goals, which merely confuse when they are supposed to be everything, Christianity introduced weight, and this weight was intended to regulate temporal life, both its good days and its bad days, etc. And because the weight has vanished—the clock cannot run, the ship steers wildly—and for this reason human life is a whirlpool" (JP 1:1003).

19 So Kierkegaard adds: "It has always been difficult for me to present Christianity in its true rigorousness, for it seemed to be that way only for me, because I had sinned more than others. It has always been my desire to be rigorous with myself in order to be all the more lenient with others, but this is still only a misunderstanding, for it was most rigorous in the Holy One himself. But just as a parent does not consider a child's possible iota of guilt worth mentioning, so in comparison to me other men have always seemed to me to be innocent" (JP 6:6411). See also his autobiographical note from 1851: "[In] one sense I am tired of life. For myself I fear nothing. But just as I stood there and was ready to thrust the sword into its sheath, something happened to prevent it. It seemed to me that my dead father put this demand to me: You must present Christianity in its utmost rigorousness, but you must keep it poetic, you may attack no one, and on no account may you make yourself out to be better than the most insignificant person, for you know very well that you are not better, ... yet you must not make any compromise in presenting Christianity" (JP 6:6748, p. 397).

extremity in the very ideals of the New Testament itself. Speaking against Rudelbach's praise of him,[20] he confesses his commitment to Christian ideals:

> I have not "sacrificed," not "my time," not "my diligence"—the most that can be said is that I have dedicated or devoted my time and my diligence in a part of my life to the service of an idea; and least of all have I sacrificed—"my life." No! *Essentially* I am only a poet who loves what wounds: ideals, what detains: ideals, what makes a man, humanly speaking, unhappy: ideals, what "teaches to take refuge in grace": ideals, what in a higher sense makes a man indescribably happy: ideals—if he could learn to hate himself properly in the self-concern of infinity. Indescribably happy, although humbled, deeply, profoundly humbled, before the ideals, he has had to confess and must confess to himself and to others that there is the infinitely higher that he has not reached, yet unspeakably happy to have seen it, although it is precisely [the ideals] which cast him to the earth, him, consequently the unhappy one . . . . No, no, the eternally happy one. For eternity! For one can grow weary of all temporal and earthly things, and so it would be tormenting if they were to continue eternally. But the person who

---

20 On Andreas Gottlob Rudelbach (1792–1862), see Julia Watkin, *The A to Z of Kierkegaard's Philosophy* (Lanham, Maryland: The Scarecrow Press, 2010) 220: "In his journals, Kierkegaard's view of Rudelbach seems to shift from respect of his learning and firmness of standpoint, to criticism of Rudelbach concerning the latter's desire for external reform of the church."

gets a vision of ideals, instantaneously has but one prayer to God: an eternity! And this prayer is instantaneously heard, for ideals and eternity are eternally inseparable . . . . And in calm weather, when life seems to be tranquilized in illusions, one may think he can do without this fantasy about ideals, think that all they do is disturb everything, and quite right—they will disturb all the illusions. But when everything is tottering, when everything is splitting into parties, small societies, sects, etc., when, just because everyone wants to rule, ruling is practically impossible: then there is still one force left which can control men: the ideals, properly applied. (JP 6:6749)

These ideals include treating others the way we would like to be treated; thinking better of others than of ourselves; never seeking thanks for oneself but always giving thanks for everything; denying ourselves; never pleasing people; never doubting God; hating ourselves; testing all things; never flagging in zeal; praying constantly; loving our enemies—but not the world nor conforming to it; not tampering with nor peddling God's Word; suffering with Christ; pummeling our bodies; knowing that life does not consist in the abundance of our possessions; that all that the world exalts is an abomination in the sight of God; that Jesus is the only savior;[21] and that we should eagerly

---

21 This is one of the most hotly contested of Christian ideals: "A Buddhist, no matter how sincere, [seems] simply not [to be] relying on the work of Christ. But here we can introduce a parallel to the referential account suggested by Alston . . . . The Buddhists might very well be referring to the work of Christ even though systematically misdescribing the source of their salvation . . . . The atheist, whether Buddhist or Western post-enlightenment, may very well be referring to God's salvific work

await his return to judge the living and the dead.²² These ideals, Kierkegaard notes, control us by disturbing us, humbling us, wounding us, saddening and gladdening us, taking away our grip on the here and now, and by detaining us from wandering off into silly myths.²³

These ideals keep Christianity from being "blabbered . . . down into something meaningless, into being spiritless impotence, suffocated illusion." As such these ideals function as "a quickening whip on all [the] spiritlessness"²⁴ within the

---

in her and his life and thereby be saved. Humanity looks on the stature of a person whereas God looks at the heart, as the scriptures report. There is much more to an actual Christ-like life than believing or saying 'the right things' that we seem on shaky ground to rule out how God's grace might work in cases outside the Christian faith itself." Mark S. McLeod-Harrison, "Christianity's Many Ways of Salvation: Toward an Irrealistic Salvific Inclusivism," *Philosophia Christi* 16/1 (2014): 167. Unfortunately for this account of inclusivism, Holy Scripture says in Romans 10:9 and 2 Corinthians 6:14–18 that it is not possible.

22 In order, these references are: Mt 7:12; Phil 2:3; Lk 17:9–10; Eph 5:20; Lk 9:23; Gal 1:10; Jas 1:6; Jn 12:25; Rom 12:11; 2 Cor 4:2, 2:17; 1 Thes 5:21, 17; Mt 5:44; 1 Jn 2:15; Rom 12:2; 1 Pt 4:13; 1 Cor 9:27; Lk 12:15, 16:15; Acts 4:12; Heb 9:28; John 5:27. After reading this list of verses, Kierkegaard's awkward explanation makes more sense: "Giødvad told me yesterday that I most likely had discouraged one or two theological candidates from becoming ministers by making the conception so ideal. I answered that as far as such a person is concerned, it would be the same with everything; by presenting ideally what it is to be a man I could ultimately discourage him from being a man and thus it could end in suicide. Then I showed him that such sickness was a matter of egotistically loving oneself instead of loving the ideal and hating oneself, loving the ideal which makes one a worthless fellow— and then always cheerful and happy over existing" (JP 2:1791). And Kierkegaard has this prayer to help with any and all discouragements: "Father in heaven! When the thought of you awakens in our soul, let it not awaken like a terrified bird that flutters about in confusion, but like a child from its sleep" (JP 3:3372).

23 See 2 Tm 4:4; Eph 4:14; Col 2:8.

24 No wonder, then, that "absolute spirit is the greatest of cruelties for us

Christian church (JP 6:6943). The "decisiveness of eternity," embedded in these Christian ideals, ushers into Christian living "a fear and trembling and quaking" that cannot be found anywhere else (JP 6:6850). Unfortunately this sort of preaching can make enemies out of those who hear it: "[If] I present what Christianity is essentially [my listeners] will be furious, [they] will become my [enemies]"[25] (JP 6:6831). As a result, the preacher ends up looking more like a bloody hunting dog, than some handsomely coiffured dignitary:

> Have you ever seen a hunting dog: bloody, exhausted by his struggles and loss of blood in the battle inside the foxes' burrow—it still does not let go; it has clamped its teeth shut and dies that way. I, too, am exhausted, but I have not let go of my idea, I have not made my life more comfortable, thereby making it less obvious what my goal has been.
>
> (JP 6:6803)

This, however, is how it must be because such suffering is part and parcel of our life with God in Christ Jesus. For God can only help me by "knocking me around—and yet it is out of love, yes, out of love—would only that I were worthy of it" (JP 6:6913).[26]

---

poor men" (JP 1:347), for "the truly divine prodigality . . . is the impetuosity of martyrdom, which is to be sensitive to what belongs to God [Mk 12:17]" (JP 1:387).

25 See Gal 4:16: "Have I then become your enemy by telling you the truth?" (RSV).

26 Indeed, "God—lovingly and out of love—tortures me where it hurts the most: yet his negative is a mark of the positive, a primitivity that does not relate to the contemporary age but to coming generations, and a significance which is properly expressed by the fact that I am superfluous to my age" (JP 6:6918). Kierkegaard also notes that when

I have tried to include all of this intense struggling with the divine ideals of Christianity in this collection of Kierkegaardian sermons. And that is as it should be because of Kierkegaard's goal: "My life," he writes, will be "a complete existential study on human selfishness and the deceit and hypocrisy carried on in the name of Christianity" (JP 6:6499). Bringing up the Christian ideals in these sermons will then help flush out this chicanery and further Kierkegaard's fight against such "leering brainlessness and bestial nonsense and depravity" (JP 6:6871). Accordingly these sermons will fight against a corrupted Christianity which has given up on "any childlike naïveté about wanting to strive toward likeness to the idea"—a Christianity which "has halted in secular prudence [and] says goodbye to ideals and regards striving after them as fanaticism" (JP 6:6694). Such is a bewitched or "hexed" Christianity (JP 6:6934)—the "shabbiest [and] trickiest" of its kind (JP 6:6921). And the cost for going against this shabby prudence is to have Kierkegaard's version of Christianity called "a lunatic, wicked, blasphemous, misanthropic exaggeration and caricature of that gentle doctrine, Christianity, the true Christianity, which is found in Christendom and whose founder[27] was Jesus Christ" (JP 1:353).

So in the first sermon, "Take the Test," on Genesis 22, I use Kierkegaard's passage on unconditional love being reserved for only God (WL 19), and his idea that explaining the near sacrifice of Isaac sounds only like "speaking in a strange tongue" (FT 119, 114). And in the second sermon, "Endure," on Mathew 24:13, I explore his passages on false fears (UDVS 58), our disordered wills (PV 54) and our refuge in Christ (CD 280). In the third sermon, "Don't Doubt," on John 20:27, I use Kierkegaard's passage on finding good reasons for faith as

---

God helps us mature in the spirit (Col 1:28) he does so with the most "dreadful beating" (JP 2:1418).

27   That is so—but only tongue-in-cheek.

the wrong way to combat doubt (FSE 68), and his words on self-doubt overcoming our doubts about God (UDVS 273).

In my fourth sermon, "Fight Depression," on 1 Kings 19, I use his passage on being drawn to belief in Christ against our will (JP 5:5313). And in my fifth sermon, "Be Doers of the Word," on James 1:22, I begin with Kierkegaard's attack on busyness (WL 98–99) and end with his formula about how striving follows the gift of grace (JP 1:993). All of this leads to a close reading of Luther on the forgiveness of sins (BC 433). In the sixth sermon, "Serve," on Mark 9:35, I end it with Kierkegaard's teaching on selfless love (WL 244).

In my seventh sermon, "Hate Yourself," on Luke 14:26, I begin with Kierkegaard's point that self-hatred is for self-examination (FT 72)—which leads to fighting against ourselves (EUD 143) and self-denial (UDSV 224)—provided that we do not distort it (WL 23). I take up the same theme again in my eighth sermon, "Hate Yourself—Again," on John 12:25, which is a full presentation of Kierkegaard's five-point prayer on hating yourself properly (PC 157). And in my ninth sermon, "Thank God Rightly," on Ephesians 5:20, I focus on Kierkegaard's warning against self-serving thanksgiving (JP 2:1510), and how we should not expect thanks from those we help (WL 32–36).

In my tenth sermon, "Trust in the Serpent," on Numbers 21:8, I string together five passages from Kierkegaard—one on believers leaping into the dark (UDVS 238); another on the need for blindness in faith (WL 295); a third on God struggling against himself (JP 1:532); a fourth on how poison turns into a remedy (CD 96); and the last one on the need to starve all illusions out of the church (JP 6:6227–28). In my eleventh sermon, "Don't Be Surprised," on 1 Peter 4:12, I study three passages from Kierkegaard—one on faith as restless traveling (UDVS 218); another on godly help feeling like torment (PC 114–15); and the third on getting help from on high only when we walk alone (UDVS 220–21). In my twelfth sermon, "Pray for Servants," on Matthew 9:38, I use at the beginning three passages from Kierkegaard—one on how God changes our prayers for the better (EUD 36); another on how we should only pray that God will abide with us (EUD 392; and a third on how only God understands us (BA 92).

In my thirteenth sermon which is on Isaiah 49:6, and entitled "Rejoice in the Remnant," I use four passages from Kierkegaard against crowds—one attacking them (PV 109); another linking them to falsehood (PV 106–10); a third against fat churches (PC 229–30); and a fourth about the church taking up a polemical stance (JP 4:4147). In my fourteenth sermon, "Stand Firm," on 2 Thessalonians 2:15, I include nine passages from Kierkegaard—the first one on being scrupulous (UDVS 66–68); the second on reading Job passionately (R 204); the third on seeking out Christ alone (CD 280); the fourth on our disordered wills (PV 54); the fifth on Christ being our substitute (WA 123–24); the sixth on leaping to God (TA 76, 108); the seventh on God pulling us to him (CD 253); the eighth on longing for the Lord's Supper (CD 261); and the last one on being restless (UDVS 218). And in my fifteenth sermon, "Come to Your Senses," on Luke 15:17, I use two passages from Kierkegaard—the one on fighting against ourselves (EUD 143); and the other on the sickbed being our best preacher (CD 164).[28]

In my sixteenth sermon, "Stick to the Bible," on 1 Corinthians 4:6, I use Kierkegaard's statement that the Bible wants to change us dramatically (FSE 31). And in my seventeenth sermon, "Labor for Love," on I Thessalonians 1:3, I use a number of passages from Kierkegaard's book, *Works of Love*—the first one about love being difficult (WL 376); the next one on true love looking crazy (WL 202–203); the third on love being

---

28 See also Ronald F. Marshall, *Kierkegaard for the Church*, 51–74.

offensive (WL 200); the fourth on love going beyond eroticism (WL 140–41); the fifth on love being unworldly (WL 139–149); the sixth on love making us unhappy (WL 111); the seventh on needing a duty to love (WL 43); and the last one on how mercy surpasses money in love (WL 317). In my eighteenth sermon, "Rejoice at Christmas," on Luke 2:10–14, I use a number of passages from Kierkegaard—the first one on the centrality of Christmas (JP 1:573); the second on how Christ was born a stranger (JFY 170); the third on how faith wants to change us (JFY 189, 151); the fourth on the internal divine combat in redemption (JP 1:532); the fifth being a rhapsody on Holy Communion (WA 186–87); and the last one being his exaltation of Christ in Acts 4:12 (CD 222).

In my nineteenth sermon, "Welcome Saint Stephen at Christmas," on Acts 7:56, I use a series of passages from Kierkegaard—the first one on how we slog along in the bog (JP 6:6503); the second on how dying to the flesh brings a new birth (JP 1:568); the third on how Christianity is fanatical (JP 3:2379); the fourth on how Christianity has an inverted dialectic regarding happiness (JP 4:4680); the fifth on how Christianity allows for suffering now (JP 3:3098); the sixth on hearing Scriptures as the very voice of God (FSE 39); and the seventh one on how worldly delights are not a premium (UDVS 233). In my twentieth sermon, "Do Your Duty," on Mark 8:34, I use four major passages from Kierkegaard—the first one on our dependence on God (UDVS 182); the second on the bad side of self-hatred (WL 23); the third on the parable of the seduced lily (UDVS 167–78); and the fourth one on how Jesus is trustworthy in Holy Communion (CD 258). And in my twenty-first sermon, "Prepare Yourselves," on Mark 14:16, I use one passage from Kierkegaard which speaks about our constant need for God, even in the simplest of things (CD 64).

In my twenty-second sermon, "Glory in the Cross," on Mark 15:39, I used four passages from Kierkegaard's book,

Without Authority—the first one on conquering ourselves with God's help (WA 157); the second on the difficulty of praying the Amen (WA 169); the third on being silent before God (WA 18–19); and the fourth on how Holy Communion lightens our souls (WA 170). In my twenty-third sermon, "Rejoice in Christ's Victory," on Mark 16:8, I use two passages from Kierkegaard—the first one on Christ judging us because we fear people instead of God (TW 136–37, 132); and the second one on how hard it is to learn about Christianity (TDIO 101). And in my twenty-fourth sermon, "Follow Saint Philip," on Acts 8:35, I do not use any specific passages from Kierkegaard—just his overall perspective on law and gospel, rigor and grace, severity and mildness (JP 3:2873).

In my twenty-fifth sermon, "Overthrow the World!" on Acts 17:6, I use four passages from Kierkegaard—the first one about being "a thorn in the eye of the world" (JP 6:6492); the second on the assassination of Christianity (TM 48); the third on how the repulsiveness of Christianity finally attracts us (JP 1:455); and the last one on how the wicked world tests us (JP 2:1439). In my twenty-sixth sermon, "Fear the Fires of Hell," on Luke 12:5, I use one passage from Kierkegaard at the very end on why terror has to be included in the preaching of Christianity (CD 175). And in my twenty-seventh and last sermon of this collection, "Long for Christ's Return," on Acts 1:11, I quote at the beginning Kierkegaard's statement that all Christians should yearn for Christ's return (JP 1:340); and then close with three other statements—the first on giving up our finite clutter (JP 5:5891), the second on going against the natural in us (JP 3:2711), and then finally describing why Christianity opposes what is naturally human (JP 6:6237).

Throughout all of these sermons I also quote as many, if not more, passages from Martin Luther's vast writings. That is because his thought provides the "matrix" for Kierkegaard's perspective—and so if we do not listen to Luther we will never be able to understand Kierkegaard.[29]

My study of Kierkegaard, then, has included a parallel study of Luther, leaving me with the opinion that Kierkegaard was Luther's best student or reader. Kierkegaard's insights into the sermons he read of Luther's have propelled my further study of Luther. Years ago I wrote Jaroslav Pelikan[30] (1923–2006) to thank him for all of his hard work in making Luther's writings available to the English reader. I told him my letter to him was an odd little love letter for all that he had done to help people like me easily read through large portions of Luther's writings on a regular basis. I told him how I used his edition of Luther's translated writings every week in preparation for my sermons. In response, he wrote back that it was "profoundly gratifying to hear words of appreciation, not from some academic prize committee somewhere, but from someone on the firing line." Being on the firing line, as he says, would for me have been far less bearable without Luther's writings and those of his best student.

---

29 On this connection between Luther and Kierkegaard, see Ronald F. Marshall, *Kierkegaard for the Church*, 21n1, 58n21, 62n31, 76n4, 115n58, 197n68, 207n15, 249, 251, 268, 292, 302–303, 309–311, 340n6. See also Kenneth Hagen, "An Ethic for the Left Hand: Luther on Vocation," Luther Digest 20 (2012): 35: "Kierkegaard's voice was a Luther-voice of protest against Christendom in Denmark."

30 See Robert Louis Wilken, "Jaroslav Pelikan, Doctor Ecclesiae," *First Things* 165 (August/September 2006): 20: "Most other scholars were specialists in a particular historical period, but Pelikan roamed freely and confidently over the whole history of Christian thought—and that history was never simple history for him. He had a certain diffidence about the merits of modernity. The great thinkers of the past were living interlocutors whose ideas, ways of reasoning, and imagination commended them to Christian thinkers today." Note also that it is Pelikan who said that Luther's thought was the "matrix" for Kierkegaard's writings. Jaroslav Pelikan, *From Luther to Kierkegaard* (Saint Louis: Concordia, 1950) 21. See the complete letter on p. li

The Bottleneck

Yale University

Jaroslav Pelikan
Sterling Professor
Department of History
P.O. Box 1504A Yale Station
New Haven, Connecticut 06520-7425

Campus address:
234 Hall of Graduate Studies
320 York Street
Telephone:
203 432-1375

24 August 1993

Dear Pastor Ronald,

I have been deeply moved by your "odd little love letter," which awaited me on my return from a Yale Alumni College Abroad in Siberia (for which, indeed, we traveled through Seattle).

For someone who, more than fifty years ago, elected a life of scholarship rather than the sacramental ministry, it is profoundly gratifying to hear words of appreciation, not from some academic prize committee somewhere, but from someone on the firing line — all the more so because I had to decide, exactly forty years ago, that the only way to render this service to the institutional Church was to get off its payroll.

If, as you (and I) hope that "Luther's witness to the Triune God" can still do something for the bankruptcy of so many of the churches, it will have been worth the effort.

With sincere gratitude and assurance of my prayers for you and your people,

Fraternally in Our Lord,

J. P.

I also include in this book two major essays that buttress my collection of sermons. The first is my opening chapter on judgment, which includes four major passages from Kierkegaard—the first one dealing with dodging judgments (JP 4:4569); the second on not everything about us being open to judgment (WL 229); the third that judgments are needed to fight mediocrity (TM 92); and the last one on how judging others is best done by helping them do it for themselves (JP :6726). The other essay is the first appendix on Judaism. In it I used passages from Kierkegaard on the misery of Christianity (TM 169); its negative contrast with Judaism (JP 2:2227); how Christianity is alienated in this world (JP 2:2221); and how it also stands up against false comfort (EUD 298–303; TM 110). I conclude with Rollie Storbakken's review of my predecessor book, *Kierkegaard for the Church*—to help tie together my two books on Kierkegaard as well as four brief studies on Postmodernism, criticism, the story of Mary and Martha, and the parable on the lilies and the birds.

Chapter 1

On Judging Others

The sermons in this book seep with judgments.[1] And so if it cannot be shown that judgments play a positive role in the Christians life, then none of them will fly. All these sermons will fail. For if Christians believe that there is no positive place for judgments in our lives, then we will not be able to adjudicate any disagreements we might have with each other.[2] And that is

---

1 Another way of putting this would be to borrow the title from an article by Stanley Hauerwas in *First Things* 53 (May 1995): "Preaching As Though We Had Enemies."

2 See Letha Scanzoni and Virginia Ramey Mollenkott, *Is the Homosexual My Neighbor? Another Christian View* (New York: Harper and Row, 1978) 116: "Jesus warned us that judgment is a boomerang (Mt 7:1); and that the cumulative effect of scapegoating has been a legalistic and fearful withdrawal from the unlimited and unconditional love of God." See also David Kinnaman, *Unchristian: What a New Generation Really Thinks About Christianity and Why It Matters* (Grand Rapids: Baker Books, 2007) 191–92: "[Jesus'] teaching is unambiguous: do not judge others (see Mt 7:1–5). How have Christians gotten so far from this? . . . The Bible makes it clear that God, not humans, should judge. It is God's job, and he does it impartially while exposing the true motives of

because we will have nothing to argue over and debate if we cannot judge each other—since debates and arguments hinge on pointing out the mistakes that we make, which is simply what judgments are. Even so, many Christians are still inclined to give up on judgments because they can be so cold, mean-spirited and unloving[3]—traits universally deemed unbecoming

---

    people's hearts." My book stands against these two statements.

3   Kierkegaard, in part, agrees with this criticism: "The one who judges, even if he goes at it slowly, the one who judges that the other person lacks love—he takes away the foundation; he cannot build up, but love builds up by patience" (WL 220). So inasmuch as love builds up, and judgment blocks that from happening, judging others is unloving and therefore not Christian. And even regarding positive judgments, such as praise, we are also warned that they can lead to egotism which pulls us away from faith in Christ (Jn 5:44). On this threat, Kierkegaard warns that when we are admired and praised we "forget that it is all God's gift and help [and] fritter away [our] lives in the old rut that makes existence insipid because it is without salt, makes existence a confection because it is without earnestness." So if praised, we should follow the example of the New Testament apostle, who when praised, would have "ripped off these chains of lace" and sadly recalled "the joy [Acts 5:41] he sensed when existence had pith and had flavor . . . after having been flogged and [being] bound to be joyful over it!" (UDVS 339). For Saint Augustine's similar view on praise, see *Augustine: Select Letters*, Loeb Classical Library 239, ed. G. P. Good, trans. James Houston Baxter (Cambridge, Massachusetts: Harvard University, 1998) 453, 455: "[We are] not to live right . . . with the object of being praised by men [Mt 5:16], that is, not to make the praise of men the motive of our doing right, and yet [we are also told that] for men's sake to seek men's praise [1 Cor 10:33]. For when good men are praised, the praise confers a benefit on those who bestow it, not on those who receive it . . . [Yet this] benefits not only you [the one bestowing praise] but me too [the one receiving praise], for if they are lacking in me, it is wholesome for me to be shamed and inflamed with desire to acquire them. And so the qualities I recognize in your praises as my own I rejoice in possessing and in having you love them and me for their sake; those on the other hand that I fail to recognize as mine I yearn to acquire, not only in order to possess them for myself, but also to keep those who

to Christians.[4]

Even so, I think that judgments and the judging of others have a positive place in Christian living—and by extension, in Christian sermons. And so I will dwell on four areas of concern—the first being the example of Jesus himself. I will then move on to show how wisdom requires judgment. Third, I will show how Matthew 7:1–5 allows for making judgments even though many mistakenly think it does not. And fourth, I will show that we cannot be responsible without making judgments. I will then close with a six-fold practical guide on judging others according to John 7:24.

Imitating Jesus

My first point is that we are supposed to "imitate" Jesus Christ (1 Cor 11:1; 1 Pt 2:21) and he judged others—so we also should be able to do the same. And Jesus was even harsh about it[5]—criticizing, refuting and condemning people for what they said and did. He did not do this in such a way, however,

---

have a genuine love for me from being deluded when they praise me." So both negative and positive judgments are fraught with peril for the Christian.

4 Note, by the way, that this observation itself is a judgment.
5 On this matter Kierkegaard notes that "worldly wisdom has a long list of various expressions for sacrifice and devotion . . . I wonder if among all these you will find the suffering of having to seem to hate the beloved, of having to have hate as the final and sole expression of one's love because there is the infinite difference of Christian truth between what the one and what the other understand by love? . . . . Christ's life is really the only unhappy love. In the divine sense, he was Love . . . . *For this reason his whole life was a horrible collision with the merely human conception of what love is* . . . . We pretend that only ungodliness had to collide with Christ. What a misunderstanding! . . . No, it is indeed madness, humanly speaking: he sacrifices himself—in order to make the loved one just as unhappy as himself." (WL 109–11) (italic added).

that excluded all comfort and support. But even at that, he still was tough—combining his comfort and support with times of biting criticism.[6] Jesus could rebuke Saint Peter, for instance, for disagreeing with him over his need to suffer (Mt 16:23). And Jesus also condemned the scribes and Pharisees for being hypocrites (Mt 23:13–36). He also chided a group of women on the *via dolorosa* for their misdirected lamentations (Lk 23:38). He famously threw merchants and their customers out of the temple because they were abusing God's house (Jn 2:15–16). He told a sinful woman to quit sinning (Jn 8:11). He called the plaintive woman, with a languishing child, a dog (Mt 15:26). He said we should rebuke the unrepentant (Lk 17:3). He even rebuked his mother—telling her to mind her own business (Jn 2:4). He chastised his disciples for being weak (Mt 26:41). He slammed his family for being superficial (Mk 3:32–35). He condemned those who practiced the bad business practice of Corban (Mk 7:10–13). And Jesus threatened with eternal damnation people he called goats (Mt 25:41, 46). So saying that Christians should never judge other people flies in the face of the example Jesus set. That would mean, then, that we have no choice but to judge others as Jesus did—taking on, for instance, the lazy and sexually deviant, who are chastised in the New Testament (1 Thes 5:13; 1 Cor 5:1–5).

---

6   Even so, Kierkegaard rightly insists that, "as a rule Christianity is dismaying rather than consoling . . . . But if I am a Christian clergyman, I am obligated to bring consolation in the Christian way. The question remains whether I would have the courage to be Christianly cruel . . . . Christianity . . . educates with the help of eternity and to eternity. Therein lies the dismaying aspect of Christianity's help, for when a person suffers, Christianity's help begins by turning the whole temporal life into suffering . . . . [And so] Christianity denies all temporal help—in order to educate for eternity" (JP 6:6262).

Wisdom

But would not love block us from judging others? Well, even though Christians are called to love (Jn 15:12),[7] that is not the sum and substance of Christianity. We are also supposed to be wise (Mt 10:16)—and that is the second part of my defense. This wisdom requires Christians to be perceptive, with good timing, in making apt assessments and evaluations of whatever comes our way. We have been told to test everything (1 Thes 5:21).[8] In order to do that, we have to be able to discern what is going on, with keen insight. When acting wisely, we differentiate the good from the bad. Therefore Christians would be gullible and stupid if they did not navigate their way, making good judgments, on a daily basis (1 Pt 2:15).[9] And Jesus also taught us not to be in the fog about other people—but to stay alert and on our guard for every wolf coming down the road dressed up like a sheep (Mt 7:15–20). Therefore if we were not able to make good judgments, we would be nothing but shoddy disciples (Lk 11:35). And so Jesus expects us to be

---

7   But even love is not without its critical component for Kierkegaard: "What frightful severity! That love, that it is love, the forgiving love, which, not judging, no, alas, itself suffering, is nevertheless changed into the judgment! That love, the forgiving love, which does not want, like justice, to make the guilt manifest but on the contrary wants to hide it by forgiving and pardoning, that it nevertheless is this which, itself suffering, makes the guilt more frightfully manifest than justice does!" (WA 173).

8   See also 1 Cor 5:12; 2 Cor 13:5; Gal 6:4; 1 Jn 4:1.

9   See Terry D. Cooper, *Making Judgments Without Being Judgmental: Nurturing a Clear Mind and a Generous Heart* (Downers Grove, Illinois: IVP, 2006) 26–27: "A world without judgments would be a world without conviction, principles and ethical concerns . . . . Our values reside beneath every decision we make . . . . If we . . . embrace a judge-nothing philosophy, . . . the end result is . . . moral indifference."

cautious (Mk 13:33; Lk 14:9, 28) and critical (Lk 9:5). We are to test everything and take nothing for granted. And we cannot do that without making good, solid judgments. This does not mean, however, that we are to be so cautious and careful that we never take any risks. No, that would be to succumb to worldly sagacity, Kierkegaard warns:

> One person may have more sagacity and more common sense than another and therefore be able to venture more and to endure more, but it continually holds true that common sense and sagacity can count on one thing—that when the suffering and strain are endured for a longer or shorter time, the way becomes easier and one is victorious even in this life. On the other hand, a way that becomes narrower and narrower unto the end, along that way sagacity and common sense never walk—"that would indeed be madness." (FSE 61–62)

But it is along that mad,[10] narrow road that Christians apply their wisdom, that they may know the lay of the land as they proceed forward, so that when they act, they will be in line with God's word and have a good chance of making a difference—just as the good Samaritan did (Lk 10:37). This is the wisdom from above (1 Cor 2:7)—which calls us to judge others.

---

10 Kierkegaard thought it was crazy—but still wonderful—to love others, expecting nothing in return (WL 108, 111, 132, 185, 203, 238, 287, 290, 318, 321).

Miscontruing Matthew 7

Unfortunately Matthew 7:1 has confused many and provided safe haven for those who have wanted to put an end to the judgment of people. "Judge not," it says,[11]—and they take this to mean that any and all judgments of others are wrong. This reading, however, pays too little regard to the way this first paragraph at the beginning of Matthew 7 ends—and this is the third point in my defense. At the end of this paragraph, it says that if you proceed properly, you may then "take the speck out of your brother's eye" (Mt 7:5). If you refrain from judging, as it states at the beginning of the paragraph, then you can go ahead and make your judgment at the end. Such judgments would be allowable. For taking out this speck is actually a way of judging another person. But if we forget—or defiantly refuse—to link or assimilate the end of this paragraph with its beginning, we will then end up making a conundrum out of the whole opening paragraph in Matthew 7. That is because it will not add up—for it will begin by saying do not judge others, and then go on to end by saying you can judge others—and it is all supposed to fit together somehow! But it does not. In one breath the paragraph says both to judge and not to judge—without any clarification or qualifications of the two commands.

This, however, is not the only way to read Matthew 7:1–5. If the opening prohibition is combined with the closing approval, then our conundrum is dissolved. Then the beginning and the end of the paragraph will clearly fit together with each other, since they have modified each other. Then the beginning prohibition is limited to stopping only the bad judgments, and

---

11 See also 1 Cor 4:3–5; Rom 2:1 and Jas 4:12—which all speak against some form of judging others.

the closing permission is confined to only good judgments. On this reading, the opening prohibition would then say: "Do not judge *poorly*," instead of not to judge at all. By dissolving the conundrum in this manner, we can then see how Matthew 7:1 does not condemn all judgments of other people, but only the bad ones. This is the way Luther understood this passage. First he says that when we judge we cannot do whatever "we please," because then our judgments would be based on our own flimsy opinions and not on God's sturdy word. Next, our judgments should never be aimed at taking out "revenge" on another person, because then our judgments would not be for our neighbor's well being, as they are supposed to be (Mt 22:39). Finally, we have to judge one another as best we can, because if we do not, we will eventually "sanction a wrong," which would be immoral of us.[12]

Being Responsible

All of this leads to the surprising conclusion that it is not those who want to judge, but those who do not want to judge, who

---

[12] Martin Luther, "Sermons on Mathew 5–7" (1532) LW 21:223, 106, 112. And on the matter of being judged by the same judgment you level against others (Mt 7:2), see Mikal Gilmore, "Bob Dylan: The Rolling Stone Interview," *Rolling Stone* 1166 (September 27, 2012) 81: "Everything people say about you or me, they are saying about themselves. They're telling about themselves. Ever notice that?" These are the poor judges: "Sure, I had a motorcycle accident . . . . And sure, I sounded different. So . . . what? They want to know what can't be known . . . . [They're] trying to find [their] way to 50 million fables. For what? . . . They don't really know. It's sad. It really is. May the Lord have mercy on them. They are lost souls" (80). But if the criticism is reasonable and "constructive," Dylan notes, "if someone could point out here and there where my work could be improved upon, I guess I'd be willing to listen. The people who are obsessed with criticism—it's not honest criticism" (81).

are the real culprits in this matter.[13] Kierkegaard helps explain this fourth part of my defense:

> [It] is part and parcel of . . . rascality that no one is inclined or cares to judge in any way. The smart thing is to leave judging alone, since everyone knows best for himself how the shoe fits. [And so] a rare Christianity prevails in which men refrain entirely from judging one another . . . . No, . . . the concern of Christianity [is always] to get men to judge—in order to get them out of their masks, to get a little personality into this objective rascality or this rascality with objectivity.
>
> (JP 4:4569)

Here we see how it is irresponsible of us to avoid making judgments—"like a school where the record book has disappeared" (JP 1:995). This is because dodging judgments enables us to hide behind a mask of impersonal objectivity, Kierkegaard says—avoiding all responsibility for what we say and do. By avoiding judgments, we think we can blend into the crowd and pretend that we are just doing and saying what everybody else is doing and saying. But judgment will not

---

13 See Terry D. Cooper, *Making Judgments Without Being Judgmental*, 14–15: "What I . . . did not realize was that my harsh condemnation of judgmental people was every bit as judgmental as anything *they* were saying. I was becoming a narrow-minded defender of open-mindedness. I was intolerant of tolerance . . . . While the content of what I was saying may have differed from the judgmental attitudes I had encountered, the process of my thinking was the same . . . . Again, it is easy to become self-righteous precisely when we are pointing out the self-righteousness of others."

stand for this since it affixes responsibility individually. So if a person holds a view, they have to explain and defend it—rather than say that it is what everyone else is saying and doing and so we are immune from any responsibility for holding it.

Yet, even so—as an astute dialectician[14]—Kierkegaard also warns against the opposite pitfall—that of charging ahead with abandon,[15] relishing the chance to expose and condemn

---

14 On Kierkegaard's dialectical method, see David F. Swenson, *Something About Kierkegaard* (1945) ed. Lillian Marvin Swenson (Macon, Georgia: Mercer University, 1983) 117–18: "The existential dialectic bears *qua* dialectic the stamp of its origin as a philosophical term in the dramatic dialogue. It is, namely, a mutual confrontation of opposites in their logically developed consequences. As existential it seeks to mediate a clarification of the issues of life, paving the way for a decisive personal commitment . . . . The dialectic is the unrest in the forward movement of learning, the existing individual being always a learner in the sense that his life is a constant striving."

15 This is the person who is "so avid to judge, to vent his resentment, his powerful or powerless indignation, upon someone else without really knowing anything about what he [is] judging" (WL 234). This is also seen in our reluctance to forgive: "To forgive sins is divine not only in the sense that no one is able to do it except God, but it is also divine in another sense so that we must say that no one can do it without God. If men really were able to forgive sins, they still are not adequate for it. Indeed, how poor, pinched, and reluctant, how very conditional is their forgiveness" (JP 2:1224). These considerations also help us sort out destructive from constructive criticism and conflict in the church. On this matter see Kenneth C. Haugk, *Antagonists in the Church: How to Identify and Deal With Destructive Conflict* (Minneapolis: Augsburg, 1988) 21–22: "Antagonists are individuals who, on the basis of non-substantive evidence, go out of their way to make insatiable demands, usually attacking the person or performance of others. These attacks are selfish in nature, tearing down rather than building up, and are frequently directed against those in a leadership capacity." For a recent example of balanced, constructive criticism, see Michael Eric Dyson, "The Ghost of Cornel West," *The New Republic*, April 19, 2015 (online)—even though Dyson has been vilified for it.

another's foibles with our biting, albeit well-formed, judgments:

> How inventive is hidden inwardness in hiding itself and in deceiving or evading others, the hidden inwardness that preferred that no one would suspect its existence, modestly afraid of being entirely disclosed! Is it not so that the one person never completely understands the other?[16]
> (WL 229)

Because we hide ourselves, so effectively, judging others is very difficult, if not impossible. We cannot assume then that the judgments we make always hit the mark squarely. That is because they will never have all the relevant information—since some will remain beyond our reach. And so Kierkegaard continues his cautionary note:

> But if he does not understand him completely, then of course it is always possible that the most indisputable thing could still have a completely different explanation that would, note well, be the true explanation, since an assumption can indeed explain a great number of instances very well and

---

16 This is in part inspired by 1 Samuel 16:7 which says that only God can see into our hearts. So Kierkegaard adds: "Ostensibly it is an imperfection in earthly life that basically a person cannot entirely, cannot thoroughly make himself understandable to others; on closer inspection one will surely be convinced that it is a perfection, since it suggests that every individual is religiously structured and is to strive to understand himself in confidentiality with God" (BA 92).

thereby confirm its truth and yet show itself to be untrue as soon as the instance comes along that it cannot explain—and it would indeed be possible that this instance or this somewhat more precise specification could come even at the last moment. (WL 229)

So we cannot be too careful when judging others! We will even have to be ready to change our minds at the very last moment when some new material comes in on the person we are judging. Because people are in part opaque, this caution is crucial, as Kierkegaard further explains:

> Therefore all calm and, in the intellectual sense, dispassionate observers, who eminently know how to delve searchingly and penetratingly into the inner being, these very people judge with such infinite caution or refrain from it entirely because, enriched by observation, they have a developed conception of the enigmatic world of the hidden, and because as observers they have learned[17] to rule over their passions. Only superficial, impetuous, passionate people, who do not know themselves and for that reason naturally are unaware that they do not know

---

17 Gal 5:23 however says that this self-control is a gift from God. But either way, it is still indispensable: "As you see, it is already upbuilding to bear in mind that the one who loves builds up by controlling himself! . . . . [For] love that builds up has nothing to point to, since its work consists only of presupposing [love in others] . . . . [So] one who loves works very quietly and very solemnly, and yet the forces of eternity are in motion. Love humbly makes itself inconspicuous just when it is working the hardest—indeed, its work seems as if it did nothing at all" (WL 217–18).

others, judge precipitously. Those with insight, those who know, never do this. (WL 229)

It is easy to see how this "enigmatic world of the hidden" could keep a person from making any judgments at all. But Kierkegaard finally resists saying that.[18] He instead stands against only *precipitous* judgments. And he furthermore condones ruling over our passions so that we can develop the art of delving, penetratingly and searchingly, he says, into another person's inner being in order to make a good judgment.[19] Indeed, only "half-experienced and very confused people think of judging another person on the basis of knowledge" (WL 231)—since there is always more relevant information to gather, and principled considerations to include.

Even so it may still seem that the disadvantages far outweigh the advantages in judging others. Our limitations are so great that they may well render all good judgments impossible. Against this view, however, Kierkegaard writes:

> [Now] a break must be made with all . . . considerations of tender love. And . . . there will be some people to whom I owe it, at least at times, to take into consideration all the trivialities that mediocrity with great pompousness didactically

---

18 For indeed, Kierkegaard did oppose his contemporaries: Peder Ludvig Møller (1814–1865) (COR 38–46; JP 5:5887), Andreas Gottlob Rudelbach (1792–1862) (COR 51–59; JP 3:2961; 4:3869, 4164, 4209; 6:6223, 6725, 6851), Nikolai F. S. Grundtvig (1783–1872) (TM 207–208; JP 2:1860; 5:6097; 6:6876), Jacob Peter Mynster (1775–1854) (TM 3–8; JP 6:6853), Hans Lassen Martensen (1808–1884) (TM 79–85), and Adolph Peter Adler (1817–1869) (BA 61, 68–70, 239).

19 And by so doing, we are also constantly testing ourselves—"since to live is to judge oneself, to become disclosed" (WL 228).

> recites, all the gibberish that they, by bringing it along themselves, get out of what I write, all the lies and slander to which a person is exposed, against whom the two great powers in society, envy and obtuseness, must with a certain necessity conspire. Why, then, am I willing [to do this]? I am willing to do it because I would eternally regret [letting] the contemporary generation . . . remain quite calmly where it is, in the delusion . . . that the pastors' play-Christianity is Christianity. (TM 92)

And what he brings by way of judgment on such mediocrity is not his own estimations based on cloudy personal perceptions, but "how Christ judges official Christianity," by way of the revelations in the New Testament (TM 131).[20] So Kierkegaard does not care so much about making political and interpersonal judgments, as he does about making religious ones, based on the teachings of the New Testament.[21]

But when he makes his judgments he mostly carries out "flank attacks, wounding from behind" (JP 6:6477).[22] By

---

20 And so "God regards it as presumptuousness for a human being to pretend purity and to judge the splinter in his brother's eye . . . . God will do unto you exactly as you do unto others. In the Christian sense, you have nothing at all to do with what others do unto you—it does not concern you; it is a curiosity, an impertinence, a lack of good sense on your part to meddle in things that are absolutely no more your concern than if you were not present. You have to do only with what you do unto others, or how you take what others do unto you. The direction is inward . . . . (but without taking you out of the world)" (WL 383–84).
21 And it is just these judgments that the sermons in this book are full of—and so a positive assessment of judging others is essential for understanding them.
22 See Part Three of *Christian Discourses*—"Thoughts That Wound From Behind—For Upbuilding: Christian Addresses" (CD 161–246). Note especially: "In Christendom . . . Christianity is continually still mil-

proceeding indirectly, Kierkegaard can then accentuate the "existential consequences" of our lives:

> I never deny directly what a man says about himself. The usual thing is for someone to make some inflated statement about himself and then to be told that it is a lie, a delusion—and there is a quarrel. I do not do things that way. No, when a man says something like that, I answer: If you yourself say so, then I believe it. Then I take his statement and think it through to all its existential consequences. I confront him with them. One of two things happens—either he more or less accepts them and then there is more or less truth in him, or he does not accept them—and then he has judged himself. I judge no one, but this brings things into the open. (JP 6:6726)

This is Kierkegaard's compromise—how he both judges and refrains from judging at the same time This compromise fits exactly with the best way to read Matthew 7:1–5—a passage which also calls us to both refrain from judging and to make

---

itant" (CD 229). This approach follows Socrates and Jesus: "Even in Christendom, you know, the catechetical art is patterned on him [Socrates], but no catechist has ever been able to ask questions as he did. Imagine this simple wise man, this determined hater of all evasions and excuses and muddleheadedness and dubiousness, and in addition, the equally shrewd, cunning, deft, and undaunted ferreter of the same [Jesus]; he who had no doctrine that he expounded at a distance to people but as a teacher so probed people to the core that to the person conversing with him it seemed as if he were conversing with himself [Mk 10:22; Jn 4:29], as if his innermost being became disclosed to him; he who not only fetched wisdom down from heaven but knew how to make it penetrate into 'the single individual'" (CD 218–19).

good judgments simultaneously. This compromise avoids judging, as Kierkegaard says—while still confronting the person and opening up matters of great importance. This method also nicely promotes the facilitation of self-judgment—both in the self-control of the one making the judgment (WL 217–18), and in the one receiving the judgment, which reduces the likelihood of quarrels breaking out that muddle what is in play. And what we do not want to lose sight of, in this whole discernment process, are just those important matters—the existential consequences of what we say and believe in our daily lives.

John 7:24: Judging Others Rightly

So rather than dwelling on the supposed prohibition against all judging in Matthew 7:1, it would be better, in light of my four part defense, to follow a more nuanced verse, John 7:24, which says that we should judge others *rightly*—instead of never at all. Given the four points that I have made in my defense, the following six pieces of practical advice provide a straightforward guide on how to make right judgments of others—something I also try to do in the sermons collected in this book.

No Double Standards. First, it would be wrong to use a double standard when judging other people. For the basis upon which we judge others, must not apply just to them, but also to ourselves (Rom 2:3). After all, what is good for the goose is good for the gander. This is because the only fair way to judge others is to have one standard for everyone in the same station of life. This last provision takes into account that police officers, for example, should not be judged by the same standards used to judge janitors or dentists, and visa versa. And neither should adults be judged by standards reserved only for children, and visa versa. But when police officers are judging each other, then one standard should apply for all—as with any other profession or walk of life. Christians, after all, are expected to treat others in the same way as they would want to be treated—it is our golden rule (Mt 7:12). At a very minimum, that would include having no double standards when judging others. So if I were to chastise someone for drinking too much alcohol,[23] while drinking too much myself, and without any twinges of shame or intentions to reform, that would be an example of judging with a double standard. All fair-minded, loving Christians, must never chastise like that, and if they do, they should promptly and sincerely apologize for doing so.

Bona Fide Norms. Second, we cannot judge others based on what we think would be better for them. That would only result in bickering, since our judgments would not be based on any compelling bona fide norms. Christians, however, must always appeal to a higher authority when making judgments of others. They need to ask what the Bible has to say about how we are living and how we should improve. So if we criticize someone for being greedy, we must never do so because we want money from them for our pet projects. No, we should instead appeal to the parable about hoarding wealth in Luke 12:16–21, and the story about Zacchaeus helping the poor in Luke 19:1–10.[24] Then, on the basis of those holy words,[25] we could judge

---

23   Christians, before making their judgments, will also want to be informed on all the complicating factors involved in alcoholism. On this matter see, for instance, Herbert Fingarette, *Heavy Drinking* (Berkeley: University of California, 1988), especially his fifteen page bibliography and chapter five on "Understanding Heavy Drinking as a Way of Life."
24   For a more complex Biblical account of this issue, see John C. Haughey, *The Holy Use of Money: Personal Finances in Light of Christian Faith* (New York: Crossroad, 1989).
25   Ideally we would hope that the norms were shared, but even when they are not, the judgment should still proceed on the basis of the higher authority that we hold sacred. When the norms are not shared, it is of

another for not being generous. In this way, the judgment is not made in self-defense or for self aggrandizement. Luther understood well the need to have our judgments steer clear of any such self-interest:

> Our enemies want to be considered peaceful and humble, and we must pass for unrepentant, stubborn, and impetuous hotheads. Yes, in matters involving Christ we want to be just that; here do not expect any concessions or any patience from me. Here I am stiff-necked, for my person is not concerned. You are attacking me at a point that does not pertain to me. On the other hand, if you assail me, my physical goods, life, or limb, I shall gladly give way to you . . . . I will gladly humble myself and even let you walk all over me.[26]

Revisable. Third, our judgments can never be final. We must always keep them open to revision—no matter how long ago we made them. This is because we might learn, for example, that we misunderstood some feature of our friend's poker playing habits that we were critical of.[27] Or we might discover that we misunderstood or misapplied some Biblical admonition used in our judgment. As a consequence, we would

---

course much less likely that our judgments will be accepted as being worthwhile by the person we are judging.

26 Martin Luther, "Sermons on John 6–8" (1531), LW 23:330.

27 On this many faceted game, see Andy Bellin, *Poker Nation: A High-Stakes, Low-Life Adventure Into the Heart of a Gambling Country* (New York: HarperCollins, 2002). Note especially: "The trick to becoming a decent poker player is . . . . never call the first bet unless you've got the goods . . . . But to become great . . . you have to be able to read people. That's what puts you over the top" (235).

have to either withdraw the judgment and apologize for it, or revise it and ask for a reconsideration to be made of it—being newly revised. Since we are finite and limited creatures (Rom 1:25; 2 Cor 4:7), we cannot pretend that any of our judgments will ever be final, absolute and beyond criticism. We are not God, after all—and so we cannot see those whom we judge with absolutely impeccable vision and perfect discernment (Ps 119:75; Mt 5:48). That makes all of our judgments tentative—never being able to close the book on any given person. Nor can we assume that we will always be free of all hatred or envy when we judge others. If and when this happens, and we repent of it and apologize for it, we then would also have to revise our judgments to rid them of these mistakes. This is one clear and significant way that self-control enters into making good judgments. We must always examine ourselves with a critical eye to see why we want to judge someone in the first place. Any good judgment of another person will then always begin with robust self-evaluation and acute self-criticism (2 Cor 13:5–9)[28]—taking the log out of our own eye, before we try to help out another person with our judgments (Mt 7:5).

Constructive. Fourth, our judgments must always be constructive. When criticizing someone, we must always include in the judgment a better way to go. That is because Christian judgments are not supposed to discourage or destroy the person being judged. They are instead given with the hope of helping the person improve—their only aim is to build up people (1 Cor 8:1). So when Luther criticizes pastors for being anemic, he adds:

---

28 "On the whole I think that one cannot truly speak of Christianity without perpetual self-accusation" (JP 1:108).

> The true shepherd must keep watch. He must be zealous in the Word. He must give consideration to consciences, to comfort the sad, strengthen the afflicted, lest they despair, call back those who wander away, in short, he must win many for Christ.[29]

These lines fill in what pastors should be doing, but only partially. Elsewhere Luther provides more detail. Being zealous for the word, for instance, would require of the pastor to emphasize that everything depends on God's word.[30] And comforting the sad will at times mean being rough in order to bring about true healing.[31] Calling back those who have wandered away, Luther notes, is anything but easy and smooth.[32] And conversion to Christ must be based on a strong dose of fear and trembling.[33]

---

29 Martin Luther, "Lectures on Zechariah" (1526) LW 20:127.
30 Martin Luther, "Against the Heavenly Prophets" (1525) LW 40:212, 214.
31 Martin Luther, "Commentary on Psalm 118" (1530) LW 14:60–61: "Let everyone become a falcon and soar above distress . . . . [So when distress comes, do] not sit by yourself or lie on a couch, hanging and shaking your head . . . . [Do] not brood on your wretchedness, suffering, and misery. Say to yourself: 'Come on, you lazy bum [*du fauler schelm*]; down on your knees, and lift your eyes and hands toward heaven!' Read a psalm or the Our Father, call on God, and tearfully lay your troubles before Him. Mourn and pray . . . . [God wills] that you lay your troubles before Him . . . . He wants you to grow strong in Him . . . . Otherwise, men are mere babblers [*eitel plaudere*]."
32 Martin Luther, "Lectures on Galatians 1–4" (1535) LW 26:310: "[The] presumption of righteousness is a huge and horrible monster. To break and crush it, God needs a large and powerful hammer, that is, the Law, which is the hammer of death, the thunder of hell, and the lightning of divine wrath. To what purpose? To attack the presumption of righteousness, which is a rebellious, stubborn, and stiff-necked beast."
33 Martin Luther, "Commentary on Psalm 51" (1538) LW 12:390: "[If] you want to be converted, it is necessary that you be terrified or killed,

So if Luther believed it was wrong for pastors to be cowardly, he was also quick to point out just how they should behave constructively—and in some detail.

Slowly. Fifth, our judgments must never be hasty—for haste makes waste. Snap judgments are almost always wrong. Christians therefore believe that being slow to talk is not a sign of dullness or distraction, but rather one of respect (Jas 1:19). So we must take our time to mull over any judgment that we are planning to make. We must carefully review what we are going to say before we say it. We must check out any and all references to the Bible and other sources that we include in our judgment to make sure that they are cited accurately, and that they are appropriate. Being methodical, in this way, makes for good judgments. If we are too busy to be deliberate about what we want to say, then we should put off making our judgments until sometime later when we have more time to do it rightly—and carefully.

Collaboration. Finally, when we are working on the judgments we want to make, we should always consult with others, whom we respect, to see if they think we are on the right track (Mt 18:15–20; 1 Cor 5:1–13, 14:21). If they cannot confirm our judgments, then we should reconsider them and possibly make some changes to them. But if they think our judgements are

> that is, that you have a timid and trembling conscience. When this has happened, then you ought to accept the consolation not of some work of yours but of the work of God, who sent His Son Jesus Christ into this world to preach the consolation of free mercy to terrified sinners. This is the way of conversion; other ways are the ways of error . . . . Those who are . . . heirs of eternal life through Christ, whose merit they accept by faith—they [also] do good, [but] not with the purpose of attaining eternal life, to which they are already entitled by an alien merit, namely, Christ's, but with the purpose of being pleasing and obedient to the divine voice, so that the glory of God as well as holy teaching and life are promoted."

pretty good, then we should feel encouraged to proceed with them as planned. This is part of what Kierkegaard called being included in "the great fellowship of existence" (UDVS 183).

It is in this fellowship that the sermons in this book have been written—even though that does not mean that I am not responsible for what I have preached in them. But it does mean that I would covet your evaluation of my sermons—just as I have looked to Kierkegaard and Luther for help in writing every one of them.

Chapter 2

Sermons

When preaching has been done away with, faith, prayer, and the right use of the sacrament will not be able to exist.
(LW 2:84)

In *Kierkegaard for the Church* I describe Kierkegaardian sermons.[1] First they are didactic discourses—based on Biblical texts. They explicate and unfold the Biblical message rather than spin yarns of human delight and affluent sentiment. Second they are aggressive in spirit (PC 242)—as if there were enemies going against every word of the sermon. Third they follow the Lutheran threefold format: condemning sin, proclaiming Christ, and leading to good works (BC 185–86). Fourth they emphasize the good works that are fitting for those who believe in the Gospel of Jesus Christ (JP 6:6717). Fifth they go against the prevailing theological mediocrity infecting the church far and wide (JP 6:6743). And finally they are not timely—following the cultural trends and intellectual fads (WL 366). Instead they long for what is eternal and godly.

All the sermons in this collection struggle to exhibit these same half dozen sermonic traits. All of them were preached at

---

1   Ronald F. Marshall, *Kierkegaard for the Church: Essays and Sermons* (Eugene, Oregon: Wipf & Stock, 2013) 247–60.

my parish—First Lutheran Church of West Seattle, between 2007 and 2012. While writing them and delivering them I have also kept in mind Kierkegaard's notion of the living voice or apostolic nature of the preached sermon:

> Just as apostolic speech is essentially different in content from all human speech, so it is also in many ways different in form . . . . Apostolic speech is concerned, ardent, burning, inflamed, everywhere and always stirred by the forces of the new life, calling, shouting, beckoning, explosive in its outburst, brief, disjointed, harrowing, itself violently shaken as much by fear and trembling as by longing and blessed expectancy, everywhere witnessing to the powerful unrest of the spirit and the profound impatience of the heart [being] as impatient as that of a woman in labor. (EUD 69)[2]

This feature is not as apparent when reading the texts of these sermons—but I hope it was for those who heard them when they were first preached. Kierkegaard cared overall about *how* the truth was stated and not just about being clear about *what* was true (JP 1:678, 4:4558).[3] So this matter of the apostolic voice, in the delivery of the sermon, should probably also be included as a seventh trait of Kierkegaardian sermons.

So these sermons are not designed to smooth things over and make life easy. They instead actually try to upset their hearers, as Kierkegaard taught, and for the better:

---

2   See also *Kierkegaard for the Church*, 62–63 and 103.
3   See also CUP 1:202–203.

> If I were a clergyman and could preach in such a manner that the individual would go home from church wanting to hear me again, extolling me and exulting over me—however, if by studying his individuality I learned the way influence should be brought to bear with him and then proceeded to thrust him away so that he finally almost became angry with me and went and shut his door and prayed to God—in which case would I benefit him the most.
>
> (JP 5:5883)

But that does not mean that these sermons try to lord it over the bewildered congregation.[4] No, Kierkegaard instead thought that the first target of every sermon should be the one preaching it:

> What actually has made me a religious speaker? The fact that I am a listener. That is, my life was so complicated and intense that I truly felt the *need* to hear words of guidance. I listened and listened, but if what I heard was supposed to be Christianity, then there was no help for me. So I became a speaker myself. This accounts for my knowing with certainty what our pastors seldom know, that there *is* one who benefits

---

4   See also Luther's measured twofold remark from 1522: "Preach gently to the young and weak Christians. Let them enrich themselves and grow fat in the knowledge of Christ. Do not burden them with strong doctrine, for they are still too young. But later, when they grow strong, let them be slaughtered and sacrificed on the cross" (LW 30:49).

from these discourses: I myself. I am the exact opposite of other speakers: they are preoccupied with speaking to others—I speak to myself.

(JP 6:6424)[5]

---

5 Kierkegaard finishes this entry by adding: "And it is also a fact that insofar as others think it impossible to benefit from my discourses, then it must be because their lives are far too superficial, all too lacking in intensity, insulated from dangers." So while the preacher is supposed to be the first target of any given sermon, that does not prevent others from getting hit later. And so the unpopularity noted in footnote 12 on page 336 in *Kierkegaard for the Church*, also applies to this book, *Kierkegaard in the Pulpit*. Because of this trait in Kierkegaard's writings, I agree with Paul Tillich (1886–1965) that a preacher can find in them "more ideas for sermons than he can use even in a long lifetime." *The Ground of Being: Neglected Essays of Paul Tillich*, ed. Robert M. Price (Mindvendor Publications, 2015) p. 135.

Sermon 1

Take the Test

Today we're radicals because we've read Genesis 22 out loud in church on the near sacrifice of Isaac. Many Christians today are saying that these Bible verses shouldn't be read in church because they scare children—traumatizing them with the thought that God might also ask their parents to kill them.[1] So why have we today, blithely and a bit recklessly, waded into these deep and dangerous waters?

The Gushing Fountain

Some may think we actually haven't been so reckless, since Genesis 22 is assigned to be read only once every three years—and that's not so bad. What's more, having been read, it doesn't have to be preached on. So why are we being so brash today and doing that? Why am I preaching on it after it's been read, instead of pretending that no one was paying attention to it when it was read—and then just simply skip over it? We want some answers.

Well, the short answer is because Abraham was blessed when he passed the test up on Mt. Moriah (Gn 22:16). And since we want God to bless us too, we can't skip over the test like that. So in order to take the test, Genesis 22 has to be read out loud and preached on from the pulpit. If we were to run away from

---

1 James L. Crenshaw, *A Whirlpool of Torment* (Philadelphia: Fortress, 1984).

what Martin Luther called—in his hundred page lecture from 1539 on Genesis 22—"the greatness of this trial" (LW 4:92), then we wouldn't be blessed. And the blessing we'd miss is that Abraham will have many descendants and that all the nations will be blessed through them (Gn 22:17–18). Luther points out that Christ is included in those descendants—as forecasted in Genesis 3:15 (LW 4:175)—and so what we want from God is actually "the gushing fountain" of those blessings (LW 4:151). And that is "deliverance from sin and hell" (LW 4:149). So a great deal is at stake for us on Mt. Moriah—therefore we will have to climb that mountain of sacrifice with Abraham and Isaac.

The Traumatic Walk

And when we do, it will also be traumatic for us—since the blessing we're after can't cover over the terror the test brings with it. No, the trauma goes along with the test whenever and wherever it's taken up. Søren Kierkegaard, that great admirer of Luther, wrote a famous book at the beginning of his authorship on Genesis 22, aptly called, *Fear and Trembling*. In it he argues that we can't receive the same blessing Abraham did without also enduring that slow three day journey up the mountain with him—at least in a figurative way. We can't, as he said, skip the walk and fly to the top of the mountain, in a flash, in a moment, on some "winged horse," to steal the blessing without any accompanying pain (FT 52). No, the "anxiety and distress" in the walking is the necessary precondition of the blessing itself (FT 53, 64, 65, 66, 74, 113). And it is this distress that makes the test an "unbelievable trial," as Luther notes (LW 4:106)—because for three days Isaac's life was up in the air. Would he live or would he die?—it simply wasn't known.

Pegasus Coin
345-307 BC
Corinth, Greece

"Nowhere else in Holy Scripture," writes Luther, "is a walk like this described" (LW 4:111). Well, I should hope not! One's plenty enough. For that slow walk up the mountain keeps "the reader in suspense to the point of weariness" (LW 4:112). And our anxiety in large part comes from knowing that we could not endure as Abraham did—Abraham being "the greatest among the holy patriarchs" (LW 4:91). For Abraham is called the father of the faithful (Rom 4:16)—and we are not, since none of us has the magnitude or level of trust in the Lord that he had. This is because even though Naomi (Ruth 1:3-5) and Job (Job 1:13–19, 2:7) lost more than Abraham did, neither of them was commanded to immolate their own children, as Abraham was told to do. That he had to bear the burden of that heavy command is what makes him the father of the faithful—since the command "confronts Abraham with a contradiction," which then makes his Lord and God look like "an enemy and a tyrant" (LW 4:94). Luther explains the magnitude of Abraham's faith in this way, saying that its glory is in

> not to know . . . what you are doing, what you are suffering, and, after taking everything captive—perception and understanding, strength and will—to follow the bare voice of God [*nudam Dei vocem*] and to be led and driven rather than to drive . . . . It is certain that Abraham had many who found fault with . . . this faith and . . . out of some pernicious piety advised him not to believe that what was happening was from God.
> (LW 29:238)

Here we see that the magnitude of his faith rests on his trust in that bare, uninterpreted word of God (2 Cor 4:2; 2 Pt 1:20)—the *nudam vocem*. This is a faith that does not waver when challenged, since it rises above it all—for your life is "hid with Christ in God" (Col 3:2). For, properly understood, faith is not grounded in what is seen or handily managed (Heb 11:1; Jn 3:8, 20:29; Rom 10:17; Acts 14:22). No, it's based on hearing the word of God and keeping it (Lk 11:28; Rom 10:17).

Abraham's Silence

Now what's so terrifying about Abraham's trial is that he says virtually nothing about what's going on during it. If we knew, for example, that he had private assurances from God that he wasn't going to have to kill his son, then we could much more easily go along with it. Then our fear and trembling would be abated to a great extent. But all we have instead is silence—infuriating, exasperating, silence (FT 60). Nowhere does Abraham argue with God over this command (LW 4:107)—as he earlier did regarding Sodom and Gomorrah (Gn 18:20–32). No, they just walk along calmly to their dreaded fate without saying much of anything. There's only silence as they go. And that's not because Abraham is reticent about what he knows, but because he just "can't . . . explain" what's going on (FT 115, 80, 71). It would be as if he were speaking in a "strange tongue" if he had tried to explain his ordeal (FT 114, 119). So he wouldn't have been understood if he had talked about it. Maybe that's why the little bit we do get from him is fraught with ambiguity—namely, that God will provide the lamb (Gn 22:8). But couldn't that be Isaac himself, we wonder, in some symbolic way? And that maddens us—that we don't know exactly what God will provide as the burnt offering. And come to find out, it's not a lamb [שׂה] at all, but a ram [איל] instead (Gn 22:13). In addition, when Abraham speaks about

God providing the sacrifice, he does "not... disclose [the plan] that Isaac himself must die" (LW 4:112)—which is something of a lie which also complicates the silence all the more.

So there's trauma galore in Genesis 22. At the end of this reading, we learn that Sarah, the mother of Isaac, dies (Gn 23:2). The old rabbis, we're told,[2] thought they knew what happened before she died. Abraham and Isaac came home from Mt. Moriah and Sarah asked them how their trip had gone. Abraham told her that he almost killed their boy in a sacrifice to the Lord. Sarah then "uttered six cries and . . . died"—probably of cardiac arrest—maybe screeching out at the end, "What! Have you gone mad, you old fool?!" That's not much of a stretch, it seems to me, even though it's only legend. And from this we see that the trauma in this trial endures even after it's over and the blessing has come. So the blessing cannot wipe away the fear it's everlastingly built upon.

Our Modified Exam

So what about us, now? What's it like for us up in the thin air atop Mt. Moriah? What will our trial look like? Will it be exactly the same as Abraham's was? Luther argues that our test will differ from his because we, unlike Abraham, haven't been commanded by God to kill our children (LW 4:124). King Ahaz thought Abraham's command extended to all of us, and so he "burned his son as an offering" (2 Kgs 16:3). But by so doing, Luther argues, he committed "a grievous sin; for God did not command this" (LW 4:180). Our trial, then, will be different—"from afar, so to speak" (LW 4:96). This is because Abraham's command is not repeated to us. If

---

2   Gerhard von Rad, *Biblical Interpretation in Preaching* (Nashville: Abingdon, 1977) 38.

it was intended to be, some monument would have been built on Mt. Moriah to draw our attention, but that wasn't done (LW 4:178–79). What then will our trial be like? How will it differ from Abraham's? How will it look to us—from afar?

We can only approach Genesis 22 from the perspective of the New Testament. Just as "an eye for an eye, and a tooth for a tooth" (Lv 24:20) isn't carried over into the New Testament (Mt 5:38-39), and Psalm 8 isn't really about exalting us, but praising Christ our Lord (Heb 2:5–9), so, too, Abraham's trial isn't the same for us. Our version of it is in Matthew 10:37-38:

> He who loves father and mother more than me is not worthy of me; and he who loves son or daughter more than me is not worthy of me; and he who does not take his cross and follow me is not worthy of me.

That's the New Testament version of Genesis 22. That means our test will be a matter of getting our priorities right. It's not that we love God and kill our kids—but that we love God more than our children. It means having our priorities set straight. That's our test—to love God more than anything else. And that's not too far away from Genesis 22:12 about fearing God more than anyone else.

Martin Luther digs deeply into this test in Matthew 10. For him it's about keeping the creator above the creatures. The creator is the ocean and we are but little drops of water by comparison. "Let the drop" therefore "yield submission to the ocean," he charges (LW 26:107). This does not mean, however, that we should disregard one another, abandon our families, practice social irresponsibility and become disrespectful children or dead-beat parents. No,

in the absence of an emergency everyone must remain in his town, place, and calling, and not forsake his family; all should remain together where they belong. But if the alternative ever confronts us—either to leave our calling and position or to deny Christ—then I declare: "Rather than deny Christ, I will sacrifice life, house, home, etc."
(LW 23:202)

That's because God is most important. He trumps everything—for in our test he has "commanded confidence and condemned despair" (LW 4:105). As such, we must keep our priorities straight and know what's most important in our lives. When creatures aren't challenging God's superiority, then it's fine for us to care for them—and diligently at that (LW 6:27). But when they want to usurp God's place, then there's an emergency and we must put them in their place—demote them, if you will—but not try to kill them. This means that being steadfast in faith is the limit that our love for one another must face. Therefore

> a curse on a love that is observed at the expense of the doctrine of faith, to which everything must yield—love, an apostle, an angel from heaven, etc. (LW 27:38)

For "love and faith are exact opposites in their intentions, their tasks, and their values" (LW 26:119). When they conflict, love must lose out (LW 14:244). That's because if "love is the most important, ... I lose Christ" (LW 26:270)—which is blasphemy.

Therefore we must be dialectical about this, needing as we do, "careful distinction and accurate logic," so that we don't confuse faith and love (LW 6:28–29). An example of such an emergency would be marriage. If a non-Christian husband doesn't let his wife "be a Christian and live a Christian life, ... then divorce is in order" (LW 28:33), when otherwise it's strictly forbidden (Matthew 19:18). Another example would be the Lord's Supper. "If fickle fanatics juggle and play the clown with the words of the Supper according to their fancy," then we must "shun, condemn, and censure them" (LW 37:27). In these cases, being tolerant is out of bounds, as it would be if your children were discovered to be fornicators (Eph 5:3) or practicing homosexuals (Rom 1:26-28). Just because your children are doing this or that doesn't make it right (LW 1:122). In this case even the Muslims have it right that our children can be temptations to us (Qur'ān 8:28; 64:14–15).

Kierkegaard spells out this asymmetry very well. In Matthew 22:37–39 it says we are to love God with everything that is in us, but our neighbors we are to love only as ourselves. This is because

> a person should love God unconditionally *in obedience* and love him *in adoration*. [But] it is ungodliness if any human being dares to love himself in this way, or . . . another person in this way, or dares to allow another person to love him in this way. (WL 19)

Once again, creatures are not to be treated like the creator (Rom 1:25). This distinction must be admitted and honored.

Being Ransomed

So are you ready for the test? Or are you tormented by that recurrent collegian's nightmare—that you're lined up for an exam in a class you forgot to attend—and so you panic, since no solution is in sight. Is that how you feel—when looking at Mt. Moriah afar off? Are you rattled—unprepared for the test God has for you?

If so, how shall we proceed? Trying harder doesn't seem to get us very far. Trying to forget, never lasts very long. So it seems we need help from beyond ourselves—or *extra nos*, as Luther put it (LW 24:347; 26:387; 42:48; 51:28). At just this point the words from Mark 1:15 feel like a fresh breeze blowing gently our way: "Repent and believe in the Gospel," they say. So rather than trying to dig ourselves out of this hole, all we have to do is admit we've failed. Repent, the Good Book says. Say you're wrong and ask God to forgive you. And God will step in. But not because we're worth it (LW 30:301; 31:57). No, God will rescue us because he's loving and not because we're lovable. So don't despair. That can send you right back down into the hole you've dug for yourself earlier. No, instead do this: Repent and believe in the Gospel.

But what is that Gospel? Mark 10:45 says it's that Jesus came to give his life as a ransom for us. But what's a ransom? It's what gets you out of prison, or frees you from the oppression of kidnappers. And what is our imprisonment? Where are we in jail? Sin is our prison!—that ignorance and defiance from which we cannot free ourselves (Jn 8:34; Rom 6:20–22). Luther called that being twisted in on ourselves—or *incurvatus in se* (LW 25:291, 313, 341). This is the chief burden that weighs us down (Mt 11:28). It's what generates the "objectless anxiety" that counselors report hearing about from their mysteriously depressed clients.[1] But what exactly is that ransom that saves us from this imprisonment—from this objectless anxiety that terrifies us as long as it's allowed to go on without any identification or resolution?

The ransom is simply the cross of Christ. That's the price paid to set us free (1 Cor 6:20, 7:23; LW 47:113). For only in the crucifixion of Jesus is our poverty of spirit turned into glorious riches (2 Cor 8:9). Only on his cross are we saved from our sins. Only in his death do we find life—getting out from under the burden of sin, guilt and fear. Only in his suffering and death are we kept free from that "place of torment" (Lk 16:23, 28)—which is hell itself (LW 25:435). Only in Christ do we see that "death is nothing but a sport and empty little bugaboo of the human race, yes, an annoyance" (LW 4:116)! Therefore we must

> see the enormity of God's wrath over sin, and learn that there is no other remedy for this than the death of God's Son.... If there is no sin, then Christ is nothing. Why should he die if there is no sin or law for which he must die?
> (LW 47:110; 52:253)

Our only remedy or ransom, then, is Christ Jesus. Without this ransom, whatever else we say about Jesus will only be "preaching half of Christ." That is because Christ is fundamentally

> the Price by which satisfaction is made for divine justice and wrath on our behalf.... If He has placed Himself in His own Person to

---

3 Rollo May, *The Meaning of Anxiety* (1950), (New York: Norton, 2015) 56, 191.

turn away wrath from us, He has established Himself as the Price.

(LW 28:264)

And so we cannot settle for an idea, a concept, a narrative or some work of art. What we need instead is this person who is both human and divine—as well as his painful suffering and death for us. For in the cross the wrath of God is lifted off of our backs (Jn 3:36). Jesus is our ram caught in the thicket (Gn 22:13; LW 4:137, 11:102). No longer are we then the object of his divine fury—just as Isaac's throat was no longer under that knife's blade. For in Christ, God has sworn to be merciful (Gn 22:16; Jn 6:27). Knowing this, and believing in this, makes us "buoyant" (LW 4:158)—freed from darkness and despair. So God tests us that he might "stir up faith and love in us" (LW 4:132).

Sacrificing To The Lord

And when you come down from the mountain, see to it that you also walk in the ways of the Lord. Struggle with Luther to "carry out God's commands" —foreswearing all social "wantonness, lewdness, extravagance in dress, gluttony, gambling, [and] extortion in every trade" (BC 291, 290). And do that by heeding Romans 12:1–2:

> Present your bodies as a living sacrifice, holy and acceptable to God, which is our spiritual worship. Do not be conformed to this world but be transformed by the renewal of your mind, that you may prove what is the will of God, what is good and acceptable and perfect.

For this is "the most useful knowledge" of all (LW 25:438). Amen.

Sermon 2

Endure

Matthew 24:13 says whoever endures to the end will be saved. Why does our Lord Jesus say that? Why does he want us to hang in there, not give up, keep our nose to the grindstone and toe the line? Why does he want us to tough it out and endure—endure, endure to the end? Why all of this pressure on us?

Giving Up So Quickly

Saint Paul answers our question for us in Galatians 1:6. There he says to the Christians in Galatia how shocked he is that they have so quickly abandoned the Gospel of Jesus Christ which he had proclaimed to them. This is indeed shocking news because it says, in effect, that the seal of our salvation (Eph 4:30) can be broken—due to our "willful" turning away from God (BC 623, 35). So if we've been saved, that doesn't mean we'll always be saved.[1]

---

1 On this questionable Calvinist teaching on the perseverance of the saints, see J. Walls and J. Dongell, *Why I Am Not a Calvinist* (Downers Grove, Illinois: InterVarsity, 2004) 79–84.

No, matters in this life are up for grabs—that's why we are to work out our salvation in "fear and trembling" (Phil 2:12), with all spiritual cockiness purged from us (1Cor10:12). As long as we live, it remains uncertain whether or not we'll "continue in the faith" (Col 1:23; Lk 17:5, 18:8). And if we are to be saved, we must do just that—believe to the end (Jn 3:16; Rv 2:10). It is therefore wrong of us to suppose that it's "enough merely to accept the Gospel, [for] acceptance must be followed by that spiritual power which renders faith firm . . . in conflicts and temptations" (SML 8:267). We must "lead the life of active soldiers" (LW 20:8) for by such pugilistic, spiritual efforts we are then able "to remain steadfast" (LW 13:177). We must not willingly remain "hardened, impious [and] insensitive" (LW 25:478).

So beware. Don't forget Alexander and Hymenaeus who made a "shipwreck of their faith" (1 Tm 1:20). The same could happen to you. And this can also come about quietly by "drifting away" from so great a salvation (Heb 2:1–3). How ghastly!

Grievously Tempted

The reason our faith gives way is because we shamefully give in to temptations. And they're all around us—as well as within us. The devil, we are told, prowls around like a lion, seeking to devour us (1 Pt 5:8). And, as if that were not enough, from within us also come all sorts of evils which defile us, "reptilian thoughts" (LW 51:25), as Luther called them—such terrible things as pride and foolishness, fornication and murder (Mk 7:20–23).

We are vulnerable to these temptations because we fear people instead of God. Søren Kierkegaard, whom we remember this time of year—thanking God for his abiding witness to the riches of Christ Jesus—aptly describes these false fears:

> Instead of impressing upon [one another] a holy fear and a sense of shame before the good, [we teach others] to fear financial loss, loss of reputation, lack of appreciation, disregard, the judgment of the world, the mockery of fools, the laughter of light-mindedness, the cowardly whining of obeisance, the inflated insignificance of the moment, the delusive, misty apparitions of miasma [or swamp gases]. (UDVS 58)

These false fears make us "effervesce," Kierkegaard says, and we then end up loving the moment, fearing time and counterfeiting eternity—by turning it into "the deceptive illusion of the horizon, . . . the bluish boundary of time, . . . [and] the dazzling jugglery of the moment" (UDVS 62–63).

Deeply Distracted

Kierkegaard further explains that these temptations are so deep, that they are even rooted in time itself:

> Alas, time and busyness think that eternity is very far away, and yet in drama the producer has never at any time had everything in readiness for the stage and the transformation of the performers in the way eternity [or God] has everything ready . . . at every moment—although it holds back. (UDVS 66)

Time nit-picks our souls to death with its myriad distractions. We have lists of things to do each day—and none of what we write down has anything to do with eternity. Time not only envelops us—but it also seems to consume us. We can't get free of it and we can't save ourselves from it either. Time is a strange thing to talk about—and yet we must because eternity is at stake. The temporal flow tries to rob us of eternity. Kierkegaard says it tries to make us think that eternity is very far away. "Goaded on," he continues,

> in superstitious delusion one would rather hope for [temporality's help] than grasp the eternal . . . . Ah, it is a foolish sagacity (however much it swaggers, however loquacious it is) that foolishly defrauds itself out of the highest comfort and by means of a mediocre comfort helps itself into an even more mediocre comfort, and ultimately into certain regret. (UDVS 114)

No wonder we're told not to set our minds on earthly things, but on the things that are instead above (Col 3:2).

No Ability Implied

Yet even with this clarification and authorization for the call to endure, we still find ourselves waffling. It's clear that we are to endure, but we cannot seem to pull it off—the good that we would do, we just can't do (Rom 7:18). Why, then, are we told to do it? Is this command itself somehow incoherent? Or is it just sheer mockery of our miserable incapacities?

Well, actually, it's neither. This is because commands in Christianity do not imply ability—by necessity. That is to say, just because we're told to do something, does not mean we can.

Now if that is so, then why are we told to do it in the first place? The sense in all of this seems to escape us—to say the very least. So what's up? How should we understand these Biblical commands?

In Christianity, commands don't act normally but function differently. Luther explains their unusual purpose in this way:

> Moses . . . issues commandments about doing, but does not describe man's ability to do. The inference tacked on by [foolish reason] however concludes: Therefore man is able to do such things, otherwise they would be commanded in vain . . . . [But this] reasoning is bad . . . [For] the commandments are not . . . . either inappropriate or purposeless, but are given in order that blind, self-confident man may through them come to know his own diseased state of impotence if he attempts to do what is commanded. (LW 33:128)

Our inability is therefore to lead us to despair over our own infected or disordered capacities (PV 54), so that we might long for someone else—who is stronger—to save us (Rom 7:24–25).

The Steadfastness of Christ

Our failure to do what we should do, could easily drive us to despair and unbelief. We could lament our failure and end up with "darkness" as our only companion (Ps 88:18). But that malaise is not the only possible outcome. From early on the hope has instead been that we'll be driven to Christ (LW 16:232; 26:126).

And in our despair if we look to Christ we'll learn that he is the one who strengthens us so we can endure (1 Thes 3:12–13)—in spite of ourselves. And this he does by way of his "steadfastness" (2 Thes 3:5). Great power is manifest in that steadfastness. We first and foremost see this in his crucifixion. He was "obedient unto death—even death on a cross" (Phil 2:8). That resolve to sacrifice his life for sin (Heb 9:26) takes great intestinal fortitude. It takes sterling singleness of purpose. On the cross he was taunted: "Save yourself! . . . . Come down from the cross . . . . and we'll believe in [you] . . . . Let God deliver you now, if he desires you" (Mt 27:40–43). But Jesus doesn't budge. He is not swayed by their mockery. His face, after all, has been "set . . . to go to Jerusalem," so he can die for the sins of the world (Lk 9:51, 53). There's no turning back now. He'll bear the sins of the entire world in his body (1 Pt 2:24; 1 Jn 2:2) —regardless of how painful it is (Heb 12:2, 13:13). He will become sin who knew no sin (2 Cor 5:21; Rom 8:3; 2 Cor 8:9; Heb 4:15). He will become a curse to save us from the curse (Galatians 3:13). None of this ignominy will sway him—for he is steadfast, obedient and resolved to save us from our sin by being punished "in our place"—as our very substitute—*Ich trit an deine stat* (LW 22:167). He'll take what we had coming.

And in his suffering and death, Christ will move "the Father to grace" (LW 51:277) so that "God is reconciled to us" (BC 121)[2] by way of the stilling of his wrath (BC 138). For indeed, Christ

---

2   See also BC 137, 140, 142, 147, 149, 152, 153, 165, 166, 216, 253, 257, and 260. Note also that these passages on reconciling God go against Robert W. Jenson, *Systematic Theology*, 2 vols. (New York: Oxford, 1997–1999) 2:187.

was placed under the law for us, bore our sin, and in his path to the Father rendered to his Father entire, perfect obedience from his holy birth to his death in the stead of us poor sinners, and thus covered up our disobedience, which inheres in our nature, . . . so that our disobedience is not reckoned to us for our damnation but is forgiven . . . by sheer grace for Christ's sake alone. (BC 550)

No wonder, then, that Kierkegaard erupts at the end of his 1848 book, *Christian Discourses*, saying: "I will seek my refuge with . . . the Crucified One, ... to save me from myself" (CD 280)!

And the second way Christ's steadfastness helps us is by strengthening us now, in this life (1 Tm 4:8). Christ's victory becomes ours right now. It doesn't just open the gates of heaven in the end (Heb 10:20), but helps us endure right now. This is a strange notion—since we know that other important qualities, like the talent to play baseball, for instance, cannot be shared. But Christ's victory over "sin, death, God's wrath, the devil, hell and eternal damnation" (LW 23:404) can be shared with us (2 Cor 4:14). Through this sharing, when we believe in his victory and entrust our lives to his care, he becomes "our righteousness," though we remain "ungodly" (1 Cor 1:30; Rom 5:6).

With this strengthening, we, like Saint Paul, can then shout out that we can now "do all things" (Phil 4:13)! This is because, as Saint Paul also says, "it is no longer I who live, but Christ who lives in me" (Gal 2:20). But when he shares his steadfastness with us, it does not mean we're perfect (Phil 3:12; SML 8:280; LW 27:26). No, all it means is that we can now persistently press on to that "upward call of God in Christ

Jesus" (Phil 3:14). All it means is that we need not "grow weary in well doing" (Gal 6:9). All it means is that a Christian "should not bear the name without the works" (SML 7:161).

Lord, Forgive Us!

In the face of our "spiritual fornication" (LW 25:346) with temporality and finitude (*contra* Jn 15:18-19), we must now repent of our filthy, sinful descent into time. This is because we were not made to be absorbed into time. So with Kierkegaard, we should sneer in the face of temporality, and query:

> Why was an immortal spirit placed in the world and in time, just as a fish is pulled out of the water and cast onto the beach? (UDVS 62)

Therefore let us repent now. Let us crawl back into the water, as it were. Do not therefore "weary your soul with makeshift, temporary palliatives; do not grieve the spirit with temporal consolations" (UDVS 101)! Repent instead. All those temporal consolations do is make your mind vacillate between "drowsiness and a burning tension" (UDVS 112). Therefore repent, even though it isn't popular. Kierkegaard puts it this way, on a related matter:

> If adhered to it will make your life strenuous, many a time perhaps burdensome; if adhered to it will perhaps expose you to ridicule by others, not to mention that adherence might ask even greater sacrifices from you. It goes without saying that the ridicule will not disturb you, that is, if you hold fast to the conviction;

the ridicule will even be of advantage to you also by convincing you even more that you are on the right path. (UDVS 136)

So repent and bear the burden and the ridicule—you're on the right path. And do that by praying to God to forgive you your sins.

Martin Luther, in his *Large Catechism*, explains that prayer for forgiveness in this way:

> There is great need to . . . pray, 'Dear Father, forgive us . . .' Not that he does not forgive sin . . . before our prayer . . . . But the point here is for us to recognize and accept this forgiveness. For the flesh in which we daily live is of such a nature that it does not trust and believe God and is constantly aroused by evil desires and devices, so that we sin daily in word and deed, in acts of commission and omission. Thus our conscience becomes restless; it fears God's wrath and . . . loses the comfort . . . of the Gospel. Therefore it is necessary constantly to [pray this prayer. This serves] God's purpose to break our pride and keep us humble . . . . If anyone boasts of his goodness, . . . he should examine himself in the light of this [prayer]. He will find that he is no better than others, that in the presence of God all men must humble themselves and be glad they can attain forgiveness. Let no one think that he will ever in this life reach the point where he does not need this forgiveness. In short, unless God constantly forgives, we are lost. Thus this [prayer] is really an appeal to

> God not to . . . punish us as we daily deserve,
> but to . . . forgive as he has promised, and grant
> us a . . . cheerful conscience. (BC 432)

These powerful words will help keep you on the right path. For in them we have the motivation and requirements for forgiveness, as well as the dangers and fears clearly stated if it's rejected and lost.

Abiding in Christ

Now, all of you who have heard these words of Christ regarding his steadfastness, come to the Altar, bow down and receive him this day—"in, with, and under" (BC 575) the bread and the wine of the Lord's Supper. Bow down knowing that "to be lifted up to God is possible only by going down" (WA 132). Know that when you receive this sacrament, Christ himself will abide in you that you may abide in him (Jn 6:56). And when you abide in Christ, his steadfastness will become yours as well. Rejoice in the strength it provides for you—making you "divinely strong in weakness" (WA 176). Do not doubt that it is here for you—"to bring . . . refreshment" (BC 449). Know that in it there's "abundant life" for you (Jn 6:53, 10:10) or *zoe*, ζωη, in the Greek. This isn't sheer existing (βιος)—this is a rich life with God.

Welcome the Prophets

And when you leave church today, do good works in Christ's name. Practice what's been preached. Live a life worthy of the Gospel you've heard today (Phil 1:27). Follow Jeremiah 26:5 which says "heed . . . the prophets" whom God urgently sends. They are the ones who call us to greater faithfulness. They are the ones who insist that God wants us to live "a vastly higher life than others know" (SML 8:282). And rather than rejecting them and even killing them because of the pressure they place on us, let us simply bless them in the name of the Lord (Mt 23:39).

And may we do the same with those prophets who have followed the Biblical ones and witnessed among us in our time. See them as your friends—even though they too bear down on you in order to hold your feet to the fire. Welcome them even though they press for greater dedication and discipleship (LW 26:99).

May we this day so regard Søren Kierkegaard, from Copenhagen, Denmark, whose writings have blessed us these last one hundred and fifty years. Let us honor him as did the poet, W. H. Auden (1907–1973), winner of the Pulitzer Prize (1948), Bollingen Prize (1954) and the National Book Award (1956). Let us say of Kierkegaard this day—in Auden's words[3]—that

> a great deal of Kierkegaard's work is addressed to the man who has already become uneasy about himself, and by encouraging him to look more closely at himself, shows him that his condition is more serious than he thought . . . Nobody except Christ and, at the end of their lives perhaps, the saints are Christian. To say "I am a Christian" really means "I who am a sinner am required to become like Christ."

---

3   *The Living Thoughts of Kierkegaard* (1952), ed. W. H. Auden (New York: New York Review Books, 1999) xxv, xxviii. For a contemporary account of this uneasiness, see Julie Holland, "The Medicated States of America," *The Seattle Times* (October 9, 2015): A13: "Americans suffer from an over-abundance of processed foods, synthetic hormones, virtual relationships, silicone breasts and, now, fake moods, brought about by and ever-increasing percentage of us taking psychiatric medications. The patients I meet in my Manhattan psychiatric practice are stressed, sad and scared."

To that I say Amen—and again I say, Amen.

Sermon 3

Don't Doubt

These are great days—the seven weeks of Easter. They're even better than Christmas—and longer too. That's because it takes seven full weeks to sing all our Easter Alleluias. And that's because we're celebrating the victory over sin and death—which is great indeed. So don't start planning for Mother's Day and Memorial Day just yet. We still have lots of Alleluias to sing!

Learning from Doubt

Why then do we take today to remember the doubting Thomas? Every year we do this on the second Sunday of Easter. Why is that? Doesn't dwelling on doubt dampen our celebration—and rain on our parade? Why then do we give him so much attention? Shouldn't we be devoting today to singing more Easter Alleluias instead? Well, not really. And the reason for this is that there's so much to learn from the doubting Thomas and his skeptical ways. And so we give him more time than one would expect.

Controlling Doubt

Now the first thing we learn from him is the very anatomy of doubt. This is important because by understanding its structure, we can better avoid the pitfalls of doubt. And that's a good thing, because Jesus said—"Don't doubt, but believe" (Jn 20:27). Don't doubt like Thomas did. How much clearer could this be? So those who would celebrate doubt, as what makes us religiously mature,[1] or who imagine that faith and doubt actually go together—saying that "serious doubt is confirmation of faith"[2]—well, they have it all wrong. We shouldn't be open "to new ideas—to truth wherever it is," and trust in that process of discovery.[3] That's because our Lord Jesus said—"Don't doubt, but believe." He wouldn't have said that if doubt was truly grand and glorious. He wouldn't have said that if what he really wanted for the church was the "tentative" attitude of the scientist.[4]

No, Jesus wasn't some sort of skeptic, who along with the father of modern philosophy, René Descartes (1596–1650), peddled doubt to make us mature and secure. Unlike Jesus, Descartes' philosophy was founded on the dictum—*dubito ergo sum*, "I doubt therefore I am."[5] Jesus rather said, "When you have lifted up the Son of man, then you will know that I am," or *tunc . . . ego sum*, in the old Latin Bible (Jn 8:28). So a life of doubt and hesitation would be a disaster for Christianity. It would send us on wild goose chases—for as the philosopher Peter Strawson puts it, in the swimming pool of philosophy, "there's no shallow end."[6] For once doubt takes hold, we are forever paddling just to keep our heads above water. That's

---

1 See Val Webb, *In Defense of Doubt: An Invitation to Adventure*, (St. Louis: Chalice, 1995).
2 Paul Tillich, *The Dynamics of Faith* (New York: Harper & Row, 1957) 22.
3 Contra John B. Cobb, Jr., *Doubting Thomas* (New York: Crossroads, 1990) 83, 33.
4 Bertrand Russell, *The Will to Doubt* (New York: The Philosophical Library, 1958) 22.
5 *The Philosophical Works of Descartes*, 2 vols, trans. Elizabeth S. Haldane and G. R. T. Ross (Cambridge: Cambridge University, 1969–70) 1:219, 324.
6 *Analysis and Metaphysics* (New York: Oxford, 1992) vii.

because doubt cuts our legs out from under us—gleefully throwing our daily lives into question.[7] No wonder, then, that "plain showing off is . . . a feature of the philosophical life."[8]

But in our life with God, there's no place for all this caution. Before him we are instead to trust, obey and follow—not hesitate, look back (Lk 9:62) or doubt! If we were to do that, we would look like crazy beggars—as Martin Luther put it long ago. And that's worth pondering since he's our "most eminent teacher" (BC 576). His words then are:

> Our Lord God can give a wavering heart nothing, even though he would dearly love to do so . . . . We stand there like crazy beggars. We hold out our hat, hoping God will put something into it, but we keep moving it around, refusing to hold it still. (LHP 2:423)

That's what doubt does to us—it keeps us from holding our hats still. And as long as we keep pushing them out and pulling them back, moving them from side to side, over and over again, we'll fumble all the blessings God sends our way! And this is the height of recklessness. No wonder Luther went on to say that doubt is a horrifying and "dangerous plague" (LW 26:377).[9]

---

7   Robert Fogelin, *Walking the Tightrope of Reason* (New York: Oxford, 2003) 67.
8   Colin McGinn, *The Making of a Philosopher* (New York: HarperCollins, 2002) 63.
9   And once it sets in, Epicurus of old looks very attractive. On this see George Santayana, *Three Philosophical Poets: Lucretius, Dante, Goethe* (New York: Doubleday Anchor, 1953) 34: "Epicurus . . . . denied the supernatural, since belief in it would have a disquieting influence on the mind, and render too many things compulsory and momentous. There was no future life: the art of living wisely must not be distorted

But even so, doubt has a place when it comes to building good bridges and performing life-saving surgeries. Then we want our engineers and physicians to test materials and plans with a careful and critical eye in order to make sure no mistakes are being made. But when it comes to God, we have to shift gears and simply "hear the word and keep it" (Lk 11:28, 8:21)! To allow doubt to spill over into our religious lives only destroys faith. For "doubt . . . . is by far the gravest of all the sins which condemn the world and the unbelievers" (LW 4:147). So the "effrontery to teach . . . that one should doubt," is nothing less than the devil's work (LW 8:312).

The Show Me State

Now why was Thomas so skeptical? And why do any of us doubt, for that matter (Matthew 14:31)? Well, it's because we're from Missouri—the "Show Me State."[10] For Missourians are no fools. They're hard-headed skeptics who have to be shown what is true before they'll believe it. So Thomas, true to form, wouldn't believe what he couldn't confirm with his own eyes. He was obsessed, if you will, with empirical evidence. This accounts for his bravado after Easter when he says of Jesus, that "unless I see in his hands the print of the nails, and place my finger in the mark of the nails, and place my hand in his side, I will not believe" (Jn 20:25). Thomas wasn't going to be taken in. And he believed that the way to steer clear of being snookered, was to test everything physically. The old adage that "a bird in the hand is better than two in the bush"[11] is founded on such a hope.

---

by such wild imaginings."
10 See John W. Brown, *Missouri Legends* (Saint Louis: Reedy, 2008).
11 See John Bunyan, *The Pilgrim's Progress* (1768).

Now Jesus surprisingly goes along with Thomas on this matter. He shows up again and invites him to take a look and to take a touch—or two. But in the process this turns out to actually be a test for him and for all of us, instead of a verification of the resurrection of Jesus Christ. For no sooner than Thomas comes to faith at the wonder of seeing the risen Christ before him, Jesus nails him by saying, "Blessed are those who have not seen and yet believe" (Jn 20:29). Note that it doesn't say that they are "more blessed" than those who do see. That would imply that those who see in order to believe, would also be blessed—just not as much as those who don't see and yet believe. But that isn't it at all.

No, what we have instead is a blessing reserved just for those who don't see. And that's radical, for it demeans eyewitnesses from then on. So what begins with eyewitnesses and empirical evidence, ends differently (1 Jn 1:1–5). That's because there is a little noticed weakness in empirical evidence. Luther elaborates this point:

> [Jesus] offers us peace . . . . in the Gospel as certainly and clearly as it was . . . shown to the disciples bodily . . . . And it is much better that it is done through the Gospel than if he now entered here by the door; for you would not know him, even if you saw him standing before you, even much less than the Jews recognized him. (SML 2:373)

Here Luther builds on the fact—which is quite contrary to popular opinion—that not everyone who witnessed the miracles of Jesus believed in him because they saw them (Jn 12:37). This shows that empirical evidence isn't all that it's cracked up to be.¹² So in our life with God, being from Missouri is actually of little help—and even a disadvantage! Luther elaborates this point by saying:

> Reason and human nature . . . never go beyond what they perceive, and where there is no perception, they immediately deny God . . . . The natural light of man and the light of grace cannot be friends. Human nature wants perception and certitude as a condition for faith. Grace wants faith prior to perception . . . . Grace happily steps out into the darkness and follows nothing but the word and the Scriptures. (LW 52:196)

So believing is seeing—and not the reverse, as Thomas, the philosophers and those from Missouri would have us think. For only "the deaf and ignorant . . . will hear" (LW 16:248; Jn 9:39).

Fighting Doubt

So doubt is neither to be celebrated nor endured. This is because a "Christian should . . . not doubt" or "be content with anything" other than a firm faith, which is the confidence by which we "gain the victory" (SML 6:229, 247, 260). When doubt creeps in, as it did with Thomas, we shouldn't settle for that thinning out of our faith. We shouldn't "float and bob in uncertainty" (SML 2:401). No, we should instead "engage in a continual struggle against doubt" (LW 6:10). We have to

---

12 Think of the dispute over the Rodney King video—apparently its record of him being beaten up by LA police wasn't as plain as first supposed. See Lou Cannon, *Official Negligence: How Rodney King and the Riots Changed Los Angeles and the LAPD* (New York: Random House, 1999).

fight against that "devil's yeast," as Luther called it (LW 7:233), which persistently clings to our hearts—perniciously holding us back from a rich and robust faith in our Savior, Christ Jesus. Our goal should be to "strive for certainty," and "believe with complete certainty" (LW 26:379). So just because we doubt, doesn't mean we should continue to (Mk 9:24).

How then should we go about fighting against doubt? Søren Kierkegaard, that great admirer of Martin Luther, warned against the wrong way to wage this war against doubt:

> Some . . . sought to refute doubt with reasons . . . [So they] first of all . . . tried to demonstrate the truth of Christianity with reasons . . . . And these reasons fostered doubt . . . . [For] these reasons . . . are already a kind of doubt—and thus doubt arose and lived on reasons . . . . [For] offering doubt reasons in order to kill it is just like offering the tasty food it likes best of all to a hungry monster one wishes to eliminate. No, one must not offer reasons to doubt—at least not if one's intention is to kill it—but one must do as Luther did, order it to shut its mouth, and to that end keep quiet and offer no reasons.
> (FSE 68)

The point is that if reasons are given not to doubt those reasons will be twisted to defend doubt all the more. Why is this? Why don't reasons against doubt, put an end to doubt?

It's because these reasons keep the matter on an intellectual plane where doubting can go on forever. This plane leaves "everything in abeyance"—it "cannot fasten down anything" or "tie the knot at the end" (JFY 196). The immensely popular

American horror story writer, Stephen King, has written that writing is a strange "act of telepathy"[13]—whereby the writer tries for a meeting of the minds across time and space. Many think conversations try to do the same. So if just the right words are said, we think a breakthrough will come and end doubt.

But that's too intellectual of a solution. No, the only way to stop doubt is by suffering for the sake of righteousness (Mt 5:10; 1 Pt 3:14). Kierkegaard explains this tough idea this way:

> So it always is with need in a human being; out of the eater comes something to eat;[14] where there is need, it itself produces, as it were, that which it needs . . . . But someone who sits in idleness and ease through good days or is busily astir in busyness from morning to night but has never suffered anything for the sake of truth actually has no need . . . . [So if] you doubt, ... say to yourself: No sense making a fuss over that kind of doubt; I know very well its source and nature—namely, that I have . . . too easy a life, spare myself the dangers bound up with witnessing for truth against untruth. Just do that! But above all do not become self-important by doubting. (FSE 69)

Doubt therefore comes to an end through self-denial. Anything else only furthers doubt. So in combating doubt, it's easy to go down the wrong road. Kierkegaard explains this further:

---

13 *On Writing: A Memoir of the Craft* (London: Hodder & Stoughton, 2000) 106.
14 See Jgs 14:14.

> When one, entirely innocent, suffers, then it
> . . . seems as if the struggle were about justifying God, something only the conceit of fools and conceited wisdom can regard as the easiest—because for a human being that is really presumptuousness. . . . It wants to reverse the relation, wants to sit quiet and safe, . . . it wants to make God the defendant, to make him the one from whom something is required. . . . Right here is faith's struggle: to believe without being able to understand. And when this struggle of faith begins, . . . then the consciousness of guilt comes to the rescue. . . . One would suppose it to be a hostile power, but no, it specifically wants to help . . . the believer by teaching him not to doubt God but himself. Instead of the mendacity about thinking through the doubt, which is patently doubt's most dangerous invention, the consciousness of guilt thunders its "Halt." (UDVS 273)

So we are to fight against ourselves and not against God. Our best attack on doubt comes from attacking "our own feeling, . . . purpose, and will [which] we love . . . more passionately than [anything else, and which] hinders faith in Christ, [so that] unbelief follows" (LW 29:154).[15] "For our own will is the . . . most deep-rooted evil in us" (LW 42:48). So a Christian "is a man of will who no longer wills his own will but with the passion of his crushed will, . . . wills" what God wants (JP 6:6966). By crushing our sure will, we keep it from being "pernicious" (CD 211).

---

15 See also LW 44:376, 7:104–106; SML 7:229.

A Divinely Planned Sacrifice

So hold onto the word of God which tells of his "definite plan" to send his son to die for us (Acts 2:23; 1 Jn 4:10). Do not long for some cosmic Christic principle[16] that floats free of the written word—following the peculiar contours of our private experiences. Do not long for an experience of the risen Christ, appearing in your bedroom to confirm what the word already tells you.[17] No sooner than these exotic moments come and go, you're hungering for more and are never satisfied.

No, instead know this—that Christ is all tied up with the words of the Bible itself. Know that you'll find him no other way.[18] Know that all other ways lead to doubt and error (Acts 4:12, 14:15). Know that "God . . . . has circumscribed Himself with a certain . . . Word" (LW 12:352). So dwell on that word, that it may "dwell in you richly" (Col 3:16). In this way you can put your faith above your feelings (SML 7:244). For it is "the glory of faith" to take "everything captive—perception and understanding, strength and will" and to follow "the bare voice of God and to be led and driven rather than to drive" (LW 29:238). In this way you become "a knight and a hero who . . . vanquishes all," disdaining all that "the world possesses, both its good and its evil, . . . everything with which the devil can lure and entice or intimidate and threaten" (LW 24:21, 44:77).

---

16 See Matthew Fox, *The Coming of the Cosmic Christ* (New York: HarperCollins, 1988).
17 See Reynolds Price, *A Whole New Life: An Illness and a Healing* (New York: Plume, 1982) 42–46.
18 See Hans W. Frei, *The Eclipse of Biblical Narrative* (New Haven: Yale, 1974) and Jacque Ellul, *The Humiliation of the Word*, trans. Joyce Main Hanks (Grand Rapids: Eerdmans, 1985).

Therefore we should neither be amazed at nor upset with, the word "God" showing up on an alligator's side in Wisconsin—exotic though that report may be.[19]

This will put an end to us cursing God in heaven for every little "pain in the leg" we feel (LW 14:49)! And this is because Christ is our "Priest over against God, ... who sacrificed Himself on the cross," that we might "find mercy before God" (LW 23:195). Without that sacrifice of Christ, we are lost (LW 23:55). Without faith in Christ, God's wrath rests upon us (Jn 3:36; Rom 2:5, 5:9). But when we believe in Christ, our burdens are lifted (Mt 11:30) and we have hope—both for the life to come in heaven, and in this life now (Lk 18:30; 1 Tm 4:8).

Pray Rightly

And we who bask in this victory of Easter are also expected "to walk in newness of life" (Rom 6:4; 1 Pt 2:24). So we are to obey God to conquer the world (1 Jn 5:3–4). Therefore we must

> follow neither the customs of the world nor our own reason or plausible theories. We must constantly . . . control our wills . . . Always we are to conduct ourselves in a manner unlike the way of the world. (SML 7:16)

There's no better way to do that than to pray in the name of Jesus and according to his will (Jn 15:16; 1 Jn 5:14). This means our prayers won't be bundles of grab-bag requests nor dashes off to bargain sales—elbowing our way in. No, instead we'll pray with confidence, "which is the soul of prayer," asking for what is "expedient according to the will of God," without

---

19 "G-O-D Appears on Gater," *The Seattle Times*, July 24, 2006.

fixing "the manner and the time" of the answer, and waiting "patiently and diligently." For as St. Bernard of Clairvaux (1090–1153) put it:

> Do not despise . . . prayer . . . . Be sure either that what you have asked for will be granted . . . . or that what has been asked for has not been beneficial. (LW 30:322–23)

This is hard to stomach—especially when we pray for the sick. But it is God's good will. For he knows that being sick can often be better for us, than being well and forgetting him (Hos 13:6). So pray knowing that having our names "written in heaven" (Lk 10:20) matters more than succeeding in this life. That'll take some of the pressure off us, so we can pray as we should—having rejoiced in the salvation Good Friday and Easter bring, and having taken up the good fight of faith (1 Tm 6:12) against doubt. Amen.

Sermon 4

Fight Depression

In our reading from 1 Kings 19 we are ushered into a therapy session between Elijah, the famous prophet of Israel, and God himself. And we learn from this encounter that we must never give in to our despair—but fight against it with everything that's in us.

Elijah's Depression

In these verses, God shows Elijah how to fight against his despair, darkness, sorrow, sadness and depression—without the aid of any drugs or medicines. That isn't because the Bible opposes the use of medicines or psychotropic drugs. We know, after all, that leprosy, for instance, was healed by prayer—but also with the use of cedar wood, scarlet thread and hyssop (Lv 14:1–9)—which were the medicines of that day. And we know that Jesus not only healed by means of his Word—but also with the use of poultices or mudpacks, which he put on those blind eyes (Jn 9:6–7).

No, the reason medicines weren't used for Elijah was because another feature of depression was being treated—and that was anger. For unresolved anger can also make us depressed—for "depression can easily erupt as rage."[1] And so "many depressed

---

1 Andrew Solomon, *The Noonday Demon: An Atlas of Depression* (New York: Scribner, 2001) 180.

people have particular trouble with anger."[2] What happens is that we get upset because events or people cross us—and there's nothing we can do about it, so we stew, and turn inward, and descend into despair. This is what Elijah did—he hid in a cave in the wilderness and wished he could die (1 Kgs 19:4, 9).

Elijah was mad because God had not blessed him for risking his life when standing up for the truth against King Ahab (1 Kgs 18:18–40). Do you remember what Ahab did? He caved into his pagan wife, Jezebel (1 Kgs 21:25), and advanced the evil ways of the false god, Ba'al, throughout all of Israel–thereby doing "more to provoke the Lord, the God of Israel, to anger than all the kings of Israel, who were before him" (1 Kgs 16:33). So Elijah, that "troubler of Israel" (1 Kgs 18:17), rightly took a stand against the king and warned that if a turnabout didn't happen soon, God would strike him down, along with his wife—leaving them both to be eaten by dogs (1 Kgs 21:24; 2 Kgs 9:33–37). That threat enraged the king and his wayward wife—and so Jezebel set out to kill Elijah (1 Kgs 19:2). As a result, Elijah was on the run to save his life. And he despaired that he was alone, under threat, and with none to help, comfort or protect him.

---

[2] Richard O'Connor, *Undoing Depression: What Therapy Doesn't Teach You and Medication Can't Give You* (New York: Berkeley, 1997) 92. Knowing that depression is in some way grounded in anger, makes cognitive therapy all the more tenuous. On this see Richard Watson, *Cogito, Ergo Sum: The Life of René Descartes* (Boston: Godine, 2002) 208, 210: "Elisabeth was . . . very harassed by court life, so much so that she was in a state of slight depression. Descartes recommended that Elisabeth think joyful thoughts and then she would be happy. . . . [But] Elisabeth was not at liberty to think of 'forest greenery, the colors of flowers, or the flight of a bird' every time her unmarried sister got pregnant, her brother committed a murder, or her uncle got his head chopped off."

But rather than giving him drugs to lift his spirits, the angel of the Lord simply admonishes Elijah: "Get up and eat," get busy, get to work (1 Kgs 19:5, 15). The anger just isn't worth it (Jas 1:20). And furthermore, there's a compatriot for him—Elisha, who will support and eventually will take over for him (1 Kgs 19:21).

Lift Your Drooping Hands

The New Testament pursues this same sort of approach to depression. We're told to follow Jesus in order to jump-start our fight against depression. Look to Jesus, we're admonished,

> who . . . endured the cross, despising the shame . . . . Consider him who endured . . . such hostility against himself so that you may not grow weary or faint-hearted. In your struggle against sin you have not yet resisted to the point of shedding your blood . . . . Therefore lift your drooping hands and strengthen your weak knees. (Heb 12:2–4, 12)

These are striking words—accusing us of complaining long before we've shed any blood as our Lord did! (Mt 10:24–25). So we're just "softies" (LW 14:49)—looking for the easy way out, instead of pursuing the hard truth of God (LW 11:58) and loving it (Rom 1:18; Gal 4:16; 2 Thes 2:11–12; 2 Tm 1:13–14). There's hardly a more condemning and upsetting verse in the entire Bible! So against our sheepishness, we're admonished simply to stand up and tough-it-out—"lift your drooping hands and strengthen your weak knees." That's it—there's nothing more or less to the therapy given in the New Testament.

Luther's Anfechtung

And Luther also fought against despair or *Anfechtung*, as he called it (LW 44:63). In spite of having the joy of Christ in his heart (LW 31:190), he knew very well about a troubling internal turmoil (LW 24:399–401). He knew life could be a "vale of tears" (LW 28:122).[3] He knew that "the power of grief" can be so great that it can kill many and be "more penetrating than any sword" (LW 8:13). So it has been rightly said of Luther that he was

> haunted by anguish . . . . [since he knew that] the Gospel is not merely too complex to grasp; [but] is repugnant to everyone whose conscience seeks justification in works! . . . . We can search for a psychological explanation for these dark days . . . . [But Luther] was a highly sensitive human being afflicted by living in two eras at once, a disorder that physicians or psychiatrists might be able to ameliorate but cannot cure.[4]

---

3   See also LW 22:119, 43:30—and, of related interest, SML 2:212, LHP 1:49. Apparently it still is. In this regard see Paul Krugman, "There is a Darkness Spreading Over Part of Our Society," *The Seattle Times* (November 10, 2015): A11: "Despair appears to be spreading across Middle America . . . .with troubling consequences for our society as a whole . . . . While universal health care, higher minimum wages, aid to education, and so on would do a lot to help Americans in trouble, I'm not sure whether they're enough to cure existential despair."

4   Heiko A. Oberman, *Luther: Man Between God and the Devil* (New Haven: Yale, 1989) 324.

Luther despaired because he was angry with the church—and because he knew there was little he could do about it. What was he, after all, against the whole Holy Roman Empire? He was running up against insurmountable odds! So he, like Elijah, wished he could crawl into a hole and hide. Anger and helplessness can lead to such darkness and despair. Fed up with his ineffectiveness, Luther cried out at the beginning of his *Large Catechism*:

> The common people take the Gospel altogether too lightly, and even our utmost exertions accomplish but little . . . . [And the pastors], like pigs and dogs, . . . remember no more of the Gospel than this rotten, pernicious, shameful, carnal liberty. (BC 358–59)

And he could even despair, the following year, of preaching itself, a calling he usually loved. "Daily," he says, "the people become more obdurate, mocking, and spiteful" (LW 23:362). And he goes on to say elsewhere:

> I would rather hear no other news than that I had been deposed from the preaching office. I am so very tired of it, [because of] the great ingratitude of the people, but much more because of the unbearable hardships which the devil and the world deal . . . me. (LW 34:50)

Then in a fit of rage, or so it seems, he says that "God appears to be the biggest fool of all" because he tries "to accomplish His purposes by means of . . . preaching . . . . But He gets nowhere. [And] he has this coming . . . . Why does he not change His tactics? If I were the Lord God I would use my fists" (LW 23:382)!

Then three years later, he sizes up the situation very differently. Then he says:

> Sad to say, the godless world does not believe, ... and treats the . . . messengers like dirt under feet. That is not for the world's good. But it is good for us who are proclaiming that Word, lest we become proud and arrogate to ourselves powers that are not ours to have. [This] fact . . . . keeps us . . . humble. Otherwise, if the worldlings did believe the Word and bestowed great honors on us, . . . we might become proud and damned. (LHP 2:131)

Yet even this note of resignation has a despairing tone to it. So while he makes some gains, Luther continues to lament his lot.

STOP BROODING

But later that year, when writing on his beloved Psalm 118, his tone changes—becoming more triumphant in his admonitions:

> Do not sit by yourself or lie on your couch, hanging and shaking your head. Do not destroy yourself with your own thoughts by worrying. Do not strive and struggle to free yourself, and do not brood on your wretchedness . . . and misery. Say to yourself: "Come on, you lazy bum; down on your knees, and lift your eyes

and hands toward heaven!" Read a psalm or the Our Father, call on God, and tearfully lay your troubles before Him. Mourn and pray . . . . [For] praying, reciting your troubles, and lifting up your hands are sacrifices most pleasing to God. It is His desire . . . that you lay your troubles before Him. He does not want you to multiply your troubles by burdening and torturing yourself . . . . He wants you to grow strong in Him. By His strength He is glorified in you. Out of such experiences men become real Christians. (*LW* 14:60–61)

This great passage from Luther's pen tell us how to become true Christians. He hits us hard and then quickly comforts us with tender compassion. You lazy bums, he yells! Open up to God—for he will not turn away from you. Do that, rather than chewing on your souls like a frenzied dog with a bone. For being irascible isn't our preferred mode of interaction (BC 445, 390). Do that, knowing that God will strengthen you when you submit to him. Do that, knowing that God himself is glorified when you are strengthened.

Greater Than Our Experience

But will this work? Can we bow down and pray as we should? It is so easy for us to slip back into the darkness—even when we're trying to pull ourselves up and out of that despair. For if we stay with our experiences of sadness, in order to combat those feelings, it's easy to fall back into them repeatedly. For while we're fighting against the darkness and despair, depression continues to surround us. And though we fight diligently, we still remain in that sea of sadness—with no light shining at the end of the tunnel.

But that doesn't spell failure. That doesn't mean we have no where to turn when we're sad. No, we haven't come to the end of our proverbial rope just yet. No, there is more than sheer darkness. Indeed, we still have the glorious words from Ephesians 5:2:

> Christ loved us and gave himself up for us, a fragrant sacrifice to God.

Here we have something beyond our experience of despair. Here we have something to keep us from slipping back again into the darkness. Rather than relying on ourselves to dig ourselves out of the hole of depression, we have another. Now we can look elsewhere and see what's for us and irreversibly good. Now we can look to Christ who offered up his life as a sacrifice for sin, to God the Father. All of this is certain. Just as time cannot be reversed, so that the American Civil War, for instance, never happened—so the sacrifice of Christ is certain and sure. It can't be erased from history either. But that doesn't mean we can't belittle it, forget it, neglect it, reject it, or disbelieve it. We can still do that to Christ's sacrifice for us. But if we do, the sacrifice will still stand (LW 29:227). And it also remains certain that God has not rejected the sacrifice of his Son, but accepted it as a fragrant offering, satisfying (Is 53:11) the just requirements of the law with its legal demands (Rom 8:4; Col 2:14) that stood against us because of our disobedience, rebellion and sin.

This is the good news that cannot be found anywhere else (Jn 6:68; Lk 10:42; Acts 4:12). Regardless if we believe in it or not, it still stands. It lasts forever—"the same yesterday and today and forever" (Heb 9:26; 13:8). Because of this sacrifice of Jesus, and God's ratification of it, the blood of Jesus saves us from the wrath of God (Rom 5:9). And if we believe in this message (Jn 3:36; Rom 3:25), and entrust our lives to Christ's care (Jn 10:4, 9, 27-28), then we will no longer have to fear the threats and wrath of God (LW 13:376). Thanks be to God!

Being Drawn to Christ

But how shall we believe in Christ and entrust our lives to his care? We cannot push ourselves into belief. We cannot force ourselves to follow the Lord Jesus. That would be like trying to get a plant to grow up by pulling on it[5]—something everyone knows is stupid.

What has to happen is that God must draw us into Christ (Jn 6:44). That would be like Christ entering through the closed doors of our hearts, as Kierkegaard once noted (JP 5:5313), as he did through those closed doors when the disciples were in hiding long ago (Jn 20:19, 26). Such drawing and entering—unlike our casual picking and choosing—is traumatic. Therefore it would be right to say that this new birth of faith comes "amid penitence" (BC 164). That's because penitence means admitting that we're wrong and God is right (LW 51:318). So tribulation is our avenue into faith (Acts 14:22). Tough times don't mean, then, that God has abandoned us—they instead mean that he is "pressing [us] to His heart" (LW 6:149)! So for us to have the ability to believe, we have to see that we are not "capable of faith" (LW 51:110). This miraculous shift (LW 33:98) from incapacity to ability, happens at the cross of Christ—for it is there that we're drawn to him (Jn 12:32). For indeed, if you see in

---

5 Gerhard O. Forde, *The Preached God* (Grand Rapids: Eerdmans, 2007) 141.

> the blood and wounds and death of Christ,
> . . . . that God is so kindly disposed toward
> you that he even gives his own Son for you,
> then your heart in turn must grow sweet and
> disposed toward God. (LW 44:38)

This means that in our life of faith, "unimagined delights [sneak] in when brokenhearted."[6] From this sequence we see that we cannot believe on our own, but only when God "gathers" us to himself—and by himself (BC 345).

And while waiting for faith to spring up, we don't have to sit on our hands. "You can fall down . . . and complain to God of your inability; and say, ... my flesh, alas, will not submit; therefore help my unbelief that I may honor thy name and hold thy Word to be true" (SML 2:259).

Rely on the Supper

All of you, then, who have heard these words and believe in them, come to the Sacrament of the Altar in thanksgiving, and eat of the bread and drink of the cup—knowing that Christ is truly present in, with, and under the bread and the wine of this holy Supper, so that his abundant life might dwell in you (Jn 6:53, 10:10).

Don't miss out on this blessing. Come and receive the Sacrament of the Lord's Supper. It is here that your faith "may refresh and strengthen itself and not weaken in the struggle but grow continually stronger" (BC 449). Rely on this gift—and not on

---

6   This is my six word memoir in "That's All They Wrote," *Seattle Post-Intelligencer,* March 24, 2008.

yourself. Rely on it rather than on the American philosopher, Ralph Waldo Emerson (1803–1882), and his influential essay on self-reliance. Don't trust him when he says:

> Nothing is at last sacred but the integrity of your own mind . . . . Obey thy heart . . . . Nothing can bring you peace but yourself.[7]

Don't believe in these words. Rely instead on those sacred words in John 6:53—"unless you eat the flesh of the Son of man and drink his blood, you have no life in you."

Be Radiant

And when we leave worship today, do good works in the name of Christ, our Savior. Out of gratitude, let us serve him (BC 413). Psalm 34:5 tells us to "look upon the Lord and be radiant," נהר, or *nahar*. This is like unto Matthew 5:16, "Let your light shine before others that they may see your good works and give glory to your Father who is in heaven." So shine brightly and be radiant–*nahar*. But what does this mean? We in the Lutheran Church are blessed to have Luther as our "most eminent teacher" (BC 576)—so let us listen to what he says this verse is telling us:

> What He calls "good works" here is the . . . teaching about Christ and faith, and the suffering for its sake. He is talking about works by which we "shine"; but shining is the real job of believing and teaching, by which we also help others believe . . . . [Here we have] the distinctly Christian work of teaching cor-

---

7 *Essays: First and Second Series* (New York: Gramercy, 1993) 26, 45, 48.

rectly, of stressing faith, and of showing how to strengthen and preserve it; this is how we testify that we really are Christians . . . . Thus the most reliable index to a true Christian is this: if from the way he praises and preaches Christ the people learn that they are nothing and that Christ is everything. (*LW* 21:65–66)

So be radiant—and see to it that you are nothing and Christ is everything (John 3:30). Be radiant—and give God all the glory (1 Cor 10:31). Be radiant—and work to strengthen and preserve the faith in Christ Jesus by fighting against depression. Call on God for help to get this done—for you'll need it (Jn 15:5). Call on him for wisdom and compassion to be radiant in just the right ways. And he'll answer you because he wants you to be strong (1 Cor 16:13), and to serve him in his kingdom (Lk 10:2). Rejoice in the Lord because of his power and goodness, wisdom and mercy (Rv 5:12). For through his divine help we can serve him as we should—which today we've seen includes fighting against depression. Amen.

Sermon 5

Be Doers of the Word

Today our reading from Saint James tells us to get off the dime—to get going and get busy. It tells us that believing in Jesus is not enough—that we must also follow him. These are tough words that keep us from basking in the laurels of our faith. Why is that?

That Epistle of Straw

We would think that believing in Jesus would be enough—especially when it comes to our salvation. And that is because, for the longest time, we have been nurtured on the words from Ephesians 2:8 that we are saved by grace through faith, and this is not our own doing but a gift from God, lest anyone should boast. So why does Saint James tell us—in contradistinction to this venerable Biblical passage—that we must also be doers of the word (Jas 1:22), in addition to believing in the word of grace? Saint James creates what is called cognitive dissonance—or a collision of ideas. And the collision is, that on the one hand, we have the belief that faith is sufficient, but on the other hand, we have the opposite. And neither of these can be easily dismissed since they both come from the same sacred source—the Holy Scriptures! So what are we to do?

Some take refuge in Martin Luther's notorious statement that this Epistle of Saint James, written by the very brother of our Lord (Mt 13:55; Gal 1:19), is nothing but "an epistle of straw" (LW 35:362). Running with that statement, they dismiss Saint James—erroneously concluding that he must be without any divine merit since Luther didn't like him. But this overlooks Luther's praise for the Epistle of Saint James, which he couldn't easily live with, because it so "vigorously promulgates the law of God" (LW 35:395). Even though, then, he disputes parts of it—like what it says about temptation, justification and the anointing of the sick with oil (LW 4:92, 132–34)[1]—he cannot deny that "otherwise [there are] many good sayings" in it (LW 35:397). Even at his most perturbed, all Luther says is—"I almost feel like throwing Jimmy into the stove"—but only "almost" (LW 34:317)!

SOUNDING LIKE JESUS

The fact of the matter is, that Saint James sounds a lot like his brother at the end of the Sermon on the Mount when he says:

> Not everyone who says to me, "Lord, Lord," shall enter the kingdom of heaven, but he who does the will of my Father who is in heaven.
> (Mt 7:21)

Doing the will of God the Father sounds a lot like Saint James when he admonishes us to be doers of the word and not hearers only (Jas 1:22). On doing the will of God, Luther says that

> we should believe in Christ and be found in a calling [authorized by] a word of God.... [For instance, there] should be fidelity and obedi-

---

1 See also LW 35:396; 36:118–22.

ence from inferiors to superiors, and among the others there should be mutual love and service, and everyone should perform his office faithfully. You find nothing here about . . . any other special way of life . . . . These are the ones who belong in heaven, not the ones who neglected the Word of God and yet supposed that they were serving God very seriously and devoutly by saying the word twice, "Lord, Lord," while the rest of us hardly say it once. They are always busier and more energetic in their worship than genuine Christians; but since they have been doing their own will, they better look for another Lord to . . . open up heaven for them . . . . [So] we should be careful not to . . . be seduced . . . . We should abide by what He calls good so that everything . . . is done on the basis of His commandment, though it may not be very ostentatious or pleasing to reason.

(LW 21:269–70)

Faith in Christ, then, is supposed to result in obeying the Biblical commands of the Lord—and nothing more. Doing nothing, then, is just as unacceptable as pursuing non-Biblical life-styles. Søren Kierkegaard, that Danish admirer of Luther, also warned against such busyness:

> The one who occupies himself only with the eternal, uninterruptedly at every moment, if this were possible, is not busy. Thus the one who actually occupies himself with the eternal is never busy . . . . To be busy is, divided and scattered, to occupy oneself with what makes

a person divided and scattered. But Christian love . . . is as far from inaction as it is from busyness. It never . . . rests satisfied . . . . It is not a mood in the pampered soul that knows and wants to know no law, or wants to have its own law and listens only to songs—Christian love is sheer action, and its every work is holy, because it is the fulfilling of the Law. (WL 98–99)

So if we veer off course, all our righteous deeds will amount to sheer, wasted busyness—and of no account to anyone.

No Floating Goose

With those important refinements in hand, we return to the basic point that faith necessarily reaches out to do good deeds. Luther makes this essential point in a most unforgettable way:

Faith is a vigorous and powerful thing; it is not idle speculation, nor does it float on the heart like a goose on the water. But just as water that has been heated, even though it remains water, is no longer cold but hot and an altogether different water, so faith, the work of the Holy Spirit, fashions a different mind and different attitudes, and makes an altogether new human being. (LW 2:266–67)

So when we believe in Christ we are different—we behave differently (LW 26:405)—our faith doesn't leave us unchanged, only floating on our hearts like a goose on water, instead of penetrating it and changing our hearts. Once we become Christians, we no longer live as we used to. We talk differently. We spend our time differently. And we even spend our money differently. Have you ever heard people say they don't like to go to church because all they ask for is their money? Well, I hope so! And that's because "where your treasure is, there will your heart be also" (Mt 6:21). So we have to talk about giving ten percent of our money, or what's called a tithe, to the church where we worship (Dt 14:22; Mal 3:7–10; Mt 23:23). We have to because it's a Biblical mandate—and because how we use our money affects our hearts, which affects our faith—and ultimately even our salvation (Ez 11:19; Lk 8:15)! So these critics aren't making a moral point against greedy Christian churches—all they're saying is that they want to be watered-down Christians.

They're saying that "God wants nothing of us but that we ... believe in him."[2] They want to believe in Christ but without becoming new creations (2 Cor 5:17). They want to believe in Christ without following him (Mt 16:24). They want to live by the Spirit but without walking by the Spirit (Gal 5:25). They want faith but without having to supplement it with virtue and knowledge (2 Pt 1:5). They want faith but without having to share it (1 Pt 3:15). They want to be Christians but without lifting up the beaten down (Lk 10:37). They want the Christian blessing but without running the race (1 Cor 9:24). They want to be with Christ but without suffering with him (1 Pt 4:13). They want Christ but without eating the bread of his body on the first day of the week (Acts 20:7; Jn 6:53).

Now all of these unwarranted, illegitimate, and unauthorized cuts in the Christian faith put these nay-sayers squarely against the Bible and its saving message. They also pit them against Luther himself, who in a 1528 sermon, just recently translated anew, says that he "always taught" that God wants Christians "to live and walk in holiness and without blame" (LW 69:38). So may the Lord indeed have mercy on our souls. May he keep

---

2 Gerhard O. Forde, "Teleleshai," *Logia* 10 (Epiphany, 2001) 63.

us from watering down the Christian way of life (2 Pt 2:1) (BC 169), in spite of its appeal to our sinful selves. Supposing that we have been thoroughly "liberated by the gospel," we end up "misusing" it and saying there's "no further need to do anything [or] give anything" (LW 51:207). Alas.

THE IMPLANTED WORD

Saint James goes on to say that we are justified by these works we're called to do—and "not by faith" (Jas 2:24). This puts a huge burden on us to do even more and better good works—for our justification and salvation are now hanging in the balance. But that's not quite right. We have misread Saint James. This is because our efforts are not really pitted against our saving faith and trust in the Lord (Eph 2:8–10). For "'to do' includes faith at the same time" (LW 26:255). So all that our works do is refuse to let our faith float free. This is because Saint James says works "complete" our faith (James 2:22). "Therefore justification does not demand the works of the Law but a living faith which produces its own works" (LW 25:235). So in, with, and under our works is our saving, living faith—which is being completed by our works and not replaced by them. So while our works are necessary, they do not save us—that's what faith does. Furthermore, James 2:21 clinches the matter, which if cast aside, grievously and shamefully twists, distorts, corrupts and clouds over all that Saint James has to say:

> Rid yourselves of all sordidness and rank growth of wickedness, and welcome with meekness the implanted word that has the power to save your souls. (Jas 2:21)

Here it's clearly and powerfully stated that salvation does not depend on our doing of the word, but on the fact that the word has already been implanted in us. And that implantation happens by simply hearing it (Rom 10:17).

In his 1536 sermon on this verse, Luther erupts, "What more could be desired?"—that God's word has been "planted or engrafted within" us (SML 7:299)! That's because that's as good as it gets—having the saving word there, within us, well before our welcoming of it takes place. But this doesn't mean everything is then settled. No, there's still more to our salvation than this implantation—wonderful though it may be. We must also welcome that implanted word in all meekness—knowing that our welcoming is parasitic on the implantation of the word itself. Therefore "take heed," Luther says,

> to accept in purity and to maintain with patience the Word so graciously and richly given you by God without effort or merit on your part. (SML 7:300)

So when you grow weary in your well-doing (Gal 6:9), do not despair. All is not lost or in vain. The implanted word remains—even apart from you being tired out doing or practicing or welcoming it. Work diligently, then, to implement God's implanted word in your lives—but not in such a way that you rely on those efforts of yours, diligent though they may be. Rely instead on what God has so graciously and richly given you in what you've heard (Rom 10:17)—and then let it "dwell in you richly" and simply (Col 3:17). Kierkegaard, in a journal entry from 1851, also strikes just the right balance when he says:

No, infinite humiliation and grace, and then a striving born of gratitude—this is Christianity.
(JP 1:993)

Forgiving & Forgiven

A good example of this combination of our implementing and God's implanting is that petition in the Lord's Prayer where we say—"forgive us our trespasses as we forgive those who trespass against us" (Mt 6:12). Luther explains this dialectic between forgiving and being forgiven in his profound, but largely under-read and unstudied, *Large Catechism*—which he thought was "one of his best books" (LW 50:173).[3] There he writes:

> God has promised us assurance that everything is forgiven and pardoned, yet on the condition that we also forgive our neighbor who does us harm . . . and . . . bears malice towards us, etc. If you do not forgive, do not think that God forgives you. But if you forgive, you have the . . . assurance that you are forgiven in heaven. Not on account of your forgiving, for God does it altogether freely, out of pure grace, because he has promised it, as the Gospel teaches. But he has set up this condition for our strengthening and assurance as a sign along with the promise. (BC 433)

---

3 On this judgment, see Martin Brecht, *Martin Luther,* trans. James L. Schaaf, 3 vols. (Philadelphia: Fortress, 1985–1993) 2:280.

Forgiveness is at the heart of our salvation in Christ (LW 30:236), and so we would do well to follow the catechism carefully at this point. This passage trades on the connections between the words condition, assurance and accounting.

Condition. First we are struck with the condition—that if we don't forgive others, we'll never be forgiven by God. That is the plain and simple condition for our forgiveness from him. This condition is so important that Jesus reinforced it in one of his most strident parables (Mt 18:23–35). In Luther's 1530 sermon on this parable, he says that it teaches us "the state and regimen of the forgiveness of sins" (LHP 3:138). Regimen? Yes! For there's nothing sloppy, cheap or undisciplined about God's forgiveness. Thus the condition before us—if we are unmerciful, God will never forgive us. Period. Luther sees a *quid pro quo* in this condition:

> We should not misuse God's . . . forgiveness. Our Lord God has given us more than enough proofs that our sins are forgiven, namely, the proclamation of the gospel, baptism, the Sacrament, and the Holy Spirit in our hearts. Now, it is important that we, too, give proof by which we testify that we have indeed received the forgiveness of sins. The proof that is expected of us is that [we] forgive the faults of [others].
> (LHP 3:144)

Assurance. Luther then turns this condition on its head. What was first over-bearing, has now become gracious. For when we forgive others, we have a certain assurance that God truly has forgiven us. This is renewing because often our guilt over what we've done seems greater than God's mercy (1 Jn 3:19–20). So this unexpected assurance is deeply and mercifully gracious. The very fact that we forgive others means that we also have taken God's mercy to heart and have "not forgotten . . . the grace of God and become more wicked and rebellious than before" (LHP 3:141).

Accounting. Finally we cannot say that God forgives us on account of our mercy toward others. Even though our forgiving others is the condition for God forgiving us, our forgiving doesn't make God forgive us. That's because he's already waiting in the wings with his absolution on the tip of his tongue. We don't have to make him want to forgive us. He already does (Ex 34:6–7). So follow the regimen of forgiveness, as Luther put it, and fulfill the condition by showing mercy to those around you, and then rejoice in God's goodness, mercy, kindness—and forgiveness.

Abundant Life

Furthermore, you who have welcomed that implanted word into your lives, receive him now, made flesh, in, with, and under (BC 575) the bread and wine of the Lord's Supper. For in this sacrament there is abundant life (Jn 6:53; 10:10) that enables you to do all things through Christ (Phil 4:13). That is because through the immortality of Christ's divinity, he completely swallowed up death (LW 29:135). This covers not only the death that tries to keep us from eternal life in heaven, but also the spiritual dying that plagues us all now. So do not depend on yourselves—for you have no abundant life in you. Look instead to Christ. He is bodily here today in this "most venerable" Sacrament (BC 577) with his abundant life. And he has promised to lighten your load by helping you carry your burdens. Come to me, he says (Mt 11:28). Just as he carried our sins in his body on the cross—that by dying for them he might free us from God's wrath (1 Pt 2:24; Rom 5:9), so he helps us now. Rejoice, then, in Christ today.

True Religion

And then when you leave this place, continue to do good deeds in the name of Jesus (Col 3:17). James 1:27 says that these works come in two types that make up true religion—helping the lonely and needy, the widows and orphans, and also pursuing personal decency by keeping yourselves unstained by the world. So work to perform both types of works in your lives. First do so by helping the needy. Feed the hungry. Encourage the depressed. Protect the abused. Sit with the lonely. House the homeless. Do all of these things as if you were helping Christ himself (Mt 25:40). And then secondly, be sure to keep yourselves unstained by the world. Don't follow the dominant value system of consumerism and violence that engulfs our world. Strive instead to live a simple, peaceful life (Rom 12:16–18)—not based on getting more and more, nor on walking over whoever crosses you. Call on God to help you, for without him you will surely fail at these tasks (Jn 15:5). And he will answer you, for today we have seen how he is at work in us to turn us into doers of the word. Amen.

Sermon 6

Serve

Have you ever wanted to be great? Have you ever wanted to be of some significance? Then today you've come to the right place! For today our Lord Jesus tells us what it takes to become great. The only problem with this is that what he says is disquieting.

Building on Self-Denial

What Jesus told his first disciples long ago he repeats to us today in Mark 9:35—that whoever would be great must be last and servant of all. So great people are not those who get a lot, but who give a lot. That is because it is "more blessed to give than it is to receive" (Acts 20:35). We would think it was the other way around. We would think that great people are those who have huge talent, great power, much luck and plenty of respect. But Jesus doesn't agree for a minute. The great are those who are servants of all. They are the last—not the first in this, that, or some other thing. So greatness is not about being a "gimme, gimme" person. It's rather about being a sacrificial, generous person. Greatness, according to Jesus, is based on giving—not on getting.

This definition of greatness shouldn't surprise us—even though society and its prevailing cultural norms run contrary to it. That's because in the New Testament life is based on self-denial (Mt 16:24) rather than on self-fulfillment (Mt

16:25; Jn 15:13). Life, according to Jesus, is based on humility rather than on self-aggrandizement (Lk 18:14; Jas 4:6; Lk 12:15). It's about being other-directed, as Dietrich Bonhoeffer (1906–1945) taught[1]—and not about being self-absorbed. It's about looking to God and neighbor—our "greatest" obligations (Mk 12:30–31)—and not dwelling on our self-preoccupied lives.

Giving the Best

So greatness, according to Jesus, comes through service to others. It's not about accumulating the most money, power and prestige. But this service to others isn't about giving them whatever they want—regardless of its quantity and quality. No, our service to others isn't about making them self-indulgent, degraded, and corrupt. No, our service to others is rather designed to make their lives as good as they can be in the eyes of the Lord.

Martin Luther, in his *Large Catechism*, ties this into the First Commandment about having no other gods:

> Man's whole heart and confidence [should] be placed in God alone, and in no one else.... To cling to him with all our heart is nothing else than to entrust ourselves to him completely. He wishes to turn us away [*abstrahere*] from everything else, and to draw us [*attrahere*] to himself, because he is the one eternal good.
> (BC 366)

---

1 *Letters and Papers From Prison*, trans. John W. de Gruchy, Dietrich Bonhoeffer's Works, Volume 8 (Minneapolis: Fortress, 2009) 500–503.

In our service to others, then, what we want to provide is this "one eternal good"—even though it means brutally turning us "away from everything else." But we have something better to offer than this—and so we cannot settle for less. "Serve only God," we're told (Matthew 4:10)! My friend, the Rev. James H. Wessel, formerly the pastor of the huge Upper Arlington Lutheran Church, in Columbus, Ohio, used to say—"Why should we feed hungry children just so they can go to hell?" So even though his church spent thousands of dollars on human service projects—they spent even more on evangelism. For they not only wanted the needy to have food, shelter, clothes and medical care—but most of all they wanted them to be baptized with a saving faith in Christ Jesus. So our service to others must concentrate on nurturing a life with God.

God = His Word

But bringing about this life with God will be easier said than done. That's because a life with God is always a very difficult row to hoe, as they say (Mt 7:14).[2] And it doesn't help that God is the invisible One—inscrutable and almighty (Rom 11:33; 1 Tm 6:16; Rv 1:8). For how can we have a life with a God like that? How can we even get started on such a life? And where would we go if we were finally to get going? What would we do in such a life with God? Unfortunately all of these questions go begging—as long as God remains the invisible and inscrutable One.

But what if God is his Word to us (Jn 1:1)? What then? What if God binds himself to his revelation to us in the Holy Bible (LW 42:147; 46:276)? What then? Well, then he would no longer be distant and removed from us. Then we would know what he has given us and what he expects from us—for

---

2   See also BC 143, 161; LW 12:217, 21:191, 28:72.

he would have revealed himself to us. Then we could have a life with him—one based on his Word. It would be preoccupied with reading, studying, memorizing, obeying, and following that Word. People, then, who live with God would be those who have a life with his Good Book—we would be people of the Holy Scriptures (LW 25:261).

As such we would no longer define right and wrong by ourselves (Is 5:20; Dt 12:8). We would instead follow the Holy Scriptures and believe what they say is right—being "regulated by the Word" (LW 17:144). And this is because, as Luther argued,

> the Word of God . . . is eternal [and applies] to all men of all times. For although in the course of time customs, people, places, and usages may vary, godliness and ungodliness remain the same. (LW 14:290)

Now according to the holy words of Scripture, we learn that all of us are sinners and deserve eternal punishment in hell (Rom 2:5, 3:23), and that we cannot save ourselves (Ps 49:7–9; Rom 7:24, 9:16–18). But we learn also that if we believe in Jesus and follow him we will be saved from the fires of hell (Jn 3:36; Mt 7:21; Acts 4:12). These assertions (LW 33:21) are at the heart of what God tells us about godliness and ungodliness.

Being Offended

But these are tough words—and many find them to be not the least compelling (Mt 7:13–14, 11:6). They offend the positive image we have of ourselves (Job 27:5–6), as well as the independent streak that runs through us all (Dt 8:17). Because of our pride, we are unable to push ourselves in the right direction. Try though we may, we keep tripping up ourselves. Our pride goes before us—and we fall (Prv 16:18), over and over again.

As long as our pride reigns in us, we cannot give ourselves over to this new life with God. For our pride is a monster of "self-righteousness" (LW 26:310) which suppresses the truth about us and God (Rom 1:18)—a truth that could save us (Jn 8:32)—albeit a truth that is "harsh" [*aspra veritas*] (LW 11:58). It is a word that cuts deeply into us (Heb 4:12) and exposes us for what we are (Jn 3:20). And we quite naturally resist this assault (Mal 3:2–3). No one in their right mind would find this to be "pleasant" in any way (Heb 12:11). So rather than enduring and learning and being strengthened (Rom 5:3-5), we, like the disciples, flee from the sufferings of the cross (Mt 26:56).

BEING STOPPED COLD

But we're not left with that plight. It can be stopped. We're not some ineluctable runaway train. And what stops us is James 4:6—"God opposes the proud, but gives grace to the humble." Without this word we are a runaway train. But with it there is hope that we'll be saved from the impending wreck ahead.

How so? By sheer fright, my friends in Christ! That line—"God opposes the proud"—stops us cold. Now we have a tiger by the tail—and that changes everything. As of old, we hear again the words in Job 41:8, "Lay hands on him; think of the battle; you will not do it again!" I should say not! When God is after us, our goose is cooked (Hos 13:8; Am 5:19). And when we come to know this for sure, the game changes. For his pursuit of us is much worse than that of any IRS agent, crazed mother-in-law, drug-addicted robber, Middle-East terrorist or escaped psychopath! For he is the king of creation, who is able to hurl earthquakes, storms and pandemics our way (Nm 16:31–32; Ez 13:13, 14:21). No other opponent we will ever meet could be so fierce.

With that thunderous, divine assault upon us, we are pulled ahead to where we belong. No longer do we have to try to push ourselves in the right direction. Now, finally, we're pulled ahead—finally heading on the path of righteousness (Prv 4:18).

Paying What We Owed

But there's more than this thunder. If that were all—we would be crushed. But there's more. James 4:6 goes on to say that God also "gives grace to the humble." Once humbled, then, we are given grace. We are lifted up (Ps 75:7)—just think of it! Pulled ahead for sure—but also lifted up. "By grace you have been saved through faith; and this is not your own doing, it is the gift of God—not because of works, lest anyone should boast" (Eph 2:8–9).

And what does this grace give? Just how does it lift us up? And where do we go when we have been lifted up? Luther spells it out:

> Jesus Christ . . . . has snatched us, poor lost creatures, from the jaws of hell, . . . and has restored us to the Father's favor and grace, ... not with silver and gold but with his own precious blood—[making] satisfaction for me and [paying] what I owed. (BC 414)

How much more graphic could it be—hell having jaws and wanting to eat us up!? It's this horror that grace saves us from. And why is hell so ferocious? Because God's wrath is breathing down the necks of unrepentant sinners! He wants to torment sinners in hell by bearing down upon them—mercilessly (Dt

13:6–11; Lk 16:23, 28; Rv 9:5). But grace frees us from all of this—from God's wrath and hell (Jn 3:36). And that happens when Jesus meets God's demands by paying what we owed.

How does Jesus do that? Well, not with silver and gold—that's for sure (1 Pt 1:18). No, he does it with his precious blood. By dying on the cross, he puts away our sin (Heb 9:26). And that he does by paying what we owed God. And what we owed was punishment for our sins. Now, it's right at this point, that we see the grace of God most vividly—for our gift from Christ Jesus is that he was punished in our place (LW 22:167; 26:284). He is our substitute—and in that great turn-around is grace and salvation. For only then can God become our loving heavenly Father (Jn 10:29) instead of our cosmic, fire-spitting Judge (Mt 3:12; BC 419). By being punished in our place, Jesus moves God to mercy (LW 51:277).[3] Or as Luther puts it in our passage from the *Large Catechism* just quoted, he restores us "to the Father's favor and grace" (BC 414). This includes changing God or reconciling him (BC 121).[4] As strange as this may seem, for an immutable and eternal God (Heb 13:8), our salvation requires it. Without reconciliation, a wrathful God (Is 13:9; Mi 6:2) and defiant, rebellious humanity (Job 9:32–35; Acts 7:51), would remain in conflict forever (Rom 5:2; LW 26:325).

---

3   See also my "Moving the Father to Mercy," *Dialog* 35 (Fall, 1996) 309–310.
4   See also BC 137, 140, 142, 147, 149, 152, 153, 165, 166, 216, 253, 257, and 260.

A Peculiar Phraseology

But when we believe in "the reconciled God" (LW 12:377, 399),[5] we too are changed. We become new creations (2 Cor 5:17). When that happens, we can then say with Saint Paul, "I can do all things in Christ who strengthens me" (Phil 4:13).

But this could sound crazy and be summarily dismissed. That's because being grandiose is a sign of psychological instability[6]—rooted in damaging delusions. And so over-estimating ourselves—or saying that we can do all things, that is, being grandiose—hurls us into personal as well as inter-personal collapse—because of the inflated self-importance it breeds (LW 52:208). But what if this grandiosity wasn't rooted in ourselves? What if it wasn't delusional? What if it were factual? What if we could manifest it in our lives without bringing it into being by ourselves? What then?

Well, that's exactly what we have! And that's because we are able to do all things—but only because Christ dwells in us (Gal 2:20). This is the power of salvation (2 Tm 3:5)—concrete and practical. Nothing abstract or ethereal here—but new people with new capacities, emerging on the scene (LW 26:375). Even so, we know with Luther that this indwelling is "a peculiar phraseology" (LW 26:168)—for to say that Christ lives in us isn't standard fare. But be that as it may, we would still highly prize such a person. Just think of it—a person who is a humble, thankful servant. And that's the way people are when Christ dwells in them. Humble—not always pushing themselves on you and making everything be about them. Just think of it! Thankful—not bitter and complaining about everything because nothing is ever quite right and so nothing is ever any

---

5 See also LW 24:163; 30:12, 280.
6 See Karen Horney, *Neurosis and Human Growth* (1950) (New York: Norton, 1991).

good either! And serving—always getting things done so that there's room for those sweet little moments of quiet repose together. Who wouldn't want a son or daughter-in-law like that? Who wouldn't want a friend like that—humble, thankful, and a hard-working servant?!

Thank the Lord

So rejoice in Christ for all his mercies. For he not only died to save us from our sins, but by so doing, he also leads us into newness of life. He bore our sins, after all, "that we might die to sin and live to righteousness" (1 Pt 2:24)—by walking "in newness of life" (Rom 6:4). So we aren't saved to take time off, or to go on spiritual vacations, or to lounge around theologically on some backyard deckchair in the afternoon sun. No, we rather are saved so that we can work in the kingdom (Lk 10:2; Eph 2:10). For as Luther wrote in his beloved *Smalcald Articles*, "if good works do not follow, our faith is . . . not true" (BC 315).

So give thanks to the Lord for he is good (Ps 118:1). And bring that thanksgiving with you to the Altar of the Lord and receive the sacrament this day. All of you who believe in Christ and follow him, come forward, bow down, and eat and drink. For in this sacrament is the gift of refreshment (BC 449). So come and be refreshed. Know that your sins are forgiven for Jesus' sake. Come and be refreshed. Know that there's power here for you to fight against sin and death—for, as Luther said, in this sacrament we have "a pure, wholesome, soothing medicine" and "a precious antidote" to the poison that infects us (BC 454). So come and give thanks and be refreshed and walk in newness of life.

No Partiality

But this new life in Christ isn't vague or dreamy. No, there are moral details galore. Take, for instance, James 3:16–17:

> Where there is envy and selfish ambition, there will also be disorder and wickedness of every kind. But the wisdom from above is first pure, then peaceable, . . . full of mercy, . . . without a trace of partiality or hypocrisy.

This passage drives toward wiping out every trace of partiality and hypocrisy. Attacking envy, selfish ambition and disorder serves that goal—as does the pursuit of purity, peace and mercy. So let us first work to wipe out partiality. But what does this entail?

Partiality is the playing of favorites—which has no place in Christianity. We are to be kind to everyone. For there is no greatness in loving those who love us—for unbelievers do that (Lk 6:32). No, the truly remarkable thing would be to love the unloving. For this would be a truly sacrificial act. It would be to give without expecting anything in return. The best book on this is Søren Kierkegaard's *Works of Love*. In it he shows, in great detail, how true Christian love is grounded in self-denial (WL 7).[7] Without that component, Christian love would be just ordinary human mutuality—enmeshed in a "lower" conception of love (WL 244), deluded by the "glittering externality" of life (WL 328). But there's no denial or sacrifice in that. Kierkegaard expounds:

> Since the neighbor is . . . every human being, all dissimilarities are . . . removed from the object . . . . Yet this love is not proudly independent of its object. Its equality does not appear in love's proudly turning back into itself through indif-

---

7 See also WL 55, 223, 258, 268, 364–66.

ference to the object—no, the equality appears in love's humbly turning outward, embracing everyone, and yet loving each one individually but no one exceptionally. (WL 66–67)

When we do this we become "invisible" and "anonymous" (WL 274, 276). And then we can finally practice true impartiality.

No Hypocrisy

Furthermore, let there be not even a trace of hypocrisy among us. Let us rather be genuine and not phony—given that our Lord despised hypocrites (Mt 23:13–33). Let us practice what we preach, stand by our words, and "walk the talk." A few years ago I re-read J. D. Salinger's famous novel, *The Catcher in the Rye* (1951). I was struck by how the book's hero, Holden Caulfield, rants against the phoniness he finds all around him in New York City. Everywhere he looked he found a "glaring disparity" between what people say, and in fact do.[8] So let us not be like the rank and file phonies of life. Let us throw off deceit. Call on God for help with both of these—being genuine and impartial—and he will strengthen you—for he wants us to serve as we should. Amen.

---

8   See the readings on the *Catcher in the Rye*, ed. Steve Engel (San Diego: Greenhaven Press, 1998) 80.

Sermon 7

Hate Yourself

Jesus tells us in Luke 14:26 to hate ourselves. This is shocking! It seems the exactly wrong thing to say. So why does he say it? No one else tells us this—except, perhaps, homicidal monsters and sexual perverts. So why does Jesus tell us to hate ourselves? He's not a wicked person. He's not a pervert. He's the good shepherd, after all (Jn 10:11). He's the one on whom we depend for our safety and salvation. So what's up here? Is there any method to his madness? Why does he tell us to hate ourselves? This instruction seems wild beyond measure. Surely there seems to have been a mistake made somewhere. But as Søren Kierkegaard writes in his famous book on the near sacrifice of Isaac, in Genesis 22, entitled *Fear and Trembling*:

> Luke 14:26 offers a remarkable teaching on the absolute duty to God .... This is a hard saying. Who can bear to listen to it?[1] This is the reason ... that we seldom hear it. But this silence is only an escape that is of no avail ... The context in which these words appear, ... indicate that the words are to be taken in their full terror in order that each person may examine himself.   (FT 72)

---

1   See Jn 6:60.

Dodging Self-Hatred

So it's no surprise, then, that some say the word μισεω, usually translated as hate, actually means something else. It means something softer, like "give up," "love less" (TEV 1976; CEV 1995) or "let go."[2] But that word μισεω won't budge under these clever, definitional revisions. Μισεω has been translated as hate for generations, and hate it must remain. We cannot dodge so easily the command to hate ourselves.[3] So the word misogyny, for instance, or the hatred of women, comes from μισεω, and rightly so—as does misanthropy or the hatred of humanity. Hatred then—and no less offensive other word—is the only correct translation of μισεω—whether we like it or not.

Others try to head self-hatred off at the pass by saying it's not about hating *ourselves*. No, they say, it's rather about hating *our lives*—which they think is less than ourselves. But when Luke 14:26 says we are to hate our lives it means ourselves. The two expressions mean the same—so the distinction between self and life is without any difference. This is because the word at stake here, ψυχη or psyche, means our entire life or self (see Lk 6:9, 9:24, 12:23, 17:33). Ψυχη therefore leaves nothing out of ourselves that could be loved instead of hated. For "from the sole of the foot even to the head, there is no soundness" in us (Is 1:6). So "we are all utterly lost [and] there is no good in us" (BC 309, 519). What must be hated, then, is our entire being—or at least that's what the word ψυχη means in Luke 14:26.

---

2 Eugene Peterson, *The Message: The Bible in Contemporary Language* (Colorado Springs, CO: NavPress, 2002).

3 See Gerhard O. Forde, "Fake Theology," *Dialog* 22 (Fall, 1983) 246–51.

Defying Self-Hatred

But these linguistic, Biblical facts don't stop the critics. They're convinced—even against these facts—that self-love trumps self-hatred in the Bible. They're convinced that those who think Jesus taught self-hatred are maliciously deluded. "Such attitudes are dangerous distortions and destructive misinterpretations of scattered Bible verses grossly misread by negative-thinking Bible readers who project their own negative self-image onto the pages of Holy Scripture." So sin, rather than coming from self-love, actually springs up from being a "non-self-loving" person. And salvation isn't aided and abetted by self-hatred, but rather comes only through acquiring "a noble self-love."[4]

In this critique, self-love and self-hate are switched around—making self-love good and self-hate bad. In the last half of Saint Augustine's (354–430) massive and magisterial *The City of God*, he wrote the exact opposite:

> Two cities have been formed by two loves: the earthly by the love of self, even to the contempt of God; [and] the heavenly by the love of God, even to the contempt of self.[5]

This venerable teaching is now being brazenly assaulted with impunity. For generations it guided the church in the way of salvation. But now it's thought to be passé, simply because it offends "the dignity of the person."[6]

---

4   Robert H. Schuller, *Self-Esteem: The New Reformation* (Waco, Texas: Word, 1982) 113, 128, 49.
5   *The City of God*, trans. Marcus Dods (New York: Random House, 1950) 477.
6   R. H. Schuller, *Self-Esteem*, 31.

And what's more, Jesus tells you to love your neighbor "as yourself" (Mt 22:39). Now some think this rule implies that we should love ourselves and only then love others. So this verse, they say, trumps Luke 14:26. But as Luther points out, this cannot be so, since nowhere in the Bible is there a command to love ourselves (LW 25:513). So what we have in the line ως σεαυτον or "as yourself," is actually a call to love your neighbor *instead* of yourself (LW 26:355–57). This line, then, isn't about self-love at all.

Defining Self-Hatred

Now when Jesus tells us to hate ourselves, this coheres with other Christian teachings. So this isn't an aberrant idea. In line with it we're told to "deny" ourselves (Mt 16:24; Mk 8:34; Lk 9:23). We're also told to "lose" our lives for Jesus' sake (Mt 10:39, 16:25; Mk 8:35; Lk 9:24, 17:33). And we're told to "die" to ourselves (Rom 6:4; Gal 6:14; 2 Cor 5:14). All these verses go down the same road that self-hatred does. Its meaning therefore is to stand against ourselves—for we are our own worst enemy (LW 27:364, 42:48)! We don't have our best interest at heart. We shoot ourselves in the foot repeatedly. So hating ourselves means we don't like our interests and instincts. It means we reject our chosen values and ways. Self-hatred, then, is about saying "not as I will," but as God wills (Mt 26:39). This is because we're terrible sinners (Lk 5:8; Mk 7:21–23; Jer 17:9)—and, indeed, in self-hatred there's "nothing to hate but sin" (LW 14:162)! As such we must not be followed but opposed—for we are grievous sinners.[7]

---

[7] Therefore "truly loving oneself is akin to worrying about the kind of person you are becoming." The *Quotable Kierkegaard*, ed. Gordon Marino (Princeton, New Jersey: Princeton University Press, 2014) xl.

The Lutheran Confessions elongate this judgment saying "man is. . . so miserably perverted, poisoned, and corrupted that by disposition and nature he is thoroughly wicked . . . and hostile to God" (BC 524).

Self-hatred, then, is not about depression, despair, lethargy, or pushing us to the brink of suicide. It's rather about fighting against ourselves so that we might serve God and care for our neighbors (Lk 10:27). Kierkegaard put it this way:

> The single individual [is to fight] for himself with himself within himself . . . . in the fight to free himself in equality before God.
> (EUD 143)

In this battle—which is "the good fight of faith" (1 Tm 6:12)—we fight against our sinful self so we might live a righteous life—that we might stand before God in equality, as a sinner, with all the rest of humanity, pleading for mercy. So hating ourselves serves a good end. It's not only about destruction. In it we indeed break up the "fallow ground" or hardened crust of our lives, but only so that new life may spring up (Jer 4:3; Hos 10:12). This is an odd battle, no doubt. For in it we are both the pugilist and the one fought against. So with ourselves, within ourselves, we fight against ourselves, for ourselves—that we might be blessed. Strange as this may seem, this struggle (Phil 2:13; LW 35:377) is essential, for it puts us on the road to salvation.

So what seems only negative, is actually positive. Self-hatred therefore works for our well-being and sounds an alarm against perversions of itself—

> when the bustler wastes his time and powers in the service of futile, inconsequential pursuits . . . . [and] when the light-minded person throws himself almost like a nonentity into the folly of the moment and makes nothing of it . . . . [and] when the depressed person desires to be rid . . . of himself . . . . [and] when someone surrenders to despair because the world or another person has faithlessly left him betrayed . . . . [and] when someone self-tormentingly thinks to do God a service by torturing himself.
> (WL 23)

Self-hatred expects too much from us to be a party to any of these distorted, mistaken ways (LW 31:160). For we stand against ourselves in self-hatred for only two reasons: [1] so we can honor God and [2] so we can serve our neighbor as we should (Mt 22:36–40). Anything that holds us back from these two projects isn't part of self-hatred—regardless of what the critics say.

Defending Self-Hatred

But is self-hatred the only way to reach these goals? Surely there must be a far less offensive way to do it. Why does honoring God and helping our neighbors require us to hate ourselves? Well, it's only because we are such terrible sinners—being sinful even "beyond measure" (Rom 7:13). If it were not for that, we wouldn't have to hate ourselves. So if we deny that, self-hatred no longer makes sense and can be willfully disregarded. But as long as we belong to a crooked, perverse, adulterous generation (Mk 8:38; Phil 2:15), we'll have to hate ourselves if we are going to save ourselves "for eternal life" (Jn 12:25). We're going to have to earnestly "attack" the old Adam and Eve in us (BC 445). We're going to have to crush this huge and horrible monster of self-righteousness with "the hammer of death, the thunder of hell, and the lightning of divine wrath" (LW 26:310). If we refuse to do that, we're nothing but "damnable knaves" (LW 43:228, 18:98)! But how are we members of such a fallen humanity? What's the evidence for this? In the Bible there seems to be at least four descending degrees of degradation that testify to our wretched, sinful, disgusting state, which justifies our hatred of ourselves.

1. Dullness. First, we suffer from dullness—we're asleep at the switch. Like the people of Laodicea, we're in a fog and distracted by life. "For you say, I am rich, I have prospered, and I need nothing; not knowing that you are wretched, pitiable, poor, blind, and naked" (Rv 3:17). So we drift through life not knowing how bad off we really are. Our eyes are glazed over—and if told of our plight, we don't listen because we don't care because we don't know any better. So we're indeed asleep. Because of this, God grabs us in his word, saying, "Awake O sleeper, O drunkard, be aroused from your stupor and live" (Eph 5:14; Joel 1:5; 1 Thes 5:6; Mt 25:5). Get a grip, he says! So with Antonio Machado (1875–1939), we should be led on to confess:

> What was your word, Jesus?
> Love? Affection? Forgiveness?
> All your words were
> One word: Wakeup [*Velad*].[8]

---

8   *Times Alone: Selected Poems of Antonio Machado,* trans. Robert Bly (Middletown, Connecticut: Wesleyan University, 1983) 109.

2. Laziness. And secondly, when we do awake, we become defensive, working to shield ourselves from unpleasantness—thereby showing our devilish "dragon's tail" (LW 22:397). And so we work hard to amass wealth—for ourselves—to help ourselves idolatrously feel "secure, happy, fearless, as if [we] were sitting in the midst of paradise" (BC 365)—in clear defiance of the "flaming sword" posted to keep us from re-entering paradise (Gn 3:24). This pursuit of ease and tranquility is foolishness, says Luke 12:16–21, for the way to life is the hard, narrow way which few favor (Lk 13:23–24; Mt 7:13).

3. Recklessness. But we also defend ourselves by redefining goodness. We say evil is good and good is evil (Is 5:20). This enables us to love darkness rather than the light (Jn 3:19). And so quite gleefully, we're "hell-bent for leather." We throw all caution to the wind and pursue our basest desires. And we love sinning (LW 22:390). For deeply rooted in our sinful hearts we have the "desire to seek life where there is certain death and to flee from death where one has the sure source of life" (LW 43:183)! So indeed we're like the prodigal son, wallowing in "loose living" (Lk 15:13). And none of this bothers us because we have redefined goodness so it can be included in our perverted morality. But this too is condemned when Jesus says he has come to poke out the eyes of those who see life in this distorted way (Jn 9:39).

4. Disability. Finally, we're further mired in sinful filthiness by being unable to do the good we should do, and helplessly dragged into doing the evil that disgusts us (Rom 7:18–24). This captivity makes us wretched and pitiful. And it is unavoidable, since everyone who sins is a "slave to sin" (Jn 8:34). So if we try to improve, our efforts will fall under their own weight. Any self-confidence, then, runs aground (LW 3:4; 26:171; 31:371).

DISPLAYING SELF-HATRED

We should then follow Proverbs 9:8 and love the one who rebukes us. We shouldn't resist the call to hate ourselves. We should instead say: "Thank you Lord! I needed that hit up the side of the head. It hurt alright, but nothing else could help and only you loved me enough to tell me this saving, offensive truth!" These should be our words because as Proverbs 16:18 says, "Pride goeth before a fall." So no wonder "the Lord of hosts . . . is against all that is proud and lofty, against all that is lifted up and high" (Is 2:12). For it's precisely this pride that tries to keep us from the cleansing abrasives in self-hatred. And pride strikes us all. For each of us has a "philosopher in us."[9] And "philosophy and ego are never very far apart." In fact, "philosophical discussion can be a kind of intellectual blood sport, in which egos get bruised and buckled, even impaled . . . . Plain showing off" is also a part of it.[10] So because of our supposed superiority, we think we're better than others, believing we're more talented, harder working and better educated than most (LW 18:263; *contra* Phil 2:3).[11] But this isn't the Biblical way. Even so, we still hold back and resist the self-hatred in Luke 14:26.

Therefore God sends a Savior for us, Christ Jesus, who suffers the same humiliating humility that is required of us in hating ourselves. In this way he shows us that he doesn't ask of us anything he'll not himself do first. So Jesus leaves his heavenly abode, filled with all the glory, honor and respect of the angelic hosts, and takes on "sinful flesh" (Rom 8:3). And

---

9   Anthony Kenny, *The Legacy of Wittgenstein* (Oxford: Blackwell, 1984) 48.
10 Colin McGinn, *The Making of a Philosopher* (New York: HarperCollins, 2002) 63.
11 Robert Taylor, *Restoring Pride* (Amherst, New York: Prometheus Books, 1996) 31.

this descent is no cake walk, even for the only Son of God (Lk 22:44). For he comes to be "obedient unto death, even death on a cross" (Phil 2:8). And in the process he is mocked, bound, spit upon, slapped, kicked, stripped, whipped and forsaken (Mt 26:67, 27:2, 28–31, 39–44, 46). And he endures all of this voluntarily—as he did the washing of the foul feet of his faithless disciples (Jn 13:12–17; Mt 26:31, 56). In this display you have "an example, that you should follow in his steps" (1 Pt 2:21)—even with the humiliation included![12] So Jesus, though he didn't need to hate himself because he was sinless (Heb 4:15; 1 Pt 1:19), did so anyway. He denied himself and gave up his life in the most degrading, painful way on the cross—becoming even "a curse for us" (Gal 3:13). And in this he "was self-denial" himself (UDVS 224).

But even this powerful example will not suffice. In addition we need redemption and forgiveness. This is because—try though we may to hate ourselves—we will fall back again and again into being "lovers of self, lovers of money, . . . lovers of pleasure rather than lovers of God" (2 Tm 3:2-4; LW 29:119). For we continue to have a "mad passion for [our] own glory" (LW 33:226). So we need deliverance from ourselves, from beyond ourselves (Rom 7:24). And this we have in Christ Jesus. For the one who gave us this model of humiliation, also frees us from our sin through his very humiliation. This he does by taking our sins upon himself, suffering the punishment for them, and then sharing his victory with us, though we didn't deserve it (Rom 5:8). By his wounds indeed we have been saved (1 Pt 2:24; 2 Cor 8:9; Is 53:5).

---

12 *Contra* Robert H. Schuller, *Self-Esteem*, 84.

Developing Self-Hatred

But it isn't enough to talk about and even affirm self-hatred as we have done today. We must also implement it and develop it in our daily lives—"walking by" it, if you will (Gal 5:25). Now the key[13] to this is Christian actions—like those two dozen listed in Romans 12:9–21. This is what self-hatred does to us—it puts work and action in the place of feelings and sentiment. Self-hatred displaces those hurt, offended, complaining, exhausted and bruised feelings. Now we no longer dwell in them, but put our head down and plow straight ahead (Lk 9:62; LW 15:113; 44:77). This gives us new power. For serving God and neighbor usurps our feelings—whether disrespected or honored, sullen or thrilling.

But we can't do any of this on our own. Only God can fill us with the competence and confidence we will need to quit living for ourselves (2 Cor 3:6; 5:15). Only then can we do all things through Christ who strengthens us (Phil 4:13). Only then can we hate ourselves while never hating others (1 Jn 2:9–11). And this we do, giving all the glory to God (1 Cor 10:31). For this righteousness of ours doesn't belong to us, because of our sin, so it remains alien to us, *extra nos*—on loan from God (LW 12:367).[14] Amen.

---

13 See also Ronald F. Marshall, *Kierkegaard for the Church*, 37, 86n31.
14 See also LW 24:347; 25:137, 415; 26:170, 387; 27:21; 51:28.

Sermon 8

Hate Yourself–Again

Once again we see how tough Jesus can be on us. In John 12:25 he tells us not only that we will lose out if we love ourselves, but that we must hate ourselves if we want to go to heaven. So what shall we make of these words which seem so crazy to us? Does our Lord really want us to be suicidal or abnormal psychologically? What's up with his emphatic regard for self-hatred?

Denying Yourself

These startling words are not about self-mutilation or anything of the sort. They instead are about self-denial (Mt 16:24)—which runs throughout the entire New Testament in various manifestations. So self-hatred is about self-denial and not about self-destruction. We are to lose our lives for the sake of the Gospel (Mk 8:35). We are to die to the world and to our sinful ways (Gal 6:14; Rom 6:11). And to die to ourselves means no longer living for ourselves alone, but "for him," who was crucified and raised from the dead for us (2 Cor 5:15).

To deny ourselves, then, is to demote ourselves (Jn 3:30), or put ourselves on the back burner, if you will. And we are to deny ourselves so that we can follow Jesus (Mt 16:24). Self-hatred therefore has a purpose beyond itself—beyond simply denying ourselves, dying to ourselves, or hating ourselves. Its purpose is to enable us to follow Christ—that we might walk "in newness of life" (Rom 6:4; 1 Pt 2:21). So anything that would damage us or in any way impede or compromise our discipleship, wouldn't be *bone fide* New Testament self-hatred. Self-hatred in the New Testament is supposed to be invigorating—not demoralizing. It's supposed to make us robust saints of God (2 Tm 1:7)—not damaged creatures, diminished in mind and body. It's supposed to help us become "wise as serpents and innocent as doves" (Mt 10:16). And to be like that takes agility and savvy, compassion and nerve.[1]

GOING ABOUT HATING YOURSELF

But what if I were to tell you now to hate yourselves on the count of three. What would you do? Poke yourself in the eye? I think not. You would most likely just sit there—and a bit befuddled at that. You would probably think I was joking around. And that's because we have no tools for getting going on hating ourselves. We have nothing to grab on to, as it were, to try to hate ourselves.

In one sense this is as it should be since hating ourselves is an attitudinal or dispositional matter—it's about how we see ourselves. So it's not about particular actions—doing this or that on command. However, in another sense, this is all wrong, since we should know what to do when trying to hate ourselves. For if we are to hate ourselves in order to follow Christ—then there must be something to do as we walk down that path of righteousness (Ps 23:3). Our problem is knowing exactly what that is.

In this regard there is a helpful prayer by that admirer of Martin Luther, who lived in Copenhagen, Denmark, over one hundred and fifty years ago—Søren Kierkegaard by name. You may have heard of him. But you might not have known that

---

1 On these points, see my previous sermon, "Hate Yourself."

he not only believed that Luther was the master of us all, but that next to Jesus Christ, he was the truest figure (JP 3:2465, 3:2898). So Kierkegaard's words should perk up your Lutheran ears. His prayer comes from the end of his book, *Practice in Christianity*. In it Kierkegaard, under his complex pseudonym Anti-Climacus, meditates over and over again on John 12, about Jesus drawing us to himself when he's lifted-up on the cross. In this little prayer we have five ways to hate ourselves:

> Lord Jesus Christ, our foolish minds are weak; they are more than willing to be drawn—and there is so much that wants to draw us to itself. There is pleasure with its seductive power, the multiplicity with its bewildering distractions, the moment with its infatuating importance and the conceited laboriousness of busyness and the careless time-wasting of light-mindedness and the gloomy brooding of heavy-mindedness . . . . But you, who are the truth, only you . . . can truly draw a person to yourself, which you have promised to do. (PC 157)

And indeed Christ does just that—drawing us to himself—when he dies for the sins of the world on the cross (Jn 12:32; LW 44:38). Just think, for a moment, of that unbelieving centurion, who, upon witnessing the crucifixion, said: "Truly this was the Son of God" (Mt 27:54). In this prayer Kierkegaard gives us five ways, then, to hate ourselves so that we too might make a similar confession.

PLEASURES

The first way he gives us in this prayer to hate ourselves is to battle against the seductions of pleasure. His point isn't that we should forgo all pleasure, but that we shouldn't become Epicureans (Acts 17:18) and wallow in pleasure, wrapping up our whole life in the pursuit of pleasure. This is the height of self-indulgence—and self-hatred aims to purge us of this self-aggrandizement which we find in our scandalous identification with pleasure. Each one of us will have a different set of pleasures that woo us into this trap. The power in these pleasures is truly seductive, as Kierkegaard says—in that they won't settle for anything less than everything we are and have. And so we must corral them before they consume us.

This is the great value in "self-control"—which is one of the hallmarks of the spiritual life (Gal 5:17; 2 Tm 1:7). Through self-control we corral the wild horses of pleasure. And precisely in that curtailment we see self-hatred at its best.[2] It cuts the nerve of the "fleeting pleasures of sin" (Heb 11:25). It keeps our lives from being built upon sand (Mt 7:26). For our lives are not to be driven by pleasure, but in giving God all the glory (1 Cor 10:31).

DISTRACTIONS

Next we are to oppose the "multiplicity" in our daily lives "with its bewildering distractions." Think of all those to-do lists we carry around with us. They both control and consume us on a daily basis. Not that we should be slouches or irresponsible slugs, but our life isn't about getting tasks scratched off our lists. That would be too fragmented of a life for a Christian. We are instead to be more focused than what the multiplicity of distractions brings. Being "tossed to and fro and carried about

---

2   See also Ronald F. Marshall, *Kierkegaard for the Church*, 86n31.

with every wind" (Eph 4:14) isn't Christian discipleship. Christ tells us that our lives should be organized around loving God and caring for the neighbor (Mt 22:37–39). But we rush after these distractions anyway, eager for another thrill from that teeming multiplicity.

And that's how the new affects us (Acts 17:21). So we suffer from a love for it or neophilia.[3] Luther therefore warned that it's wrong to yearn for "something new," supposing that the "old and . . . ordinary . . . count for nothing" (LW 41:127; 22:486).[4] That's what boredom does. So pitting self-hatred against this love of the new goes a long way toward freeing us from the bewildering distractions of multiplicity.

Busyness

Hating ourselves also frees us from excessive busyness which feeds our conceit and exalted sense of self-importance. We like to think that the world couldn't make it without us—crazy though that may sound to the sober-minded. So we keep bustling around not just to fight off boredom—but even more to feed our egos. If I have so much to do, I imagine, it must mean that I'm very important.

Gone from this way of life is waiting quietly upon the Lord, the maker of heaven and earth (Pss 37:7, 46:10, 62:5). Gone from this way of life is the quiet time of prayer—where we wait silently on the word of the Lord. All of these spiritual wonders are gobbled up by the rush, by the hurricane of busyness. Gone is taking time every day "to collect yourself in the impression of the divine" (FSE 50). Hating yourself, then, is a way to make room for prayer and quiet—which are the opposite of

---

[3] Desmond Morris, *The Naked Ape: A Zoologist's Study of the Human Animal* (New York: Dell, 1967) 130, and Richard John Neuhaus, *American Babylon: Notes of a Christian Exile* (New York: Basic Books, 2009) 59.

[4] See below, "Conclusion: Old Christianity."

busyness, since they teach us how to forego our will and obey God alone (Mt 6:10; LW 42:48–49). So in self-hatred, Christ is rebuking the storms of our busyness, that "a great calm" may come upon us too (Mt 8:26).

Light-Mindedness

The fourth way this prayer helps us hate ourselves is by putting the kibosh on wasting time in light-mindedness. We waste time when we're driven by trivialities—worrying, for instance, as this Sunday's news has, over whether or not movie stars Jennifer Aniston and Brad Pitt will ever get back together again.[5] We get obsessed over these matters—calling our friends to weigh in on the odds and even changing our schedules so we don't miss these stars on TV. It's not that a little light-mindedness is bad in helping us unwind. No, again, it's a matter of going hog-wild over all of this careless time-wasting of light-mindedness. It's as if the weighty matters of life are more than we can bear, and so, in self-defense, we escape into the trivialities of popular culture—whatever they may be. I can do that, for instance, by calling up a fellow pastor to gossip over the latest sexuality research published in a psychological journal—all under the pretense of enriching our marital counseling skills.

But escaping the traumas of life isn't Christian. We know that those who try to save their lives in this way will lose them (Mt 16:25). We know that it is the way of the fool to take-it-easy, "eat, drink and be merry" (Lk 12:19; Eph 5:4). We know that we are here instead to share in the sufferings of Christ and walk in his steps (1 Pt 4:13, 2:21). And he was hardly a man of

---

5   See Walter Scott's "Personality Parade" in *Parade* Sunday magazine, March 29, 2009.

light-mindedness—coming nowhere close to being the jovial, back-slapping type (LW 22:236–37, 377).[6] Hating ourselves, then, is about quitting obsessing over trivialities.

Heavy-Mindedness

But Kierkegaard also says we are to hate ourselves so as not to sink into the gloomy brooding of heavy-mindedness. Who would have ever thought that Kierkegaard would fight against such brooding—being himself famously characterized as gloomy and brooding.[7] This is as strange as President Nixon opening up trade in 1972 with our then sworn enemy, China.[8] So while Kierkegaard indeed suffered from sadness, he never thought of it as being virtuous. He instead battled against his recurring melancholy—in the name of the joy found in Christ (Phil 4:4). For he believed that "never, never did the parched and drought-stricken earth sense the rain's refreshment as deliciously," as when the sinner, who rests in the joy of Christ, celebrates the forgiveness of sins (CD 132).

So brooding gloom is not a sign of self-hatred but of self-indulgence and the very self-love that damns us to hell (2 Tm 3:2–4; Is 30:9–11). Self-hatred, to the contrary, is actually about freeing us from such heavy-mindedness. We aren't to be serious about the big issues of death and wrath, wickedness and judgment, in order to despair over them, but that we might praise God for his wisdom and mercy and then also help our

---

6 See, for example, the famous laughing Jesus drawing by Fred Berger in *Playboy* Magazine, January 1970; and the 1999 *Jesus* movie—screenplay by Suzette Couture—where a light-hearted, silly Jesus plays tag with his disciples.

7 See H. V. Martin, *Kierkegaard, the Melancholy Dane* (New York: Philosophical Library, 1948); and Theodor Haecker, *Kierkegaard, the Cripple* (New York: Philosophical Library, 1950).

8 Margaret McMillan, *Nixon & Mao: The Week that Changed the World* (New York: Random House, 2007).

neighbors live a decent life. So self-hatred is paradoxically the cure for depression—little known as this might be among practicing therapists and counselors.

Beyond Us

Now as illuminating as Kierkegaard's prayer is, we cannot simply take up his five points and sail-off, unimpeded, into a righteousness based on self-hatred. That is because all our capacities are tainted by sin, and so our attempts to use these Kierkegaardian tools, if you will, won't help much, simply because in our using of them, we will in fact distort and otherwise corrupt them. I'm reading a new book by Anne Harrington called, *The Cure Within*,[9] which goes against what I'm saying, albeit in another context. Nevertheless, we must not let her argument sway us in the wrong direction regarding our souls. For on this religious point, if we are to find any help at all, it will have to come from outside of us. For as Jesus taught, it is not what enters us that defiles, spoils or harms us, but what already is in us—from the beginning (Pss 51:5, 64:6; Jer 17:9). For from within, he says, comes every sort of waywardness—"fornication, theft, murder, adultery, coveting, wickedness, deceit, licentiousness, envy, slander, pride [and] foolishness" (Mk 7:21–22). There is enough here to defeat anyone—regardless of how many blessings we've received from on high. And that's breathtaking!

No wonder, then, that we run to Hebrews 5:9 which says that the "source" of our salvation lies outside of us in Christ Jesus our Lord. This is good news because it means that our salvation cannot be destroyed by our sin. For Christ became perfect by his own suffering and obedience—and not because

---

9   *The Cure Within: A History of Mind-Body Medicine* (New York: Norton, 2008).

of any help from us. And so he'll remain perfect because his perfection is not based on anything outside of him. Therefore in Christ we actually have pure compassion and fortitude—unstained by us or anyone else. We see this in Jesus rescuing us by his death on the cross (Heb 9:26). Only his purity can do this. By sacrificing himself, Jesus was punished in our place (2 Cor 8:9)—that we might be forgiven, and then glorify God, serve our neighbor, and live in heaven forever.

Within Us

But how exactly will this happen? Christ indeed is great, but doesn't sin hold us back from him? How, then, can he help us? Hebrews 11:6 says that only faith in God pleases him and knowing that he rewards those who obey him. So being morally pure won't please God. That's because we couldn't be even if we had eternity to try to do it. We are just too weak for that (Mt 26:41; Rom 7:18). Therefore all we need is simply to believe in Christ—which means trusting in him and entrusting our lives to his care (Pss 23:4, 91:14; Jn 10:28; Rom 8:28, 38–39). With such faith we refuse to say with Job that God is "against me . . . against me, . . . against me" (Job 10:16–17). No, faith knows that God is on our side even when we are assailed by troubles in this life.

And when we trust in God in this way, a miracle happens. He whom we believe in, actually, then, enters into us. And so with Saint Paul we can say and sing that it is no longer I who live but "Christ who lives in me" (Gal 2:20). How so? Well we know about demon-possession alright—how those demons can thrash us about mercilessly, overpowering us from within (Mk 5:2–5, 9:20–22). Just so, Christ likewise can enter into us. But rather than beating us down like the demons, he lifts us up as if "with wings like eagles" (Is 40:31). Then we can sing with

Saint Paul, "I can do all things in Christ who strengthens me" (Phil 4:13)—maybe even pray Kierkegaard's five-point prayer and mean it!

Food of the Soul

Come then, and receive Christ at the Altar today. For he is truly present there. Bow down at the Altar and receive him—in, with and under the bread and the wine of the Lord's Supper. See in it the clearest testimony that our eternal salvation lies outside of us. Just as none of us will bring bread and wine with us to the Altar, but only receive it from the Lord, consecrated by his word and given to us for the forgiveness of sins and our salvation—just so our hope for goodness and mercy, and for heaven itself, is also not provided by us. It can only be received from beyond us. Therefore Luther rightly calls this sacrament "food of the soul" in his *Large Catechism* (BC 449).

Better Than Us

And when you leave today, do good works in the name of the one who saved you, Jesus our Lord (Col 3:17). For we who live in his Spirit must also walk in it (Gal 5:25). During Lent our good deed is to fast the foods we especially enjoy (Mt 6:16). But we also care about the implications of this fast—wanting to extend it to other parts of our lives, besides our eating. Today Philippians 2:3 helps us with that by telling us to count others as being better than ourselves. This extension is something of a psychological fast—weaning us from our deeply held pride.

Now I know most of you here today and I know that you are in fact better than most other people—in terms of your intelligence, diligence and kindness. That makes this verse very disturbing and difficult for us. But while we notice your superiority over others—God doesn't. For *sub specie aeternitatis* (Spinoza, 1632–1677)—or from God's bird's eye viewpoint—

these differences don't matter. To disrupt our perception, then, we are told that everyone else is better than us—even if it's not the case according to what we see and understand on our own. But this fasting of our pride is necessary if we are to be as humble as we're supposed to be (Mi 6:8; Lk 18:14). So extend your fast beyond food, and take on your pride as well. Call on God to help with this, otherwise you'll surely fail (Jn 15:5). And he will bless you because he wants you to walk in humility, for that is a big part of the glorious, sacred self-hatred by which he has designed to keep you safe for all eternity. Amen.

Sermon 9

Thank God Rightly

Today we gather to give thanks on the occasion of our national holiday—established by President Abraham Lincoln (1809–1864) in 1863. Normally we only observe church holy days, but this is different because Christians think so highly of thanksgiving.

Ungrateful Bipeds

We prize thanksgiving and encourage gratitude because the Holy Scriptures teach us to do so. And this sacred admonition takes precedence over any declaration or encouragement from our government. The Russian author, Fyodor Dostoyevsky (1821–1881) bemoaned our ingratitude—defining man negatively as an "ungrateful biped."[1] And we see this same negative view when Jesus heals the ten lepers (Lk 17:11–19)—and only one returns to thank him. This may well have inspired Martin Luther to conclude that only "one tenth of the people really perceives God, while the other nine tenths begin" but don't stick with it (LW 23:400). It is right, then, for us to use this national holiday of Thanksgiving Day to promote and defend thanksgiving since ingratitude is rampant. And this widespread influence is a terrible predicament because, as Luther warned,

---

1   *Notes From Underground,* trans. Constance Garnett (New York: Dell, 1960) 49.

> ingratitude is an evil damnable and pernicious enough to quench all the springs of grace and blessing, . . . it is like a poison-laden, burning, destructive wind . . . . For God cannot bless you if you are ungrateful. (SML 8:336)

Ephesians 5:20

Even so, all our efforts to promote and increase thanksgiving will be in vain if it isn't done properly. In our society, gratitude or being thankful, doesn't measure up to what Holy Scriptures say it should be. That's because most Americans, if they are grateful, give thanks without directly thanking God in Christ Jesus, and furthermore, are only grateful for the good things in life and not the bad things as well. But that's not what the Bible teaches. Take Ephesians 5:20, for instance. Here is something quite different:

> Always and for everything, [give] thanks in the name of our Lord Jesus Christ to God the Father. (Eph 5:20)

In this little verse we have three radical claims completely missing from our society today. The first claim is that being grateful isn't enough. That's because it's too general. It needs to be directed explicitly to God the Father, if it's going to be true gratitude.

We have a very helpful elaboration in the Lutheran Confessions of this hotly contested point:

> Although much that is good comes to us from men, we receive it all from God through his command and ordinance . . . . So we receive our blessings not from them, but from God

through them. Creatures are only the hands, channels, and means through which God bestows all blessings . . . . [So] we must acknowledge everything as God's gifts and thank him for them. (BC 368)

Behind all our blessings, then, stands God the Father (Jas 1:17)—which when either unknown or denied, is a "horrible blindness" (LW 1:128). So when we thank our parents for raising us, for instance—we must not forget about God and thank him primarily, since he is the one who made their care possible in the first place.

And the second radical claim is that even this thanksgiving to God cannot be in general, but must be done in the name of Christ Jesus. This is because our thanksgiving—even when it is directed to God—remains corrupt. Søren Kierkegaard, that great admirer of Luther who lived in Denmark, explains this complication:

> We hanker after and chase after earthly goods and then—in order to rid ourselves of anxiety—thank God. Aha! This is precisely the way in which such a Christendom becomes even more secular-minded than paganism. Thanking God for good days should first and foremost mean undertaking to examine oneself, how one clings to such things; it should mean that one learns to think lightly of all such things. But, instead, we clutch even more tightly and then thank God—in order to keep on possessing these things with complete complacency and security. (JP 2:1510)

Because of such corrupt, self-serving thanksgiving, we need to be purged, corrected, and cleaned out. Thanking God in the name of Jesus does this for us in two ways. First it filters our thanksgiving through his words and those he inspired:

> Seek first the kingdom of God.[2] Life does not consist in the abundance of your possessions.[3] Don't lay up for yourselves treasures on earth.[4] Learn to be content in whatever state you're in.[5] Do not set your minds on things that are on earth.[6]

By so doing, our thanksgiving is jolted and given a form that "the world cannot give" (Jn 14:27). But to make sure this sticks, Christ also "perfects" (Heb 12:2) our thanksgiving by sharing with us his perfection (1 Cor 1:30). Through our faith in him, his righteousness becomes ours. Then we can glorify him in our thanksgiving—rather than ourselves (1 Cor 10:31).

And the third radical claim is that we should also thank God for our sorrows and pain, losses and suffering—and not just for the blessings and pleasures of this life. That is because—

> God wants us to regard the evils that we experience as coming to us with His permission . . . . God permits evils to come to us; for it is His will that, when we have been chastened, we

---

2   Mt 6:33.
3   Lk 12:15.
4   Mt 6:19.
5   Phil 4:11.
6   Col 3:2.

cast ourselves on His mercy . . . . By . . . these works God aims to humble us that we might . . . obey His will. (LW 13:155)

So "God alternates in what he does . . . . He brings an end to suffering, grants a break, and then lets it soon begin again" (LHP 3:244). This is because "sin is rooted" in our "flesh and blood," and so God has to send our way, "great misery and anxiety, poverty, persecution and all kinds of danger, . . . until the flesh becomes completely subject to the Spirit" (SML 3:130). By suffering so, we learn the hard lesson that our flesh and blood cannot fulfill or save us (LW 14:335)—it's too weak (Mt 26:41).

And in addition to this breathtaking claim, the last part of Ephesians 5:20 also adds the lesser, but still radical, admonition that we should always give thanks for our blessings and not toss them off, quickly forgetting about them (Hos 13:6). For indeed, when compared to our many and great blessings, what ails us is "barely a drop of water on a big fire or a little spark in the ocean" (LW 14:50)!—and so we shouldn't let our troubles consume us.

Luther's Thanksgiving

But how are we going to be able to pull off all of this? For we can't seem to do the good we want to do (Rom 7:18–19)! Therefore we need Christ to go beyond his words and save us by his power (Heb 7:25). This power is given to us through prayer and the sacrament of the Lord's Supper—the Great Thanksgiving, the Holy Eucharist. Regarding the power of prayer (Mt 17:21), a wonderful way into it is through Luther's words.[7] From those words I have assembled a ten-part prayer which can pull us into true thanksgiving:[8]

1. In the first part of this prayer we ask for power to use God's gifts properly so that our discipleship may become all the greater:

> Give us grace, dear Father, to use your gifts to the saving of our souls and to the betterment of our lives. Thus may the fruits of the earth serve to maintain and improve the health of both body and soul.

This prayer admits by implication that without God's help, his blessings will become curses because of our abuses of them.

2. The second part of this prayer asks God to fight against our abuses—which include laziness, lustful distortions, and gluttony:

> We ask you to give us the grace to expel the lusts of the flesh. Help us to avoid excessive eating, drinking, and sleeping, and to resist laziness. Grant that by fasting, careful eating, and proper clothing and care for the body we may watch and toil to become useful and fitted for good works.

---

7   *Luther's Prayers*, ed. H. F. Brokering (Minneapolis: Augsburg, 1967) §§ 204, 64, 50, 205, 81, 59, 52, 45, 44, 14.

8   See Prayers at flcws.org.

Here we ask for protection from wealth and pleasure. This is because abundance in hoarding and gorging must give way to frugality, modesty and discipline—which only God can provide (Lk 18:27). Then our blessings will serve good works which is precisely why God so graciously gives them to us in the first place!

3. And in the third part we ask for power to rejoice in God's coming kingdom instead of in this wicked world (1 Jn 5:19):[9]

> Help us to hate this life and to long for the life that is to come. Enable us not to dread death but to welcome it. Release us from the love and attachments of this life, so that your kingdom may be totally completed in us.

It's hard on us to pray for help in welcoming death (LW 44:85, 114). But if heaven is our home (Phil 3:20), then we must look forward to dying—for in death we will also be set free from sin and corruption (Rom 6:7, 8:19–21).

4. In the fourth part of this prayer we ask for power to use God's gifts wisely—spending them in keeping with his will:

> Come to us and use our bread, silver, and gold. How very well they are spent if we spend them in your service.

Notice that we use these gifts rightly only when God takes them up and uses them for us in our lives. This can only happen when we let the Holy Scriptures "regulate our lives" (LW 17:144) by making us follow their line of reasoning (LW 25:261)—rather than our own way of thinking things through.

---

[9] See also 1 Jn 2:15-17; Mt 17:17; 1 Cor 5:10; BC 434.

5. And in the fifth part of this prayer we ask for help in becoming hard workers who are also modest. Our tendency is to want to be queen bees rather than worker bees.[10] We prefer being waited on over serving others (contra Acts 20:35). Therefore we need God's help in transforming our lives (Romans 12:2):

> Keep us wide awake and active, eager and diligent in your word and service. May we not be overconfident, idle, and indifferent, as though we owned all things.

This prayer will keep us from trying to turn the creatures into substitutes for the Creator (Rom 1:25)—which is at the heart of all idolatry itself (Ex 32:4).

6. In the sixth part we pray for protection for nature and from nature—which we often let usurp the place of God. This helps us keep nature in its place—as the material support for service to God and neighbor:

> Protect the fruit of the fields and all the cattle from lightning, poison, wild beasts, and every possible injury.

In these words the truth that we cannot rely on ourselves to keep ourselves safe is reinforced. We are fragile creatures in an inhospitable world (Eccl 4:3; Acts 27:14–20; LW 15:26)—and so it is only God who can help us make it through this life (John 15:5).

---

10 See, for example, William F. Longgood, *The Queen Must Die and Other Affairs of Bees and Men*, Illustrations by Pamela Johnson (New York: Norton, 1985).

7. And in the seventh part of this prayer we ask for help in enduring calamity—which only happens when we see how helpful these traumas can be (Rom 5:3–5; Heb 12:7–11):

> Give us grace to willingly acknowledge and bear all sickness, poverty, shame, suffering, and misfortune as coming from your divine will to crucify ours.

These words drive us to the demanding heart of Christianity—which admonishes us to follow God's will alone, and never our own hopes and plans and schemes (Mt 26:39; LW 42:48).

8. And in the eighth part we ask God to help us pray properly—since we don't even know what's best for us (Is 5:20, 30:10):

> Keep us from desiring anything temporal or eternal that does not praise and honor your name. If we should ask you for any such things, we pray that you would not hear our foolishness.

This prayer keeps us from doting on ourselves since it admits how foolish we can be (BC 360, 568). When we admit this, then we are beginning to move in the direction of thanking God for all of his goodness and mercy—challenging though it may be.

9. And in the ninth part we ask specifically for a thankful heart—knowing full well that we cannot make ourselves be grateful:

> Help us that with all our possessions, words, and works we may praise and honor only you, and not through them seek to win a name for ourselves. We glorify you alone to whom all things belong. Guard us against the shameful evil of ingratitude.

The reason given for being thankful is that all depends on God—which then is pitted against our deep yearnings and corrupt longings for self-glorification.

10. And in the tenth part of this prayer we ask for clarity and courage of mind so that we can exalt Christ Jesus above everything enjoyable in this life (Phil 3:8; LW 23:55):

> O Lord, you have given us your Son, Jesus Christ, who is far more precious and dear than heaven, and much stronger than sin, death, the devil, and hell. For this we rejoice, praise, and thank you. In the name of God the Father, Son and Holy Spirit. Amen.

This prayer helps us see that salvation from sin and the gift of eternal life in heaven are what matter most—which is why we are supposed to seek after them before anything else (Mt 6:33).

The Great Thanksgiving

And secondly Christ empowers us through the Lord's Supper—the Holy Eucharist or Great Thanksgiving (LW 35:98).[11] For when we eat of the bread and drink from the cup, knowing that "in, with, and under" (BC 575) the consecrated bread and

---

11 See also LW 36:19, 171; 37:144, 313; 38:122–23.

wine we mysteriously receive Christ himself (Jn 6:56), we can then walk in righteousness and thank God as we should. For in "this most venerable sacrament," we have

> an abiding memorial of his bitter passion and death and of all his blessings, a seal of the new covenant, a comfort for all sorrowing hearts, and a true bond and union of Christians with Christ their head and with one another.
> (BC 577)

This memorial, seal and bond are all powerful. They give us the "abundant life" (Jn 10:10) that only Christ Jesus can give, which turns us once again into children of God (Jn 1:12, 14:6; Eph 2:3–7). This comes from his death on the cross (Jn 12:32). And for this we remember and give thanks (Lk 22:19).

No Thanks

And precisely because faith in Christ makes us children of God, we also want to do good works in his name (Col 3:17). On this national holiday there can be no better work for us to do than giving up on expecting people to thank us for helping them (Lk 17:9). So while it is important for us to be grateful, and for all people everywhere also to be grateful, we can never demand that of them—nor even expect it from them. This is so even when scientists are mounting proofs that being grateful "leads to increased life satisfaction and optimism."[12] The reason, however, for giving up on being thanked is not because we know people are ungrateful bipeds as Dostoyevsky said. It rather has to do with why we help people in the first

---

12 M. Y. Bartlett & D. DeSteno, "Gratitude and Pro-social Behavior," *Psychological Behavior* 17 (April 2006) 14.

place. And the point is that we are not supposed to do this to be thanked—and to feel good about ourselves. No, we instead are to help simply because it's our duty (Lk 17:10). So if people aren't grateful for what we do, that's no reason to stop helping them or despair—provided that what we're doing is still of some help. No, our only motivation should be to fulfill our duty and help others.

Once again it is Kierkegaard who explains this best. In *Works of Love,* he shows how our duty to love is what enriches love—saving it from both the "heat of spontaneous love" which is the "sickness of jealousy," and the "sluggishness" of a love that has been "dissipated in the lukewarmness and indifference of habit." Love gains this "enduring continuance" when it has "undergone the change of eternity by having become a duty"—which makes our help as glorious as "sterling silver" (WL 32, 35, 36). Being enriched through duty, the help we give is then made steady and truly loving—having been freed from the need to be thanked. And it is this same change of eternity that also helps us thank God in the way that pleases him. Amen.

Sermon 10

Trust in the Serpent

What is the most important Old Testament passage quoted in the New Testament? Is it the one about the Creation of the world? Or the Ten Commandments? Or David killing the giant Goliath? Or could it be the one about the fiery snakes in the wilderness? Now what if it were that last one? What would that mean for us?

A Peculiar Quotation

John 3:14–15 would have us believe that it is indeed this last one about the fiery snakes. That passage from the Old Testament about the poisonous serpents in the wilderness is given a most important place in the New Testament. There are a couple other Old Testament passages that vie for this honor—like Jonah in the belly of the whale which is cited as proof that Jesus would be resurrected after three days in the grave (Mt 12:40). But no other Old Testament passage ties in with the central event of Christ's crucifixion the way those fiery snakes do in Numbers 21:4–9.[1] This is surprising since the Old Testament hardly remembers this episode from Numbers 21—unlike the Exodus from slavery in Egypt which is cited all over the place in the Old Testament. But in the New Testament there are, what appear to be, minor episodes from the

---

[1] The only possible exception is that of the Paschal Lamb in 1 Corinthians 5:7 from Exodus 12:13.

Old Testament that are high-lighted—like Balaam (2 Pt 2:15) and Enoch (Heb 11:5) and Rahab the whore (Jas 2:25). This is especially odd given that the major figures—Jeremiah and Ezekiel, Joseph—the favored son of Jacob, and Samson—the protector of Israel, as well as Job and Solomon are passed over in silence or hardly mentioned at all. And the minor, though esteemed, Old Testament figures of Deborah and Ruth aren't even on the radar screen of the New Testament.

But Numbers 21:4–9, about those poisonous serpents killing the disobedient children of God in the wilderness—that passage is given very high profile by linking it directly to Jesus dying on the cross for the sins of the world. This Old Testament passage is right there at the burning hot center of the message of the New Testament—for it is Jesus dying on the cross that the church is to proclaim over everything else (1 Cor 1:23, 2:2). Martin Luther even once said that we should praise Christ's suffering and death "to the utmost" (LW 13:319).

Those Deadly Snakes

Now just what's behind this episode about the snakes in the wilderness? What leads up to this ghastly event when God's children are killed by poisonous snakes? Well, it's actually all about disobedience—our disgusting ingratitude. That's what's behind it all. For after 430 years of terrible pain in Egypt (Ex 12:41), God hears the cry of his people begging him for release (Ex 3:7–8). And he sends Moses to lead them out of slavery into the freedom of the Promised Land (Ex 14:30). Now that short journey to freedom could have been about a three month walk along the Mediterranean coastline—but it was lengthened wildly into forty years of wandering in the wilderness (Ex 16:35)! This was because they disobeyed God in the wilderness (Nm 14:26–35), when they complained about having nothing good to eat (Ex 16:3).

This complaining, whining, and squealing ingratitude enraged Almighty God. In a watered down version of the wrath he unleashed in the flood (Gn 7:21–22), he attacks his own people once again. But this time—forgoing the mighty rushing flood waters—he sends slithering, frightening snakes to bite his people and their children with poisonous venom. God sends these snakes to punish them knowing how afraid we are by nature of snakes.[2] So God hits them with a one-two-punch—killing them with venom and reptilian terror.

That Ridiculous Remedy

And it works. His attacks on them scare his people straight. They figure out right away that it's God who is sending the snakes to punish them. They don't have to first find labels on the backs of little snake shirts saying **MADE BY GOD**® to know that it was God who was doing this. Oh, no. The pattern was clear from the time of the flood, that God uses nature to scare us and hurt us when we repeatedly shake our fists in his face:

> Thus shall my anger spend itself, and I will vent my fury upon them and satisfy myself; and they shall know that I, the Lord, have spoken in my jealousy, when I spend my fury upon them.
> (Ez 5:13)

And God does that by way of earthquakes, hurricanes, firestorms, wars, diseases, famines and "evil beasts" (Nm 11:1, 16:31–32, Ez 13:13, 14:21). So when dying from the snake bites and watching their children writhing in pain and terror, they beg Moses to plead with God to take away the snakes. Just

---

2 See *Scary Creatures: Snakes Alive* (Brighton, United Kingdom: Salariya Books, 2002) 19—where an anaconda squeezes a crocodile to death!

as he sent them without warning, so they hope he will take them away—in a moment, in a flash, and in that way free them from all harm.

That's what happened with the mysterious Spanish flu that hit America without warning in 1918—randomly killing over six hundred thousand in just three short months—and then, inexplicably, vanishing on Armistice Day, November 11, 1918, never to be seen again. What a catastrophe that was—people dying so fast and in such large numbers that they had to be buried by steam shovels in New York City—just to keep up with the morgues.[3] So those ancient people of God were hoping for the same sort of quick fix. But that was not in the cards.

God had something else in mind—something far stranger up his sleeve. His answer was that the snakes would stay—remaining as deadly as ever. This is not like Daniel in the lions' den, when God "shut the lions' mouths," so they wouldn't hurt him (Dn 6:22). No, in the case of the snakes in the wilderness, Moses would take a dead snake, put it on a pole, and stand it upright in the middle of the bitten people—right at the scene of the crime. If bitten, all they would have to do is look at the dead snake on the pole—now turned into bronze—and they would be healed. Then those poisonous bites which had threatened them, would no longer be lethal—if they but gazed upon the bronze serpent. But looking at a bronze snake after having been bitten by a real one, would be the last thing they would want to do. Luther imagines them spouting off:

> Ha, what a ridiculous medicine it is that you propose for the. . . bite of the serpents! Moses, have you lost your senses? How are we to be

---

[3] See Pete Davies, *The Devil's Flu* (New York: Henry Holt and Company, 2000).

helped by looking at this bronze serpent, which looks like those that bit us? We are so terrified that we cannot stand the sight of them! If only you would, instead, give us ... a cooling plaster ... to take away the venom and the fever! .... How can that dead ... object up there benefit us? .... Moses, are you insane? Do you want to terrify us still more with your cure and scare us out of our wits? How could that serpent help us? (LW 22:338–39, 341)

Even so, some miraculously believed in the cure and were healed—in spite of the fact that it's natural "to shy away from anything that has harmed us" (LW 22:341). So the snakes stayed, and healing came through them, instead of by killing them off. How strange a cure! So why did God take up such a weird way to rescue his people? Why didn't he just dispose of the snakes, as he was asked to do? What was he trying to do in this crazy sounding cure for his people?

Destroying Death by Death

Well, we don't know for sure since he doesn't tell us in the text. That leaves us to piece together what his rationale could have been. And we can do that by assembling Biblical verses that shed light on God's mysterious, healing ways (Mal 4:2).

The first verse is Hebrews 2:14 which says that Christ destroyed death by death. This parallels what happened in the wilderness—the dead, bronze snake overcomes the deadly snake bites. So the death lurking in those poisonous bites is neutralized by the dead bronze snake upon the pole. This is much the way that vaccines work—introducing "a whole or partial version of a pathogenic microorganism into the body in order to train the immune system to defend itself when the organism threatens to cause an infection through natural means."[4] Here we have death doing in, or destroying death—through a weakened form of itself that can be more easily wiped out. Christ as the bronze snake, "does us no harm with its venom; for this is a healing serpent, without venom" (LW 22:342). This image of the bronze serpent works, then, by showing how the death of Jesus resembles the healing that comes from that serpent. For both do the same thing—making death itself, destroy death itself.

And that's helpful because we're not inclined to think that death could save us from itself. So if we're going to go against common sense, it would help to have a compelling image—and that we surely have in the bronze snake on the pole. It was in fact so compelling for Israel that later on that bronze serpent took on the exotic name Nehushtan, became an idol, and had to be destroyed (2 Kgs 18:4). What in part is so riveting here is seeing "sin . . . destroyed by its own fruit,[5] and . . . slain by the death to which it gave birth,"—similar to the way "a viper is devoured by its own offspring" (LW 42:151). That odd power could tempt one to view all of this superstitiously. Guarding against that, our teaching is that "in death itself there is life, something which is unknown to and impossible for . . . reason" to grasp (LW 4:116).

Going Against Reason

And this takes us to our next verse, John 9:39, which says that those who can see, need to lose their sight. This is because we naturally love what is wrong—we sinfully prefer darkness to the light (Jn 3:19). So we need to have our reason, or our seeing mind, thwarted, since it loves the darkness. And that is what the bronze serpent does. It pushes us beyond reason into faith.

---

4   Arthur Allen, *Vaccine* (New York: Norton, 2007) 14.
5   See Rom 6:23.

As Luther points out, "just looking at the serpent did not effect the cure; it was faith in the Word that did it" (LW 22:339). And the word said to "look at the bronze serpent and live" (Nm 21:9). Simply looking at the snake was baffling because it seemed useless. That was all one's reasoning could come up with.[6] But faith goes further and gives the cure a try. Believing in what Moses said about the bronze serpent was the basis for trusting in this cure. And yet even with that there weren't any guarantees. So they had to take a risk and leap beyond their reasonable, good sense findings, and try out the cure—in spite of the way it all looked.

Søren Kierkegaard, who learned a great deal from diligently, if not daily, reading Luther's sermons (JP 3:2465),[7] helps with this leap. And we need that because believing in such a cure makes us look crazy. On this matter Kierkegaard writes that "when in the dark night of suffering sagacity cannot see a handbreadth ahead of it, then faith can see God, since faith sees best in the dark" (UDVS 238). There is then a seeing or even a sort of thinking in faith that apprehends God's healing.

---

6   And vaccines aren't even altogether reasonable as an analogy to the poisonous snakes. See the modern uprising against them—*Vaccine Epidemic*, ed. Louise Kuo Habakus & Mary Holland (New York: Skyhorse Publishing, 2011).

7   See also JP 3:2485, 2493, 2516, 2530, and 3515. Note as well Harold J. Grimm, *Martin Luther as a Preacher* (Columbus, Ohio: Lutheran Book Concern, 1929) 122: "Martin Luther as a preacher will always stand out as one of the greatest teachers of Christ and the Word of God, and his sermons will be read by thousands of ardent admirers for ages to come." Kierkegaard was clearly one of those ardent admirers of Luther's sermons. And he would further agree with Grimm when he writes about Luther that the "man who sang the Word of God, talked about it in the lecture room and with his friends, saw its power in nature, felt it permeate his entire being and dominate his entire life, certainly was preeminently fitted to be the preacher who could well rank among the foremost pulpit orators of all times" (44).

It's just that this thinking is "illuminated" by the grace of God to see what our minds would otherwise miss (LW 26:268; 34:144). So Kierkegaard says "the unseen is that what is seen is nevertheless not seen, for if it is seen, it obviously is unseen that it is not seen" (WL 295). Now that's a fancy, detailed way of saying that believing is seeing—and not the other way around (Jn 20:29). And this we need because God values obeying over comprehending in our saving relationship with him (Lk 11:28; BA 5, JP 2:1129).

God Against God

Finally this strange cure pits a snake against a snake—the bronze one against the living, poisonous ones. This reptilian contrast points to the depth of our salvation where, as the Lutheran Confessions teach, the death of the Son of God is "pitted against" the wrath of God the Father (BC 136). What we have in this strange encounter is God going against himself in order to bring about our salvation (JP 1:532). This confrontation trades on distinguishing "between God and God" (LW 12:321)—between his wrath and mercy. The goal is to have his mercy prevail over his wrath.

Hosea 11:9, our last verse, shows this struggle when God says, "my heart recoils within me"—which is God fighting "against his wrath."[8] Even the rainbow in the sky which was to settle this conflict in God (Gn 9:15), warns us, in its red colors, of our coming "fiery . . . judgment" (LW 2:149). And God's wrath continues to restrict his love until the blood of Christ satisfies that wrath—saving us from it (Rom 5:9; Col 1:20; Jn 3:36). By being punished in our place, Christ removes the need

---

8   Hans Walter Wolff, *Hosea* (1965), trans. Gary Stansell (Philadelphia: Fortress. 1974) 201.

for God to punish us for our sins in hell (2 Cor 8:9). That's why he makes his sacrifice to God (Eph 5:2; Heb 9:14)—which stabilizes God's love for us.[9]

Our Serpent of Salvation

So take a second look at that bronze serpent—for it's not supposed to scare you away. In it we are instead to see Jesus who is "the serpent of our salvation" (LW 22:340). For inside those snake-skins is the Lamb of God who takes away the sin of the world (Jn 1:29; LW 22:343). Because of that sacrificial Lamb, dressed in snake-skins, we're strangely drawn to him (Jn 12:32). For in him is performed "the difficult task of turning poison into a remedy" (CD 96). Therefore we confess that

> the foolishness of the Gospel . . . reveals another righteousness, namely, that because of Christ, the propitiator, we are accounted righteous when we believe that for Christ's sake God is gracious to us. We know how repulsive this teaching is to the judgment of reason and law and that the teaching of the law about love is more plausible. (BC 189)

Indeed it is so. We would rather hear that all we have to do to be saved is live a decent life and care for one another—rather than all this repulsive business about turning poison into a remedy (CD 96). The simple life of love is far more plausible to us than the repulsive one about sacrifice, wrath, faith and love. We would rather save ourselves than do so through some lamb in snake-skins!

---

9   *Contra* Jack Miles, *Christ: A Crisis in the Life of God* (New York: Knopf, 2001) 50.

But this is our plight—trapped in sin before an angry God who saves us only through the most strange divine self-sacrifice. But don't settle for your sin. Don't "be faithless, but believing" (Jn 20:27). Don't give up the repulsive in the name of the plausible. Don't sacrifice faith for a life of reason. And don't run from the only thing that will bring God's grace to you.[10]

Starving Out Illusions

Furthermore, do good works in Christ—knowing that "every sound tree bears good fruit" (Mt 7:17). This is so even though "sometimes, through the weakness of the flesh," as Luther takes pains to point out, "something wrong creeps in" and we

> bear wormy fruit, [but it] is still good fruit and has no . . . thorns. [So] rather than . . . being fruitless, the tree will bear fruit that is wormy, though that is not its fault. So all the works of a Christian are of a good kind because the tree is sound. (LW 21:267)

With that warning against perfectionism in hand, we are nevertheless to press on, that we may glorify Christ in our deeds (Col 3:17). During Lent our good deed is fasting the foods we especially like. But we also want to extend our fast beyond foods into other areas of our lives. Today let that area be our thinking.

Let us then dethrone the arrogance of our thought that likes to stand in judgment over what's plausible or not (*contra* 1 Cor 2:4). Our reasoning therefore has a way of hamstringing

---

10 See my "Our Serpent of Salvation," *Word & World* 21 (Fall, 2001) 385–93.

the great claims of our faith—thinking it can rule them out of court on grounds of implausibility. Let us counter that ploy by fasting our minds of its yarns. Kierkegaard put it this way:

> The situation calls for Christianity to be presented once again without scaling down . . . . but as . . . a dialectician does it, in Socratically starving the life out of the illusions in which Christendom has run aground. For it is not that Christianity is not proclaimed, but it is Christendom which has become sheer expertise in transforming it into illusion and thus evading it. (JP 6:6227–28)

So we are to fast our thinking as well, by depriving ourselves of those mental reductions by which we evade what is offensive about Christianity—sin, wrath, judgment, sacrifice and faith.

Therefore let us pray that God would save us from "unprofitable and dangerous enquiries [and] from difficulties vainly curious."[11] Let us recall Luther's warning that reason is a whore (LW 40:175). And so while reason might be "a sun and a kind of god appointed to administer" many areas of our lives (LW 34:137),[12] it fails when it comes to understanding sin and salvation (LW 17:76).[13] May God then keep us ever mindful of the right way to follow Christ in our thinking. Amen.

---

11 *Samuel Johnson: Diaries, Prayers, and Annals,* (New Haven: Yale University Press, 1958) 383–84.
12 See also LW 3:320–24; and 44:336.
13 See also LW 22:69, 319, 458; 23:51, 80, 84, 350–352; 26:228; 51:377, 384; 52:167, 196.

Sermon 11

Don't Be Surprised

On this fourth day of Christmas, we wish you all once again a very Merry Christmas! Unfortunately we must also remember today the slaughter of the Holy Innocents. Christians have been doing this for hundreds of years. But why continue to dredge this up?

Fourteen Thousand Children Killed

On this day we remember how King Herod, long ago, just after Jesus was born on the first Christmas day, in a furious rage, killed all the male children in Bethlehem (Mt 2:16). And he did so to try and kill the newborn Jesus whom he feared had come to take away his throne. Not knowing where to find him, he decided to kill all the little boys in the area—hoping that somehow Christ Jesus would be included among those slaughtered. Even though the New Testament does not tell us how many were killed, the church has estimated that there were around fourteen thousand slaughtered![1] What a travesty! Ghastly beyond measure, we would all agree. No wonder Rachel, "weeping for her children, refused to be consoled" (Mt 2:18; Jer 31:15). We get her point.

---

1   See P. H. Pfatteicher, *Festivals & Commemorations* (Minneapolis: Augsburg, 1980) 470.

And it only gets worse as the plot thickens. Why, we ask, was Jesus and his family warned of this slaughter so they could escape into Egypt and be saved, but the other fourteen thousand were not (Mt 2:13)? Why did God allow them to become collateral damage, as contemporary military parlance puts it these days? They were just in the wrong place at the wrong time—at no fault of their own. Why let these little ones be mowed down so mercilessly?

Tribulations Remain

Well, there are a couple things to say—unsatisfactory though they may be. And the first is that this happens so we'll know that Christ's coming at Christmas is not for the purpose of ending all sorrow now. 1 Peter 4:12 therefore tells us "not to be surprised at the fiery ordeal" that is to come. For while Christmas promises peace (Lk 2:14), it will have to wait (Lk 12:51). Worldly peace will have to wait until Christ's second coming in glory (Lk 21:27; Acts 1:11; Heb 9:28). Then, and only then, will the wolf dwell peacefully with the lamb, and all tribulations come to an end (Is 11:6). But before that, we will have to learn how to endure misfortune because it's not going away until Christ returns—long after his crucifixion, resurrection and ascension.

Luther spells this out, in breathtaking detail in his *Large Catechism*—telling us just what we'll have to learn to endure:

> The devil .... cannot bear to have anyone teach or believe rightly .... Therefore, like a furious foe, he ... rages with all his power and might, ... in order to hinder us, put us to flight, cut us down, and bring us once more under his power .... Therefore we who would be Christians must surely count on ... the devil with all his

angels . . . inflicting every possible misfortune and grief upon us. For where God's Word is preached, accepted or believed, and bears fruit, there the blessed holy cross will not be far away. Let nobody think that he will have peace; he must sacrifice all he has on earth—possessions, honor, house and home, wife and children, body and life. Now, this grieves . . . the old Adam, for it means that we must remain steadfast, suffer patiently whatever befalls us, and let go whatever is taken from us . . . . [So] the devil and all his host [will surely] storm and rage furiously against the [Gospel] in their attempt utterly to exterminate [it]. (BC 428–29)

In the face of this massive assault, our goal must be to confess with Saint Paul (2 Cor 4:8–9):

We are afflicted in every way, but not crushed; perplexed, but not driven to despair; persecuted, but not forsaken; struck down, but not destroyed.

So no complaining or despondency. Instead we are to be resilient under pressure and buoyant under duress (Heb 12:12–13). Once we know that our life on earth is not supposed to be a rose garden, but the very "vexation of life" (LW 8:114), then we can lower our heads and move forward, knowing what lies ahead. Indeed, life is "like a picnic in which the basket eats the food"![2] Once we know what race we're in, we can run it to the end (2 Tm 4:7)—tough though it may be (1 Cor 9:24).

---

2   Robert Bly, *Talking into the Ear of a Donkey: Poems* (New York: Nor-

The Big Test

And secondly these tribulations are here to test us to see whether we can believe in God even though he allows such horrible things to happen—including the slaughter of the Holy Innocents (1 Pt 4:12). Can we believe in him for who he is, rather than for what he does? That is our biggest test. Can we believe that he is a loving God when what we see happening under his watch is so horrible?

That is our test (Gn 22:1),[3] and our leaning is to flunk it. That is because we care so much for our immediate physical welfare in this life. So we're very reluctant to say that "the sufferings of this present time are not worth comparing with the glory that is to be revealed to us" (Rom 8:18). We instead are like the fool who wants to take his "ease, eat, drink and be merry" (Lk 12:19). We want our reward now, in this life. We want uninterrupted peace and prosperity now. We want health and satisfaction now. Now, now, now!

Another example of this same problem is when Jesus castigates his followers after he miraculously multiplied the loaves (Jn 6:11) since they were only looking for "food which perishes" (Jn 6:27). Never mind that this bread was miraculous—it still was just temporary! Christ would rather they cared about the bread "which endures to eternal life," which he himself was. So he says "I am the bread of life, ... I am the living bread which came down from heaven" (Jn 6:35, 51). On this contrast between time and eternity, between common bread and heavenly bread, Luther writes:

---

ton, 2011) 51.
3 See also Ps 66:1; 1 Pt 1:7; 2 Cor 2:9; and Jas 1:12.

Today the Gospel finds disciples who imagine that its teaching affords nothing but a gratification of the belly, that it brings all manner of earthly delights, and that it serves solely the wants of this temporal life . . . . They [have] no other interest than . . . to indulge their selfishness . . . . It is quite common to regard the Gospel as a belly sermon . . . [But] that is not the purpose of the Gospel. Yet people still cling to this illusion, ... that Christ came into the world solely for the sake of our physical well-being . . . . [Christ however wants] to turn the people away from such an illusion, . . . to draw them from the belly to the Spirit . . . . But when the people hear that Christ wants to direct them away . . . from the field and the earth to heaven, they are displeased . . . . For flesh and blood is interested only in bodily nourishment . . . . The entire world seeks nothing but money and goods, food and drink . . . . [But this food is] only a perishable food, which does not endure eternally. The term "perishes" connotes contempt for such food. For this food is destined to perish; it is used up; it is of no help . . . . Then why should you despise the imperishable food and eternal life, and rate it lower than the perishable bread? . . . Isn't that madness . . . on your part? . . . . Yet it is customary in the world to be concerned only with what is ephemeral and to disregard what is eternal . . . . Thus we senseless fools make bold to defy God. But in the end we shall see who will be the loser . . . . [So] the Lord wants to teach [us] not to cling so tenaciously to temporal goods.... Christ tears the hearts and ears of us all away from all bakeries and granaries,... yes, from all labor, and directs them to Himself.... He is the true Chef and Miller, who supplies us with a different kind of corn from that commonly found in the world .... People are good evangelicals so long as... the Gospel will... enrich them.... But when they hear that through its message they will be delivered from sin, death, and the power of the devil, they... despise the Gospel.... [But] God does not have His Gospel proclaimed for the sake of the belly, but for the... salvation of our souls.... The Christian adheres to such a foolish message and believes in that stupid God. (LW 23:5-13)

So resist the pull of temporal goods—necessary though they may be for this life. Cling instead to Christ—"that stupid God"—knowing that when you have him you have everything (LW 23:55). Resist all the Christmas glitz. Cling to Christ—even when everything else is falling down all around you. Do not let that collapse rob you of Christ.

Job 13:15

This is the same test Job had. In Job 13:15—that great verse which translators have repeatedly tried to mangle[4]—Job says "though God slay me, yet will I trust in him" (KJV). What he says in this powerful verse is that he will love God for who he is—the source of all human goodness (Jas 1:17)—regardless of

---

4   See D. J. A. Clines, *Job 1–20* (Dallas, Texas: Word Books, 1989) 313.

what he does or allows him to suffer. Job lost everything—except his life and wife. He could have become bitter—and almost did. But he finally entrusts his life to God's safe keeping—even though God himself has caused him to suffer so much. Let us then be like Job. Let us pass the test with flying colors as he did.

Traveling Faith

But to do so will take a faith that is "exceedingly arduous" (LW 29:185). This is a faith that knows its fair share of despair and restlessness (LW 40:241). Søren Kierkegaard, that Danish lover of Luther, describes it well. Faith, he writes,

> expressly signifies the deep, strong, blessed restlessness that drives the believer so that he cannot settle down at rest in this world, and therefore the person who has settled down completely at rest has also ceased to be a believer, because a believer cannot sit still as one sits with a pilgrim's staff in one's hand—a believer travels forward . . . . Their way through the world is not as light as a dance but it is heavy and hard, although faith for them is still also the joy that conquers the world.[5] Just as a ship as it lightly proceeds at full sail before the wind at the same time deeply cuts its heavy path through the ocean, so also the Christian's way is light if one looks at the faith that overcomes the world, but hard if one looks at the laborious work in the depths. (UDVS 218)

---

5 See 1 Jn 5:4.

This is as it should be, for faith draws us away from the temporal, in which we are so deeply embedded, and directs us to a heavenly, eternal life with God. As a consequence, we do not sail through this world unscathed. Again Kierkegaard explains this well:

> Christianity does indeed proclaim itself to be a comfort, cure, and healing—that being so, people turn to it as they turn to a friend in need ... And then—then the very opposite happens. They go to the Word to seek help—and then come to suffer on account of the Word. And with this suffering it is not as when one takes a medication or undergoes a treatment in which healing can involve some pain, to which one submits and in which there is no contradiction. No, tribulation and persecution come upon one because one has turned to Christianity for help . . . . Now the understanding is brought to a halt . . . . What is Christianity, then, and what is it good for? . . . . The help looks like a torment, the relief like a burden . . . . Now the issue is: will you be offended or will you believe. If you will believe, then you push through the possibility of offense and accept Christianity on any terms. So it goes; then forget the understanding; then you say: Whether it is help or torment, I want only one thing, I want to belong to Christ. (PC 114–15)

So Christianity isn't a life enrichment plan. That's what makes faith in it so difficult. The help it provides isn't basically for this life. What it does is make us fit citizens for heaven.

On those terms, whether we're protected now or not, matters little—strange though that may sound to our earth-bound ears. No, the help we receive now is of an invisible sort as Kierkegaard again explains:

> Alone! When you have chosen, you will surely find fellow pilgrims, but in the decisive moment and every time there is mortal danger you will be by yourself. No one, not one, hears your ingratiating appeal or heeds your vehement complaint—and yet there is help and willingness enough in heaven. But it is invisible, and to be helped by it is to learn to walk alone. This help does not come from outside and grasp your hand; it does not support you as a kind person supports the sick one; it does not lead you back by force when you have gone astray. No, only when you completely yield, completely give up your own will, and devote yourself with your whole heart and mind—then help comes invisibly, but then you have indeed walked alone. We do not see the powerful instinct that leads the bird on its long journey. The instinct does not fly ahead and the bird behind. It looks as if it were the bird that found the way. Likewise we do not see the teacher but only the follower, who resembles the teacher, and it looks as if the follower himself were the way, just because he is the true follower who walks by himself along the same road. (UDVS 220–21)

Once again the help Christianity provides looks like nothing at all—since it doesn't provide earthly prosperity and protection. But that is the wrong conclusion to draw. Faith alone knows that.

Sharing in Christ's Sufferings

Once said, however, faith still remains arduous. Under that weight we can stumble and fall. So we are told to rejoice when we suffer for then we are "sharing in the sufferings of Christ" (1 Pt 4:13). This may not seem like much help, but it is. You may think all that would help is to have Christ free you from all suffering, but it is not so. Instead in this sharing there is true solidarity and companionship which emboldens us. For now we know that the One who throws us into the fray, actually suffers too, right along side of us.

I once had a college instructor who took the same essay tests he gave out. When we turned in our papers he would hand us a copy of his completed exam. He was a hard man with little human warmth. But that practice of suffering with his students, if you will, gave that class an aura like no other class I ever took over my eleven straight years of college, seminary and graduate school. And what that aura did was motivate his students and strengthened our classroom performance. So while sharing in Christ's sufferings doesn't seem like much help, there are human analogues to suggest it deserves a second look. And when we give it a chance, we will find power in his mercy to suffer with us, along side of us.

And we also learn that his suffering with us is greater than ours. For he suffered to "die for sins . . . [in order] to bring us to God" (1 Pt 3:18). In that great feat we who believe in it are set free from the debilitating trauma of our guilt for having sinned against God and his law. Christ dies in our place, bearing the punishment for our sins, that God may bless us rather than condemn us. This is a breath of fresh air—spiritually put. And it makes us stronger than we ever could be on our own. So thank God for the Savior, Christ Jesus, and his love for us, shown in his sacrifice for our sins. Rejoice and be glad that you believe in him. And then come to the altar today and receive him in the bread and the wine of the Holy Eucharist—that your faith may abound and flourish.

A Strange Comfort

Now the best good work we can do on this feast of the Holy Innocents is to "comfort those who are in any affliction, with the comfort we ourselves have received from God" (2 Cor 1:4–5). This comfort is what we should strive to learn about and practice.

And it is hardly some sort of pious claptrap, without any oomph to it. Rather it is filled with dynamite. How so? Because it says we should pass on the comfort God himself has comforted us with—rather than some comfort of our own making. We do this regularly—you know. We say to our suffering friends: "You'll be fine. Everything is going to be alright. Things will get better." But this isn't a Bible verse! No, this is something we've made up. The comfort we should give is this: Rejoice that you're sharing in the sufferings of Christ.[6] But that scares us. We're afraid our friends we're trying to comfort will think we're being rude and cruel to them. But it doesn't matter. This is our calling. So pray to the Lord that you might say these words the right way and at the right time. Timing can be everything. And he will bless you with an answer. For he wants you to be his powerful disciples—spreading his Word everywhere. So he'll give you the wisdom and compassion you'll need to comfort others as you've been comforted. For he loves you and wants

---

6   See Acts 5:41 and 1 Pt 4:13.

you to share that love with others. And so today he has helped you do just that through the Holy Innocents—that in the traumas of life you will not drop a step by being unjustifiably surprised by the coming fiery ordeal. Amen.

Sermon 12

Pray for Servants

In Matthew 9:35–10:8 Jesus gives us our marching orders. And they are shocking and disturbing—to say the least! We are to cast out demons (10:1, 8); raise the dead (10:8); preach only to the Jews (10:5–6); and take no pay for our work (10:8). But even more upsetting than those tough words is the command to pray to God to find and send people to go out and get his work done (9:38).

Signing-Up the Misfits

That's right—we're not to recruit, train and select these servants of the Lord. No, that's for God to do. All we are to do is to pray to God—asking him for help with this. What a strange way to get things done. It flies in the face of common sense which trades on searching out candidates with particular talents and abilities, who are diligent, reliable, educable and likeable. But God doesn't seem to care about any of these criteria. He seems to pride himself in having losers to do his work for him. If a company or corporation tried to run their store in this way, they would go out of business in no time. So why is God so reckless?

Well, if he wasn't, we never would have had the likes of Moses leading God's people. Do you remember that he was a murderer (Ex 2:12), insecure (Ex 3:11; 4:1), tongue-tied (Ex 4:10), defiant (Ex 4:13, 24; 5:22; 6:12), uneducated—and even despondent and suicidal (Nm 11:15)? And yet Moses is praised (Josh 4:14) and even returns from the dead to be with Christ on the mount of the holy transfiguration (Mt 17:3). And think of David, who is praised (Ps 132:17–18) and even called a father of Jesus Christ (Mt 1:1)—and yet he was an adulterer and a murderer (2 Sm 11:4, 15, 24). Then there's that angular John the Baptist who ate bugs and lived in the desert (Mk 1:4–6) whom God highly prized (Mt 11:11)—even though his lips dripped with biting condemnations (Lk 3:7–9)—which inspired Martin Luther to call him a "fiery angel" (BC 308).

And Saint Paul, the greatest Christian preacher and missionary of all time, was called a "pestilent fellow" (Acts 24:5) and was hard to understand (2 Pt 3:16). He killed Christians (Acts 7:58; 8:3; 26:10; 1 Cor 15:9)—and yet Christ himself saw to his conversion (Acts 9:3–6, 15–16). This hothead could vilify Elymas the magician, a potential convert, yelling at him—"You son of the devil, you enemy of all righteousness, full of all deceit and villainy" (Acts 13:10). And Paul couldn't get along with Peter (Gal 2:11) or Barnabas (Acts 15:39–40), his brothers in Christ. And we can't forget Martin Luther who was famous for, of all things, speaking crudely of human waste.[1] No wonder he thought Christians should be "bold and reckless" (LW 23:399)—himself being biting, stubborn and arrogant (LW 31:335; 23:330; 24:118). And his admiring follower, Søren Kierkegaard thought Christianity, when rightly understood, justifiably drives us to the brink of suicide (JP 3:2454).

None of these faithful servants were pleasant or polite. If it had been left up to us, they all would've been cut from the hiring process. So thanks be to God that he ignored us and our standards for bringing into being faithful servants. From this

---

[1] See, for example, LW 51:376: "I wish they had to eat their own dirt [shit];" and also LW 14:93.

we can see again the great wonder, love and grace in God not answering our prayers as we first frame them. On this vexing matter of our prayers going unanswered, Kierkegaard writes:

> God surely did not deceive you when he accepted your earthly wishes and foolish desires, exchanged them for you and instead gave you divine comfort and holy thoughts; that he did not treat you unfairly when he denied you a wish but in compensation created this faith in your heart, when instead of a wish, which even if it would bring everything, at most was able to give you the whole world, he gave you a faith by which you won God and overcame the whole world. Then you acknowledged with humbled joy that . . . from your impatient and inconstant heart he created the imperishable substance of a quiet spirit. (EUD 36)

Now that's a mighty compensation. And with a quiet spirit firmly in place, we even leave off caring about what we originally asked for. Then we find ourselves praying prayers like this:

> Lord, my God, I really have nothing at all for which to pray to you; even if you would promise to grant my every wish, I really cannot think of anything—except that I may remain with you, as near as possible in this time of separation in which you and I are living, and entirely with you in all eternity. (EUD 392)

Only God Knows Our Hearts

Another reason why it is good that this selection process is in God's hands and not in ours, is that we don't even know who the right person for the job would be. We've all had this experience. We have family and friends whom we can't get through to in matters of religion and morality. We've tried and tried and we get nowhere with them. So we long for some other person to talk to them—just the right person, whoever that may be. And God can make that happen, because he alone sees into the human heart (1 Sm 16:7). All we can do is guess who it might be—and we don't even do that very well. But God nails it every time. He knows exactly what they need and who can deliver it. That's because we're structurally aligned with God, like no other in our lives:

> Ostensibly it is an imperfection in earthly life that basically a person cannot entirely, cannot thoroughly make himself understandable to others; on closer inspection one will surely be convinced that it is a perfection, since it suggests that every individual is religiously structured and is to strive to understand himself in confidentiality with God. Most people probably do not notice either this imperfection or that it is a perfection. (BA 92)

Because of this odd, yet wonderful, perfect imperfection, God alone is the one who picks the right person for the right job.

And our own lives confirm this to be so. Each of us have people in our past whom God gave us to speak his challenging and redeeming word to us, in ways no one else could have done. In my life it was my maternal grandpa, Harry J. Lien (1892–1966) and my college pastor, the Rev. Karl A. Ufer (1913–1981). I have vivid memories of both of those men, to this very day, with their sage words and durable examples on how best to live a Christian life, day by day, in a hostile world and in a wayward church.

God's Unusual Kingdom

But we still need to know more. We need to have a more straightforward explanation for God's quirky selection process since it goes against common sense. So recalling wonderful examples of tried and true servants in the past is not enough. We also need to know what the rationale behind all of this is. Why does God go against common sense?

The answer is that God and the world are at enmity with each other (Jas 4:4; Jn 15:18–19; 1 Jn 2:15–17), and so the natural, customary, worldly way of selecting servants isn't appropriate in God's kingdom. And that explains the fruit-basket-upset when it comes to the nature of God's servants—as Luther writes:

> [When considering the] best qualified for service in his kingdom, ... Christ studiously avoided the city of Jerusalem with its royal throne, the residence of the mightiest, richest, and wisest. He refrained from calling the high priests and rulers into His ranks. He gave the nation's sovereign the cold shoulder, and He did not invite men of distinction. He journeyed through the wilderness, through hamlets and market towns, and selected the poorest and the most wretched beggars He could find, such as poor fishermen and good, simple, uncouth bumpkins. (LW 22:189)

And why again was that a good idea? Because Christ "wanted to establish a kingdom . . . in which nothing but God's grace would have currency, no matter how good and valuable it might be otherwise." This is similar to God's point made to Gideon on the eve of his battle against the massive armies of the Midianites and Amalekites (Jgs 7:12). God tells Gideon to weaken himself by cutting back the size of his army, so that when victory comes, the Israelites will not be able to claim it for themselves (Jgs 7:2). Luther continues this train of thought by saying that Christ

> wanted to drive home the truth that such a kingdom was not based on reason and human wisdom . . . . Thus the kingdom was constructed, and thus it is sustained to this day. Christ is not greatly impressed by great kings or powerful lords, by the rich of this world, or by royal lineage and great pomp, which otherwise carry weight in the world . . . . As Saint Paul declares (1 Cor 1:27): "God chose what is weak" when He established His kingdom through none but beggars, clumsy louts, and lowly people, namely the apostles . . . . He wants to be honored as one who is motivated by grace and not by our golden hair or some other virtue of which we may boast or be proud.   (LW 22:189–90)

So pretty people may make for good movie stars—but not very good servants of the Lord. And that's because "God saves no one but sinners, He instructs no one but the foolish and stupid, He enriches none but paupers, and He makes alive only the dead; not those who merely imagine themselves to be such but those who really are this kind of people and admit it" (LW 25:418–19).

Luther therefore makes the highly contentious claim that "venison, properly seasoned and prepared, tastes just as good in a wooden dish as in one of silver." Extending this image, he argues that "a poor speaker may speak the Word of God just as well as he who is endowed with eloquence." But try to explain that to people who sell dinner plates. Or try to convince people that their favorite preacher is expendable. To clinch the point, Luther concludes that whoever disagrees with him would be "like a tired and hungry man who would refuse to eat unless the food is served on a silver platter. . . . One dare not despise the treasure because of the person" (LW 22:529). And the Lutheran Confessions drive Luther's point home saying—equally contentiously—that

> Christ . . . built his church not on the man but on the faith of Peter. . . . [Consequently] the person adds nothing to this Word and office commanded by Christ. No matter who it is who preaches and teaches the Word, if there are hearts that hear and adhere to it, something will happen. (BC 325, 324n.4)

Just think of it—we add nothing to the word with our faithfulness, rhetorical inflections, subtle literary nuances, personal sincerity, historical insights, philosophical acumen and encyclopedic grasp of world affairs. None of this is worth anything—at least when it comes to God's word getting through to us. Therefore

> [God's] Word should be allowed to work alone, without our work or interference. Why? Because it is not in my power or hand to fashion the hearts of men as the potter molds the clay and fashions them at my pleasure. I can get no farther than their ears; their hearts I cannot reach . . . . That is God's work alone, who causes faith to live in the heart. Therefore we should give free course to the Word and not add our works to it. We have the *jus verbi* [right to speak] but not the *executio* [power to accomplish]. We should preach the Word, but the results must be left solely to God's good pleasure. (LW 51:76)

So if the sermons we hear extol God's word but still are not helping us any, we shouldn't complain to, or attack the preacher (Lk 10:16). What we need to do instead is pray to God that in his great mercy he would open our hearts so that his word would become a blessing to us (Lk 11:13). However, if the sermons do not glorify God's word, then Luther thought the preacher should be "chased out by dogs and pelted with dung" (BC 360)!

Good servants of the Lord, then, are not the good looking, well educated, highly skilled, deeply compassionate, richly talented, creatively imaginative, hard working, and immensely popular ones. No, they're not the best servants. And this is because

> Christ wants to have disciples who are simple-minded, who will humble themselves, who will give ear to the Word of God, cleave to it, and be willing to learn. When they hear the

> Word, they do not presume to criticize and master the teaching; they let the divine Word reform, rule, and teach them. They become disciples of the Word. (LW 23:51)

Our Great High Priest

This puts God's servants both on a higher and a lower plane than before. They're on a higher level because they're chosen by God himself. But they're also on a lower level because in the eyes of the world they are losers. But that doesn't matter since Christ himself is actually our one and only, victorious and "great high priest" (Zec 9:9; Heb 4:14)—by any standard of evaluation whatsoever. And that's because only Christ Jesus shields us from the wrath of God by his blood (Rom 5:9). No other servant of the Lord can help us out in that way—for only Christ, "the mediator, can be pitted against God's wrath" (BC 136).

This is regularly skipped over in the church today because all we hear about it, if anything, is that Christ redeems us from our sins (Heb 9:15). But it shouldn't end there. We also should hear about "how and by what means" this redemption is accomplished (BC 414). If we don't hear about that too, then it's a problem because our salvation is thereby severely blunted because its costs are ignored (1 Cor 6:20; 7:23). And when they are skipped, the greatness of God's love is diluted (1 Jn 4:10).

Now we don't have to dream up the mechanics of our redemption in order to fill out the picture. Romans 3:24–25 tells us that it happens by God putting forth his own Son "as an expiation by his blood, to be received by faith." As an expiation, Jesus is far more than an innocent victim (Jn 10:17), done in on the cross by a band of first century thugs. No, his death is also a sacrifice offered up to God for the sins of the world (Eph 5:2; Heb 9:14; 1 Jn 2:2). This was needed in order to satisfy God's demand that the sins of the world be punished (Is 53:11).[2] So in the death of Jesus, God was punishing Christ in our place, and for our sins, to free us from the consequences of them (Is 53:4–5; 1 Pt 2:24).[3] Without Christ's sacrifice, we would all be headed straight to hell. Only his death makes salvation possible.

But what makes it actual—going beyond being merely possible—is our faith in it. Without our faith in his blood, salvation is ineffectual—lying there "in a heap" on the floor, as Luther said, good for nothing (SML 7:333). But when we believe and entrust our lives to Christ, then his victory over sin becomes ours too. For we, by our faith, in fact end up dying with Christ (Rom 6:6; 2 Cor 5:14–15). And this faith and trust in the Lord is not squeezed out of us by our own exertion (Rom 9:16), but is a gift from on high (Eph 2:8; Jas 1:17). It doesn't just pop into our heads willy-nilly. No, it is generated only by hearing Christ preached for our salvation (Rom 10:17). So rejoice in the Lord and give thanks for his mercy. Through Christ's sacrifice and your faith in it, you are given the forgiveness of sins and the hope of everlasting life—and a more faithful and righteous life now as well (1 Tm 4:8). In that more faithful life now, we will see the wisdom in the lowly, humble, despised servants that God picks to be the leaders in his church on earth.

Pray Constantly

Now we also know that "it is God's will . . . that believers walk in good works [since] faith is a . . . mighty thing, so that it is impossible for it not to be constantly doing what is good"

---

[2] See also BC 309, 328, 414, and 549.
[3] See also BC 561–62; and LW 26:284.

(BC 552–53). So let our good work this day be 1 Thessalonians 5:17, which admonishes us to "pray constantly." Now what holds us back from doing this? It's our doubt that God hears our prayers and answers them. Against that doubt pit these two texts. The first is the parable in Luke 18:3–8 which says:

> There was a widow who kept coming to the [unjust] judge and saying, "Vindicate me against my adversary." For a while he refused, . . . [then he said] "Because she bothers me, I will vindicate her."

This parable is given that we "not lose heart" when praying (Lk 18:1). So pray, knowing that eventually God will surely help you—even if it's not in the way you wished. And take heart in the example of Luther who prayed three hours a day—in addition to his daily chores.[4]

And remember also, when you pray, to say: Not my will be done, but "thy will be done" (Mt 6:10, 26:39). That will help keep your prayers "brief, frequent, and intense," as they're supposed to be (LW 21:143). Amen.

---

4 Marva J. Dawn, *Morning by Morning*, ed. Karen A. Dismer (Grand Rapids: Eerdmans, 2001) 242.

SERMON 13

Rejoice in the Remnant

In Isaiah 49:6 God tells us to take care of the "survivors in Israel." They are the ones among the chosen who actually follow God's will and way in the world. These survivors or remnant—שארית, or *sha-reet*, in the Hebrew—are revered in the Bible (Is 46:3; Rom 9:27). They are the ones who prevail in spite of the difficulties and attacks upon them (*contra* Mt 13:20–22).

ON BIG BEING BETTER

We are told to revere this remnant because we don't. If we did, we wouldn't be told to do so. Therefore in this admonishing there is condemnation. We are attacked for succumbing to the temptation to favor crowds over God's dear remnant. And so we're sinners.

Now why are we that way? Why do we succumb to this temptation? Why do we favor crowds and belittle the remnant—when God explicitly tells us not to do so? Why do we think big is better—completely disregarding contentment (*contra* Phil 4:11)?

1. Human Confirmation. Well, one reason for this is that we fear being hoodwinked—and so the confirmation we get from crowds of people agreeing with us is a kind of proof that we're right. For it's not enough that the Bible says our faith is true (Jn 14:6). We think we need more than that. So one of my brothers-in-law told me how thrilling it was to sing the hymn "Amazing Grace" with twenty thousand other Christian men at a Promise Keepers[1] event some ten years ago in Seattle at the Kingdome. I asked him why he believed that. He said the huge gathering convinced him of the truth of his faith as nothing else could. But that can't be true. For Jesus told his little flock to have no fear since their size wouldn't keep them from gaining the kingdom of God! (Lk 12:32).

And that little word "little" isn't a word of endearment—but a literal word of tiny measurement. It's μικρος [*mikros*] in the original Greek from which we get such words as microscope, microbe, microphone, and microwave. No wonder then that Jesus chooses to be with just two or three (Matthew 18:20)—and not with huge crowds. And so Martin Luther—the progenitor of our little segment of the church catholic—said that size doesn't make the church (LW 2:101). He knew long ago, what we have only later come to see, that numbers manipulate and stigmatize.[2]

So Søren Kierkegaard, who admired Luther, attacked our love for crowds:

> To win a crowd is not such a great art; all that is needed for that is some talent, a certain dose of untruth, and a little familiarity with human passions. But no truth-witness . . . dares to become involved with a crowd. . . . [He wants] to become involved, . . . but always individually

---

1   A conservative Christian men's organization established by Bill McCartney in 1990 and supported with materials by Dr. Bruce Wilkinson.
2   T. M. Porter, *Trust in Numbers* (Princeton: Princeton University, 1995) 77.

... in order to split up a crowd .... But when "the crowd" is treated as the authority, ... the truth-witness shuns the crowd more than the young virtuous girl shuns a low dance hall.
(PV 109)

And this is because regarding God, "the crowd is untruth" (PV 106, 107, 108, 110). And that's because God doesn't want "to save people in general .... No, he sacrificed himself in order to save each one individually" (CD 272; 1 Cor 9:24)!

2. *Strength in Numbers.* Another reason we disregard the faithful remnant is that life in groups looks easier. Having people help us seems to lighten our load. But as Luther pointed out—such team-work is illusory. For just as we must die alone—since "no one can die for another" (LW 51:70)—so we must believe by ourselves, since "nobody else can believe ... for me" (LW 45:108; Phil 2:12). Hoping then for a team of Christian friends to lighten our load is beside the point. For we each have to run the race of faith by ourselves. Noah, remember, opposed everyone and built the ark anyway—even though it looked silly to those who watched (LW 2:56). And Jonah also shows us that "we must all act alone" (LW 19:49). Now these examples are worth following—rather than the "more probable" ways of the crowds (PV 106).

Obese Churches

But this defense of the remnant will mostly fall on deaf ears in our American society which delights in super-sizing its food.[3] And that's because there's actually "another brand of obesity" among us that's worse than our fast food industry:

---

3   See the popular movie, *Super Size Me* (2004).

A stranger obesity for which the reputed expansion of bodies is perhaps only a metaphor . . . . A social obesity. An economic, financial, and political obesity. Obesity of cities. Obesity of malls, as in Minneapolis. Obesity of churches, as in Willow Creek. Obesity of parking lots . . . . Obesity of SUVs. Obesity of airports . . . . Obesity of election campaign budgets . . . . Obesity of Hollywood box-office sales . . . . Obesity of large memorials, like the one for Crazy Horse in [Custer, South Dakota]. . . Greed is good . . . . The bigger it is, the better it is, says America today. Large is beautiful, it repeats over and over in a kind of hysterical reversal of the 1960s slogan . . . . [America] has lost control of its own situation . . . . One feels [it] has strayed from, or broken, that secret formula, that code, that prompts a body to stay within its limits and survive . . . . That immoderation, excessiveness, force of stress and unreason, . . . leads, inevitably, to death.[4]

And it is precisely in this socially chaotic environment that we are called to conduct our ministry—and quite against the grain at that!

But lamentably that counter-cultural maneuver seldom occurs. More often than not, the church instead longs to super-size itself—maybe because fully half of the three hundred and twenty-five thousand Protestant congregations in America have less than seventy-five in worship on a Sunday, and the

---

4 Bernard Levy, *American Vertigo* (New York: Random House, 2006) 240–41.

average is between eighteen and forty![5] It's no wonder then that Kierkegaard regarded this longing for numerical greatness to be the devil's ploy:

> Little by little he deluded the Christian Church into thinking that now it had been victorious, now it should have a good rest after the battle and enjoy the victory. And it certainly looked seductive, because during the time the Church was militant, a man of course thought twice before joining it; thus its growth was not very great. But after it has been victorious—well, then it won followers by the millions. What more does one want, for if there should be any misgiving connected with a victorious Church, it would have to be that it would gradually decline, decrease in numbers. But the very opposite was the case. Indeed, the Church did not decline, decrease in number; no, it increased, it is true, as a person with dropsy increases; it swelled up in unhealthy fat, almost nauseatingly expanded in carnal obesity, scarcely recognizable.
>
> (PC 229–30)

Kierkegaard is right about this—that the fear of shrinking is what propels the church into becoming an over-eater. It therefore loses its essence—which Luther knew meant being an *ecclesiola* or "small church" (LW 2:37). Even though small—and not much for marketing analysts to admire—these churches were still "palaces of ivory" in God's sight (LW 12:255)! Even

---

[5] Lyle E. Schaller, *Small Congregation, Big Potential* (Nashville: Abingdon, 2003) 14.

though they might shrink to just eight people—as was the case on Noah's ark (LW 1:311, 2:101)—they still would be palaces of ivory, provided they upheld the word—in all its purity. For where "the Word of God is present in its purity and is active, the church is there" (LW 28:302).

And it's just that diminutive essence that makes the church militant and lean—and thereby ready to fight the good fight of faith against the world (1 Tm 6:12)[6]—or as Kierkegaard put it, ready to take up its "polemical stance against the great human society" (JP 4:4147).[7]

A Ghost Town

The essence of the church, then, is to be a cultural minority or remnant. That's because getting big is dangerous. In our day we have the notorious example of the granddaddy of the mega-churches, Willow Creek Community Church, founded in 1975 by Pastor Bill Hybels, which now has over twenty thousand at worship each week. But when they recently undertook an exhaustive, multi-year, self-study to see how many were taking Matthew 22:37–39 to heart—about loving God with all your heart and your neighbor as yourself—they were sorely disappointed by the meager results.[8]

---

6   See also Jas 4:4, Mt 10:16, 25, 37; Lk 16:15; Jn 15:19; Acts 14:22; Rom 12:2; 2 Cor 10:5; Gal 5:17; Eph 4:14; Phil 3:8; Col 3:2; 1 Thes 2:4; Heb 12:4; 1 Pt 2:11, 5:9; 2 Pt 3:17; 1 Jn 2:15.
7   See also the "showdown" in JP 1:516.
8   Hawkins & Parkinson, *Reveal: Where Are You?* (Barrington, Illinois: Willow Creek Resources, 2007) 29.

So we're finding out that the one thing needful, that little pearl of great price (Lk 10:42; Mt 13:44), gets lost in big churches. And that's because in these religious enterprises, Christian discipleship wanes.[9] Eugene Peterson, then, is right to issue his biting warning:

> Is [the] suddenly prominent preacher with a large and admiring following a spiritual descendant of Peter[10] with five thousand repentant converts or of Aaron[11] indulging his tens of thousands with religious song and dance around the golden calf?[12]

While being small is no guarantee of faithfulness,[13] smaller churches do provide greater opportunity for the pursuit of discipleship.[14]

Luther, therefore, said that the best churches will look like ghost towns. He doesn't mean by this that churches should wither away on a lonely, dusty road. No, what he means is that

> according to the appearance of the flesh, ... the Christian church is like a devastated and ruined city; as the saying goes, Christians are sparsely sown, so the church is like a ghost

---

9   Daniel V. Biles, *Pursuing Excellence in Ministry* (Washington DC: Alban Institute, 1988) 5–10.
10   Acts 2:37.
11   Ex 32:4–6.
12   Eugene H. Peterson, *Under the Unpredictable Plant* (Grand Rapids: Eerdmans, 1988) 14.
13   Dennis Bickers, *The Healthy Small Church* (Kansas City: Beacon Hill, 2005) 37.
14   K. L. Callahan, *Small, Strong Congregations* (San Francisco: Jossey-Bass, 2000) 196.

> town. This city is inhabited by few citizens and is deserted, so that one citizen lives where 300 ought to be . . . . On the contrary, the whole world is fertile, abounding, rich, copious, and crammed full everywhere. [But the true] church is indeed a forsaken widow.   (LW 17:186)

Even though this isn't as it should be, "the Christian church remains forever a widow" (LW 52:119; 13:285). And so the perennial lament of all faithful pastors throughout the generations has been—that there are "so few disciples" (LW 17:173).

Our Repulsive Message

Now why is it that there is only one disciple where three hundred ought to be? It can't be because we're providing less entertainment and recreation than secular enterprises do—especially since more congregations are now providing such things as nurses[15] and aerobics classes.[16] No, the problem is that our message is "repulsive"—as Lutherans rightly teach (BC 139). This is because it's too "difficult and dangerous" (LW 12:217) on the one hand, and too thin on the other (LW 23:11, 26:134).

So first Christianity is too dangerous and difficult. That's because we must renounce everything and seek first the kingdom of God (Lk 14:33; Mt 6:33). This includes exposing wickedness (Eph 5:11) and forgoing the gratifications of the flesh (Rom 13:14). This is a narrow way that only a few go down (Mt 7:14) and which unsurprisingly offends the worldly (Jn

---

15 G. E. Westberg, *The Parish Nurse* (Minneapolis: Augsburg Fortress, 1990).

16 DeHaven, et al, "Health Programs in Faith Based Organizations," *American Journal of Public Health* 94 (June 2004) 1030–36.

15:19). And so Luther says of it that it's like walking on razors (LW 21:245)! "No life or existence on earth," then is "more wretched than that of a Christian" (LW 28:106). How could we not then think of Christianity as being repulsive—since it so clearly and relentlessly goes against our nature (Rom 11:24)?

And secondly it offends us by being too thin. Christianity gives eternal life (Jn 3:36)—but what we want is an easy, fulfilling life now, before we die (Mt 26:39; Lk 12:19; 1 Cor 15:32; 2 Cor 12:8). So even though eternal life is promised to be better than this temporal life, that's still the one we want to enjoy all the more right now. We want resilient health; loads of money; uninterrupted joy; and endless amusement—right now, and forever. We want to float through this life "on velvet cushions and on roads paved with silk" (LW 22:108)! But then, as Luther points out, we'd be "slithering along, ... just like a serpent, . . . softly and peacefully" (LW 23:291). Because of this hazard, the boom days for the churches in the 1950s—"artificial" though they were—still left us "ill-prepared to live in a world which contradicts [our] most cherished assumptions."[17]

One By One

But God can deliver us from this—however he does so only one at a time. For Christianity is not a mass movement—even though we live all over this terrestrial ball. That's because faith never comes to us *en masse*—like those huge group weddings the Moonies perform.[18] No, Christians aren't carried in by the tide like a load of driftwood. We instead must be born again, each according to his or her own individual time (Jn 3:3–5).

---

17 Richard E. Koenig, *A Creative Minority: The Church in a New Age* (Minneapolis: Augsburg, 1971) 29.
18 F. Sontag, *Sun Myung Moon and the Unification Church* (Nashville: Abingdon, 1977) 108, 83, 165–167.

This salvation comes by way of faith in the one who died for us—Christ our Lord. He shed his blood on the cross for each of us—individually (1 Jn 2:2, 4:10). And when we believe this—our hearts are cheered by being turned "from God the Judge to God the Father" (LW 19:79). Through this faith in Christ's crucifixion we "re-enter the good graces of God," and are thereby "restored . . . to the Father's favor" (BC 561, 414). Without his sacrifice and our faith in it, none of this can happen. All we would have then would be the wrath of God upon us (Jn 3:36; Rom 5:9).

This message of salvation is addressed to each one of us individually—and demands from each one of us an individual response. This is how it went with Zacchaeus. "Come down!" Christ demands of him—perched up in that sycamore tree (Lk 19:5). Little did Zacchaeus know that when he was seeking [ζητεω] after Christ (Lk 19:3, 10), he already was "being sought [ζητεω] after and saved."[19] And so it is with us as we fight to believe (Phil 2:12–13).

Burdens & Joys

Now even though we're saved by grace through faith—we're also saved for good works (Eph 2:10). So we're expected to do them after we believe—and these good works come in two basic types. There are the obvious good works which are devoted to caring for others—like feeding, clothing and sheltering the needy. The second type regards personal decency—like keeping oneself "unstained from the world" (Jas 1:27; Eph 4:17–18).

Today when we rejoice in that small faithful remnant that believes and follows Christ—our good work should be to care for our fellow Christians. In 1 Corinthians 12:26 we read that

---

19 Luke T. Johnson, *The Gospel of Luke* (New Haven: Yale University, 1991) 285.

> if one member suffers, all suffer together; . . .
> if one member is honored, all rejoice together.

This verse is about sharing our lives in church. And we are to do that by bearing one another's burdens (Gal 6:2) and rejoicing in each other's accomplishments (Phil 4:1; 1 Thes 2:17–20). But that can't be done if we don't beat back jealousy (1 Cor 13:4; Jas 3:16) and self-absorption (Rom 12:16; Phil 2:3). For jealousy keeps us from rejoicing in each other's accomplishments, and self-absorption keeps us from bearing each other's burdens. And against these two sinful inclinations we simply have to take our stand, as Luther warned:

> The German poets prefer the Germans, the French the French. And these . . . they regard of the highest worth, almost unmindful of the fact that we are Christians . . . . We are all strongly inclined to this fault with a strange propensity, and most rare is the man who does not possess it. So we yield to the advice of no one, even though we are convinced by the reasoning.
> (LW 25:464)

This self-absorption and disdain for others keeps us from sharing our lives with each other—and tears apart the church, which is the very body of Christ (Eph 1:23; Col 1:18). So let us have nothing to do with such recklessness and instead "outdo one another in showing honor" (Rom 12:10). Call on God to help you with this for without him you can do nothing (Jn 15:5). And he will hear your prayer and bless you since he wants you to share your lives with each other—just as he has done for you in bearing your burdens (Mt 11:28) and in rejoicing with you (Lk 15:7). So pray that you might become as generous as he has been (Eph 4:32). And he will surely bless you because then you will also be able to do as he has commanded you this day—which is, as we have learned, to rejoice in the remnant. Amen.

Sermon 14

Stand Firm

Saint Paul worries about us losing our faith and so he calls us to "stand firm" (2 Thes 2:15). He worries because we are so careless about all of this. So he further says: "Let any one who thinks that he stands take heed lest he fall" (1 Cor 10:12)!

Opposing the Darkness

Søren Kierkegaard, whom we remember today before God—as we have in November here since 1980 for his abiding and profound witness to the Savior Christ Jesus—he also knew about this threat to our faith. He knew that we were too casual about the risks involved—imagining that we are decidedly *not* "contending against . . . principalities, against the powers, against the world rulers of this present darkness, against the spiritual hosts of wickedness in the heavenly places," as Ephesians 6:12 says we are. He knew that few Christians worry any longer, or so he supposed, about making a "shipwreck" of their faith, as Hymenaeus and Alexander of old did (1 Tm 1:19). And so he laments that

> in the busy life, in all the dealings from morning to night, it is not such a scrupulous matter whether a person completely wills the good . . . . And in the world there is always hustle and bustle . . . . But in eternity it will make a

> tremendous difference whether or not one was scrupulous . . . . [So] just like poisonous fumes over the field, like the hosts of grasshoppers over Egypt, so excuses and the hosts of them become a general plague that nibbles off the sprout of the eternal. (UDVS 66–68)

These words echo those of our Lord Jesus when he laments that those invited to his banquet whine—"I have bought a field, and I must go out and see it; I pray you, have me excused," or "I have married a wife, and therefore I cannot come" (Lk 14:18–20). So we ever so gently refuse to sell all that we have to obtain the pearl of great price (Mt 13:46). We cannot see our way clear to love God with all of our heart, soul and mind (Mt 22:37).

And it even gets worse. In addition to this "drift" away from our faith in Christ (Heb 2:1–3), we also rebel against the Lord our God. We shake our fists against the heights of heavens—because of the suffering, loss and sacrifice we are forced to endure here (Mt 13:21)—ostensibly to strengthen us (2 Cor 12:9; Rom 5:4; Rv 3:19; Heb 12:10). And so with Job of old we cry out, protesting aloud: "Out of the city the dying groan, and the soul of the wounded cries for help; yet God pays no attention to their prayer" (Job 24:12)! Kierkegaard, in one of his pseudonyms, underscores the human persistence of this protest:

> If I did not have Job! It is impossible to describe all the shades of meaning and how manifold the meaning is that he has for me. I do not read him as one reads another book, with the eyes, but I lay the book, as it were, on my heart and read it with the eyes of the heart . . . . Every

word by him is food and clothing and healing for my wretched soul. Now a word by him arouses me from my lethargy and awakens new restlessness; now it calms the sterile raging within me, stops the dreadfulness of the mute nausea of my passion. Have you really read Job? Read him, read him again and again. (R 204)

And so we cry out in manifold ways because of the sadness and confusion of life—for we believe with the early Job that God has set himself against us (Job 6:4, 10:2, 14:20, 16:9, 19:11). And so our faith shrinks—and our trust in him dwindles (Job 6:11, 30:26).

Therefore whether it is due to busyness or open rebellion, the "calamity of our age . . . is disobedience" (BA 5)! That's because deep in our hearts we refuse to say to the Almighty One, "thy will be done on earth as it is in heaven" (Mt 6:10).

Stepping Aside

And so in our sadness, confusion and disobedience, our hope in God gives way. And the more we look inwardly the less chance we have of coming back to faith in God. And so we must be directed away from ourselves to "the steadfastness of Christ" (2 Thes 3:5). For he has what we need and want—his very steadfastness—or as the old Latin Bible puts it, the *patientia Christi*. Looking to him with eager anticipation, Christ will then share with us his *patientia*. What we are unable to make for ourselves, he will share with us. For as Luther liked to say, our salvation can only come from outside of us, or *extra nos* (LW 24:347).[1] So Kierkegaard, who greatly admired Luther, writes in his *Christian Discourses* (1848):

---

1   See also LW 26:387; 33:176; and 51:27–28.

> I will seek my refuge with him, the Crucified One. I will beseech him to save . . . me from myself . . . . He moves me irresistibly; I will not inclose myself in myself with this anxiety for myself without having confidence in him . . . . [And so] nailed to the cross . . . . He moves every person who has a heart! (CD 280)

We must seek this refuge because we are "wretched" and cannot stop from doing what we know we shouldn't do (Rom 7:18–24). Or as Kierkegaard flatly put it, our "ability to receive" the blessings of God is not "in order" (PV 54). This is because, as Luther said, we are twisted up within or *incurvatus in se* (LW 25:245).[2] This is the damage that our sin does to us—the veritable hanging of Judas, if you will—that traumatizes, in one way or other, all who would follow Jesus (Mt 27:5).

And the reason it's the crucified one who saves us is because it is precisely in his suffering and death that he is steadfast and obedient, even unto "death on a cross" (Phil 2:8). Nowhere else do we see his steadfastness and his glory (Jn 12:32; 1 Cor 2:2). So we "step aside," as Kierkegaard argued, and let Christ save us and bring us new life—through his suffering and that alone:

> If the Redeemer's suffering and death is the satisfaction for your sin and guilt—if it is the satisfaction, then he does indeed step into your place for you, or he, the one who makes satisfaction, steps into your place, suffering in your place the punishment of sin so that you might be saved, suffering in your place death so that

---

[2] See also LW 25:291, 313, 345, and 513.

you might live—did he not and does he not then put himself completely in your place?. . . [And] so the satisfaction of Atonement means that you step aside and that he takes your place . . . . What is the comfort of Redemption but this, that the substitute, atoning, puts himself completely in your place! . . . . [Therefore] you, behind him saved, the judgment past, may enter into life, where once again he has prepared a place for you. (WA 123–24)

Living With Christ

So rejoice in Christ for he is your light and your salvation (Ps 27:1). Trust in him and have a peace which the world cannot give (Jn 14:27). Don't hold back. Don't be "offended" (Jn 6:61). Don't be "ashamed" (Mk 8:38). Instead let us take these words of encouragement from Kierkegaard to heart:

> Decisiveness in life tries in vain to snare the individual, but the benediction upon the moment of decision waits in vain . . . . And if this keeps on for a long time, we finally are captured . . . . Then it will be said: "Look, everything is ready; look, the cruelty of abstraction exposes the vanity of the finite in itself; look, the abyss of the infinite is opening up; . . . God is waiting! Leap, then, into the embrace of God."
> (TA 76, 108)

So believe in Christ (Jn 14:1)—for God himself is pulling on your soul to believe in him (CD 253). Then receive him in the Lord's Supper this day, for in this bread and the wine is life (Jn 6:53). Come to the table of God, and bring these words with you:

> I long with all my heart for this supper, for this supper that is in his remembrance . . . . But the longing for fellowship with your Savior and Redeemer should increase every time you remember [Christ]. He is not one who is dead and departed but one who is living. Indeed, you are really to live in and together with him; he is to be and become your life. (CD 261)

Eating and drinking to remember Jesus therefore involves far more than recalling a bygone teacher. It means to embark on a new life.

Traveling Forward

Now since the word and sacrament this day have come to us, they also equip us to do good deeds in Christ's name (Eph 4:12; Col 3:17). And that is because, as Kierkegaard once said,

> faith expressly signifies the deep, strong, blessed restlessness that drives the believer so that he cannot settle down at rest in this world [for] a believer travels forward. (UDVS 218)

And where should we go? What should we do—by the mercy of God? Well, let us do this—"hold fast to the traditions" of Christ that save us (2 Thes 2:15)—and to them alone! Amen.

Sermon 15

Come to Your Senses

Today we have before us the famous Parable of the Prodigal Son—perhaps the best known parable of Jesus, next to the one on the good Samaritan (Lk 10:30–37). This parable on the prodigal son is truly great—inspiring the text of the beloved hymn, *Amazing Grace,* by John Newton (1725–1807), and also the radio humorist, Garrison Keillor, to say that the only eulogy he wants read at his funeral is this parable.[1]

THE PRODIGAL SON

This parable is also internally great for its three leading figures—the woebegone son, after whom it's named, and then the forgiving father and jealous older brother. The famous German Lutheran scholar, Helmut Thielicke (1908–1986), argued in his popular book, *The Waiting Father,* that this parable should actually be named after the father since it's "only because . . . [he] was open and receptive . . . that [the son] was able to . . . be reconciled."[2] But that's not quite right. For if that naughty boy hadn't repented of his dissolute, "loose" (RSV) or "riotous" (KJV) ways (Lk 15:13)—he never would have gone home to look for reconciliation with his father in the first place. On that

---

1 See Todd Etshman, "Visiting Lake Wobegon," *The Lutheran* (February 2002) 22.
2 *The Waiting Father: Sermons on the Parables of Jesus,* trans. John W. Doberstein (New York: Harper & Row, 1959) 28.

score, then, the younger, disobedient son is the key figure—as has been said for years—because repentance is so central to forgiveness—as Martin Luther long ago pointed out, calling it in fact "a requirement" of forgiveness itself (LW 12:333).

So the heart of this parable is the line that "he came to himself" (Lk 15:17). That's because this line is a euphemism for repentance. When the younger son comes to his senses he realizes how wrong he is—and that admission starts the ball rolling in the right direction of a new life (Lk 15:24, 32). But many don't see it that way. Barbara Grace Witten has written a whole book on this theological rebellion. In it she tells of her survey of contemporary American preaching on this parable and how, by and large, preachers skip or gloss over repentance or the changing of the prodigal son's mind—μετανοια or *metanoia*.[3] And if they somehow do manage to touch on repentance, what they have to say is so watered down that the difficulty in repenting and the dangers in dissolute living are all lost. Sweetness and light trump fear and shame.

Reversus

In the old Latin Bible our key line from Luke 15:17, "he came to himself," is given a helpful twist—*in se autem reversus*. Here the note of reversal is sounded—with the putting of pressure on the boy to repent and live a new life. This is illuminating because it captures what's so difficult about repenting. Søren Kierkegaard—that avid reader of Luther's sermons—expresses this *reversus* and its inherent internal turmoil in a memorable way. "Only in this way is . . . the struggle the truth" he writes, "when the single individual fights for himself with himself within himself" (EUD 143). It's just that sort of inner battle

---

3 *All Is Forgiven: The Secular Message in American Protestantism* (Princeton: Princeton University, 1993) 35, 39, 65, 78, 82, 107, 140.

that brings about the *reversus* of repentance, the turning around to our new life with God—whereby we admit he's right and we're wrong (LW 51:318).

And all of us need to learn from this *reversus*—because all Christians are threatened by drifting away from our great salvation (Heb 2:1–3). Once we've been saved by grace through faith (Eph 2:8)—we can still make a shipwreck of our salvation (1 Tm 1:19). So when we're told that nothing can snatch us from our Father's hand (Jn 10:29)—that doesn't mean that we can't ruin our faith all on our own (*contra* Lk 11:28; 1 Pt 5:9) (LW 28:252–253; 51:128). No, for God's faithfulness doesn't keep us from being faithless (2 Tm 2:13). Therefore Lutherans condemn "those who teach that persons who have once become godly cannot fall again" (BC 35). Because of that danger and risk we need to "live in harmony" with our baptism and keep it as a "daily" preoccupation (LW 35:39; BC 445)—seeing to it that we're even converted on a "daily" basis, over and over again [*quottidie converti*] (LW 17:117).

Sexual Filth

By studying the prodigal son carefully we'll be able to work more diligently on being converted daily. And the first thing we learn from such a study is our weakness for sexual filth. In the parable we're told that he wanted to run off to a far away country so he could have sexual dalliances with whores and not be seen or caught by his family and friends (Lk 15:13, 30). That's what he spent his fortune on—illicit sexual favors. And that tempts us all.

Just think how advertisers use immodestly clad women to sell nearly anything![4] Or think how the brawny, sexy fireman's calendars are quickly sold out every year to women of all ages!

---

4   See *Sex in Advertising: Perspectives on the Erotic Appeal*, ed. Tom Re-

The prodigal son escaped to that far away place because he refused to be bound by the vows of the holy estate of matrimony. God gives us those confinements in which to express ourselves lovingly and sexually. But we want to burst our bonds asunder (Ps 2:3; Jer 2:20)! We refuse the sexual confinements set within the restrictions of the marriage vows—forsaking all others and keeping ourselves only for our husband or wife. This freedom-in-confinement is the glory of Christianity (Rom 6:16–18) and is well-expressed in that all but forgotten hymn by George Matheson (1842–1906), "Make Me a Captive Lord, and Then I Shall Be Free."[5] So let us beware and struggle not to make the same mistake.

In Luther's *Large Catechism* he tells us that keeping marriage holy will make for "less of the filthy, dissolute, disorderly conduct which now is so rampant everywhere in public prostitution and other shameful vices" (BC 394). This theological conviction is confirmed in anthropological studies which have shown that humans—if not constrained by the Spirit of the Lord—are promiscuous like sexually wild chimpanzees are.[6] This shameful behavior hasn't abated much over the last four hundred and fifty years—but keeps up at its depressing rate.[7] Just think of the rampant prostitution in AIDS-infested, sub-Saharan Africa![8]

---

ichert and Jacqueline Lambiase (Mahwah, New Jersey: Lawrence Erlbaum Associates, 2003).
5   *Service Book and Hymnal* (Minneapolis: Augsburg, 1958) Hymn 508.
6   Jared Diamond, *The Third Chimpanzee: The Evolution and Future of the Human Animal* (New York: HarperPerennial, 1992) 25, 70.
7   See Don-David Lusterman, *Infidelity: A Survival Guide* (Oakland, California: New Harbinger, 1998); and Lora Shaner, *Madam: Inside a Nevada Brothel* (First Books, 2001).
8   See Keith B. Richburg, *Out of Africa: A Black Man Confronts Africa* (New York: Harcourt Brace & Company, 1998) 124!

The Battleground

These same sexual allurements—that the prodigal son caved in to—throw us all into the battle between the spirit and the flesh. The classic Biblical passage on this struggle is in Galatians 5:16–24:

> Walk by the Spirit and do not gratify the desires of the flesh. For the desires of the flesh are against the Spirit, and the desires of the Spirit are against the flesh; for these are opposed to each other, to prevent you from doing what you would . . . . Now the works of the flesh are plain: fornication, impurity, licentiousness . . . . But the fruit of the Spirit is . . . patience, . . . faithfulness, . . . self-control . . . Those who belong to Christ Jesus have crucified the flesh with its passions and desires.

On this battlefield we learn that flesh and Spirit don't co-exist together peacefully. So if it feels good—that doesn't mean you should do it, as that old mantra from the Summer of Love in 1967 had it.[9] No! we are to crucify the flesh instead with its passions and desires rather than simply give in to them. Those wayward desires always make it look like the grass is greener on the other side of the hill. But that's a lie—and that's why there's an adage against it. What's on the other side of the hill

---

9   See P. Braunstein and Michael W. Doyle, *Imagine Nation: The American Counterculture of the 1960s and 1970s* (New York: Routledge, 2011) 330; and *The Times Were a Changin': The Sixties Reader*, ed. Debi Ungar and Irwin Ungar (New York: Random, 1998) 159. On the Dionysian background of this expression, see Todd Gitlin, *The Sixties: Years of Hope, Days of Rage* (New York: Bantam, 1993) xix, 167, 213–217, 237.

is actually only a herd of pigs eating their slop. That's what the prodigal son found out—the hard way, after he had squandered all his inheritance. So heed the wisdom of the Lord. See in the licentiousness of the flesh, destruction and gloom—rather than some garden of delights. And see in the patience and self-control of the Spirit, life and freedom—rather than drudgery and despair.

Nose to Nose With Pigs

The prodigal son turns away from his dissolute life and sexual filth when he bottoms-out—finding himself starving while feeding the pigs. At that moment of degradation and humiliation and despair, he comes to his senses. This is our second lesson to learn from this parable. It tells us that we'll continue in our sin as long as we wallow in its deceits and passing pleasures (Heb 3:13, 11:25). But once we've been cut to the quick (Acts 2:37), then our eyes will be opened. It's as if some one had grabbed us and shook us until we came to our senses and discovered how we'd been hurting ourselves. That's exactly what extreme situations are for. They clear the fog so we can see what's going on. That's why we're told that no one will enter the kingdom of God except through "many tribulations" (Acts 14:22). And that's why Kierkegaard called the sickbed the best preacher (CD 164). As long as we're sailing along without a care—we'll continue sinning without any misgivings at all. For it's only when our life comes crashing down around us that we have a chance to break free from our dissolute ways. So in order to help us, God must be hard on us and send us disasters. For without them, we are lost. If the prodigal son had not ended up nose to nose with those filthy pigs, he never would have repented.

So the Lutheran Confessions rightly teach that the prophet in Isaiah 28:21

calls it God's alien work to terrify because God's own proper work is to quicken and console. But he terrifies, he says, to make room for consolation and quickening because hearts that do not feel God's wrath in their smugness spurn consolation. (BC 189)

Luther famously called this terrifying quickening being "driven to Christ" or *agitatur ad Christum* (LW 16:232). Furthermore he writes that

> the righteous, while they live here, have flesh and blood, in which sin is rooted. To suppress this sin God will lead them into great misery and anxiety, poverty, persecution and all kinds of danger . . . until the flesh becomes completely subject to the Spirit. That, however, does not take place until death. (SML 3:130)

The prodigal son well found out about this great misery and anxiety, poverty and all kinds of danger—and so shall we when we sally off to some far place for our dabbling in dissolute delights!

No Excuses

Finally mark well what the prodigal son said when he repented. He doesn't blame his father for giving him his inheritance too soon—before he was mature enough to handle it (Lk 15:12). No, he heaps all the blame upon himself. Nor does he blame the women he abused for sexually selling themselves to him. No, he takes all the blame himself. *Mea culpa, mea culpa, mea maxima culpa* he cries—"by my most grievous fault" he bewails his sins.[10] So he emphatically resolves (Lk 15:19) that he must go and tell his father that

> I have sinned against heaven and before you;
> I am no longer worthy to be called your son;
> treat me as one of your hired servants.

And so he grovels in abject self-abasement—and rightly so, for he has been willfully and defiantly reveling in sexual filth and deep rebellion. Now all excuses have come to an end (Lk 14:18).[11] Now all explanations of extenuating circumstances count for nothing. Now he must confess his sins in contrite repentance and nothing more. For only that will do. Anything else—God will surely despise (Ps 51:17). So learn this lesson well from the prodigal son. Don't try to defend yourself before the Almighty God—for that would be nothing more than demonic (LW 22:397)! But instead simply say, "God, be merciful to me a sinner!" (Lk 18:13).

Knowing How It Ends

But what if the spirit is willing and the flesh is weak (Mt 26:41)? What then? What if we can't muster the *reversus* of the prodigal son? What if that act of self-accusation seems like a super-human feat for us? What then? Are we finished off? Are we doomed to an eternity of eating slop with the pigs?

---

10   *Lutheran Book of Worship* (Minneapolis: Augsburg, 1978) 155.
11   See also Bill Cosby and Alvin F. Poussaint, *Come On, People: On the Path from Victims to Victor* (Nashville: Thomas Nelson, 2007); and Alan M. Dershowitz, *The Abuse Excuse and Other Cop-Outs, Sob Stories, and Evasions of Responsibility* (New York: Little, Brown and Company, 1994).

No! for we have more than the prodigal son had in that distant land where he found himself wallowing in dissolute waste. We have the whole parable before us. We know how it all ends. We have seen his father running to him, embracing him and kissing him—while he was still far off (Lk 15:20). And that picture pulls us ahead. It can do for us what we cannot do for ourselves (Jn 6:44; Rom 8:3). It changes us from within (2 Cor 3:18). It gives us hope—hope in someone other than our sinful selves (Heb 12:2). From our perspective, the weakness of the prodigal son seems awfully mighty to us. Why does he pick himself up and go home in shame and not just die in the pig sty? How does he summon the strength to pivot around like that—in the slippery mud and in the disgusting filth? Well, we don't have to spend too much time on that—wondering if we could do the same.

And that's because we know about God's love for us in Christ Jesus. In Christ Jesus, God's love for us is not unpredictable and uneven. In him God's love for us is sealed (Jn 6:27)—that is to say, it is certain and nothing we can do or will do will ever be able to dislodge it. And that's because his love for us is not grounded in our lovability (LW 31:57; 30:30)—but in the fact that he sent his only Son Jesus Christ to be a sacrifice for our sins (1 Jn 4:10).

Keeping the Cross in the Parable

We have been warned that the church has within it those who are enemies of the cross of Christ and who will try to empty it of its power (Phil 3:18; 1 Cor 1:17). And it's no different now. Today there are those trying to use this profound parable of the prodigal son to show how God doesn't need Christ Jesus to die for us so that he can love us.[12] On this view, grace doesn't

---

12 Michael Winter, *The Atonement* (Collegeville: Minnesota, 1995) 89;

have to wait for the crucifixion before it can be lavished upon us (*contra* Jn 1:17, 19:30; Eph 1:7–8). That's because the father loves the prodigal son without any intervening sacrifice being made (*contra* BC 414, 541, 550, 561)—nor, for that matter, with any repayment of his squandered inheritance to his father. He simply sees his prodigal son coming home and welcomes him lovingly. Nothing more happens—nor is needed to happen. And all of that takes place simply because God is love (1 Jn 4:8). No miraculous, divine sacrifice is needed to "move the Father to grace" (*contra* LW 51:277). He just loves us—pure and simple.

But this revision of Christianity and Holy Scriptures is a travesty, designed to drive a wedge between this glorious parable and the death of Christ on the cross at Golgotha, so that these two Scriptural truths may be pitted against each other. All of this is easily avoided, however—and its disingenuousness exposed—by simply reading this parable in the context of the whole of Scripture, as it should be (LW 48:54; 9:21; 29:27). Then the wedge drops out—and the crucifixion of Christ is clearly seen to be assumed in the parable. Then Christ's sacrifice for sin (Heb 9:26) is clearly seen as the rationale for the father welcoming his bad boy home. Then Christ, offering up his life as a sacrifice for sin to his father in heaven,[13] is seen to be what turns our sinful poverty into the riches of God's blessings (2 Cor 8:9). And only then can we see the light shining in our darkness (Lk 1:79)—as it did when the prodigal son finally made it home. And with all of that in hand, we can then see

---

and *The Nature of the Atonement*, ed. James Beilby and Paul R. Eddy (Downers Grove, Illinois: IVP Academic, 2006) 104.
13 See Lk 23:49; Heb 9:14; Eph 5:2.

with Luther what is truly assumed about the death of Jesus in this parable—which Luther himself expresses so well in the following harsh, sarcastic and sharp rhetorical question:

> Why else did Christ die, except to pay for our sins and to purchase grace for us [so that God, for his sake, could] forgive us our sins?
> (LW 52:253)

Indeed, all other suppositions are false. That's because they're built on a disregard for Christianity, and vainly supposes that

> a God without wrath brought men without sin into a kingdom without judgment through the ministrations of a Christ without a cross.[14]

Foreswear all such perversions![15] Rejoice in the cross of Christ instead (Gal 6:14)—which undergird the love of God in this parable. Rejoice and come to the altar today—to receive the bread and wine of the Lord's Supper, for the newness of life it brings (Jn 6:53).

---

14 H. Richard Niebuhr, *The Kingdom of God in America* (1937) (Middletown, Connecticut: Wesleyan University, 1988) 193.

15 Another way to do that would be to see—in a shocking way—the prodigal son (Lk 15:11-32) as a symbol for Christ himself! The father in the parable is widely regarded as a symbol for God the Father—and so, on this account, in a commensurate way, the son becomes God's Son, who, as the prodigal, becomes sin for us in order to redeem us (2 Cor 5:21). Then when the son squanders his inheritance (which is Christ the Heir), the son dies—which is why upon his return the father says that his son had been dead, but is now alive. This account of the parable, corrects mistaken readings of it, by grounding the father's mercy in the son's atoning sacrifice, and so to that extent is helpful. See Peter M. Berg, "Christ as the Prodigal," *Gottesdienst: The Journal of Lutheran Liturgy* 20 (Michaelmas 2012) 5–7.

Fearing Food

And then, for the good work which faith requires, continue to fast in Lent—that you may draw closer to God, and he to you (Jas 4:8). Do that being guided by the Lutheran Confessions which say that fasting is a "spiritual exercise of fear and faith" (BC 221).

So register the fear of food—noting its dangers. For we're often out of balance—either due to stuffing ourselves or starving ourselves.[16] This might be because we're "first of all bodies" and only second of all minds.[17] So because of that bodily hazard, be more serious about controlling yourselves by fasting. Don't underestimate food. By eating of the forbidden tree, we lost paradise (Gn 3:6); and by eating of the miraculous loaves, Christ was obscured (Jn 6:26–27). So beware. Fear food that you might fast and fight against the hold it has on us.

But also note that this discipline needs faith. So call on God for help—that you might also keep your senses about you. Amen.

---

16 See Carolyn Costin, T*he Eating Disorder Sourcebook*, Third Edition (New York: McGraw, 2007); and *Food and Philosophy: Eat, Think and Be Merry,* ed. Fritz Allhoff and Dave Monroe (Oxford: Blackwell, 2007). For life is not some "well-ordered faculty meeting in which each member feels free to state his position. [Instead chicanery], corruption, self-interest, and domination are defended with threats, deception, bribes, cronyism, and the like." Nicholas Wolterstorff's review of *Civil Disagreement* (2014) by Edward Langerak, *Faith and Philosophy* 32 (July 2015): 339-40.

17 Paul R. Sponheim, *Faith and Process* (Minneapolis: Augsburg, 1979) 176.

Sermon 16

Stick to the Bible

Today we hear the demanding words that we should never go beyond the Bible (1 Cor 4:6), or *ne supra quam scriptum est*, as the old Latin Bible puts it.[1] But these words are also very controversial.[2] And so these constraining words from Saint Paul will never illuminate our lives, as they're supposed to do (Ps 119:105), unless we can first see (1) why they were said, and (2) how we might heed them.

Our Unreliability

So why are we told this? Why can't we go beyond what the Bible tells us to think and do? Isn't this pretty bad advice? We're not book worms, after all! We learn from more than books—even the Good Book! We take in all kinds of facts from all around us and then sort them out, for the greatest good, for the greatest number. So why should we hit the brakes and confine ourselves to the Bible—as our "only judge, rule, and norm" for all doctrines, so that we can know what's "good or evil, right or wrong," as the Lutheran Confessions say (BC 465)? Why tie ourselves up in this straightjacket?

---

1 On this rendering of the verse, see Saint John of Damascus (676–750), *De Fide Orthodoxa*, I.1.
2 See Joseph A. Fitzmyer, *First Corinthians* (New Haven: Yale University, 2008) 215–16.

Now if we were free from all damning character flaws, we might have a point here. But that's just not the case. We instead are all slaves to sin, with no good in us at all (Jn 8:34; Rom 7:18). "From the sole of the foot even to the head, there is no soundness" in us (Is 1:6; BC 309)! Now that's a stinging word if there ever was one! And so we have to give up on all self-reliance (Jer 17:5; Lk 18:9). When properly grasped, this leaves us in utter darkness and despair (Col 1:13; Rom 7:24).

Now it is precisely because of this forlorn state—our deep unreliability—that we need help from on high. Left to ourselves we will foul up our lives over and over again. So we need, as Martin Luther said long ago, a word that doesn't "spring from the soil of the earth" (LW 22:484). That is to say, we need help from somewhere that isn't contaminated by our corruption and sin.

The Holy Bible

Such a pure, reliable word is what we have in the Bible—a word that is free from our foibles and failings. Written by many different people—all right—but fully and truly inspired by God (2 Tm 3:16), the Bible is his very word to us. "Thus saith the Lord," we hear in it (Jer 2:5; Acts 9:5; Rv 1:10), and rightly so, for it is God speaking to us through the words of such suspect characters as King David and Saint Paul. That makes it unlike any other book on the face of the earth—in that it is the only one that we "have not invented . . . ourselves" (LW 12:186). And so we say it's holy or godlike, if you will. Luther even argues that God binds himself to this word (LW 12:352) and so—in fact—is the word himself (LW 13:386)![3] For that reason we are to confine ourselves to what the Bible

---

3   See also LW 17:93; 21:190; 46:276.

says as Saint Paul charges us to do—*ne supra quam scriptum est!* Going beyond the Bible in matters of life and faith, then, would be foolhardy in the extreme.

But over the years many from both outside and inside the church have mounted a mighty onslaught. The mere fact, they say, that God used sinful people to write his holy words taints them. Or the fact that the books of the Bible weren't even set until hundreds of years after Jesus, discredits it.[4] And so we have Gerd Lüdemann's book, *The Unholy in Holy Scriptures*[5] and Bishop Spong's *The Sins of Scripture*[6]—and from over a hundred years before them, lest anyone should think this is only a modern problem, we have William Henry Burr's *Self-Contradictions of the Bible!*[7]

Just think of it—Christians ripping up their sacred book (LW 32:175)! Even so, just as Jesus took on sinful human flesh (Rom 8:3) and yet was still fully divine (Col 2:9; Jn 5:18), so too the Bible, while written by sinners all right, still comes from God.[8] So don't look at the Bible and see just another book from a bygone time and place, for that would be to make the same mistake as those who looked at Jesus, the great Son of the Most High (Lk 1:32), and saw nothing but a common carpenter's lad (Mt 13:55)!

---

4   See Jaroslav Pelikan, *Whose Bible Is It?* (New York: Viking, 2005) 117.
5   Gerd Lüdemann, *The Unholy in Holy Scripture: The Dark Side of the Bible* (Louisville: Westminster John Knox, 1997).
6   John Shelby Spong, *The Sins of Scripture: Exposing the Bible's Texts of Hate to Reveal the God of Love* (New York: HarperCollins, 2005).
7   William Henry Burr, *Self-Contradictions of the Bible* (1860) (Amherst, New York: Prometheus, 1987).
8   See Pope Pius XII, *Divino Afflante Spiritu* (September 30, 1943) §37.

No Wax Nose

How then should we read this unusual book and see it for what it is—the very word of God? Well, it says of itself that it doesn't want to be interpreted, tampered with or cheaply disseminated (2 Pt 1:20; 2 Cor 4:2; 2:17). Or as Luther said, we must not turn it into a wax nose that we can form into any shape we like—so that it says whatever we want it to (LW 10:36).⁹ Now if that's the case, how shall we pick it up and read it? Luther charts the following course in his Easter Monday sermon of 1534:

> To understand the Scripture, there is need for the Holy Spirit's enlightenment, as the true interpreter [otherwise the Bible is] like flint and obscure gloom.... [So] we should gladly ... receive Holy Scriptures [as] God's Word .... If we will approach it with earnestness, we will find to our heart's great joy that we perceive Christ rightly, how he bore our sins, and how we shall live everlastingly, ... if only we remain simple students and fools.... There's no room, therefore, for a smart intellectual .... when it comes to this book.... God gave other disciplines—grammar, dialectic, rhetoric, philosophy, jurisprudence, medicine—in which we can ... question as to what is right and what is not. But here with Holy Scripture ... let ... questioning cease, and say, God has spoken; therefore, I believe .... [Therefore] be baptized, believe on the woman's seed, Jesus Christ, true God and man, so that you

---

9   See also LW 14:338; 39:81; 42:63.

might have forgiveness of sins and everlasting life through his death and resurrection. Don't ask, Why and how can this be? If you [stop such questioning], your heart will burn within you and you will rejoice. But if you want to dispute and ask, How is this possible? you will distance yourself from the truth.... [So] bind [yourselves] to [the Scriptures] and obediently accede to what [they say. Then] the Word [will] penetrate mightily within [you] ... so that [you] are buoyant, on fire, and glad.
(LHP 2:30–31)

There you have it—"God remains custodian of the word he speaks and can by the Holy Spirit effect things through a word delivered once upon a time, heeded or unheeded, at yet a later time."[10] No one else can do this. So Saint Augustine (354–430) was right—I trust in God in order to understand him, or *credo ut intelligam*—and never the other way around.[11] We don't figure out the Bible first by doubting it and then making our own sense of it.[12] No, we must be ever vigilant against the "blasphemous anxiety to do God's work for him"—*irreligiosa solicitudo pro Deo!*[13]

---

10 Christopher R. Steitz, *Figured Out* (Louisville: Westminster John Knox, 2000) 32.
11 *De Symbolo*, IV.
12 Contra John J. Collins, *The Bible After Babel* (Grand Rapids: Eerdmans, 2005).
13 Quoted in *The Catholic Biblical Quarterly* 71 (October 2009) 858.

Unbelievers are always free to dabble in this, if they want, and at their own peril, for Christians allow for freedom (2 Cor 3:17). But in the church, you must toe the line and walk by the rule of God (Gal 6:16). Otherwise our time will be like Luther's, when

> everything was so confused and upside-down with sheer discordant doctrines and strange new opinions that no one could know any longer what is certain or uncertain, what it means to be a Christian or not a Christian .... For proof of this [Luther says] I refer to all the books of [the] theologians .... If you can learn from them correctly [any] one part of the Catechism, I will let myself ... be shredded.
> (LW 34:28)

In the face of this threat, we must "stick rigidly" to the Bible (LW 19:45), keep it upon hearing it (Lk 11:28)—or "wait" on it until we can (LW 22:283), since the Bible's hard to absorb. For as students of it know, it aims to "affront, perplex, and astonish" us[14] in order to "radically change [our] whole life on a prodigious scale," as Kierkegaard argued (FSE 31)!

Our Only Savior

But even though the Bible's tough, its Savior Jesus still brings us salvation. For only he was crucified to make peace with God for us (Rom 5:1-2; Acts 4:12; BC 292; LW 69:262). So believe

---

14 Thomas Merton, *Opening the Bible* (Collegeville, Minnesota: The Liturgical Press, 1986) 11.

in him (Jn 14:1). And know also that he's here today in the bread and wine of the Lord's Supper, which brings strength and refreshment for you (BC 447, 449). So receive him with joy!

Memorizing the Word

And in gratitude for this mighty Savior, memorize the holy words which bring him to us today (BC 339). But don't struggle on this alone—instead link arms in the church, which is Christ's body (Eph 1:23). Don't peer into the Bible alone—thinking that your eyes are the only ones that matter (1 Cor 12:17). Instead, ponder the Bible together in church.[15] Pray it together at home. And trust in the Bible for it is eternal and applies to all times and places, just as Luther says (LW 14:290). Even though few who hear it ever assent to it (LW 16:95), find in the Bible, with the whole church on earth, wisdom worth sticking to for all of eternity (SML 1:288). Amen.

---

15 Stanley Hauerwas, *Unleashing the Scripture* (Nashville: Abingdon, 1993) 27.

Sermon 17

Labor for Love

Saint Paul believes that our love for one another isn't easy but a divinely sanctioned work or labor (1 Thes 1:3). Just as he thought faith was a labor or struggle or fight (1 Tm 6:12), so he also thought the same about love. Now since we are called to follow Saint Paul's lead, for by so doing we'll also be imitating Jesus himself (1 Cor 11:1), let us today take up his labor of love.

Bad Sentimentality

And that labor is good because it also teaches us how to love as Christ did (Jn 15:12). Now the one whom I believe has written most cogently and faithfully on this topic is Søren Kierkegaard, whom we commemorate today.[1] In his big book, aptly entitled, *Works of Love*, where he celebrates Christian love, he gives us many helpful insights. There he battles against sentimentality and ease in matters of love (WL 376)—much like Saint Paul himself. William Shakespeare (1564–1616), that bard of Avon, whom Kierkegaard also highly prized (BA 174), poked fun as well at such watered down love, which leads only "to rhyme and . . . melancholy."[2] And this he did even though he honored love's labor with the longest word in any

---

1 *Lutheran Book of Worship* (Minneapolis: Augsburg, 1978) 12.
2 *Love's Labour's Lost* (1597) IV.iii.11–13.

of his plays—"honorificabilitudinitatibus."³ Going against the grain like this, makes both Shakespeare and Kierkegaard look a little crazy or "eccentric"—and Kierkegaard, for one, would agree (WL 202–203)!

But rather than letting that deter us, let us instead simply move steadily forward with Kierkegaard's *Works of Love*—as Martin Luther might well advise us to do—as he used to do long ago (LW 22:305).⁴

Love Gone Awry

So what does he say? At the end of his book, Kierkegaard writes:

> Christianity is [often] presented in a certain sentimental, almost soft, form of love. It is all love and love; spare yourself and your flesh and blood; have good days or happy days without self-concern, because God is Love and Love—nothing at all about rigorousness must be heard; it must all be the free language and nature of love. Understood in this way, however, God's love easily becomes a fabulous and childish conception, the figure of Christ too mild and sickly-sweet for it to be true that he was and is an offense, . . . that is, as if Christianity were in its dotage. (WL 376)

In its dotage? Yes indeed! For to reduce Christianity to sentimentality is to render it senile—thereby weakening it hopelessly!

---

3   *Love's Labour's Lost*, V.i.43–44.
4   See also LW 52:143; 28:106; 12:388.

Offensive Love

Kierkegaard believes that the only way to save Christian love from this senility is to have "the possibility of offense . . . thoroughly preached back to life again" (WL 200). That means seeing how offensive Christian love is. And he shows this in *Works of Love*—and in many ways, with the clearest case coming from 1 Timothy 1:5, where love is said to be properly at home in the heart or conscience. This means that love isn't based fundamentally in the

> self-willfulness of drives and inclination. Because the man belongs first and foremost to God before he belongs to any relationship . . . . To drives and inclination this is no doubt a strange, chilling inversion; yet it is Christianity and no more chilling than the spirit is in relation to the sensate; . . . moreover, it is specifically a quality of the spirit to burn without blazing. Your wife must first and foremost be to you the neighbor; that she is your wife is then a more precise specification of your particular relationship to each other . . . . Without really being aware of it ourselves, we talk like pagans about erotic love and friendship, arrange our lives paganly in that regard, and then add a bit of Christianity about loving the neighbor.
> (WL 140–41)

But that would be to get it all backwards. Instead we must begin with God and "the spirit's love," which "you cannot point to"—weaning ourselves "from the worldly," and then build on that purified, "bound" or "transformed" love (WL 146, 145, 149, 139).

So let this witness to the spirit's love strike you and change you—with powerful words that "want to lift cars off pinned children, rescue lost and frozen wanderers—they'd bound out, little whiskey barrels strapped to their necks."[5] But even so those loving words may still sputter and run aground.

OUR DOUBLE MEDIATOR

And so we need Christ himself, who in "madness, humanly speaking, . . . sacrifices himself—in order to make the loved ones just as unhappy as himself" (WL 111)! But by so doing we not only become unhappy—because we're no longer looking to this world for our salvation (1 Jn 2:15)—but we also rejoice in the cross of Christ, for "Christianity's hope is eternity, and Christ is the Way" (WL 248)! For he is our "sacrifice of Atonement" (WL 112)—for Christ, as Luther said, "is not the Mediator of one; He is the Mediator of two who were in the utmost disagreement, . . . a damned sinner [and] the wrathful God" (LW 26:325)!

So come, receive him today, for he is here for us in the sacrament of the Lord's Supper. But note that this is no ordinary meal—where "perishable food," as Luther taught, "is transformed into the body which eats it." No, this food is holy—and so it "transforms the person who eats it into what it is itself" (LW 37:100). So eat and drink, saying with Luther: "I

---

5   Ellen Bass, *Mules of Love* (Rochester, New York: BOA Editions, 2002) 65.

take to myself the blessed sacrament, when I eat his body and drink his blood as a sign that I am rid of my sins and . . . have a gracious God" (LW 51:99)!

Be Merciful

And finally with Kierkegaard, thank God for the "royal law" (Jas 2:8) that tells us to love (Mt 22:39). Even though this law doesn't hinge on our insights and efforts (Jn 15:5; Lk 18:9), but on faith (Eph 2:8–10), by which we're given the ability so we "can" perform these loving deeds (WL 41), it is still holy and good (Rom 7:12). So don't recoil from this command as other Lutherans do,[6] but with Kierkegaard, celebrate it, saying:

> Wherever the purely human wants to storm forth, the commandment constrains; wherever the purely human loses courage, the commandment strengthens; wherever the purely human becomes tired and sagacious, the commandment inflames and gives wisdom. The commandment consumes and burns out the unhealthiness in your love, but through the commandment you will in turn be able to rekindle it when it, humanly speaking, would cease. Where you think you can easily go your own way . . . [or] despairingly want to go your own way, there take the commandment as counsel; but where you do not know what to do, there the commandment will counsel so that all turns out well nevertheless. (WL 43)

---

[6] *Contra* Steven D. Paulson, *Lutheran Theology* (London: T & T Clark, 2011) 230.

No wonder, then, that Luther called the law "the greatest treasure God has given us" (BC 411)! Even though it cannot save us from our sins (Rom 10:4), it surely can help us do good deeds.

One such good deed is the famous one to be like the Good Samaritan in showing mercy. "Go and do likewise" (Lk 10:37), Jesus commands us. And Kierkegaard takes up this charge at the end of *Works of Love*. There he reads it in light of the story about the widow's mite whose tiny gift into the temple treasury was deemed "more than" those who put in large sums (Lk 21:1–4):

> If . . . the merciful Samaritan had come not riding but walking along the road from Jericho to Jerusalem, where he saw the unfortunate man lying, if he had been carrying with him nothing [to help him with], if he had carried him to the nearest inn, where the innkeeper refused [to help because the Samaritan had no money, and if] the Samaritan . . . had [then] sought a softer resting place for [him], had sat by his side, . . . but the unfortunate one died in his hands—would he not have been equally merciful? (WL 317)

Kierkegaard asks this question to refute the saying that "mercifulness that is without money [is] a kind of lunacy, a delusion." "Therefore," Kierkegaard goes on to say, "have mercifulness; then money can be given—without it money smells bad" (WL 321).

So "mercifulness works wonders. It makes the two pennies into a large sum when the poor widow gives them" (WL 323). So give it priority! Yet, even so, the world, as Kierkegaard notes, "certainly must think this the most annoying kind of arithmetic, in which one penny can become so significant" (WL 318)! So be not conformed to the world (Rom 12:2)—"keep within your bosom [a] heart that despite poverty and misery still has sympathy for the misery of others. [For] if I myself am lying with a broken arm or leg, then I cannot plunge into the flames to save another's life—but I can still be merciful" (WL 322, 324). And then, by so doing, you'll also be laboring to love one another. Amen.

SERMON 18

Rejoice at Christmas

Today is Christmas Day, a time to be glad and celebrate the Holy Incarnation of Our Lord—for "the Word became flesh and dwelt among us, full of grace and truth" (Jn 1:14). Indeed, we had been hoping for the coming of the Messiah, for the longest of time (Is 9:6–7).[1] And finally, when the time was right (Lk 2:6), Jesus was born of Mary—over two thousand years ago now. But each year, as our celebration of this day draws near, we still long for its coming. The tension builds and builds, and then finally we burst out and sing for joy with the angels of long ago (Lk 2:10–14)!

Born a Stranger

But will our songs of joy be right on this holiday—since we're sinners who fail to do what we're supposed to do (Rom 7:15–20)—brimming, as we are, with defilements from within (Mk 7:20–23)? No wonder then, that there are many ways to be happy, and many things to rejoice over (Pss 4:7, 19:10, 62:10; 84:10). So how should we rejoice at Christmas? When we greet one another with MERRY CHRISTMAS, what should we mean by that?

---

1 On this Isaiah passage, see Sigmund Mowinkel, *He That Cometh* (1951) trans. G. W. Anderson (Nashville: Abingdon, 1954) 17, 109.

Good question! But where should we go for an equally good answer? That Lutheran Dane from Copenhagen, Søren Kierkegaard, is a good source, since he cherished Christmas—seeing in it "the strongest expression for our being saved entirely by grace, [since] the Savior is a child [and so] there can be no talk at all about imitating [him]" (JP 1:573)! And he probably learned this from Martin Luther himself, who was to him the truest figure of all, next to Jesus (JP 3:2898)! And what Luther had to say was that God couldn't have "demonstrated more pleasantly that he is gracious to all those who are lowly and despised on earth than by [Christ's] lowly birth" (LW 52:14).

So Kierkegaard begins his Christmas meditation in his last published book, *Judge For Yourself!*, stating that Jesus was born "unconditionally a stranger in the world, . . . where everything is actually a matter of alliance" (JFY 170)—being based on who you know. So the Christ child was "laid in a manger [where] if there was any alliance," Kierkegaard famously adds, "it had to be with the horses" (JFY 161)!

Proper Joy

For Kierkegaard, then, "Christianity did not enter the world [at Christmas] as . . . human whimpering . . . to win many by scaling down [the faith]" (JFY 208)! No, that would be to "seize every possible worldly enjoyment for oneself" (JFY 168). Against this "nibbling away" at eternity (JFY 157), Kierkegaard says:

> No, in order to worship God properly and to have the proper joy from worshipping, a person must . . . strive [to] accumulate, and the more the better, . . . good deeds. And when he then takes them and deeply humbled before God

> sees them transformed into something miserable and base—this is what it is to worship God—and this is a lifting up. (JFY 154)

What a complex and strange joy this is—being lifted up to God!

> [For] I do not turn on my heels, . . . I do not allow what I become in the world to be the earnestness of life—no, I let the unconditioned requirement incessantly transform into worthless rags and wretchedness myself and what I have become—on the condition that I can still . . . be involved with you, O God. (JFY 167)

Otherwise our joy is phony and we would hog-tie our faith and

> the unconditioned requirement becomes a Sunday ceremony, an entertainment put on by the pastors—and a person's life otherwise continues in total security, unmoved by the wounding restlessness of the unconditioned requirement. This emaciates Christianity, creates a façade, converts Christianity into platitudes, which it least of all wants to be! (JFY 159)

So God wants the "quiet hour on Sunday [to] alter the actual state of affairs on Monday," that we serve him alone (JFY 189, 151)!

Unholy Peanut-Brittle

This is true rejoicing at Christmas. It isn't self-indulgent joy, that tries to "defend and explain away one's own contemptibleness and mediocrity" (JFY 157), but the transformative joy that glorifies God for the Savior Jesus and admits that without him we are nothing—even though that seems to turn Jesus into "a much more terrible robber" than Barabbas himself (Mt 27:21), since Jesus levels "his assault upon the whole human race and upon what it means to be a human!" (JFY 177). But without that assault, Kierkegaard says our Christmas joy would be shamefully reduced to the "unholy sentimentality of peanut-brittle" (JP 1:568)!

Even so, we can't on our own, rejoice as we should. For "no one" can fulfill this calling, and so, "says the Gospel, that is precisely why I proclaim an Atonement" (JFY 152)! So Jesus born this day, sent by the Father to save us, has come to die for us—which is his atoning sacrifice (1 Jn 4:10). Therefore he offers up his life as a sacrifice to God (Lk 23:46; Eph 5:2), to free us from having to be punished for all of eternity for the sins we have committed (1 Pt 2:24; Rom 8:3). And that's because while God sends his son out of love (Jn 3:16), if we don't believe in him and follow him, his wrath will rest on us, all the more heavily (Jn 3:36).

Our Hiding Place

This dialectic between divine love and hatred offends many. But Luther says we instead should "distinguish between God and God" (LW 12:321). What an idea! And Kierkegaard mulls it over, meditating on what he calls "divine sublimity" (JP 3:2442):

Christianity is the combat of divine passion with itself, so that in a sense we human beings disappear like ants (although it still is infinite love for us). (JP 1:532)

The joy from this combat is what's promised at Christmas—"God and sinners reconciled," as we sing.² So it's not about being happy-go-lucky (*contra* Jn 16:33) or making the world a paradise (*contra* Gn 3:24). No, it's about Christ alone—since "our sins can be expiated only by a price commensurate with the God they offend" (SML 6:181). So Luther concludes:

> The Son . . . is my Savior; and if you . . . believe it in your heart, then your heart will be filled with assurance and joy and confidence, and you will not worry much about the . . . best that this world has to offer. (LW 51:215)

Say yes, then, to this heavenly message—do not fault it as some ridiculous mythology. And watch out, as Kierkegaard warned, for "if you do not become unconditionally joyful in this relationship, then the fault lies unconditionally in you" (WA 43)! Or as Luther says, four years into the Reformation, in another of his Christmas sermons:

> The lesson is just like the sun: in a placid pond it can be seen clearly and warms the water powerfully, but in a rushing current it cannot be seen as well nor can it warm up the water as much. So if you wish to be illumined and warmed here, to see God's mercy and wondrous

---

2 *Lutheran Book of Worship* (Minneapolis: Augsburg, 1978) Hymn 60.

deeds, so that your heart is filled with fire and light and becomes reverent and joyous, then go to where you may be still and impress the picture deep into your heart. (LW 52:8–9)

Quit stirring up the waters of your hearts, then, and rejoice. Do so by receiving the Lord's Supper today, for in it the Lord gives you something material to "cling" to (BC 440). And so Kierkegaard sings of it:

> O safe hiding place for the sinner! O blessed hiding place, especially after first having learned what it means when the conscience accuses, and the law judges, and justice punitively pursues, and then, exhausted to the point of despair, to find rest in the only hiding place that is to be found.... Only Jesus Christ can do that; [for] he gives you himself.... at the Communion table. (WA 186–87)

The Only Savior

Then, finally, also be "zealous for good deeds" (Titus 2:14) by inculcating Acts 4:12 about salvation coming through no other name than that of Jesus Christ. Of late this teaching has come under attack.[3] Prestigious Christian scholars say that Acts 4:12 isn't about eternal salvation, but only about physical healings.[4] But this can't be right since it says that healings come from our

---

3 On this attack, see *The Myth of Christian Uniqueness*, ed. J Hick & P. Knitter (Maryknoll, New York: Orbis, 1987).
4 *Christ's Lordship & Religious Pluralism*, ed. G. H. Anderson and T. F. Stransky (Maryknoll, New York: Orbis, 1981) 11–15.

faith in Christ (Acts 3:6–8, 16, 4:2, 10, 16–22). So there's no wedge here. And the Lutheran Confessions say the same (BC 292). And so Kierkegaard adds that Acts 4:12,

> compared with all earthly goods, is solid and unshaken like a mountain, and similarly . . . elevated like a mountain over the low-lying regions. (CD 222).

May we then be equally unshaken and elevated mountains in our defense of Acts 4:12—letting our strange and unpopular view be part of the meaning of our greeting: MERRY CHRISTMAS. Amen.

Sermon 19

Welcome Saint Stephen at Christmas

Today is the Feast of Saint Stephen, the first martyr of the Church—who died because he spoke out for Christ (Acts 7:51–53). But "what a difference a day makes"—as Dinah Washington sang on her Grammy award winning record back in 1959! For this transition from Christmas day to today—the second day in the twelve days of Christmas—is anything but smooth! For we have gone from singing, "Repeat the sounding joy," to killing Saint Stephen (Acts 7:57–58). So what's up? Why this "most glaring contrast" between these first two days of Christmas?[1]

Delaying Peace

Now it is precisely because we heard yesterday those heavenly, angelic words, "Peace on earth!" (Lk 2:8), that we wonder why, all of a sudden, Saint Stephen is being stoned to death by an angry mob. Have we missed something? The Christmas decorations are still up—but to no avail, for this wretched brutality still befalls us!

Well, in fact, the sad truth is that we have missed something. And what we've failed to consider sufficiently is that our Lord didn't come to bring peace on earth right away (Lk 12:51)! For on earth, for now, we must instead endure tribulation (Jn

---

1   Kaj Munk, *Four Sermons* (Blair, Nebraska: Lutheran Publishing House, 1944) 20.

16:33; Acts 14:22). But that doesn't mean that we won't have a peace of mind which the world cannot give (Jn 14:27). All it means is that we'll be the "off-scourging" of the world because we follow Christ (1 Cor 4:13). So having a peace of mind rooted in knowing to whom we belong, and the blessedness that awaits us when we die (Phil 4:4–7)—that will not and cannot keep us from running the risk of being tortured, mocked, imprisoned, wandering over deserts and mountains, living in dens and caves, and even being "sawn in two" or stoned to death (Heb 11:35–38).

Slogging in the Bog

Now that being said, how in the world can we live with the threats in these tribulations? How can we, as Martin Luther said—who is our most eminent teacher (BC 576)—how can we put up with this "vexation of life," a life which is so "horribly wretched, difficult, and troubled" (LW 8:114)? In his *Large Catechism* he even goes on to say that when we do follow Christ, we will never "have peace"—even though God "faithfully provides for our daily existence" (BC 429, 431). And if we eke out some worldly peace anyway, that can only be because we—as Luther's relentless logic again has it—have abandoned Christ (LW 13:415)[2]—by avoiding the "hard knots" intrinsic to Christianity (LW 21:62; 23:402), like self-denial, eternal damnation and the uniqueness of Christ. So Søren Kierkegaard—who thought preachers could do no better than read aloud Luther's sermons every Sunday in church rather than writing their own (JP 3:3496)—he felt that we were left, because of this tribulation, to "slog along as if in a bog" (JP 6:6503), finding our help from God, as Luther said, "in the midst of opposites" (LW 4:232). Lord have mercy!

---

2   See also LW 51:112; 52:117–19; LHP 1:163.

Because of this trouble, Luther believed that "there is no life . . . on earth more wretched than that of a Christian" (LW 28:106)—and the stoning of Saint Stephen underscores that most emphatically. And Kierkegaard, for one, took Luther's insight to heart. For he argued that it would be a bad "slogan" for the Christian life, to think that if you are loving and kind, then "it will go well with you in this world" (JP 3:3527; Hebrews 10:34)! So by including Saint Stephen's stoning at the start of the season of Christmas, the point is made that the birth of Christ means "that the natural man should die," and that, to die in this way means, "to be born" (JP 1:568).

Abounding in Adversity

To be able to rejoice in this redefined birth of the Savior, we will have to follow the wisdom of God. But if we do, as Kierkegaard warned, we will run the risk of "fanaticism" (JP 3:2379). Even so, Luther is fearless and says that the Biblical message holds that the Christian "knows how to rejoice in sadness and to mourn in happiness" (LW 25:347; Psalm 90:15). For the true Christian is "uplifted in adversity, because he trusts in God" and is "downcast in prosperity, because he fears God" (LW 27:403)! Kierkegaard called this strange flip-flop an "inverted dialectic" (JP 4:4680).

But it is just this inverted dialectic that gives us the calm to face any situation in life and to learn to be "content," as was the Apostle Paul when he suffered adversity (Phil 4:10). So the secret to enduring tribulation is in this very inversion or flip-flop—whereby adversity becomes a blessing, or as Luther said, we learn by it to be uplifted in adversity—following Romans 5:3. By so doing, Kierkegaard notes, Luther doesn't put us to sleep spiritually but instead preaches us "farther out" (JP 3:2462)—out on a limb, if you will—beyond a mere "human cause," whereby we are busy about only "finite matters" (JP

3:2570). Moving out into a realm where, if one were stoned to death for the truth, it wouldn't be the end of what matters most, but its beginning. For when the world shuts its doors on us, "heaven opens up" (JP 4:4508). That's why we are to rejoice in our adversity and not collapse under it—being only "struck down, but not destroyed" (2 Cor 4:12).

> So we do not lose heart. Though our outer nature is wasting away, our inner nature is being renewed . . . . For this slight momentary affliction is preparing for us an eternal weight of glory, . . . [for] we look not to the things that are seen but to the things that are unseen; for the things that are seen are transient, but the things that are unseen are eternal.
> (2 Cor 4:16–18)

This is what Saint Stephen knew! No wonder, then, that when the thief on the cross cried out to Jesus, "Are you not the Christ? [Then] save yourself and us!" (Lk 23:39), it fell on deaf, albeit divine, ears. And that was because "in Christianity everything is aimed at eternity—therefore a lifetime of suffering, therefore no help in this life, no victory in this life" (JP 3:3098; SML 8:356). Or as Jesus said: "Do not fear those who kill the body but cannot kill the soul" (Mt 10:28)! So Kierkegaard writes that if this earthly tribulation and anguish is lost, then we might as well "lock the churches and convert them into dance halls," because that higher divine cause of spiritual renewal and salvation will have been lost, for it is what prepares us for that eternal weight of glory (JP 3:2461). To guard against this, Kierkegaard says that the human skull is the most fitting object for "prolonged meditation" on the meaning of Christian living, because it symbolizes "that to love God is: to die, to die to the world, the most agonizing of all agonies" (JP 3:2455).

Seeing Jesus

Therefore we will surely need help if we are ever going to turn our anxieties and tribulations into blessings, like Saint Stephen did. Somehow we'll need to know that God is "swift to help,"

> even if everything is to be rendered futile, is to be blown away like a fantasy, even if nothing, nothing whatever, is to be achieved and the suffering is the one and only actuality, even if the unremitting sacrifice of a long life is to become meaningless like shadowboxing in the air.
> (EUD 334)

We cannot come by such knowledge intellectually. But we are told in no uncertain terms that God has "delivered us from the dominion of darkness and transferred us to the kingdom of his beloved Son" (Col 1:13), that we might go "through life to life" (UDVS 217)! And these words are good-as-gold, for in them we hear, Kierkegaard would say, the very "voice of God" (FSE 39), and not some human interpretation (1 Thes 2:13) of an old, disputed text. All of this happens through faith in the sacrifice of Jesus whereby he cancels what's against us (Col 2:14).

This sterling sacrifice, Kierkegaard notes, reveals that "Christianity is the divine combat of divine passion with itself" (JP 1:532). For the very blood shed in the sacrifice of the Son of God, saves us from the wrath of God (Rom 5:9)! In that salvation we are shocked by the internal combat of God "recoiling" within (Hos 11:8). But in this sacrifice is life. And so when Saint Stephen is stoned to death, he sees the heavens open, with Christ standing—not sitting as usual—to welcome him (Acts 7:56) because "dangers threaten" (JP 1:300). In death, then, Christ "strangles" death for us, so that our death—strangely—is in him and not in us (LW 42:105)! Therefore our reward comes after we die (Lk 14:14). So we are to struggle to remain faithful unto death, that we might then receive "the crown of life" (Revelation 2:10), since Jesus refuses to magically turn "mortal life into worldly delight" (UDVS 233). And to remain faithful to this promise, receive the Lord's Supper today, for it is "new strength and refreshment" for all who believe (BC 449).

Being Angelic

And then, in thanksgiving for our salvation (Col 2:7), may we also "walk as children of light," holding on to what's "good and right and true" (Eph 5:8-9)! So be angelic under attack, as Saint Stephen was (Acts 6:15). Don't seek suffering (LW 30:110), but don't flee from it either (LW 35:56). And pray for your enemies, after you rebuke them, as Saint Stephen did, and so show that love is "like a nut with a hard shell and a sweet kernel" (SML 6:208). Amen.

Sermon 20

Do Your Duty

Jesus tells us in Mark 8:34 to deny ourselves. But what does that amount to? Are we, for instance, to deny all medical care, education, friendship, job training, food, and housing? Søren Kierkegaard, that keen Lutheran author, measures and weighs this self-denial or self-hatred in *Works of Love*. In that book he does this by warning against five of its abuses:

> When the bustler wastes his time and powers in the service of futile, inconsequential pursuits . . . . When the light-minded person throws himself almost like a nonentity into the folly of the moment and makes nothing of it . . . . When the depressed person desires to be rid of life, indeed, of himself . . . . When someone surrenders to despair because the world or another person has faithlessly left him betrayed . . . . When someone self-tormentingly thinks to do God a service by torturing himself.
> (WL 23)

This futility, this folly, this depression, this despair, this torture—all of these are fueled or encouraged when we deny ourselves in the wrong way. So how can we heed our Lord's admonition, deny ourselves properly, and, at the same time, avoid these five pitfalls?

A Tale of Seduction

In Kierkegaard's little book, also published in 1847, with the long title, *What Can We Learn from the Lilies in the Field and from the Birds of the Air?*—which is based on the parable of Jesus in the Sermon on the Mount (Matthew 6:25–34) on the lilies and the birds, he says that what the follower of Christ needs to deny is the desire "to compare himself to God [or] to have a security by himself" (UDVS 178). This is what self-denial is supposed to attack.

He takes up this horrible blunder, of wanting to be like God, which self-denial is to unravel, in a little parable in that book, about a seduced lily. It's out in the field, where "imperceptibly and blissfully time slipped by, like running water that murmurs and disappears" (UDVS 167). Then a little bird visits in the beauty of the field—coming and going at will—almost capriciously. "But as so often happens," Kierkegaard writes—forebodingly, "the lily fell more and more in love with the bird precisely because it was capricious" (UDVS 167)! Can you hear in this the echo of John 3:19—"the light has come into the world, and men loved darkness rather than the light"?! Kierkegaard then goes on to say that

> this little bird was a naughty bird. Instead of ... delighting in [the lily's] loveliness, ... the bird would show off in its feelings of freedom by making the lily feel its lack of freedom. Not only that, but the little bird ... talked

> . . . truthfully and untruthfully, about how in other places there were . . . gorgeous lilies in . . . rapture and merriment . . . . And it usually ended its story, . . . humiliating to the lily, that in comparison . . . the lily looked like nothing. (UDVS 167)

And with that the lily was crushed. So what happened next? The naughty bird agrees to peck the soil away "from the root of the lily," take it under its wing, and fly off to the place of beautiful lilies, and plant it there, so that it "might succeed in becoming a gorgeous lily" too (UDVS 168–69)! Sounds pretty good, doesn't it? But what happens? "Alas, on the way the lily withered" (UDVS 169)! Alas, indeed—for now its dreams of glory are over!

Doing Your Duty

Kierkegaard concludes by saying that "the lily is the human being. The naughty little bird is the restless mentality of comparison, which roams far and wide, fitfully and capriciously, and gleans the morbid knowledge of diversity . . . . The little bird is [what's] seductive in [us], ... the conflict of discontented comparison" (UDVS 169, 181). And this seduction is morbid—for it destroys the life of peace that God has in mind for his children (Phil 4:4–13). It keeps us from exclaiming: "O Lord, my heart is not [occupied] with things too great and marvelous for me" (Ps 131:1)!

In whatever we do, then, we must not think we're in control (Jn 15:5). For that would be to long to be like God (Rom 1:22–25). In whatever walk of life we pursue, where ambition and hard work definitely have their place (Gal 6:4–5), we must give all the glory to God (1 Cor 10:31). Self-reliance is always wrong for the Christian (Dt 8:17).¹ We instead, should think of ourselves as servants—and unworthy ones, at that—who are only doing our duty (Lk 17:10). So if we're teachers or mechanics, lawyers or artists, presidents or entrepreneurs, truck drivers or restaurant employees, don't forget you're still unworthy servants just doing your duty—ambassadors for Christ in whatever walk of life you're in (2 Cor 5:20). That's your most resilient, basic identity—and it holds even if your vocation fails. For everything else is secondary. So don't succumb to "inflated self-importance," as Martin Luther warned (LW 52:208). Say with Kierkegaard:

> Dependence on God is the only independence, because God has no gravity; only the things on this earth, especially earthly treasure, have that—[so] the person who is completely dependent on him is light! (UDVS 182)

So don't compare yourself to those above you socio-politically, as Luther again warned (LW 21:320). Remember you're a person like everyone else—or just a "man," as Kierkegaard puts it. Deny everything else that wells up within you to seduce you—as happened to our poor little lily in Kierkegaard's parable. And then, with our astute Danish writer,

> consider Solomon. When he puts on his royal robes . . . there is . . . ceremonial address, and the one speaking says: Your Majesty. But when the most solemn term of address is to be used in the eternal language of earnestness, then we say: Man! We use the very same term of address

---

1   See also Is 64:6; Lk 18:9, Jas 4:14–15.

for the lowliest person when he like Lazarus [Luke 16], is sunk, almost unidentifiable, in poverty and wretchedness—we say: Man! . . . . And in the decisive moment of death when all diversities are abolished, we say: Man!
(UDVS 170–71)

Depend on Christ

But maybe we still want to play one-upmanship! We still want to think of others as being beneath us by making ourselves better than all of the rest (*contra* Phil 2:3)! To break this, we need to look to Christ—the "pioneer and perfecter of our faith" (Heb 12:2). And when we do, we see one who "must undergo great suffering, and be rejected by the elders, the chief priests, and the scribes, and be killed" (Mk 8:31). Yes! And he is killed so that he might "destroy . . . death" and open heaven for all who believe in him (Heb 2:14, 9:24)! By worrying about being better than others, we can't add "one cubit" to our span of life (Mt 6:27). But Christ is "able" to (Heb 2:18)—and for all of eternity at that (Jn 14:3), which is considerably more than one lousy cubit of time or stature! So deny yourself and believe in Christ, your Mediator and Redeemer (1 Tm 2:5; Col 1:14)! In his death he bears our sins (1 Pt 2:24) and so saves us from the wrath of God (Rom 5:9) and gives us eternal life (Jn 3:36)!

Long for the Supper

And he is not now long gone, after he has done this for us, but is with us today, and until "the close of the age" (Mt 28:20). Receive him then—in the bread and the wine of the Lord's Supper, where he promised he would be for us (1 Cor 11:24–25). Receive Christ, as Kierkegaard loved to do, in this magnificent sacrament. Receive it, for in it is life, the abundant life (Jn 6:53; 10:10), through the forgiveness of sins (Mt 26:28). Long for it—for as Kierkegaard said about its splendor:

> Oh, there is indeed only one . . . trustworthy friend in heaven and on earth, our Lord Jesus Christ . . . . He who went to death for me—should I not long for fellowship with him [in his supper]! No friend has ever been able to be more than faithful unto death, but he remained faithful in death—[for] his death was indeed my salvation . . . . He gave me life by his death; it was I who was dead, and his death gave me life. (CD 258)

Guard Creation

And, then, by the power of the Spirit of Christ himself (Jn 14:12–26), do good deeds in his name (Col 3:17). And do them out of gratitude to God for the mercy he has shown you in Christ Jesus. For without our works of righteousness—based on faith in Christ Jesus (Eph 2:10)—faith is dead (Jas 2:26).

Let us then follow the summary of the law—and love God above all and then our neighbors (Mt 22:36–40). One good way to love both God and neighbor would be to guard the earth (Gn 2:15)—thereby glorifying God's work, as well as cleaning up where we live together. Luther says this work is now "sad and difficult," whereas before Adam and Eve dragged us all down into the doldrums of sin, it was a "most pleasant" activity. But now "only faint and almost extinct traces" of this care for the earth remain (LW 1:103). But let that not deter us! For God has called us to this task. See in it then, yet one more noble duty to do. Amen.

Sermon 21

Prepare Yourselves

Today is Holy Thursday and on this day we give thanks to God for the sacrament of the Lord's Supper. On this day we remember our Lord keeping and then transforming the Jewish feast of the Passover—his Last Supper—on the day before his crucifixion.

Discerning Christ's Body

In Mark 14:16 we learn that the disciples prepared for the Lord's Passover. And they did this by getting a room ready and preparing the lamb, the unleavened bread, and the rest of the food for that Jewish meal. Just so, we must also get ready to receive the Lord's Supper today. But our preparation won't be the same as theirs.

In 1 Corinthians 11:29 Saint Paul says that whoever eats and drinks of the Lord's Supper "without discerning the body" will be judged, condemned and damned. This then is the key element in our preparation. So if we're going to be ready to receive the Lord's Supper properly today—we'll have to discern the body of the Lord and not just prepare a room and a meal like the first disciples did. This is the only way that we'll be blessed on this most holy day—by discerning the body of our Lord before we eat of the bread and drink from the cup. That's because this meal is a high risk venture and not just some easy religious ritual. No, if we don't receive it properly, we'll end up damning ourselves by way of it.

Remembering Christ

Now we can head off that disaster by attending to the words of Martin Luther in his *Large Catechism* regarding the Lord's Supper—which we also know as the Holy Eucharist, the Holy Communion, and the Sacrament of the Altar.

By so doing we'll add to the first and foremost point, that in discerning the body of our Lord we acknowledge that the consecrated bread of this sacrament is the actual flesh of Jesus Christ—raised from the dead and living. This is what the words of institution do to the bread and wine when they consecrate them—they "cause the bread to be his Body and the wine his Blood" (LHP 1:455). So as Luther put it in his *Large Catechism*, "in and under" the bread and the wine of this sacrament we have the actual, living body and blood of Jesus Christ himself—truly present to us (BC 447; LHP 1:458). So be sure to believe that, and so receive the sacrament properly. For it is precisely this miraculous feature of the sacrament that makes it "the food of our soul" which nourishes and strengthens us (BC 449).

But beyond that basic point we also hear, "Do this in remembrance of me" (Lk 22:19; 1 Cor 11:24). Luther says these "are words of . . . command . . . . addressed to the disciples of Christ [to help them] obey and please the Lord Christ" (BC 451–52). So getting ready for this sacrament will include more than receiving the gift of his presence in the consecrated bread and wine. It will also have to do with "a true understanding" (LHP 1:463) of this command to remember Christ. So while we indeed receive the great gift of our Lord's presence in this sacrament, we'll also need to feel the pressure of his command on us in this sacrament. And Luther helps us understand this. He writes:

> A promise is attached to this commandment, . . . which should most powerfully draw and impel us . . . . "This is my blood, poured out for you for the forgiveness of sin" . . . . Ponder . . . and include yourself personally in the "you" so that he may not speak to you in vain . . . . Those who feel their weakness, who are anxious to be rid of it and desire help, should . . . use the sacrament as a precious antidote against the poison in their systems. For here in the sacrament you receive from Christ's lips the forgiveness of sins, which contains and conveys God's grace and Spirit with all his gifts, protection, defense, and power against death and the devil and all evils.
> (BC 454)

So we need not force ourselves to remember Christ—for his promise to help us in this sacrament draws us to him. He comes to be with each one of us individually—that our weakness may be overcome. That poisonous sin within us that frightens us he lifts from us—through the forgiveness of sins. Because of this protection and power we're drawn to him—and thereby remember him.

Needing God

All of this is based on our need for God in Christ Jesus. It's because of the poison that's inside us that we need him so. Recognizing and nurturing this need for God is a major part of our preparation for the Lord's Supper. For indeed, true and worthy communicants or recipients, of this "most venerable sacrament" (BC 577),

> are those timid, perturbed Christians, weak in faith, who are heartily terrified because of their many and great sins, who consider themselves unworthy of this noble treasure and the benefits of Christ because of their great impurity, and who perceive their weakness in faith, deplore it, and heartily wish that they might serve God with a stronger and more cheerful faith and a purer obedience. (BC 582)

So purity and strength aren't prerequisites for receiving the Lord's Supper. No, all we need instead is to deplore our predicament and fiercely long for a purer and fuller obedience and joy.

Søren Kierkegaard, that profound admirer of Luther, helps us further understand this need we are to have for God—a need he calls our perfection:

> The Christian knows that to need God is a human being's perfection. Thus the Christian is once and for all aware of God and is saved from the presumptuousness that could be called ungodly unawareness. [But] the Christian is not aware of God . . . on the occasion of great events, . . . no, in his daily perseverance he is aware that he at no time can do without God . . . . The Christian is on the watch, and without ceasing he is on the watch for God's will. He craves only to be satisfied with God's

> grace, he does not insist on helping himself but prays for God's grace. He does not insist that God help him in any other way than God wills .... The Christian has no self-will whatever; he surrenders himself unconditionally.
>
> (CD 64)

We surrender, or bow down before God so resolutely, because only he can maintain our lives on a daily basis. No one else can. For it is God who maintains our *nephesh* or נפש in the Hebrew—which is our spirit or breath of life. Without that breath we know we would simply dry up and die away (Ps 104:29). And so we give up on our own will and follow God's will—regardless of what he commands (LW 16:183). And that's because we depend on him and need him more than anyone else—for he is all-powerful and won't abandon us, even if, for example, our parents do (Ps 27:10)!

So turning the Lord's Supper into a frivolous event to make it more relevant and meaningful is a travesty. In the 1970s I saw this happen at Saint Anthony Park Lutheran Church in Saint Paul, Minnesota, when the pastors, Richard L. Foster and Rolf G. Hanson, dressed up in full clown outfits and handed out ice cream Dixie cups for the wine and Oreo chocolate cookies for the bread—honking their clown horns along the way! On that day I saw the truth in Luther's quip that God punishes his church for its waywardness by sending "empty talkers and garrulous chatters" for pastors (LW 25:447)!

Getting Loose

But we long for more than this, even though we often forget it all and go our own way—swept away by "the fleeting pleasures of sin" (Heb 11:25)! Oh, how wretched we are (Rom 7:24)!

What then can we do? If we can't rely on ourselves to even trust in God, depend on him and nurture our deep need for him—what's left for us? Have we dug a hole so deep for ourselves that we cannot get out of it? Not quite. And that's because the Lord has freed us from our bonds (Ps 116:14). Glory be to God! But wait a minute. By what "means" are we lifted up (BC 414)? How are we freed from our bonds? Are these just pious, sentimental words with no existential impact on our daily routines?

Not according to Colossians 2:13–14! There we read that

> God made us alive, forgiving us all our sins, having canceled the bond which stood against us with its legal demands; this he set aside, nailing it to the cross.

These bonds that bind us up are the legal demands from the law of the Lord. Trust in God rather than in others—the law thunders down at us from on high (Ex 20:3–6; Jer 17:5–7). Do not rejoice when your wealth increases—thinking that prosperity will make you better (Dt 8:17). Think better of others than you do of yourselves—humiliating though that be (Phil 2:3; *contra* Jgs 15:11 and Jer 50:15). Keep your marriage vows—even though adultery looks like loads of fun (Mal 2:16; Heb 13:4). All these demands from the law of the Lord weigh down heavily upon us—especially when we break them. And indeed we do—for we've all gone astray (Is 53:6; Rom 3:23). So what then? Are we done for—set to be punished as we deserve (Lv 26:14–33; Lk 13:4–5; BC 347, 372)?

No, for those demands have been cancelled on the cross of Christ! But that isn't apparent—for all we see on the cross is a good guy being abused and murdered (Lk 24:7). How then does that cancellation take place on the cross—and on a cross of all places? Is there more happening there than first meets the eye? Well, yes indeed there is! For when Jesus dies on the cross he offers up his life as a sacrifice for sin to his Father in heaven (Lk 23:46; Eph 5:2; Heb 9:14). And note this point well:

> Jesus Christ, the Son of God, dies on the cross and bears my sin, the Law, death, the devil, and hell in His body. These enemies and unconquerable tyrants press in upon me and —create trouble for me; therefore I am anxious to be delivered from them, justified and saved. Here I find neither Law nor work nor any love that can deliver me from them. Only Christ takes away the Law, kills my sin, destroys my death in His body, and in this way empties hell, judges the devil, crucifies him, and throws him down into hell. In other words, everything that once used to torment and oppress me, Christ has set aside; He has disarmed it. (LW 26:160)

But just because this most moving and liberating sacrifice was missed by most who witnessed his terrible, horrifying death—that brutal fact alone doesn't make it any less true. For only in Christ's punishment on the cross (2 Cor 8:9; 1 Pt 2:24; 1 Jn 2:2) are we saved from the punishments for our sins—if we only believe in him and entrust our lives to his care (Rom 3:25; LW 32:76). So indeed his bruises do heal us (Is 53; 1 Pt 2:24).

Ending the Discord

And at the heart of this salvation is the spell-binding reconciliation that occurs between God and the sinner—which is largely ignored these days in the American church, forgotten and even defied. This disregard, however, is deeply dangerous and must not go unchallenged. For an antidote to this evil, let us heed Luther's words:

> We are the offenders; God . . . is the offended. And the offense is such that God cannot forgive it and we cannot remove it. Therefore there is grave discord between God . . . and us. Nor can God revoke His Law . . . . And we who have transgressed the Law of God cannot flee from the sight of God. Therefore Christ has stepped into the breach as the Mediator between two utterly different parties separated by an infinite and eternal division, and has reconciled them . . . . And so He is not the Mediator of one; He is the mediator of two who were in the utmost disagreement. (LW 26:325)

No wonder then that we are to "proclaim the Lord's death" whenever we eat and drink of this sacrament (1 Cor 11:26)! So use these words from Luther to fight against those who would belittle the cross. Use them to confirm the following graphic sermon—that has been trashed as divine child abuse—but which is still a sterling illustration of how Christ steps into the breach for us:

> The preacher held up a dirty glass. "See this glass? That's you. Filthy, stained with sin, inside and outside." He picked up a hammer. "This hammer is the . . . instrument of God's wrath against sinners" . . . . The preacher put the glass on the pulpit and slowly, deliberately drew back the hammer, took deadly aim, and with all his

might let the blow fall. But a miracle happened. At the last moment he covered the glass with a pan. The hammer struck with a crash that echoed through the hushed church. He held up the untouched glass with one hand and the mangled pan with the other. "Jesus Christ died for your sins. He took the punishment that ought to have fallen on you."[1]

Take these words to heart. Believe that in Christ Jesus, our mediator, we have the bread of life that will not perish, nor be taken away, nor leave us—but "endures to eternal life" (Jn 6:27).

Viaticum

And there's more still. Knowing that faith without works is dead (Jas 2:26), and that we do good deeds to help keep ourselves from being stained by the world (Jas 1:27), let us also this day prepare for the Lord's Supper—at the heavenly banquet too. For Jesus told us at the Last Supper that we wouldn't share this meal with him again until we are with him in heaven (Lk 22:18; Rv 19:9). And so let us eagerly await his return (Heb 9:28). In order to do that we'll need to fight against all that holds us back from doing so. And Luther also helps us with this struggle. He writes:

> If someone could believe with a certain and constant faith . . . that he is the . . . heir of God, he could regard all the power and wealth of . . . the world as filth . . . in comparison with

---

1 Shirley C. Guthrie Jr, *Christian Doctrine,* Revised Edition (Louisville: Westminster John Knox, 1994) 250.

his heavenly inheritance. Whatever the world has that is sublime and glorious would make him sick. And the greater the pomp and glory of the world is, the more detestable it would be to him. In other words, whatever the world admires and exalts most, that is foul and worthless in his eyes[2] . . . . Nothing more delightful could happen to him than a premature death [for] through it he comes into his inheritance.[3] In fact, a man who believed this completely would not go on living very long but would soon be consumed by his overwhelming joy.

(LW 26:392–93)

Now the fact that we haven't yet been whisked away in such a rapturous joy means that our faith is weak. But even so, we must still fight against the world's pomp, rejoice in our coming heavenly inheritance and long—against our nature—for a premature death!

But before we do that and receive our heavenly reward, we'll have to go through Judgment Day. And in fact, that's exactly what the Lord's Supper is to help us with. Luther again explains:

> We have two principal sacraments in the church, baptism and [the Lord's Supper]. Baptism leads us into new life on earth; the bread guides us through death into eternal life. (LW 35:67)

---

2 See Lk 16:15.
3 See Phil 1:23.

Having the Lord's Supper just before we die and go to judgment (Heb 9:27), has been called the *viaticum*, or the food for our journey up into heaven. This Luther graphically calls a stretcher:

> Thus the sacrament is for us a ford, a bridge, a door, a ship, and a stretcher, by which and in which we pass from this world into eternal life.
>
> (LW 35:66)

In preparing, then, for this heavenly banquet, let our good work be to get ready for that awesome and great day of judgment. But how shall we go about that when we don't even know when it's coming (Mt 24:36)? Well, once again, Luther provides instruction:

> We ought . . . to prepare ourselves for [Christ's return] to judge the living and the dead . . . . Before [he] returns . . . [he] will be despised and the preachers of the Gospel will be regarded as fools. The wicked masses, on the other hand, will live riotously and in boisterous gaiety, as though nothing else mattered . . . . Everybody will build, marry, . . . become secure, and in so doing burden their hearts . . . . [Then] Judgment Day will suddenly [come] when they are at their securest, when things rock with drumbeat . . . . and dancing, they will suddenly be laid low and burned with a fire that will never [end] . . . . While they [live] high and carefree, fire and brimstone will fall upon them . . . . just as [it did] to Sodom! . . . . [Then]

> Lot announced to them, "God will destroy you with fire"; but they laughed at him . . . . The same thing is happening today . . . . For this reason Jesus says, "My dear . . . Christians, do not follow the ungodly, careless crowd."[4]
>
> (LHP 1:38–40)

No, follow Luther's words instead. Beware of the godless crowds and maintain doctrinal fidelity. Fear the fire that burns forever—and give up on all silliness. Endure rejection—knowing that Christ also was despised. Keep yourself from being stained by the world (Jas 1:27). And ask God to help you with all of this (Jn 15:5)—knowing that you'll then also be ready to receive the Lord's Supper. Amen.

---

4 See Lk 21:34–36. And so our land would be "better off with an evangelical consensus that limited consumerism's inroads into family life, motivated altruistic attempts to help the underclass and tamed the antisocial, pop culture." Steven Keillor, *This Rebellious House: American History & the Truth of Christianity* (Downers Grove, Illinois: InterVarsity Press, 1996) 293-94.

SERMON 22

Glorify the Cross

Today we have before us the Passion of Jesus Christ—culminating in his death on the cross. Now even though its impact on us is huge, we still wonder what to make of it. Shall we, like some early Christians, "live as enemies of the cross" (Phil 3:18)?—either, deplorably, by disdaining salvation by the shedding of blood (Lk 18:9–12; Col 1:20), or simply, by lovingly wishing, that our Savior Jesus be spared all the shame and pain (Mt 16:22)? Either way, should we take a stand against Christ's horrible death? Or should we, with Martin Luther, the progenitor of our little corner of Christendom, exclaim instead with full hearts:

> The cross was the altar on which [Christ], consumed by the fire of the boundless love which burned in His heart, presented the living and holy sacrifice of His body and blood to the Father with fervent intercession, loud cries, and hot, anxious tears (Heb 5:7). That is the true sacrifice. Once and for all it takes away the sins of all the world and brings an everlasting reconciliation . . . . It deserves to be praised to the utmost and to have every honor given to it . . . . What man can praise and exalt Him enough? . . . . Willingly . . . He has mediated

between God's wrath and our sin. By His blood and death He gave Himself as the sacrifice or ransom and thereby far outweighed both of them. No matter how great or burdensome sin, wrath, hell, and damnation may be, this holy sacrifice is far greater and higher!
(LW 13:319–20)

What Luther says here rings true with Galatians 6:14—"far be it from me to glory except in the cross of our Lord Jesus Christ!"

Struggling to Say Amen

But can we follow suit? Can we glorify Christ's gruesome, salutary crucifixion just like Luther does, or will we—and shamefully at that—become modern day enemies of the cross of Christ? Will we join the Muslims and follow their teachings (Qur'an 4:157), that Jesus didn't die for us on the cross to save us from our sins?[1] Joining Luther then, and saying Amen to Christ's crucifixion, won't be at all easy (Mt 7:14). That's because entrusting our lives to the glories of the cross, by faith in Christ—and exclaiming that the crucified One is God (Mk 15:39)—that is a fight (1 Tm 6:12, 1:18, 4:10). It's a war (Rom 7:23). It's a battle (1 Cor 9:27; Phil 2:12). To believe, then, is to "slug it out with death" (LW 17:389). And when we do, we

---

1 See Ahmed Deedat, *Was Jesus Crucified?* (Des Plaines, Illinois: Library of Islam, 1992); and Louay Fatoohi, *The Mystery of the Crucifixion: The Attempt to Kill Jesus in the Qur'an, the New Testament, and Historical Sources* (Birmingham, United Kingdom: Luna Plena, 2008) 133–34.

> cling fast to celestial things and [are] carried away and ... dwell in things that are invisible[2] [and so] the believer hangs between heaven and earth, ... suspended in the air and crucified.
>
> (LW 29:185)

That makes this battle very unusual—hanging there, being crucified and all the rest! It turns the battle of faith into more than our effort, but a gift as well (Eph 2:8; Rom 3:24). And so in this battle, unlike almost every other altercation we will ever encounter in this life, we "fight most effectively when [we] fight the least" (LW 16:90)! Just think of it. And Søren Kierkegaard does just that. This devout Lutheran author writes:

> How true it is that the one who conquers himself is greater than someone who captures a city.[3] Greater than the one who sets everything in motion in order at least to do something himself is the one who, in relation to God and to receiving the forgiveness of sin, is able to become still[4] in order devoutly to let God do everything, fully understanding that in this regard he himself is able to do nothing at all, and that everything, everything a person is able to do himself, be it even the most glorious, the most amazing, still in this regard is infinitely nothing. (WA 157)

---

2   See Heb 11:1.
3   See Prv 16:32.
4   See Ps 46:10.

So there you have it—you fight the good fight of faith by being still in the presence of God, as he draws you to himself (Jn 6:44, 12:32)! No wonder then that it's so hard for us to say Amen to what God does for us! And on this Kierkegaard again helps us:

> In praying aright it is difficult to be able to reach the Amen—for the one who has never prayed, it seems easy enough, easy to finish quickly, but for the one who felt the need to pray and began to pray, it surely happens that he continually seemed to have something more upon his heart, as if he could neither get everything said nor get it all said as he wished it said, and thus he does not reach the Amen.
> (WA 169)

God Did It

What shall we then do? If we're not able to follow through on God's call to us to love and follow him, and in stillness say the Amen, are we forever lost? Are we left with nothing but the wrath of God weighing down heavily upon us (Jn 3:36)? What if we can't stop fidgeting—spiritually—before God? What then? Well, with Kierkegaard, let us just listen to the Gospel (Rom 10:17):

> Oh, but would that the Gospel, ... might teach you, my listener, earnestness, and ... to make you completely silent before God! Would that you in silence might forget yourself, what you yourself are called, your own name, the famous name, the wretched name, the insignificant name, in order in silence to pray to God: "Hal-

> lowed be your name!" Would that in silence you might forget yourself, your plans, the great, all-encompassing plans, or the limited plans for your life and its future, in order in silence to pray to God: "Your kingdom come!".... Then nothing would be impossible for you.... [For] just as the fear of God ... is the beginning of wisdom,[5] so also is silence the beginning of the fear of God. (WA 18–19)

So let's give it a try, together, today, right now. Let's listen, in silence, to Acts 2:23—"this Jesus, delivered up according to the definite plan"—*definito consilio*, in the old Latin Bible—"and foreknowledge of God, you crucified and killed by the hands of lawless men." Now mull that over—*definito consilio!* Scared yet? Yes! for our Lord's brutal crucifixion was then no accident—nor was it bad luck! Rather it was just what God wanted to have happen—lies, spitting, nails, and all! Why? Because it is only by Christ suffering and dying that sinners may have peace with our Holy, Just and Almighty God (Rom 5:2; Col 1:20). For according to our God, the forgiveness of sins requires the shedding of Christ's blood (Hebrews 9:18)! *Definito consilio!* Mull it over. *Definito consilio!* Let the fear of God well up in you. It was *his plan* to have his only begotten Son murdered, so that sinners might be saved. He loved you that much to sacrifice his Son (1 Jn 4:10)! And this is just the reversal we need—for as Luther famously explains, "the gospel teaches exclusively what has been given us by God, and not—as in the case of the law—what we are to do and give to God." And so

---

5   See Prv 1:7.

in matters of salvation, God "disannuls the old testament. For the little word 'new' makes the testament of Moses obsolete and worthless, one that is no longer in effect" (LW 35:162, 84).

Lighten Your Load

So receive Christ today in the Lord's Supper. For the one who died for you, has done more than that for you. He indeed has "lavished" his grace upon you (Eph 1:7–8). He has been raised from the dead, and so "death no longer has dominion over him" (Rom 6:9)! And so he's free—free to be with us in the Lord's Supper today. So, as Kierkegaard, lovingly reminds us all:

> Hear it aright, take it altogether literally, the forgiveness of sins. You will be able to go away from the Communion table as light of heart, divinely understood, as a newborn child, upon whom nothing, nothing weighs heavily, therefore even lighter of heart, insofar as much has weighed upon your heart. There is no one at the Communion table who retains against you even the least of your sins, no one—unless you yourself do it. (WA 170)

And maybe you will. For no one leaves the Lord's Supper "completely unburdened." But that shouldn't ruin it! No, all it does is "make us as imperfect as we are," says Kierkegaard, which keeps us from being, "intoxicated in dreams, [to] imagine that everything was decided by this one time, nor in quiet despondency, [to] give up because this time we did not succeed" (WA 170–71)! So come today, surely—but also all the remaining weeks in your life!

Sharing in Christ's Sufferings

And finally, glorify the cross of Christ by sharing in his sufferings (1 Pt 4:13)—using this question by the great Isaac Watts (1674–1748) to guide you:

> Must I be carried to the skies
> On flowery beds of ease,
> While others fought to win the prize,
> And sailed through bloody seas?[6]

Take these lines to heart—knowing that our Lord Jesus suffered mightily as did many of his early followers (Heb 11:35–38), and so we cannot expect to fare any better than they did (Mt 10:24–25). Amen.

---

6 *Service Book and Hymnal* (Minneapolis: Augsburg, 1958) Hymn 554.

Sermon 23

Rejoice in Christ's Victory

Easter is for us the best day of the year! Alleluia! Χριστος ανεστη, Αληθως ανεστη!—"Christ is Risen! He is Risen indeed!" That greeting has been exchanged by Christians for generations from all over the world because Easter is our grand and glorious feast of Christ's victory over "sin, death, God's wrath, the devil, hell, and eternal damnation" (LW 23:404)—as our blessed Martin Luther rightly puts it.[1] Alleluia!

But if that is the case, then why do we have those upsetting words in Mark 16:8—that seem to rain on our Easter parade!—saying, in no uncertain terms, that the first disciples to discover the empty tomb of our crucified Savior, Jesus Christ, which was to be proof-perfect that Jesus was alive and well—that they, instead of being merry and jubilant and sharing the good news with everyone they saw, instead "fled from the tomb, for terror and amazement had seized them, and they said nothing, . . . for they were afraid"? Unbelievable! They were afraid—or *timebant*, as the Old Latin Bible has it! *Timebant!* Can you believe it? And so we're tempted to say, "Shame on you, Mark 16:8! Why are you so sheepish?!"

---

[1] Edgar M. Carlson, *The Reinterpretation of Luther* (Philadelphia: Westminster, 1948) 68–73.

Three Reasons

And there's more. We're also shocked to discover that we're not told why they were afraid and didn't tell anyone about the empty tomb! So what we have here is actually a double conundrum—they not only didn't (1) celebrate the first Easter, but we don't know (2) why they were afraid to. So what shall we make of that? Are we left to languish in bewilderment? Well, not quite, for there are still a few Biblical pieces we can put together. For even though we don't have any straight-forward answers to our questions, we do have scattered insights of considerable worth. And the first of those has to do with fearing that the resurrection of Jesus might lead to some sort of indiscriminate resurrection—with dead people popping back to life all over the place, since death now has been defeated (Heb 2:14; 1 Cor 15:54–55). This has happened before, you know, but in small measure (Mk 5:42, 9:4), and the fear now is that resurrections will start cropping up all over. So the resurrection cat is out of the bag and we're scared!

1. Threatened. First, we're afraid because maybe now murderers from the past will come back to hunt us down. Maybe Jezebel of old, who tried to kill Elijah (1 Kgs 19:2), will come back to life and come after us! And also King Herod, who tried to kill the baby Jesus (Mt 2:13), maybe he'll spare nothing in trying to kill us! And what of all those modern day murderers like Mao Zedong (1893–1976), Josef Stalin (1879–1953) and Adolf Hitler (1889–1945)?—who wants them running around again! Now if that's what Easter is about—even in small measure—no wonder those first disciples fled in fear! Wouldn't you have done the same?!

2. Prodded. Or maybe just the good guys from the past will come back to life, like Jeremiah, Amos, Hosea and John the Baptist. But even that wouldn't be much fun for they pushed and prodded their people to live better lives back then—lambasting them when they felt they needed to! And they would do the same to us! "Everyone is greedy for unjust gain" (Jer 6:13)! "I will punish you for all of your iniquities" (Am 3:2)! "My people have left their God to play the whore" (Hos 4:12)! "You brood of vipers! Who warned you to flee from the wrath that is to come" (Mt 3:7)! Now who would want to put up with harangues like these?

3. *Embarrassed.* Finally, what about Judas (Lk 22:47)? What if he comes back to life and embarrasses us all the more with his faithless thoughts, words and antics? Who wants to put up with his ongoing betrayals of our Lord? And what's more, wouldn't his influence finally overtake us, turning us into him? That's enough to scare any Christian—and make us run in the opposite direction!

ONE MORE REASON

But maybe the real answer lies elsewhere. Those first witnesses of the grand resurrection of Christ, maybe they were afraid because they were expecting the risen Jesus—to, well, get even with them! They saw how Jesus blew up at the scribes!—saying they looked great on the outside, but in their hearts were rotten, nothing but "dead men's bones" (Mt 23:27)! They knew they broke their promise to defend Jesus to the end (Mk 14:31) —when they all fled after he was seized and taken to the cross (Mk 14:50)! And so they feared his anger against them, if he were to come back to life! For Christ is judge (John 5:22), as the creeds say! At the end of his life, that great Lutheran writer from Copenhagen, Søren Kierkegaard wrote a pamphlet on this scary matter, called, *What Christ Judges of Official Christianity.* There he says that

> if a comfortable, pleasurable life is to be achieved by proclaiming and teaching Christianity, then the Christ-picture must be changed somewhat. Adornment, no, there will be no sparing of gold and diamonds and rubies [and the pastor's mummery will] make people think that this is Christianity. But rigorousness, the rigorousness that is inseparable from the earnestness of eternity, that must go. So Christ becomes a sentimental figure, pure Mr. Goodman . . . . Above all it is connected with wanting, out of fear of people, to be on good terms with people, whereas the Christianity of the New Testament is: in fear of God to suffer for the doctrine at the hands of people. (TM 136–37)

You Are Delivered

What then are we to do to get out from under this damning indictment against us? Kierkegaard has nailed us—or, rather Christ has done it through this Danish author's writings! So what then are we to do? Well, let us cry out to the Lord in our shame—"O wretched man that I am! Who will deliver me from this body of death?" (Rom 7:24). And God will hear us! For we're told, with bold confidence, that Jesus "was put to death for our sins and raised for our justification" (Rom 4:25)! So believe in him (Rom 3:25)—rejoice and be glad! For God has set us free from all of our sins and all the flaming punishments they bring us (Gal 5:1)!

And in addition to this confession of faith, receive Jesus, your Lord and Savior, today. For he is here in the Lord's Supper. Come and bow down before him, eat and drink, that you may be confident that your sins truly have been forgiven you (Mt 26:28).

Console Others

But there's even more to our faith than believing in Jesus and receiving the sacrament today! We're also expected to do good works (Eph 2:10). Luther explains why this is the case:

> God . . . gives us His Son, who is very God. He gives us the very dearest thing He has and is . . . And what are we to give God in return for this love? Nothing. You shall not . . . perform this or that good work. Only believe in Christ, cast off your old nature, and cleave to Him. Your faith, however, must be of the sort that abounds in good works . . . . [For] when this Gift enters your heart and you sincerely believe in Christ, you do not remain your former self, as, for instance, a thief, an adulterer, or a murderer; but you become a new man . . . . Such a faith will no longer permit you to be arrogant and proud; for if the heart is cleansed, then hands, eyes, feet, and all other members are also pure, and their works are also different. (LW 22:374)

And so "we receive fire and light, by which we are made new and different," Luther adds, "and by which a new judgment, new sensations, and new drives arise in us" (LW 26:375).

Let us today agree on showing this newness (Rom 6:4) by comforting "those who are in any affliction, with the comfort with which we ourselves are comforted by God" (2 Cor 1:4). Does that mean we'll say that everything is just fine? No, for in this life we have tribulations (Jn 16:33) and sufferings (1 Pt 4:13)! And, so as Kierkegaard points out, the help that Christianity gives "looks like torment, the relief like a burden" (PC 114)! Nevertheless, we do not consider the sufferings "of this present time" worth "comparing with the glory that is to be revealed" (Rom 8:18). And believers have that glory in Jesus' words—"Because I live, you will live also" (Jn 14:19)! Death, therefore, has no dominion over any believer in Christ! So when we die, we will be raised again to live for eternity in heaven with God. When we die, the eternal Christ will meet us to take us with him into heaven (Jn 14:3; Rom 8:39; 1 Thes 4:18). Share these great words with all who will listen. But as Kierkegaard warned, this good news, by way of the resurrection from the dead,

> is not learned by rote, it is not learned by reading about it, it is acquired slowly, and it is acquired only by the person who worked himself weary in the good work, who walked himself tired on the right road, who bore the concern for a just cause, who was misunderstood in a noble striving, and not until it is well gained in this way is it in the right place and a legitimate discourse in the mouth of the Very Reverend [and any one else who wants to witness to it]!
> (TDIO 101)

With that caveat in mind, move ahead!—"knowing that he who raised the Lord Jesus will raise us also" (2 Cor 4:14)—so we can now confidently rejoice forever in Christ's victory. Amen!

Albrecht Dürer, *Christ in Limbo*, 1510.

Sermon 24

Follow Saint Philip

During these great days of Easter, it is right for us to remember the Apostle Philip's conversation with the man from Ethiopia. For this minor incident in the New Testament actually holds great importance for all of us who would follow Christ Jesus.

Loving the Lamb

What transpires between Philip and the Ethiopian is indeed both peculiar and weighty (Acts 8:26–40). Often we rush to the end where Philip is miraculously and strangely whisked away to Azotus by the Spirit of God or at the point where the Ethiopian is baptized by Philip along that desert road—both of them jumping into the water together. But the heart of the matter is actually closer to the beginning of the incident when Philip interprets Isaiah 53 for this foreigner (Acts 8:35). These words from Isaiah are those classic ones about the one whom God afflicts for our salvation—who is punished in our place, so that "by his wounds we are healed" (Is 53:5). The Ethiopian asks who this is and Philip tells him it is Jesus who was crucified for us and then raised from the dead. It has been argued that the whole book of Acts is an elaboration of Philip's response to the Ethiopian's inquiry.[1] And that makes this incident weighty indeed.

---

1 Jaroslav Pelikan, *Acts* (Grand Rapids, Michigan: Brazos, 2005) 65.

At the heart of his answer is the Lamb of God who takes away the sins of the world (Jn 1:29; Acts 8:32). Here we learn that it is only Jesus who can save us from our sins by being punished for them in our place. For he alone was "stricken by God and afflicted," Isaiah says. Indeed, "Christ himself bore our sins in his body on the tree.... and by his wounds we are healed" (1 Pt 2:24). This is why God loves his Son—because he lays down his life for us—and we are to love him as well (Jn 10:17, 14:21). Loving Jesus for any other reason would be nice—but it won't save us. So love the Lamb of God who takes away the sins of the world. Love him because he was punished for our sins so that we may go free. Love him because he is our substitute who suffers our punishments for us, as Luther said (LW 22:167)!

Therefore do not approach God apart from Christ. All that brings is wrath, punishment and condemnation. Instead bring Christ with you and "pay God with him" (LW 30:12), as Luther put it—*Gott mit Christum bezahlen.* For we cannot approach God on our own—without a mediator or an advocate (1 Tm 2:5; 1 Jn 2:1). That is because his holiness would clash with our sinfulness—bringing only wrack and ruin upon our defenseless souls. This calamity can only be averted through the mediation and advocacy of Christ Jesus our Lord. For he is our Paschal Lamb who was sacrificed for us (1 Cor 5:7). By so doing he bought us back (1 Cor 6:20), freeing us from our imprisonment to sin (Jn 8:34) and the curse of the law (Gal 3:13). Just as the blood from the first Paschal lamb protected the children of Israel from God's angel of death in Egypt (Ex 12:13), so the blood of Jesus now shields us who believe in him from the wrath of God (Rom 5:9). So love the Lamb of God who was slain. He alone is our salvation. Love the Lamb who was slain, for there is salvation under no other name (Acts 4:12)—Alleluia!

The Fifth Gospel

Because of this resolute and resounding testimony to our salvation through the sacrifice of Christ Jesus, Isaiah has been called the fifth gospel.[2] Nowhere in the New Testament do we have as clear a reason for the sacrifice of Christ as we find in Isaiah 53—for there we learn that Christ was "stricken . . . by God" and "wounded for our sins," that "with his stripes we are healed" for "the Lord . . . laid on him the iniquity of us all," and that "the Lord . . . shall see the fruit of the travail of his soul and be satisfied" (Is 53:4–6, 10–11). Even so, this effort to see Christ in Isaiah has known "long periods of deep disagreement and bitter strife."[3] But still we hold that in Isaiah 53

> the suffering servant retains its theological significance within the Christian canon because it is inextricably linked in substance with the gospel of Jesus Christ, who is and always has been the ground of God's salvation.[4]

Without this conviction Jesus wouldn't be the Lamb of God who takes away the sins of the world, for he wouldn't be that spotless lamb (1 Pt 1:19) who was so by virtue of being the Word who was "with God and . . . was God," from the beginning (Jn 1:1–3).

---

[2] J. F. A. Sawyer, *The Fifth Gospel: Isaiah in the History of Christianity* (New York: Cambridge, 1986).

[3] Brevard S. Childs, *The Struggle to Understand Isaiah as Christian Scripture* (Grand Rapids, Michigan: Eerdmans, 2004) 322.

[4] Brevard S. Childs, *Isaiah: A Commentary* (Louisville: Westminster John Knox, 2001) 423.

False Teachers

But soon after Philip faithfully witnessed to the Ethiopian that Isaiah 53 was about Jesus, storm clouds came rolling in. False teachers sprang up in the Church against this good news—denying "the Master who bought them" (2 Pt 2:1). Just think of it! This message wasn't attacked by atheists, humanists and the like—but by Christians. And this is the way it goes. The heresies that have plagued the church over the years have come almost exclusively from Christian leaders.[5] And it continues so to this very day.

Since the late 1980s Christians have been railing against the Lamb who was slain with new and concerted efforts—famously calling this message one of "divine child abuse." For God to send his only Son to die an awful death after having been beaten up and spit upon and all the rest, is simply unconscionable. It's divine child abuse, they lament. And these critics are many. The pile of books in my study, arguing for this revision of Christianity grows every year. They amount to a full-scale, broadside attack on the Christian faith. Here is my growing list of revisionists:

Parker & Brown, *Christianity, Patriarchy & Abuse* (1989).
R. G. Hamerton-Kelly, *Sacred Violence* (1992).
M. T. Thangaraj, *The Crucified Guru* (1994).
D. K. Ray, *Deceiving the Devil* (1998).
L. S. Bond, *Trouble With Jesus* (1999).
Green & Baker, *Recovering the Scandal of the Cross* (2000).
R. L. Floyd, *When I Survey the Wondrous Cross* (2000).
R. Girard, *I See Satan Fall Like Lightning* (2001).

---

[5] See Ben Quash & Michael Ward, *Heresies and How to Avoid Them: Why It Matters What Christians Believe*, with a foreword by Stanley Hauerwas (Peabody, Massachusetts: Hendrickson, 2008).

J. D. Weaver, *The Nonviolent Atonement* (2001).
Brock & Parker, *Proverbs of Ashes* (2001).
J. Nelson-Pallmeyer, *Jesus Against Christianity* (2001).
A. W. Bartlett, *Cross Purposes* (2001).
S. J. Patterson, *Beyond the Passion* (2004).
S. Finlan, *Problems With the Atonement* (2005).
J. Sanders, *Atonement & Violence* (2006).
Borg & Crossan, *The Last Week* (2006).
S. M. Heim, *Saved From Sacrifice* (2006).
Beilby & Eddy, *The Nature of the Atonement* (2006).
Jersak & Hardin, *Stricken by God?* (2007).
S. A. Brown, *Cross Talk* (2008).

Against this theological barrage I have argued elsewhere[6] that Jesus couldn't have been abused on the cross by his Father because:

He was not forced to die, but freely chose to do so.
He knew his death was good, in that it saved sinners.
He knew he would quickly be raised from the dead.
He knew his Father shared in his pain—being equal to him.
He told his followers to suffer too, since it's strengthening.
He knew that all suffering wasn't justified by his death.

But this rejoinder isn't a slam-dunk. It settles nothing. That's because their assaults on our faith gain steam every year. And that's because heretical teachings are tenacious. So they have to be fought against continually and diligently. And no Lutheran should be surprised by this. For we have been warned in our Confessions that

---

6 "Preaching Against the Cross," *Lutheran Partners* 19 (September/October 2003): 24–29.

the church [is threatened] with ruin. [For] there is an infinite number of ungodly within the church who oppress it. (BC 169)

These words have been around for hundreds of years and yet we still haven't taken them to heart. We continue to give the benefit of the doubt to our lay leaders, pastors, bishops, college and seminary professors. But that is a terrible mistake. No, everyone should be tested against the Word and our doctrinal heritage to see whether or not what is being said is right or not. We have to be ever-diligent—otherwise the light of Christ will grow dim in us (Lk 11:35). So "contend" with all of your might (Jude 1:3) for the Lamb of God, who takes away the sins of the world!

Follow Saint Philip

That means you'll have to follow in Saint Philip's steps and proclaim the Lamb of God who takes away the sins of the world—Alleluia! You'll have to be as courageous as he was—daring to declare the name of the Lord—even to foreigners. That's because this message about the Lamb of God is so integral to our Easter proclamation that it cannot be compromised in anyway whatsoever.

Therefore do not cave in to the critics who complain about a metaphysical conundrum regarding God's identity—that he has to send his only Son to die who is identical with him, but has to stand against him, in order to save us from him—and his furious wrath. Don't cave in to this supposed incoherence. See instead in this sacrifice of Christ, the Father and the Son working together for our salvation. Follow instead in the footsteps of Saint Philip and offer up the same testimony that he gave to that Ethiopian long ago. Declare that Christ Jesus is the one stricken by God for our salvation. Say this is so even though in Isaiah the name of Jesus isn't mentioned. Say this is so because of the inspiration of the Holy Spirit (2 Tm 3:16) and then sing—Alleluia!

And don't cave in to their second ploy either, when they bemoan the psychological trauma caused by the fright of the crucifixion itself. On this score they complain that the burden of the cross is too great for sinners to bear. It's too much for us to know that Jesus had to suffer and die because of our disobedience and rebellion. Jesus, who was so loving and so good, had to suffer because of us—as we sing on Good Friday, "I it was denied thee; I crucified thee"!⁷ But that, they say, is far too damning for us to bear! And so they sidestep the Lamb of God who died to take away our sins. Against that psychological dodge, let us once again follow Saint Philip. Let us rejoice in the Lamb who was slain and has begun his reign—Alleluia! Follow Saint Philip, knowing full well that this trauma is not inflicted upon us to stymie us, but to drive us instead to Christ—*agitatur ad Christum* (LW 16:232).

Cleansed by Christ

But even with all of this clarification and explanation, we still find ourselves not doing the good we would do (Rom 7:19). Alas, this is so, for the spirit is willing but the flesh is weak (Mt 26:41). So we must look to another. We cannot find salvation in ourselves (Ps 49:7–9). And we are told in the New Testament, that the one we're looking for is none other than Jesus himself, "the pioneer and perfecter of our faith" (Heb 12:2). For he is the one who cleanses us through his word (Jn 15:3).

---

7   *Lutheran Book of Worship* (Minneapolis: Ausgburg, 1978) Hymn 123.

He cleanses us from our sin by forgiving us for his sake and because of his sacrifice on the cross (Heb 9:26). And even though we are made clean by Jesus, he still prunes us that we may flourish and blossom all the more (Jn 15:2). So we must not despair when we find ourselves under his pruning knife. In those times of trauma, we must instead cling to his cleansing Word and the promise of greater discipleship by his grace. Then we will be able to tough-out the trauma and grow in grace (2 Pt 3:18). Then we can settle into the truth that we are both clean and unclean at the same time. Luther's formulation of this is classic:

> This is peculiar cleansing . . . . Man is first declared clean by God's Word for Christ's sake, in whom he believes. For by such faith in the Word he is grafted into the Vine that is Christ and is clothed in purity . . . . This is the Christian doctrine of true purity, which is so incomprehensible to any non-Christian, . . . who is unable to reconcile the two facts that a Christian is clean and unclean at the same time. They are ignorant of the power of Christ, . . . of how we are declared wholly clean for His sake through the Word, as clean as He Himself is, although in ourselves we are still, and always will be, impure because of our sinful nature.
> (LW 24:210, 212–13)

There we have equal reasons to be both joyous and sober at the same time. How grand! In this way we can have all the benefits from on high without degenerating, as a result of those blessings, into irresponsible and pompous spiritual slobs. We know we are pure as Christ in God's eyes, while still being plagued with our most loathsome sinful nature. With that balanced account of ourselves, we can face the difficulties of life and our weak flesh and still find comfort in Christ our Lord. Luther gave this balanced account in his famous Latin line—*simul iustus et peccator*—at the same time saint and sinner (LW 26:232).

Every bit of this cleansing hinges on Christ's victory on the cross—where he defeated sin for us poor weak creatures (BC 414). So let us not hanker after some watered-down explanation of the cross. Let us instead hold fast to the ancient traditions of the church (2 Thes 2:15). And let us find abiding solace in Luther's searching rhetorical question which maintains that great tradition in the face of similar opposition from his own time:

> Why else did [Christ] die, except to pay for our sins and to purchase grace for us so that we might despair of ourselves and our works, placing no trust in them, so that we might, with courageous defiance, look only to Christ, and firmly believe that he is the man who God beholds in our stead and for the sake of his sole merits forgives us our sins, deigns to look upon us with favor, and grants us eternal life. This is the Christian faith.   (LW 52:253; 76:164)

Any divergence whatsoever from this teaching, then, will drain the Christian faith of its lifeblood. Therefore we must be adamant about keeping matters straight. Luther again helps us:

> Only . . . Christ frees us from our burden. One has sinned, another bears the punishment . . . . This, then, is the Christian religion: One

has sinned, Another has made satisfaction. The sinner does not make satisfaction; the Satisfier does not sin. This is an astounding doctrine.

(LW 17:99)

Luther risks sounding mechanical here, in order to be clear about the good news that we have in Christ Jesus our Lord. What Christ does for us can be found nowhere else. What Christ does for us bears upon his Father in heaven. What Christ does for us cleanses us by moving God to mercy (LW 51:277). What Christ does for us moves God to mercy by satisfying his divine requirements for the punishment of sin, rebellion and disobedience (Lv 26:16).

So rejoice in the Lamb who was slain and has begun his reign—Alleluia! And come to the Altar of the Lord and receive this risen Lord in, with, and under the bread and the wine of the Sacrament of the Lord's Supper (BC 575) that your faith in the forgiveness of sins may grow and your love for one another abound.

Our Clarion Call

But all of these wonders are still not enough. The Apostle Paul also admonishes us to "look carefully" how we walk that we might "make the most of the time" (Eph 5:15–16). What better way would there be for us to do that during this time of Easter than to "declare the greatness of the Lord" (Ps 145:6)? And what is his greatness? Nehemiah 4:20 says that it is that "our God will fight for us" (אלהינו ילחם לנו, *elohenu yeelakem lanu*). Let us, then, get that word out—*elohenu yeelakem lanu!* Let that verse be our clarion call—to be repeated over and over again. *Elohenu yeelakem lanu! Elohenu yeelakem lanu!*

In large part this will mean not depending on ourselves (Prv 3:7; Jn 15:5). Depend instead on the Lord—for he is the one who will fight for you. He is the steady and sure one—the "rock" on whom you can rely (2 Sm 22:3; Ps 19:14; Is 26:4; 1 Cor 10:4). We, however, are but a mist, blown around by every wind of the culture (Jas 4:14; Eph 4:14). We are not a rock as our Lord God is. And as our rock, God fights for us. How does he do that? Colossians 1:13 says that he has "delivered us from the dominion of darkness and transferred us to the kingdom of his beloved son." By so doing he battles against the dominion of darkness on our behalf through his dear Son, our Savior Christ Jesus the Lord (1 Jn 3:8). He battles against darkness—which is, as Luther put it, "sin, death, God's wrath, the devil, hell, and eternal damnation" (LW 23:404). How much better could it be than to have One like this on our side to battle against such mighty foes?

So get the word out—our God will fight for us! That's a great word for this time of Easter. God fights against sin through the death and resurrection of his dear Son, Christ Jesus our Lord. This proclamation was at the heart of Saint Philip's testimony to that Ethiopian long ago. So let it be at the heart of ours as well. *Elohenu yeelakem lanu! Elohenu yeelakem lanu!* Amen.

Sermon 25

Overthrow the World!

Today, we hear the startling words in Acts 17:6, that just as the first Christians long ago were accused of "turning the world upside down," so we should follow suit and upset the world in our own day. But this is a daunting task if there ever was one. For to build a new world in the place of what we now have, goes well beyond our capacities—even when we think it doesn't![1] For the immensity of the project alone, shows that it's clearly beyond us.

Rebel & Thorn

But not for Martin Luther, after whom our church is named. Long ago he took up the task, and even said all Christians everywhere could, and should, do the same—arguing that

> all Christians ought to bear the title Christ bore on the cross . . . . [There] he is [charged with being] a rebel who wants to arouse the land against the emperor and win the people over to himself. He had to bear that title and be called a rebel. [And] there is no person in the world more wicked than a rebel, for through rebellion much blood is shed. Thus Christ dies as a . . .

---

1 *Contra* Peter L. Berger and Thomas Luckmann, *The Social Construction of Reality* (New York: Doubleday, 1966).

> rebel [and] to the emperor [is one. And] that title all Christians ... must have; [for] if we do not have this title, we do not belong to Christ.
> (LW 13:414–15)

And Luther's Danish protégé, Søren Kierkegaard, not surprisingly, being an avid reader of Luther, held a similar view. In his lengthy journals he writes:

> At times I am buoyed up by the thought that the thorn or spike I have in the flesh,[2] a suffering I try to bear patiently, will itself be or will help to be a thorn in the eye of the world.
> (JP 6:6492)

So he rebelled against nineteenth century Denmark in order not "to cover up the Christian requirement so that by suppression or by falsification a kind of decorum is produced that is to the absolutely highest degree demoralizing and is the assassination of Christianity" (TM 48). Once rid of that decorum, Christianity will be "so full of meaning that it first repels and then attracts" (JP 1:455)!

But for us mere mortals to take up this noble tradition of Christian rebellion, we'll need more information and encouragement (Col 2:2), for none of us, I do believe, can naturally take on such a harrowing task. What Jeremiah said to his weak-kneed folk long ago could just as easily apply to us: "If in a safe land you fall down, how will you do in the jungle of the Jordan?" (Jer 12:5). Precisely! For none of us, I am sure, are inclined to say with Martin Luther, "I am sure that I am a prophet" and can handle those jungles (LW 43:223; 32:9)!

---

2   See 2 Cor 12:8.

The Rationale

So, first we'll want to know why we should upset the world in any way at all. It isn't so bad, you know. Well yes, but that's precisely the bone of contention—for in the Holy Scriptures, the world is anything but a nice place. But as Kierkegaard explains,

> God does not place man in a world which forces him in every way to recognize that it is a vale of tears—and then declare in his Word that it is a vale of tears in order to see whether man will believe him. No, this would be a stupid examination.... No, the world [rather] seems a lovely, nice place, unequalled—and [then] God says in his Word: The whole thing is a lie and sin and a vale of tears; now let us see if you will believe me. (JP 2:1439)

Well put! So what do we see when we look at the world through the eyes of the Bible? We see a world in which everyone has gone astray (Is 53:6)—recklessly veering off track. No one listens to the Lord God Almighty or walks in his ways—trusting in his great revelation to us in his holy word (Ps 81:13). Therefore no one does anything that is good in his eyes (Rom 3:12, 7:19). So what we have, as Luther summarizes it, is nothing but "persistent impenitence and utmost contempt for the Word" (LW 2:39). Indeed this is an "adulterous, crooked and perverse" place (Mt 16:4, 17:17; Phil 2:15). So Luther was right to conclude that "to live rightly in this present world . . . is like living soberly in a saloon [and] chastely in a brothel, [for] the character of the world is such as to render our earthly life difficult and distressing" (SML 6:129; LW 75:198). "O how horrible and full of danger," Luther bemoans, "are the times on which we wretched men have fallen!" (LW 8:310).

The Method

How then shall we get rid of this world and replace it with a new and better one? Shall we, like those first Americans, fire another "shot heard 'round the world," like that one back in 1775—which ended up in eight years of furious fighting largely between rebel colonialists and loyal colonialists?[3] No, not at all.

Our rebellion will be verbal instead. For Jesus said that because his kingdom was not of this world, his followers were not to fight with swords and knives, clubs and fists, but only by witnessing to the truth in words and deeds (Jn 18:36–37). This is what it's like to "wage the good warfare" (1 Tm 1:18; Eph 6:10–17). So just as God called forth the first world out of the nothingness of that dark void long ago by a single divine word (Gn 1:1–3), so this new world will come into existence by that word of the Lord one more time (Rom 4:17; LW 13:52; 33:52). And that word will make a new world by keeping believers from conforming to the ghastly and disgusting old world (Rom 12:2; 1 Jn 2:15). And as non-conformists, we will be "troublers" like Elijah of old (1 Kgs 18:17).

Therefore the new world will always be struggling against the old one for prominence. And that enduring struggle (Jn 16:33) will not abate until the end of time when the enduring heavenly city, the Holy Jerusalem, descends out of the heavens (Heb 11:16, 13:14; Rv 21:1–4). But until then, as Luther

---

3 See Thomas B. Allen, *Tories: Fighting for the King in America's First Civil War* (New York: HarperCollins. 2010).

knew and taught, "the church of Satan [will be] everlastingly at war with the church of God" (LW 2:27)! So above all, endure (Mk 13:13)!

The Alternative

But what exactly will we be looking for and eagerly awaiting (Heb 9:28)? What sort of a new, alien world is on its way by the power of the word of the Lord? Well, it'll be one not based on amassing great material possessions (Lk 12:15), nor on lording it over others (Mk 10:42-43). Instead, praising God will be the major concern (Col 3:16; Heb 12:28-29). In this world we'll think better of others than of ourselves (Phil 2:3) and so there'll be no room for self-love (Jn 12:25). We'll share what we have (Acts 4:34). God's word will not be interpreted but simply believed in (2 Pt 2:20; Lk 11:28). Indecency and promiscuity will be set aside (1 Cor 6:9; Eph 5:5). Pleasure-seeking will not have a high priority (Rom 13:14; 2 Tm 3:4). And we'll help our enemies turn around to become our friends (Mt 5:44).

Our Unattractive Savior

So how can we begin to bring about this upheaval—and the sooner the better? Well, once again, all we can do is witness to the word that promises us this new world. There we learn that it is Christ who is "reconciling the world to himself," by bearing our sins in himself so that we will not be punished for them but live a righteous life (2 Cor 5:19–21). Christ's work on the cross is what brings about the new, redeemed world. But as Luther notes,

> the world has no inclination to accept Christ in . . . his unattractive earthly form. [For] he does not bring the things it desires—worldly power, honor and riches, and praise and approval of

> its own wisdom . . . . It is completely sunk . . . in lust and love of riches . . . . Especially does it repel the suggestion that worldly reputation and honor, temporal wisdom . . . and holiness should be denounced and reduced to sin and shame before God . . . . Hence the Gospel is believed only by a few simple people, who are not offended at the unattractive figure of the cross of Christ. (SML 3:326; LW 77:352)

So Christ blesses those who are not ashamed of him, and curses those who are (Mk 8:38). Therefore be sure to repent of your sins. Beg for mercy. Trust in God. And come to the Altar today for help—by eating of the bread and drinking from the cup of the Lord's Supper. For then you'll begin to live with Christ, and in his new world of love and mercy (1 Cor 10:16)! For "the Lord's Supper welcomes those who perceive their frailties and feel that they are not pious, yet would like to be" (SML 2:208; LW 76:444)!

Sacramental Neighborliness

And finally know that when we receive Christ in the sacrament

> we must not allow ourselves to become indolent, but must be diligent . . . to . . . aid our neighbor in distress . . . when he . . . requires assistance. When you fail to do this you are not a Christian . . . . You will be sure [that the Lord's Supper] is efficacious in [you] if you . . . . discover that the words and the symbol . . . . soften and move you to be friendly, . . . then it is well, [for] the sacrament is to act

upon us so that we may be transformed and become different people.(SML 2:210–11, 214; LW 76:446, 448)

Amen.

Sermon 26

Fear the Fires of Hell

Since the time of Bernard of Clairvaux (1091–1153) we have been afraid that our good intentions will do us in. For the adage probably came from him that "the way to hell is paved with good intentions." As unbelievable as it may sound, something good—good intentions—can lead us straight to hell. This, of course, is because they are not good enough. What is needed in addition to good intentions is a good life with good deeds to stay out of hell.

Now, as if this fear of hell were not enough, our Lord Jesus teaches us something even worse. In Luke 12:5 he tells us to "fear him who, after he has killed you, has power to cast you into hell, yes, . . . fear him!" Here Jesus tells us to fear something more than dying—even if our death were from some murderous rampage. No, here we are told to fear the one who can kill us and then cast us into hell. And that one is God himself (LW 67:107). So fearing hell is increased by also fearing the one who can send you there.

God Damns Sinners

God therefore is to be feared. For he is the one who has prepared hell for the damned, who are those who reject his dear Son Jesus Christ. For God is no pussy cat. He's a fierce bear or a poisonous snake (Am 5:19). He creates weal and woe (Is 45:7). He can be quite tough. This is because of our idolatry and sin. It provokes him to anger, over and over again! (Jgs 2:14).[1]

Indeed, the Lord "hates those who pay regard to vain idols" (Ps 31:6). So even though God is famously "slow to anger" (Ex 34:6), that does not mean he never blows his top. For harsh judgment is in him also. This judgment he hands down to his Son, Christ Jesus (Jn 5:27). And this includes putting into his hands "the keys of Death and Hades," or hell (Rv 1:18). So it is clear that God is the one who has prepared hell for those who cross his path (Mt 25:41)!

That Place of Torment

This place is terrible, because hell is more than an attitude, disposition or troubled state of mind. It's more than one of those dark nights of the soul which we sometimes call "hell on earth." No, hell is much more substantial than that. It isn't so ephemeral. It rather is an actual place. In Luke 16:28 Jesus says hell is a "place of torment." The old Latin Bible translates this as *locum tormentorum*. So hell is a place or a real location to be feared.

Hell is a place of torture and anguish that goes on and on without end. It is utterly horrible. When you've gone to hell you are stuck there—hemmed in, if you will, on all sides. A great "chasm" (Lk 16:26) separates you from the blessed and God's mercies (Is 59:2; 2 Thes 1:9). *Locum tormentorum*, indeed!

Hell is so severe because Christ is so wonderful. In this torment, extremes are matched (SML 6:181; LW 75:267). By rejecting Christ the Lord, one commits a horrendous wrong. Punishment for this is therefore massive and unnerving.

---

1 See also Jgs 2:20, 3:8, 12, 4:2, 6:1, 9:23, 56, 10:7.

We see this matching up of infraction and retribution in Luke 20:18. There we hear that those who reject Jesus (Lk 20:15) will be "broken to pieces . . . and crushed"!—finished off in "a miserable death" (Mt 21:41)!

Negative Pedagogy

All of this is horrible beyond measure. Human sympathy demands that we say there's nothing good in it. Clearly we would never wish anything like this even on our worst of enemies. If we did, we would be acting like bloodthirsty beasts.

But all of God's judgments are right and good and just (Ps 119:137; Rv 16:7)—regardless of how we feel about them. So those who go to hell belong there. And the extent of their pain and suffering isn't unjust—though it may seem so to us.

But this spectacle of suffering is not for divine or human entertainment. No one is to gloat over the anguished souls in hell (Prv 24:17). We are to react in quite another way. Their suffering is to be a "warning" (1 Cor 10:6, 11). It's negative pedagogy, if you will. It's a way of teaching us by a bad example. It's telling us to steer clear of that mess. It's showing us what to avoid.

Hafenreffer's Hell

So the picture of hell needs to be kept clearly before us—in all of its excruciating detail. We must not let hell—this place of torment, *locum tormentorum*—fade from our sight.

To do this, we need help. This is because it's easy for us to skip over hell. It's easy to let the word hell degenerate into slang expressions, or become the butt of bad jokes, or simply fodder for cartoon strips.

To our rescue comes Matthew Hafenreffer (1561–1619), an esteemed German Lutheran teacher, born in that first generation, shortly after the death of Martin Luther on February 18,

1546. He no doubt learned from Luther about the horrors of hell. In hell, Luther wrote, the damned shall be "afflicted with every pain, distress, grief, and misery, burn eternally without a little drop of water with which to refresh themselves, . . . and furthermore . . . they shall be bereft both of God and of all His grace and gifts . . . . How can they be plagued more horribly and severely?" (LW 28:144–45)!

So it's not surprising that in Hafenreffer's *Loci Theologici* he paints a startling picture of the ravages of hell. Here are his memorable words:

> The punishments of Hell . . . . are the most exquisite pains of soul and body, . . . arising from the fear and sense of the most just wrath and vengeance of God against sins, the most sad consciousness of which they carry about with them, the baseness of which is manifest, and of which, likewise, no remission afterwards, and, therefore, no mitigation or end can be hoped for. Whence, in misery, they will execrate [or curse], with horrible lamentation and wailing, their former impiety, by which they carelessly neglected the commandments of the Lord, the admonitions of their brethren, and all the means of attaining salvation; but in vain. For in perpetual anguish, with dreadful trembling, in shame, confusion, and ignominy, in inextinguishable fire, in weeping and gnashing of teeth, amidst that which is eternal and terrible,

torn away from the grace and favor of God, they must quake among devils, and be tortured without end to eternity.[2]

These bone-chilling words shock us—and arouse us. So they're good for us. They open our eyes. So they're worth dwelling on, bit by bit—uncomfortable though that may be. Therefore mull them over. Don't flee from them. Instead consider them carefully.

Pondering Perdition

Take to heart the following six excerpts from Hafenreffer's paragraph that your eyes may be turned "from looking at vanities" (Ps 119:37)! By way of these six lines, ponder the destruction and perdition of hell.

1. Most Exquisite Pains. No earthly pain will surpass the fires of hell. So suffering in hell will be the most exquisite—striking both body and soul. Our thoughts will terrify us and keep us awake at night. Our flesh and bones will ache with pain—leaving us weak and quivering.

2. The Most Just Wrath of God. The damned will know that hell is their just dessert. All debates will have come to an end. Contesting God's judgments will be out of the question. Why? What of all of our defiance? What's become of our sinful indignation and fist-shaking against the high heavens? It all will have been smothered by the indisputable realization that God is right and the damned are wrong (LW 51:318). Our complaining mouths will be shut tight (Rom 3:19)! The damned will know they haven't a philosophical or theological

---

2 *The Doctrinal Theology of the Evangelical Lutheran Church* (1875), Third Edition, ed. Heinrich Schmid, trans. Charles A. Hay and Henry E. Jacobs (Minneapolis: Augsburg, 1961) 658.

leg to stand on. They, like Job of old, will shut their mouths all by themselves (Job 40:4–5). God won't have to do it for them. Shame will shut them up instead.

3. *The Most Sad Consciousness.* All that's left then is sorrow. No thrashing around. No scheming to get out. Nothing but sadness. The power of God's truth will crush the excuses and appeals of the damned. None of them will be able to push off that crushing defeat. That God is right will be unassailable. Damnation in hell will be accepted and respected by all—even those in hell will bow down before the Lord (Phil 2:10)!

4. *Cursing Oneself in Vain.* Then insult will be added to injury. In addition to God's damnation, the damned will damn themselves mercilessly! Yes, because they now see the truth by the light of the fires of hell, they will curse themselves for their stupidity and stubbornness. They will bemoan that they were an "impudent and stubborn . . . . and rebellious house" (Ez 2:4–6)—that they were happy and smug participants in an "evil and adulterous generation" (Mt 12:39). Like Peter, they will "weep bitterly" for their sin (Mt 26:75). But unlike Peter, their weeping will be too late. The door to heaven, wide open for the repentant on earth, will now be slammed shut in the afterlife (Mt 25:10)! Horror of horrors!

5. *In Perpetual Anguish.* And this hell will be no purgatory, that is, some short period of cleansing before one's eventual entry into the joys and peace of heaven. No! Hell is everlasting. Period—regardless of what the Qur'an says (Q11:106–107). There are no ifs, ands or buts. Once in hell, a "great chasm" (Lk 16:26) divides the damned from heaven. That means all late entries into heaven from hell are cut off. Such an escape will be impossible. Not even death can put an end to the fires of hell (Rv 9.6). Those fires, then, are truly "unquenchable" (Mt 3:12; Mk 9:48).

6. Quaking Among Devils. In hell you are tortured relentlessly. In a supposed humor piece, the comedian Jack Handey tries to imagine what this quaking among devils would be like.³ As his first day in hell draws to a close, he sees the demons asleep. "They look so innocent," he says, "it's hard to believe that just a few hours ago they were raping and torturing us." The food there is pretty good, he writes, but the "trouble is, just about all of it is poisoned. So a few minutes after you finish eating you're doubled over in agony. The weird thing is, as soon as you recover you're ready to dig in all over again." Then after greeting Satan upon first seeing him, he was "immediately set upon by demons" for speaking out of turn. "I can't begin to describe the tortures they inflicted on me.... Suffice it to say that, even as you endure all the pain, you find yourself thinking, Wow, how did they think of that?"

SCARED STRAIGHT

So thank God for Matthew Hafenreffer! Don't listen to the therapists who say this kind of thing is psychologically damaging. No! Thank God instead for his description of hell. Don't listen to the revisionists who say it's all mythological and silly.⁴ No! Thank God instead for Hafenreffer's detailed description of hell—and that of Handey's as well.

Their words, after all, are classic. I think they even surpass those of the great John Milton in *Paradise Lost* (1667), where he says that "death be not one stroke, as I supposed, . . . but endless misery."⁵ And they also surpass those of the legendary

---

3   "My First Day in Hell," *The New Yorker* (October 30, 2006) 52. See also Ronald F. Marshall, *Kierkegaard for the Church*, 210n25.
4   See, for example, the revisionist, John Shelby Spong, *Why Christianity Must Change or Die* (New York: HarperCollins, 1998) 200–219.
5   *John Milton: The Complete English Poems*, Revised, ed. Gordon Campbell (New York: Knopf, 1992) 389.

Jonathan Edwards in his classic American sermon, "Sinners in the Hands of an Angry God" (1741), where he says that the damned in hell wrestle forever with an "almighty merciless vengeance, ... crying in extreme misery and perfect despair."[6]

So thank God for Matthew Hafenreffer and Jack Handey. Their pictures of hell are salutary. Believe it or not, they can actually scare you straight. And that's good. For just consider with Luther, that the wrath of God and the fires of hell can actually drive you straight to Christ—*agitatur ad Christum* (LW 16:232). So don't listen to those who say such words will only hurl you into despair, dread and depression. Don't listen to those who say such fear is no good for you (LW 67: 56-57). Instead trust Luther's line that such fear is what drives you to Christ—*agitatur ad Christum!*

There's More than Fear

Now, I know what you know. I know that it's true that there's more to Christianity than fearing the fires of hell. You're right. There's more than being rescued from hell. We also love Jesus now because of his wisdom. And we believe in him now so we can be more loving. We also believe so we can have peace and joy now. We believe so we can be a part of the church. We believe so we can help out in this world. For faith in Jesus makes us stronger people now.

But be that as it may, don't forget about the fires of hell. While they don't tell the whole story about our life with God, they are crucial. Forgetting them will stop our faith from growing. For we must always be watching out lest we fall (1 Cor 10:12; Heb 3:12). Lutherans teach, you remember, that just because we're baptized and believe, doesn't mean we'll never fall

---

6 *American Sermons: The Pilgrims to Martin Luther King Jr.*, ed. Michael Warner (New York: The Library of America, 1999) 361, 362.

away from Christ (BC 35). So the fires of hell are important for Christians. They help keep us serious. And they also can help show others the way to Christ (1 Cor 14:24–25; Rom 2:5–10; Acts 2:37).

Of Surpassing Worth

Now what happens when the fires of hell drive us to Christ? What can he do for us? How does Christ relieve our fears and save us from going to hell?

In Christ we have the one of "surpassing worth" [υπερεχον] (Phil 3:8–9). This is because in him we have a value or worth that goes beyond what we can muster on our own, by being good and decent. When we live with Christ, by entrusting our lives to him, we no longer worry about the past. Our mistakes and omissions no longer plague us. Now, like Saint Paul, we can truly forget what lies behind us and press on "for the prize of the upward call of God in Christ Jesus" (Phil 3:13–14).

This is amazing. It's even miraculous! Just think of it—the past will no longer haunt us. But it haunts everybody, you say! Yes indeed, but not those who entrust their lives to Christ. That burden is lifted. How does he do this?

Colossians 2:13–14 says Christ cancels the legal bond that stands against us, or *contrarium nobis*, as the Old Latin Bible puts it. This legal bond is from God's law that says all sinners must be punished. No sins escape God's judgment and all sins are punished. Because of this, God's wrath and threats weigh heavily upon us. But Christ puts an end to all of this.

He doesn't, however, lift our burden by changing the rules and saying our sin no longer matters. He doesn't cancel this debt by simple declaration. No, something far more ghastly has to happen, for indeed, there is no forgiveness without the shedding of blood (Heb 9:22).

Canceling Our Debt

And that is precisely what Jesus does. He cancels the bond that stands against us by "nailing it to the cross" (Col 2:14). This he does by being himself nailed to the cross for us. By so doing he is punished in our place. This happens by having all our sins inflicted on his body (1 Pt 2:24). The whips and rods that bruised him, the nails driven into him, the spear jammed into his side, all these were the sins of the world—piercing into his flesh (LW 42:9).

Now when he is so punished for our sins, our punishment then ends. Therefore we no longer have to fear being punished. The curse is lifted and we are set free (Gal 3:13; 5:1). So give thanks to God for this wonder! Do so by glorifying Christ himself. You can sing praise to Christ using these grand words:

> Glory be to Jesus,
> Who in bitter pains,
> Poured for me the lifeblood
> From his sacred veins....
> Blest through endless ages
> Be that precious stream
> Which from endless torment
> Did the world redeem.[7]

Preach the Whole Counsel of God

And when we're done singing, let us also do good works in honor of Christ—knowing that faith without works is dead (Jas 2:26). Let us do that by seeing to it that the whole counsel of God's word is preached (Acts 20:27). Let us therefore support sermons that testify to both the fear and the hope, the fright

---

[7] *Lutheran Book of Worship* (Minneapolis: Augsburg, 1978) Hymn 95.

and the peace. Let us not shrink back from encouraging the church to preach and teach both the kindness and the severity of God (Rom 11:22).

Søren Kierkegaard, that astute reader of Luther, gives this combination memorable formulation in his book, *Christian Discourses*. There he writes that

> it is easy to win people by enticing; it is also easy to frighten them away by repelling. But, if possible, with a fervent inwardness that no one could resist, to invite them to come, and in addition with a terror that could teach even the bravest to shudder, . . . indeed that is difficult, ... [but that is the only way] to steer rightly.
> (CD 175)

Let just that sort of difficult way, then, be our good work today (Matthew 7:14)! Amen.

Sermon 27

Long for Christ's Return

Tightly linked to the Holy Ascension of Our Lord Jesus Christ into heaven, to rule over all with his Father forever (Eph 1:20–23), is his promise to return one day to us in glory, in order to judge the living and the dead (Jn 5:22; 2 Tm 4:1), and to destroy this world and make a new and better one (2 Pt 3:11–13). Now that's a mouthful if there ever was one—but it still deserves our closest attention and praise. For so we, just like the men of old in Galilee, are told in Acts 1:11, "Why do you stand looking into heaven? This Jesus, who was taken up from you into heaven, will come in the same way as you saw him go into heaven."

Warning

Now even though this teaching is true and deeply embedded in the creeds of the church, we still bristle at hearing about Christ's return. Take, for example, the famous bishop, John Spong, who says "I must dismiss the idea of God as a record-keeping deity before whom I shall appear on the day of judgment to have my eternal destination announced, [for] my heart will never worship that which my mind has rejected."[1] Now as astonishing as this denial is, that doesn't make it unheard of. For it's even in the Bible (2 Pt 3:3)!

---

1 John Shelby Spong, *Why Christianity Must Change or Die* (New York: HarperCollins, 1998) 210.

And Martin Luther, our most eminent teacher (BC 576), is well aware of criticisms like those of Bishop Spong, and wrote many pages analyzing them. In his 1523 Sermons on Second Peter he argues against these criticisms, saying that the Holy Scripture

> warns us . . . to be prepared and to expect the Last Day every moment. [The Bible urges and impel us] not to neglect [the] understanding of what a true Christian life is. [For] the number of those who do not believe that the Last Day will come has always been rather large. [Nevertheless, Christ] will appear swiftly, unexpectedly, and suddenly, when the world will be living in the greatest smugness and will be making light of God's Word. Therefore the nearness of the Last Day will be betokened when people live just as they please, following their passions [and not worrying since] the world has been standing for such a long time and has always remained. (LW 30:191–93)

Because of these assaults, Luther not only thought that we should watch out for these false teachers, but also that we should constantly be occupied, "day to day [with] God's Word" (LW 30:199).

Christ at the Gates

And in God's word we're not left in the dark. For in Mark 13:7–29 Jesus explains in over 20 verses that just as it's a sign that summer's on its way when the fig tree "puts forth its leaves," so Christ is "at the very gates," and ready to enter in and judge us, when we hear of wars and rumors of wars, [and there are] earthquakes in various places [and famines], [and] the gospel is being preached to all nations, [and] Christians are being hated by all for Jesus' sake, [and] false Christs and false prophets . . . arise and show signs and wonders, to lead astray, if possible, the elect . . . . And when the sun [is] darkened, and the moon [doesn't] give its light, and the stars [are] falling from heaven.

This list of indicators is striking to say the least. But equally striking is the fact, that for generations and generations there have been those who have bet money on knowing, and have mounted worldwide campaigns because they were sure they knew, the hour and day when Christ was returning.[2] Most noteworthy among these debacles is the case of William Miller (1782–1849) who said Christ was returning on October 22, 1844—and when he didn't, moved it to the same day the next year. This double failure was then called "the great disappointment." Others predicted Christ's return in 1874, 1914, 1918, 1920, 1941, 1975, 1988 and in 1999. And in our day, Harold Camping predicted it on May 21, 2011.[3]

Since all these predictions leave out our Lord's words in Mark 13:32 that no one can know the exact day and time of his return—even with these indicators—the preoccupation over knowing the exact day and time is nothing but sin. So if you're caught up in it, repent in Jesus' name and give up this fool's errand. Luther, mind you, was even caught up in this—thinking

---

[2] See John MacArthur, *The Second Coming: Signs of Christ's Return and the End of the Age* (Wheaton, Illinois: Crossway, 1999).

[3] "Radio Host Says He Was Off on Rapture by Five Months," *The Seattle Times* (May 24, 2011).

that all the degradation around him was a sure sign that Christ was returning during his life time (LW 34:223; 35:315–16; 60:149, 302, 67:374). And Kierkegaard—who could be called the Danish Luther—sympathized, writing that to be a true Christian is so agonizing that it would not be endurable if one did not continually expect Christ's second coming as imminent, [and not] coming sometime many centuries hence (JP 1:340).

A Brood of Serpents

Even so, fixating on the exact time of Christ's return is like looking at a car crash—we can't seem to stop doing it. And that's because we're so corrupt. Luther spells this out with fierce sarcasm:

> There is nought in man but . . . all manner of mischief. Indeed his nature is nothing else than a liar . . . . And why? . . . . The heart is not good; therefore also the rivers flowing therefrom cannot be good. Hence does the Lord oftimes call men a generation of vipers and a brood of serpents. Is not this a beautiful title for man?
> (SML 5:301)

This devastating view of ourselves renders us helpless to improve our lot in life. That's why Saint Paul famously cries out in Romans 7:24, "Who will deliver me from this body of death?"

Seize Christ

Left to ourselves, there surely would be no hope for us—"no counsel, no help, no comfort," as the catechism puts it (BC 414). But thanks be to God that we are not left with just this! So, "cast all your anxieties on God, because he cares for you" (1 Pt 5:7). "Set your hope fully upon . . . Jesus Christ," by whom "you were ransomed from [your] futile ways . . . with [his] precious blood" (1 Pt 1:13, 18). Then, sing with Luther that "Christ is the greatest and highest person" who ever lived (SML 5:331). That's because

> through his suffering and death [he makes] satisfaction for sins and [pays] for them. This is the price that has been set, and . . . by which . . . the wrath of God [is] appeased, the Father has been reconciled [*deus placatus*][4] and made our friend. Christians alone . . . believe . . . this, [and so are] different from . . . every other [religion] . . . . For it is ordained that no one shall . . . find grace . . . except through Christ. [So] you will not find anything in your heart with which you can pay [your sins] off, nor . . . .for which God might . . . cancel your debt. . . But if you seize Christ as the one who has become your substitute,[5] . . . no sin can avail anything against you. (SML 5:221–22)

No wonder then that Luther adds that when Christ entered as the only Savior, it disrupted the peace of that famous, ancient "Pantheon, or the church of all gods," which "had more . . . idolatries than a dog has fleas." And so everyone "went quite mad [and] slew the apostles and martyrs" (LW 34:213). But don't let that stop you from believing in Christ. And don't let that stop you from receiving him today in the Lord's Supper. For as Luther says, a Christian life isn't normal, but far "above natural life," noting that

---

4   See LW 30:280; 12:377.
5   See LW 22:167.

> first, it despises self; secondly, it loves and thirsts for contempt; thirdly, it punishes everything that is unwilling to be despised, by which it resigns itself to all misfortune; fourthly, it is also despised and persecuted on account of such contempt and punishment; [and] fifthly, it does not think itself worthy to suffer such persecution. (SML 5:96)

Wow! But recall—we're supposed to be "aliens" (1 Pt 2:11)—and so we should actually be hankering after all five of these points! With Kierkegaard we should be struggling to quit being "cluttered up with finiteness" (JP 5:5891). And that struggle will make Christianity "a plague to the natural man" (JP 3:2711)—since "the natural man is lazy and weak and sensate, and Christianity is the absolute" (JP 6:6237).

Hasten His Return

So, having seized Christ through faith, and having come to an understanding of how unnatural and peculiar being a Christian is (1 Pt 2:9, KJV), let us not think that faith "is a sleepy, lazy thing in the soul, [but] a thoroughly . . . powerful thing [that] creates [an altogether] new heart, [and] a new man." And let us also recall that "the Holy Spirit is given us, who kindles a new . . . fire in us, namely, love and [the] desire to do God's commandments" (SML 5:65, 189)!

On this day, then, heed the implied command to "eagerly await" Christ's return (Heb 9:28)—even though we don't know when that exactly will be. But let us still do so in order that we might actually "hasten" its coming (2 Pt 3:12). And we should want to do this because on that day, evil will end (Rom 6:6), and all will defer to Christ (Phil 2:9–11). And that would surely be a better state of affairs than what we now have (Heb 11:16)! So that's why, even though we don't know the exact day of his return, that we still should hope—and every day hope—that today is the day when Christ returns. Amen.

Appendix One

On Judaism

What Kierkegaard has to say about Judaism goes along with his deep conviction that the Christian life, according to the New Testament, is nothing but "sheer anguish, misery, and wretchedness" (TM 169)[1]—albeit with some honor coming at the end for humble believers in Christ.[2] Kierkegaard writes about this sober understanding of Christianity again and again because the church[3] reversed it in his day—falsely making Christianity into a "gentle comfort," a sheer "enjoyment of life" (FSE 80; TM 42).[4] Because this "softening" up (JP 6:6912)

---

1 See also Mt 10:16; Lk 9:23, 16:16; Jn 15:18–19, 16:33; Rom 6:6, 7:24; 1 Cor 4:9–13; 2 Cor 6:3–10; Gal 6:14; Col 3:9; Heb 11:32–38; 1 Pt 4:12–13.
2 See Lk 6:22–23; Acts 5:41.
3 On this condemnation of the institutional church or Christendom, he writes: "It is the other and really decisive side of Christianity which has been abolished in Christendom. Christianity has become a doctrine; but conversion, rebirth, imitation, dying away from this world, renunciation, self-denial, etc.—they are as if blown away . . . . To be a Christian in Christendom in plain and simple conformity is just as impossible as doing gymnastics in a straightjacket" (JP 1:397, 409). Early on Kierkegaard hints at this same problem: "[God] does not want a person to be spiritually soft and to bathe in the contemplation of his glory, but in becoming known by a person he wants to create in him a new human being" (EUD 325).
4 Kierkegaard calls it a "downright falsehood" that Christianity is thought of in this way: "It is an extraordinary benefaction that you came into existence, it is a nice world you came into, and God is a nice

of Christianity was so entrenched and difficult to expose and correct,[5] Kierkegaard enlisted the help of Judaism to give true Christianity the bold relief it needs to correct itself.[6] "It cannot be made clear, often enough," he writes in his journal,

> that Judaism is linked to Christianity in order to make Christianity negatively recognizable—negatively, that is, by the repulsion .... [For] Christianity could not have had any

---

fellow; just stay with him, he very likely will not fulfill all your wishes, but he certainly does help" (TM 252). See also Lk 12:18–21; as well as Luther's comment in his Large Catechism that this life is not supposed to be "a nice, soft life without the cross and suffering" (BC 392).

5 So Kierkegaard writes: "Rare in any generation is a person who exercises the power over himself to be able to *will* what does not please him, so that he is able to hold firmly to the truth that does not please him, to hold firmly to its being the truth although it does not please him, and then, although it does not please him, is able to will to become involved with it" (TM 170).

6 See Kierkegaard's noteworthy fairness to the Jewish editor of *The Corsair*, Meir Goldschmidt (1819–1887). Even though Kierkegaard detested the coverage he was given in the pages of *The Corsair*, he still honored Goldschmidt's talent. Regarding his novel, *En Jøde* (1845), Kierkegaard writes: "In various countries, Jews are generally regarded as cowards, and yet it is a fact that there is a strong propensity in young Jewish men to go around dressed as officers and wanting to look like officers. Goldschmidt's novel . . . emphasizes this point with psychological mastery, which always indicates experience and familiarity with life, something for which the author of this novel must always be commended" (COR 191).

other religion as a foreground, because none[7] negatively manifests Christianity as definitely, as decisively, as Judaism does.[8] (JP 2:2227)

For some this backhanded compliment is faint praise. But Kierkegaard explains that Judaism helps out Christianity by "the deifying of marriage, . . . in the conception of the continuation of the race as a kind of divine worship—and then [for Jesus] to be born of a virgin! Fundamentally this negates the whole Old Testament or deprives it of its power" (JP 2:2227). This produces a confrontation between these two religions that

---

7   For a more extreme form of this linkage—in contrast to Kierkegaard's—see Paul F. Knitter, *Without Buddha I Could Not Be a Christian* (Oxford: Oneworld, 2009) 214–15: "There is no such thing as a neatly defined, once-for-all identity . . . . We're constantly changing and we're changing through the hybridizing process of interacting with others who often are very different from us . . . . We have an identity, but that identity in its origins and in its ongoing life comes to be and continues to flourish only through mixing it up with others. Hybrids are stronger, live longer, and have more fun than purebreds . . . . [So even] though my primary allegiance is to Christ and the gospel, my Christian experience and beliefs have not dominated nor always had to trump what I learned or experienced through Buddha."

8   Others do not see this contrast in such sharp terms. On this approach see Merold Westphal, *Levinas and Kierkegaard in Dialogue* (Bloomington and Indianapolis: Indiana University, 2008) 5: "I do not see the difference as essentially a Jewish-Christian debate, . . . it rather points to issues that arise within both traditions as they seek to answer the questions Who is the God of the Bible? and Who are we? I believe some who think primarily within Christian horizons will be conceptually closer to Levinas, and some who think within Jewish horizons will be conceptually closer to Kierkegaard. The question concerns the meaning of monotheism, prior to questions about Messiah, or Incarnation, or Trinity." Westphal's study, however, does not consider the many entries that I assemble from Kierkegaard's journals on the stark contrast between Christianity and Judaism.

sheds light on the essence of Christianity—which is otherwise obscured by the counterfeits vying to overthrow Christianity in the culture:

> Judaism established family life as a form of godliness. Christianity explodes all this by the absoluteness of the God-relationship, which can lead to hating father and mother.[9] Judaism is godliness which is at home in this world; Christianity is alienation from this world. In Judaism the reward of godliness is blessing in this world; Christianity is hate toward this world.[10] The collisions of piety which Christianity itself announces it will bring about must be regarded by the Jews as impiety, consequently as far as possible from being the expression of godliness. (JP 2:2221)

There is a judgment against Judaism in this contrast, all right, that is not universally shared[11]—which holds that Judaism is limited to prospering in this life, whereas Christianity looks

---

9   See Lk 14:26. On this verse, Kierkegaard's Johannes de Silentio says: "This is a hard saying. Who can bear to listen to it? This is the reason, too, that we seldom hear it. But this silence is only an escape that is of no avail" (FT 72). It matches for Kierkegaard the trauma of Abraham's near sacrifice of Isaac in Genesis 22.
10 See 1 Jn 2:15.
11 For a critique of this assessment of Judaism, see Jon D. Levenson, "Did God Forgive Adam? An Exercise in Comparative Midrash," in *Jews and Christians: People of God*, ed. Carl E. Braaten and Robert W. Jenson (Grand Rapids: Eerdmans, 2003) 169, 155: "[The] overwhelming tendency in the Christian tradition is to see Jesus as playing a critical role, indeed *the* critical role, in the drama of sin and forgiveness. The overwhelming tendency in the Jewish tradition, on the other hand, is to see

beyond this world.¹² So for Kierkegaard, Judaism is a form of humanism bereft of all spirit and any hope of eternal life (JP 2:2218; 1:843). He even says that "the psalms of David" lack the Christian spirit because they promise that "God will smash his enemies [or at least] hold back their attack" (JP 6:6276). In the Psalter "God intervenes in this life, jumps right in" so you will be "able to turn back quickly from the wrong way if you were on it." In Christianity, however, "God has pulled back, as it were," and lets us suffer, "for it is rigorousness on his part to deny you the childish supervision and to assign only eternity for judgment" (JP 2:2222). Unlike Judaism, Christianity says that the "more you adhere to and involve yourself with God, the worse it becomes for you" (2:1899). "For while man by nature wishes for what can give him pleasure in life, the religious person on active duty needs a proper dose of disgust with life in order to be fit for the task; disgust with life . . . is the

---

repentance as effective in reconciling sinners to God—quite without messianic intervention . . . [And] Paul's supposed pessimism [is often contrasted] with the optimism about human potential supposedly characteristic of Judaism . . . . [But] this cheery view of Judaism [I will challenge]." For a partial Jewish confirmation of Kierkegaard's views of Judaism, see Jacob Neusner, *Jews and Christians: The Myth of a Common Tradition* (London: SCM, 1991) 28: "Christians want to know . . . why the Jews did (and do) not 'accept Christ' . . . . To me as a rabbi, the answer to that question is simple: Judaism and Christianity are completely different religions, not different versions of one religion." Note also David Klinghoffer, *Why the Jews Rejected Jesus: The Turning Point in Western History* (New York: Doubleday, 2005) 100: "The Talmud is replete with discussions of the afterlife, which will follow the resurrection of the dead, and the Hebrew Bible also alludes to it, if in veiled fashion." Because this reference to eternal life is veiled may be why Kierkegaard did not think it was there.

12 See Lk 14:14; Jn 5:29, 14:3; 1 Cor 15:19; Phil 3:20; Heb 9:28.

best safeguard against getting involved in stupid nonsense" (JP 6:6932). Judaism cannot help us with that disgust because it enjoys this life too much (TM 42)—*L'chaim!*[13]

LUTHER'S ALLEGED ANTI-SEMITISM

Kierkegaard links this view of Judaism with Luther (JP 3:2525). Like Kierkegaard, Luther also saw the necessity for offense in the Christian proclamation—disgust with this life, as it were. No wonder, then, that Kierkegaard thought of Luther as "the master of us all" (JP 3:2465),[14] and that he may even be Luther's "true successor" (JP 3:2518). But this glorification of Luther creates problems. That is because many have rejected Luther because of his alleged[15] anti-Semitism or supposed hatred of the Jews—even with American Lutherans condemning him twice for it at their national conventions in

---

13 See *To Life! L'Chaim! Prayers and Blessings for the Jewish Home*, ed. Rabbi Michael Shire (San Francisco: Chronicle Books, 2000). Some take Kierkegaard's critique to be anti-Semitic. See *The Oxford Handbook of Kierkegaard*, 3, 6, referring to Peter Tudvad, *Studier på Antisemitismens Vej. Søren Kierkegaard og Jøderne* (Copenhagen: Rosinante, 2010).

14 Some see this accolade as being short-lived. See, for instance, David Yoon-Jung and Joel D. S. Rasmussen, "Martin Luther: Reform, Secularization, and the Question of His 'True Successor,'" in *Kierkegaard and the Renaissance and Modern Traditions: Tome II Theology*, ed. Jon Stewart (Surrey, England: Ashgate, 2009) 195: "Kierkegaard comes more and more to hold Luther himself responsible for the Protestant misconstrual of the law-gospel dialectic." I, however, give more prominence to Kierkegaard's own qualification of his criticisms of Luther (JP 2:1922).

15 See Carl Stamm Meyer, "Luther's Alleged Anti-Semitism," *Concordia Theological Monthly* 32 (November 1961): 695: "Luther's pronouncements against the Jews were not racial but religious."

1974[16] and 1994.[17] These critics say that Luther spews forth

---

16 See "The American Lutheran Church and the Jewish Community" (Minneapolis: ALC, 1974) Section II: Confrontation: "That the Nazi period fostered a revival of Luther's own medieval hostility toward Jews, as expressed in pugnacious writings, is a special cause of regret. Those who study and admire Luther should acknowledge unequivocally that his anti-Jewish writings are beyond any defense." See also the condemnation of Luther as an anti-Semite in "Declaration of the Bishops' Conference of the United Evangelical-Lutheran Church of Germany and of the Synod of the Evangelical Church of Germany – Martin Luther and the Jews: A Necessary Reminder on the Occasion of the Reformation Anniversary, Bremen, 11 November 2015," *Lutheran Forum* 50 (Summer 2016) 51: "According to our present understanding, Luther's view of Judaism and his invective against Jews contradict his faith in the one God who revealed himself in Jesus the Jew. Luther's judgment upon Israel therefore does not correspond to the biblical statements on God's covenant faithfulness to his people and the lasting election of Israel.... [Of particular concern are] the distinctions 'law and gospel,' 'promise and fulfillment,' 'faith and works' and 'old and new covenant'" (§§10–11).

17 Rosemary Dyson, "ELCA Rejects Luther's Anti-Semitism," *The Lutheran* (July 1994): 38: "The Declaration of the Evangelical Lutheran Church in America to the Jewish Community distances the church from Martin Luther's anti-Jewish remarks . . . . Luther shared in the cultural anti-Semitism of his time. This is especially true of tracts written in 1543 and after, including *Against the Jews and Their Lies*." On this decision see Franklin Sherman, *Luther and the Jews: A Fateful Legacy*, Revised Edition (Chicago: ELCA, 1999). Contrary to this decision, see Carter Lindberg, "Luther Not Racist," *The Lutheran* (June 1994) 56–57: "Luther was not a racist! In contrast to the medieval Catholic canonical prohibition of Christian–Jewish marriage, Luther stated that a Christian could marry a Jew, for he or she 'is just as much a man or woman—God's good creation —as St. Peter, St. Paul and St. Lucy.' Racial anti-Jewish-ness arose with pure blood laws of the Spanish Inquisition, a full century before Luther; and it was the Fourth Lateran Council (1215) that legislated degradation of Jews, including the wearing of yellow badges. For Luther, Judaism was not a racial but a theological issue. If simple causes for complex historical events are in favor, we might recall that Hitler came from a Catholic Austrian context and that Lutheran Norway resisted the Nazis."

hatred in his famous 1543 treatise *The Jews and Their Lies*[18]—a book that supposedly inspired Adolf Hitler (1889–1945) as he devised his plan to kill off the Jews throughout Europe. It has become fairly common to suppose that "Luther's diatribes in the sixteenth century are an eerie foreshadowing of Nazi practices four centuries later."[19] Even "Thomas Mann linked Luther to Hitler as did Lord Vansittart, once the highest civil servant in the British Foreign Office, Archbishop Temple and the Very Reverend R. W. Inge of the Church of England shared this opinion, and so did William L. Shirer, the author of *The Rise and Fall of the Third Reich*, a bestseller."[20]

The prestigious Luther scholar, George Wolfgang Forell concludes that in Luther's critique of the Jews, "the great theologian of the cross revealed his triumphalist Achilles' heel."[21] Other scholars agree. James M. Kittelson says this treatise is a "poison" in the church.[22] Heiko A. Oberman says Luther's attitude toward the Jews, expressed in his 1543 treatise, "becomes a pawn of modern anti-Semitism."[23] Martin Marty says that Luther is at his worst when writing this treatise. The treatise contributes to Marty's overall judgment that Luther is an unjustifiably "extreme" thinker.[24] And Eric W. Gritsch argues

---

18 Martin Luther, "On the Jews and Their Lies" (1543) LW 47:137–306. The original German title is *Von den Juden und ihren Lügen*.
19 Michael Berenbaum, *The World Must Know: The History of the Holocaust as Told in the United States Holocaust Memorial Museum*, Second Edition (Baltimore: Johns Hopkins University, 2006) 8.
20 Uwe Siemon-Netto, *The Fabricated Luther: The Rise and Fall of the Shirer Myth* (Saint Louis: Concordia, 1995) 23.
21 George W. Forell, *The Luther Legacy* (Minneapolis: Augsburg, 1983) 63.
22 James M. Kittelson, *Luther the Reformer: The Story of the Man and His Career* (Minneapolis: Fortress, 2003) 275.
23 Heiko A. Oberman, *Luther: Man Between God and the Devil*, trans. Eileen Walliser-Schwarzbart (New Haven: Yale, 1989) 297.
24 Martin Marty, *Martin Luther* (New York: Viking Penguin, 2004) 174,

that Luther "is not just 'anti-Judaic' (as some Luther research labeled him), but genuinely 'anti-Semitic.'" Moreover, Luther himself was supposedly "willing to kill 'a blaspheming Jew.'"[25]

While many who reject his 1543 treatise do not reject what Luther says elsewhere, a growing number of authors do. For instance, an increasing number of authors argue that Luther is not only too harsh on the Jews, but also too harsh in condemning homosexual behavior.[26] Words like these from Luther scholars make him appear guilty as charged. And it surely does not help that a vicious anti-Semite in Hitler's government was named Martin Franz Julius Luther (1895–1945).[27]

194.

25 Eric W. Gritsch, *Martin Luther's Anti-Semitism: Against His Better Judgment* (Grand Rapids: Eerdmans, 2012) xi. Against this judgment see Mark U. Edwards, Jr., *Luther's Last Battles: Politics and Polemics 1531–46* (Ithaca, New York: Cornell University, 1983) 139: "[The] logic of religious anti-Semitism leads to attempts at conversion, not genocide." See also Stephen R. Haynes, *Reluctant Witnesses: Jews and Christian Imagination* (Louisville: Westminster John Knox, 1995) 47: "Christians cannot force Jews to believe, but neither can they risk confirming them in their blasphemy."

26 Martin Luther, "Lectures on Genesis 15–20" (1545) LW 3:255: "The heinous conduct of the people of Sodom is extraordinary, inasmuch as they departed from the natural passion and longing of the male for the female . . . . Whence comes this perversity? Undoubtedly from Satan, who, after people have once turned away from the fear of God, so powerfully suppresses nature that he blots out the natural desire and stirs up a desire that is contrary to nature." For a condemnation of Luther's views, see David L. Balch, ed., *Homosexuality, Science, and the "Plain Sense" of Scripture* (Grand Rapids: Eerdmans, 2000) 190–91.

27 Christopher R. Browning, *The Origins of the Final Solution: The Evolution of Nazi Jewish Policy, September 1939–March 1942* (Lincoln: University of Nebraska, 2004) 342–43.

But I think these judgments against Luther are mistaken. Few who condemn Luther's four-part, one-hundred-seventy page book on the Jews have read through it carefully.[28] Others understand it quite poorly. They skim over it once or twice, searching for juicy invectives—disregarding the fact that the "greater part of the book, notwithstanding its severity, was positive."[29] They have already made up their minds against Luther on other grounds.[30] Whether they object to Luther on sacramental, Biblical, catechetical, psychological, or ecclesiastical grounds, they read the work on the Jews only to find some non-controvertible evidence to clinch their case against him. They are unaware or do not care that the great Luther scholar E. Gordon Rupp in his 1945 book *Martin Luther: Hitler's Cause or Cure?*[31] decisively refuted Peter F. Wiener's 1945 book, *Martin Luther: Hitler's Spiritual Ancestor*,[32] which accused Luther of

---

28 One mechanical way to test for this is to ask how they resolved the broken paragraph in the English translation of the treatise. If they do not know what you are talking about, they have not read the treatise carefully. See Martin Luther, "On the Jews and Their Lies" (1543) LW 47:172, lines twenty-three and thirty.

29 Armas K. E. Holmio, *The Lutheran Reformation and the Jews: The Birth of the Protestant Jewish Mission* (Hancock, Michigan: Finnish Lutheran Book Concern, 1949) 103.

30 See, for instance, John R. Loeschen, *Wrestling With Luther* (Saint Louis: Concordia, 1976) 151: "In the maddening but expected oscillation of his logic, Luther treats God's omnipresence in creation now as the premise for, now as the conclusion from, Christ's ubiquity in the Sacrament." See also Hans-Martin Barth, *The Theology of Martin Luther: A Critical Assessment*, trans. Linda M. Maloney (Minneapolis: Fortress, 2013) 469: "If there is anything that makes reading Luther's texts painful, it is the almost constant polemic.... One could almost ask: whom did he not call a 'devil'?"

31 E. Gordon Rupp, *Martin Luther: Hitler's Cause or Cure?* (London: Lutterworth, 1945).

32 Peter F. Wiener, *Martin Luther: Hitler's Spiritual Ancestor* (London: Hutchison, 1945).

anti-Semitism largely because of this 1543 treatise on the Jews. Consequently their judgment against Luther for his treatise on the Jews is skewed and hardly compelling.

LUTHER'S 1543 TREATISE ON THE JEWS

Truthfully, Luther "was not involved with later racial anti-Semitism. There is a world of difference between his belief in salvation and a racial ideology."[33] Therefore Luther can say that "we Goyim . . . confess that Mary [the Mother of our Lord Jesus] is not ours but rather the Jews' cousin and blood relative . . . [whom] we praise and laud . . . highly."[34] Now no anti-Semite could ever say this without retching. But Luther says it, not only clearly and deliberately, but also with joy, passion and pride—something that, if not noted and appreciated, misrepresents Luther completely. This is a weakness in Gritsch's book, which quotes from this page of the treatise, but not the line exalting the Jewish Mary.[35]

Since it is part of his view of salvation, Luther's critique of the Jews is really not a critique of the Jews, but of Judaism. It does not arise from any personal hatred for the Jews as a people, but only follows what the Bible has to say, especially the New Testament, about Judaism.[36] Luther believes that "it

---

33 Martin Brecht, *Martin Luther*, 3 vols. trans. James L. Schaaf (Minneapolis: Fortress, 1985–1993) 3:351. Brecht continues: "Nevertheless, his misguided agitation had the evil result that Luther fatefully became one of the 'church fathers' of anti-Semitism and thus provided material for the modern hatred of the Jews, cloaking it with the authority of the Reformer."

34 Martin Luther, "On the Jews and Their Lies" (1543) LW 47:260.

35 Eric W. Gritsch, *Martin Luther's Anti-Semitism*, 85.

36 But see also the discussion on Genesis 49:10 in Martin Luther, "On the Jews and Their Lies" (1543) LW 47:178–92. On this Biblical emphasis, see Mark U. Edwards, Jr., Luther's *Last Battles: Politics and Polemics 1531–46*, 139: "The central concern of the late treatises was not, how-

is incumbent on all to know God's book."[37] In this treatise on the Jews Luther follows the Bible, arguing against the religion of Judaism and not against the Jews in any anti-Semitic way. And it is a terrible mistake to suppose that his anti-Judaism implies anti-Semitism. While it may be so for others, clearly it does not follow for Luther. Luther, however, "did not believe the world would be a better place without Jews but he believed passionately that Christendom would be better without Judaism, just as it would be better without papalism and without Anabaptism."[38]

When Luther is attacked for his views on the Jews, more often than not the real target is the Bible rather than Luther's imagined hatred. Most critics of this 1543 treatise do not actually object to Luther's fabricated anti-Semitism, regardless of what they say. Their real objection is to Luther's harsh view of Christian salvation. Luther believes that this view is deeply embedded in the Bible itself. This is harder to admit, since attacking a deeply Biblical view on salvation can boomerang on the critics and make them look religiously suspect.

Scripture tells us two things regarding the salvation of the Jews. First, like all people, they are welcome to believe in and follow Christ, because "God shows no partiality" (Acts 10:34). The Jews are not excluded simply because of their ethnic background. Excluding them for this reason would be anti-Semi-

---

ever, these political and economic expressions of 'rough mercy' [*scharfe Barmherzigkeit*]. Luther's late anti-Jewish writings were attempts to defend and maintain theologically and exegetically the Christian sense of the Old Testament and to refute competing Jewish exegesis."

37 Martin Luther, "On the Jews and Their Lies" (1543) LW 47:280.

38 Derek Wilson, *Out of the Storm: The Life and Legacy of Martin Luther* (New York: Saint Martins, 2008) 316. See also Martin Luther, "Sermon on Matthew 23:15" (September 25,1538), LW 68:177: "[Christian] offenses, shamefulness, and vice, . . . are much greater than the vices among [the Jews]."

tism. That being said, the Bible also teaches that when a Jew (or anyone else, for that matter) follows Judaism—the view that God blesses those who keep the law—that person becomes "unworthy of eternal life" (Acts 13:46). Judaism, as a religion, cannot deliver what it promises. It has become obsolete due to the appearing of Jesus Christ, the Messiah and very Son of God.[39]

This negative judgment is not anti-Semitic but only against the saving power of Judaism, rooted in following the law. As the Jewish convert to Christianity, Roy H. Schoeman writes, it is a "pernicious error" to suppose "that the Old and New Covenants are two 'separate but equal' parallel paths to salvation, the one intended for Jews, the other for Gentiles."[40] The truth is that salvation comes only through the name of Jesus Christ (Acts 4:12).[41] It is this anti-Judaism which is at the heart of Luther's 1543 treatise on the Jews—which has nothing to do with anti-Semitism.

---

39 See Heb 7:19, 8:13; 2 Cor 3:10; 1 Pt 1:18; Rom 3:20, 8:3. This supersession, or surpassing, of Judaism by Christianity caused a firestorm in the popular culture on Easter 2001, when "the nation's most widely read cartoonist," Johnny Hart, depicted the seven last words of Jesus in his cartoon strip, "B. C.," with the candles on a Jewish menorah going out in sequence—until the eighth candle turned into the cross of Christ. Martin Miller, "Cartoon's Easter Message Offends Jews: 'B. C.' Features Crucifixion, Menorah," *The Seattle Times* (April 14, 2001).

40 Roy H. Schoeman, *Salvation is from the Jews (John 4:22): The Role of Judaism in Salvation History from Abraham to the Second Coming* (San Francisco: Ignatius, 2003) 353.

41 On this same exclusivity, see the congenial clarification in Carl E. Braaten, *No Other Gospel! Christianity Among the World's Religions* (Minneapolis: Fortress, 1992) 71: "We should aim to take seriously all that human beings have experienced and believed about God prior to and apart from the preaching of the gospel. Some argue that this concession to the revelatory quality of the religions detracts from the sole efficacy of Christ in communicating divine revelation. The answer to this fear is that the uniqueness of Christ's role is not limited to revelation but

This anti-Judaism does not imply that Christianity has received nothing beneficial from Judaism. To the contrary, Christians have received from Judaism the law; the critique of idol worship, covenants with Noah, Abraham, and David; and the stirring witness of the patriarchs and prophets, to say nothing of the Savior himself (Rom 9:4–5)![42] Christians have rightly taken these treasures and built upon them. But apart from the Savior, none of these gifts assures sinners of God's love for them and the hope of eternal life (1 Cor 15:26–56). Salvation from God's wrath only comes through "faith in Jesus Christ" (Rom 3:22, 5:9; Jn 3:16, 36; BC 136).

This is the truth given us, which we must honor, even though we "know how repulsive this teaching is to the judgment of reason and law and that the teaching of the law about love is more plausible" (BC 139). A religion based on the law, like Judaism, is more plausible to reason. But this offense does not make Christianity any less true. No, not at all. In fact, this offensiveness may even contribute to its truth (Mt 11:6). Having our feathers ruffled by Luther's treatise is not reason enough to give up on it. The Lutheran confessions show how repulsive Christianity essentially and necessarily is—and Kierkegaard takes it up as well and incorporates it into his views on Judaism. Therefore many who insist on throwing out Luther's treatise are those who have first thrown out a harsh view of

---

comes to its decisive and definitive expression in the area of justification and reconciliation. Revelation and salvation are not coterminous."

42 See also Martin Luther, "On the Jews and Their Lies" (1543) LW 47:302: "[The] kingdom of David and the King Messiah did not come from us Gentiles to the children of Abraham and Israel, but came from the children of Abraham and Israel [Jn 4:22] . . . . Even if we are all descended from Adam and partake of the same birth and blood, nevertheless all other nations were shunted aside and solely Abraham's seed was selected as the nation from which the Messiah would come."

Christianity in favor of a milder one—something which Kierkegaard vigorously opposed and was vehemently against (JP 3:2873).

When Luther says that the Jews should be punished for their rejection of Christianity and their attempts to draw Christians into Judaism,[43] he is only laying out what the Bible says. Luke 16:16 says, for instance, that "every one enters the kingdom of God violently." Saint Paul was knocked down flat on the road to Damascus, right before he "put on Christ" (Acts 9:4; Gal 3:27). And everyone since then has been required to die to themselves too—being knocked down spiritually, if you will—in order to believe in Jesus (2 Cor 5:13–17). And the Jews are no exception to this rough pedagogy. They too will have to suffer "many tribulations" before entering the kingdom of God (Acts 14:22). This is what Luther elsewhere calls *Christianissima saeveritas* or "Christian severity."[44] Those who reject Luther's 1543 treatise on the Jews therefore have a prior negative reaction to his general religious severity. Unfortunately this is rarely if ever admitted to in their critiques of his 1543 treatise on the Jews. Instead, Luther the messenger, is slain for bringing a message from God—a common, albeit deplorable, error.

---

43 See Martin Luther, "On the Jews and Their Lies" (1543) LW 47:149, 290: "[The] Jews would like to entice us Christians to their faith, and they do this wherever they can . . . . Such a mouth should be punished for two reasons; in the first place, because it confesses that it does not understand this; in the second place, because it nevertheless blasphemes something which it does not understand. Why do they not first ask? . . . . Therefore such lack of understanding cannot help or excuse them, nor us Christians if we tolerate this any longer from them."

44 Martin Luther, "Lectures on Galatians 1–4" (1535), LW 26:118.

Scared Straight

Even in the Old Testament, quite apart from Luther's treatise, God tries to scare the Jews straight. Again and again he punishes them mercilessly, especially through invading military powers under the leadership of Cyrus (Is 44:28) and Nebuchadnezzar (Jer 39:3). In Hosea, God specifically says of the disobedient Jews—quite abhorrently—that their children should be killed, their families become infertile, and that they should be driven from their homes and made to wander among the nations (Hos 9:7–17). It is important to note the similarities between this passage and Hitler's playbook. This helps one see the horrible truth about the ghastly nature of the Bible. Attacking Luther's alleged anti-Semitism, then, in the name of some fabricated and exclusively loving Bible, is to tangle oneself up in theological chicanery. The message of the Bible is tough,[45] and one has to settle for that or throw it out. All sophisticated, urbane efforts to clean up the Bible fail by "the death of a thousand qualifications."[46]

It must also be noted that these tough Old Testament words inspired Luther (who quotes Hosea eight times in his treatise) when he advises destroying Jewish synagogues, homes, religious books; preventing rabbis from teaching; ending gainful employment and safe-conduct for Jews; and imposing

---

45 Regarding the Bible, Kierkegaard thought that it was "an extremely dangerous book [and] an imperious book—if one gives it a finger, it takes the whole hand; if one gives it the whole hand, it takes the whole man and may suddenly and radically change my whole life on a prodigious scale." He concludes, saying: "I refuse to be alone with it" (FSE 31).

46 The phrase is Antony Flew's. Antony Flew, *There is a God: How the World's Most Notorious Atheist Changed His Mind* (New York: HarperOne, 2007) xi.

hard labor on them.⁴⁷ Gritsch ignores these references while quoting the less copious references to Esther, Judges, Genesis, 2 Samuel, Haggai, Daniel, and Deuteronomy, in this treatise.⁴⁸ Luther's polemic against Judaism is therefore not derived from a personal hatred for the Jews as an ethnic group, but is rather "drawn from the Old Testament . . . prophets."⁴⁹ Similarly, in the raging debate over whether or not it is right to spank our children, Luther would come down squarely on the side of spanking our children.⁵⁰ He deeply believed Proverbs 13:24, that sparing the rod spoils the child.⁵¹ This, in effect, is what he is doing in his 1543 treatise on the Jews: giving them a good licking⁵²—as offensive as that may sound to those who eschew negative pedagogy.

But if Luther rightly opposed killing the Jews for their disobedience (*contra* the Old Testament prescription),⁵³ why did he still advise other terrible punishments against them? Why did he not ignore those Biblical punishments altogether as any enlightened, urbane Christian would? Many suppose he did not ignore them because he hated the Jews and was a terrible,

---

47 Martin Luther, "On the Jews and Their Lies" (1543) LW 47:268–72.
48 Eric W. Gritsch, *Martin Luther's Anti-Semitism*, 80–87.
49 Gerhard O. Forde, "Luther and the Jews: A Review and Some Preliminary Reflections," in *Luther, Lutherans and the Jewish People: A Study Resource* (Minneapolis: The American Lutheran Church, 1977) 18. See also the reprint of this article in *Lutheran Quarterly* 27 (Summer 2013): 125–42.
50 See John Rosemond, *To Spank or Not to Spank: A Parents' Handbook* (Kansas City: Andrew and McNeel, 1994).
51 Martin Luther, "A Sermon on the Estate of Marriage" (1519) LW 44:13 and "A Sermon on Luke 6:36–42" (1535) SML 4:120.
52 Martin Luther, "On the Jews and Their Lies" (1543) LW 47:197: "I will chastise him with the rod of men (as one whips children) [2 Sam 7:12–16]."
53 See Lv 26:14–39; Ez 14:21; Hos 9:13.

evil person.⁵⁴ But what Luther says is very different. He says that he favored punishments first to witness to the Holy Scriptures, for Jesus himself rebuked the Jews.⁵⁵ Second, he intended these punishments to scare the Jews straight so that they might receive God's blessings.⁵⁶

---

54 Richard Marius, *Martin Luther: The Christian Between God and Death* (Cambridge, Massachusetts: Harvard University, 1999) 377: "Yet always beneath [Luther's] pity ran the assumption that the Jews deserved their fate because they had rejected Christ . . . . As years passed and the Jews steadfastly refused his or any other gospel, his wrath occasionally flamed into vehement hatred, culminating in his merciless tirades of 1543 . . . . [And] his fury was no less cruel and vicious because its underlying motives were different or because his suggestions for carrying his cruelty to some final solution were less comprehensive and efficient." Note also Carter Lindberg, "Tainted Greatness: Luther's Attitudes Toward Judaism and Their Historical Reception" in *Tainted Greatness: Anti-Semitism and Cultural Heroes*, ed. Nancy A. Harrowitz (Philadelphia: Temple University, 1994) 29: "The taint in Luther's greatness was that in his understanding of the Jewish faith and the Jews, he failed to be his own theologian of the cross and instead embraced the messianic pretensions of a theology of glory."

55 Martin Luther, "On the Jews and Their Lies" (1543) LW 47:277: "We . . . believe that our Lord Jesus Christ is truthful when he declares of the Jews who did not accept but crucified him, 'You are a brood of vipers and children of the Devil' [Mt 12:34]. This is a judgment in which his forerunner John the Baptist concurred, although these people were his kin. Now our authorities and all such merciful saints as *wish the Jews well* will at least have to let us believe our Lord Jesus Christ, who, I am sure, has more intimate knowledge of all hearts than do these compassionate saints" (italics added).

56 Martin Luther, "On the Jews and Their Lies" (1543) LW 47:267: "We are at fault in [allowing the Jews] to live freely in our midst despite all their . . . cursing, . . . we project and shield [them] . . . . In this way we make them lazy and secure . . . . From all of this we Christians see—for the Jews cannot see it—what terrible wrath of God these people have incurred and still incur without ceasing, what fire is gleaming and glowing there, and what they achieve who curse and detest Christ."

Luther believed that the Jews were a stubborn, stiff-necked people, as the Bible says (Ex 32:9; Ez 3:7–9; Acts 7:51–53).[57] Therefore he knew that harsh punishments were all that could help. "Harsh" or "sharp" mercy was required, rather than "gentle" mercy,[58] for that is what it takes to "soften" up recalcitrant sinners.[59] And Christians who are stubborn, Luther insists upon, need this severe treatment as well.[60] His driving

---

57   Martin Luther, "On the Jews and Their Lies" (1543) LW 47:252: "[The Jews have] always been a stiff-necked, unbelieving, proud, base, incorrigible people, and so it ever remains."

58   Martin Luther, "On the Jews and Their Lies" (1543) LW 47:268, 272, 276, 292. He had tried gentle mercy earlier in his treatise "That Jesus Was Born a Jew" (1523) LW 45:199–229. He talks about shifting gears—moving away from an irenic approach to a more polemical one—in his "Letter to Josel of Rosheim" (June 11, 1537), *Martin Luther, the Bible, and the Jewish People: A Reader*, ed. Brooks Schramm and Kirsi I. Stjerna (Minneapolis: Fortress, 2012) 127–28: "To the cautious [Josel], Jew of Rosheim, my good friend . . . . *[My] heart has been, and still is, that one should treat Jews kindly*, out of the conviction that God might now graciously consider them and bring them to their Messiah; but certainly not out of the conviction that through my benevolence and influence they should be strengthened in their error and become worse . . . . [It] is quite odd that we should have to entice and lure you to your natural Lord and King . . . . [You] should reflect on whether God will release you from the present misery, which now has lasted more than 1500 years. This will not happen unless you accept with us Gentiles your cousin and Lord, the dear crucified Jesus . . . . For . . . your imprisonment lasts too long, and yet you find us Gentiles, whom you consider your greatest enemies, favorable and willing to advise and help you, even though we can't tolerate the fact that you curse and blaspheme your own flesh and blood, Jesus of Nazareth, who has done you no harm, and that if you could you would rob his followers of everything they are and have" (italics added).

59   Martin Luther, "On the Jews and Their Lies" (1543) LW 47:206; and "The Sacrament of Penance" (1519) LW 35:18.

60   Martin Luther, "On the Jews and Their Lies" (1543) LW 47:161, 253: "We [also] perverted God's truth into lies and worshipped the veritable calf of Aaron. Therefore God also delivered us into all sorts of terrible

concern was not vengeance or anything like that, but only the "welfare" of the Jewish people.[61] He had no interest in killing them off as Hitler did, for Luther knew that vengeance belongs to God alone.[62] On the contrary, Luther wanted to end God's long-standing wrath against the Jews,[63] and he knew that would only come about through faith in the Messiah.[64] "Innumerable people, both young and old" within Judaism had accepted Christianity with sincerity down through the centuries, and Luther wanted many more Jews to do the same.[65]

> blindness and innumerable false doctrines, and, furthermore, he permitted Muhammad and the pope together with all devils to come upon us.... [So] for us Christians [the Jews] stand as a terrifying example of God's wrath." Note also Mark U. Edwards, Jr., *Luther's Last Battles: Politics and Polemics 1531–46, 141*: "[The] treatises were explicitly aimed not at Jews but at fellow Protestants. In this respect his anti-Jewish writings have more in common with his attacks on Protestant opponents [than] with his attacks on Catholics and Turks."

61 Martin Luther, "On the Jews and Their Lies" (1543) LW 47:178, 267, 274.
62 Martin Luther, "On the Jews and Their Lies" (1543) LW 47:189. So when Luther threatens the Jews with death in this treatise (LW 47:269, 287), it is only in reference to God killing them in Deuteronomy 17:12. *He is simply passing on God's bad news to them.*
63 Martin Luther, "On the Jews and Their Lies" (1543) LW 47:241, 262, 273, 292. See also Martin Luther, "Against the Sabbatarians: Letter to a Good Friend" (1538) LW 47:97: "It does not make sense that [the Jews] should suffer such misery for fifteen hundred years for unknown sins—sins which they cannot name—whereas they did not have to suffer more than seventy years [Jer 25:8–14] for sins that were more obvious, terrible, murderous, and idolatrous. Furthermore, at that time they were not without prophets and without comfort, *while in their present exile not even a fly flicks a wing for their consolation*" (italics added).
64 Martin Luther, "On the Jews and Their Lies" (1543) LW 47:215, 295.
65 Martin Luther, "On the Jews and Their Lies" (1543) LW 47:283, 306. On how this would be a reversion to early Christian practices, see Rodney Stark, *The Triumph of Christianity: How the Jesus Movement Became the World's Largest Religion* (New York: HarperOne, 2011) 79,

A Loving Treatise

Recognizing the relation between salvation and Judaism, it would be unloving and unwise to repudiate Luther's 1543 treatise on the Jews. While we may repudiate[66] the harsh tactics Luther proposed in the treatise, we ought to stand by its intent[67] to lead Jews from Judaism to faith in Jesus Christ, and join in with Kierkegaard in thinking of Luther as our wise guide in promoting the rigorousness of Christianity.[68] Luther

---

75: "[There] continued to be a high rate of Jewish conversions until about the seventh century . . . . [For] Christianity offered Diaspora Jews a chance to preserve virtually all of their religious capital, needing only to add to it, since Christianity retained the entire Old Testament heritage. Although it made observance of many portions of the Jewish Law unnecessary, Christianity did not impose a new set of Laws to be mastered. In addition, services in Christian congregations were very closely modeled on those of the synagogue and, in early days, Christian services also were conducted in Greek, so a Hellenized Jew would have felt right at home. Finally, *Christianity carefully stressed how its central message of salvation was the fulfillment of the messianic promises of orthodox Judaism*" (italics added).

66 Recall the last page to his earlier treatise, "Jesus Was Born a Jew" (1523) LW 45:229: "I would request and advise that one deal gently with [the Jews] and instruct them from Scripture . . . . Instead of this we are trying only to drive them by force . . . . So long as we thus treat them like dogs, how can we expect to work any good among them? . . . . *We must receive them cordially . . . . If some of them should prove stiff-necked, what of it? After all, we ourselves are not all good Christians either*" (italic added).

67 See Armas K. E. Holmio, *The Lutheran Reformation and the Jews*, 123: "Luther's immoderate language used against the Jew [in his 1543 treatise] is a stumbling block [when it is] forgotten that it was the general custom in polemics and *not to be taken literally*" (italic added).

68 Mark U. Edwards, Jr., *Luther's Last Battles: Politics and Polemics 1531–46*, 140: "So twentieth-century scholars may conclude that for the purposes of twentieth-century theology those aspects of Luther's theology that twentieth-century theologians deem essential need not entail the practical recommendations that Luther made." Note also the harsh

knew that many Jews believed in Jesus Christ, the Messiah,[69] and he wanted many more to follow suit. He did not want to ignore Ezekiel 3:16–21 and withhold God's warning from them—thereby "aiding and abetting" their faithlessness.[70] He wanted instead to restore the Messianic "heritage" to Israel which the Jews had "ruined" by rejecting and vilifying Jesus.[71] In order to do this he was willing for people to be "displeased" with him,[72] for he knew he had written an unpleasant, but necessary book on the Jews.[73]

---

treatment that Luther proposes in his Small Catechism for those who refuse to memorize it: "If any refuses to receive your instructions, tell them that they deny Christ and are not Christians. They should not be admitted to the sacrament, be accepted as sponsors in Baptism, or be allowed to participate in any Christian privileges. On the contrary, they should be turned over to the pope and his officials, and even to the devil himself. In addition, *parents and employers should refuse to furnish them with food and drink and should notify them that the prince is disposed to banish such rude people from his land*" (BC 339) (italic added).

69 Martin Luther, "On the Jews and Their Lies" (1543) LW 47:237, 299, 304.
70 Martin Luther, "On the Jews and Their Lies" (1543) LW 47:274–75, 279, 284.
71 Martin Luther, "On the Jews and Their Lies" (1543) LW 47:254. See also David Klinghoffer, *Why the Jews Rejected Jesus*, 144: "[Jesus was punished in the afterworld by being] boiled in excrement."
72 Martin Luther, "On the Jews and Their Lies" (1543) LW 47:185.
73 Martin Luther, "On the Jews and Their Lies" (1543) LW 47:291–92: "[It] has not been a pleasant task for me to write this book." An anti-Semite would have had fun blasting the Jews in this book. But not Luther. And he goes on to note that in Romans 9:2, Saint Paul "is saddened as he considers [the Jews]. I think," Luther writes, "that every Christian experiences this when he reflects seriously, not on the temporal misfortunes and exile which the Jews bemoan, but on the fact that they are condemned to blaspheme, curse, and vilify God himself and all that is God's, for their eternal damnation, and that they refuse to hear and acknowledge this but regard all their doings as zeal for God. *O God, heavenly Father, relent and let your wrath over them be sufficient and come to an end, for the sake of your dear Son! Amen*" (italic added).

In this way Luther's treatise is eminently—and surprisingly—pastoral. "Underlying the divine chastisement is God's 'painful grace,' the purpose of which is to strangle the old Adam so that the believer might turn to God alone for every good."[74] Condemning this treatise only undercuts these noble Christian goals, something no faithful, self-respecting Christian should ever want or dare to do. Those who condemn this treatise show a lack of understanding and compassion for the Jews. They are not willing to bear ignominy and vilification for trying to scare the Jews straight as Luther was. Instead, they are content to rest in the comfortable, unbiblical view that the Jews are safe for eternity without any belief in Jesus as their savior. Such a false comfort Kierkegaard spent his lifetime writing against (EUD 298–303; TM 110). And so should we stand against it—under the tutelage of Jesus, Saint Paul, Luther, and Kierkegaard—because "it belongs to the very essence of a faith founded on justification by grace, that there is no distinction, and that I am called to preach Christ crucified, not by Jews, but [crucified] by us all, and thus to proclaim him to all."[75] And whenever or wherever that is done faithfully, there will offense necessarily follow.

Luther's Jewish critic, Josel of Rosheim (1478–1554), however, was not impressed—ridiculing Luther in a play of his by calling him "*Martin Lo Tohar* (Martin the unclean)." *Martin Luther, the Bible, and the Jewish People: A Reader*, 180.

74 Dennis Ngien, *Luther as a Spiritual Advisor: The Interface of Theology and Piety in Luther's Devotional Writings* (Bletchley: Paternoster, 2007) 155.

75 Gerhard O. Forde, "Luther and the Jews," 19. About a week before he died, Luther says the same. See Martin Luther, "An Admonition Against the Jews" (1546) LW 58:458: "Now, we want to deal with [the Jews] in a Christian manner and, in the first place, to offer them the Christian faith, so that they will receive the Messiah, who is after all their kinsman, born of their flesh and blood . . . . If not, we will not tolerate them, for Christ has commanded us to be baptized and believe in

Luther at Sixty-three.

Him." This forced option keeps Luther's even-handedness from becoming a "counterfeit benevolence." *Philosemitism in History*, ed. Jonathan Karp, Adam Sutcliffe (Cambridge: Cambridge University Press, 2011) 1, 168.

Appendix Two

On Kierkegaard for the Church

By Rollie Storbakken

I STAND GUILTY AS CHARGED—on p. 9, footnote 34, in Pastor Marshall's book, *Kierkegaard for the Church* (2013)—of "accommodating the Christian revelation to human desires." I didn't even need my dictionary to help me figure out that part of his book, but I did find my dictionary necessary to understand most of the rest of it.

Let me explain . . .

I can only remember reading three, maybe four, books in my fifty-nine years of life—the Bible, and the biographies of Crazy Horse and Hank Williams. So this review comes from a retired Union ironworker—who was only required to use and understand four letter words for thirty-five years, and before that was raised in a horse barn.

So the reading—or studying—of this book was a lot of work for me. I looked up every word I didn't understand and penciled in the meanings, off to the side of the page, knowing that this would help me re-read the book later with greater ease and understanding. I found something on every page I felt I had to underline and stress for future study. The book is so full, in my uneducated opinion—not that I know much about books, mind you.

Just to let you know, here are a few examples of my smiles and tears as I read through this book. I had to read footnote 49 on p. 14 over a couple times to get the important difference between the theologians of glory and of the cross. (I found that my coffee always got cold while studying this book.) Footnote 18 on p. 80 is too heavy and still beyond me: "Only one's loving care for others is to be loved in self-love. The self itself is not to be loved in self-love." I still ponder this line on p. 106: "challenging ecclesiastical authority." But the quotation in the middle of p. 125 still baffles me: "If this untruth is not included, then the extraordinary does not remain the extraordinary; it is taken in vain." Even so there was also hope and relief, as in footnote 47 on p. 189: "Ah, delicious coolness," as well as Kierkegaard's love for the common man on p. 244. And I like the summaries by Pattison and Perkins in footnotes 59 and 60 on p. 195. And then there is that great footnote 15 for kids on p. 219, and the wonderful prayer at the bottom of p. 228—especially for my 9-year-old daughter, Silvie.

In spite of these difficulties, I made myself read all of the footnotes on every page of this book. I didn't skip over any of them like I thought of doing. After Matins, one Wednesday morning in December, I told Pastor Marshall I was still working on his book and that pp. 122 and 192 were two of my favorites. He later told me he looked them up and was happy to hear I liked them because he thought there were some pretty good ideas on those two pages. But that wasn't why I liked them. I later told him I had jokingly picked them because they were two of the very few pages in his book without any footnotes on them!

But by p. 63, I had settled in and started circling every little footnote number on each page to make them stand out so that going back and forth between the footnotes and the main text was easier for me to do. I highly recommend this to help you get all that is packed into this book.

For the record, I started reading it—that is, going on my educational adventure with it—in October 2013, shortly after the books went on sale in church. I finished my first reading of it on January 18, 2014.

Why did I choose this book to be one of the only books I will ever read in my lifetime? Remember I've only read three or four books in my fifty-nine years. Well, the answer is that a friend of mine—my pastor—is the one who wrote it! And how many authors do any of us know personally?

So, as an all-or-nothing type of guy, I decided to do my best to get to know this book. And that means that I'll need to keep going over it until I die, because it's about Christianity, and that's the way our faith is. So there's enough education-explanation in this work—when I go to look up the related Bible verses and footnote references—to keep me informed and busy. And then to understand and believe. In comprehending this book I feel I will stand—when kneeling—a better chance of making the team, if you know what I mean. It might take 'til I die to let go of this world and grasp what this book is about (see p. 307). That will be the moment I hope to leave you all behind.

My copy of this book, with all of its markings, is now a family treasure to be left to Silvie, to be read when she gets older. I've made notes in it like, "Silvie, look here"—with arrows ✍ and other markings to help her focus on, hear and learn about, what I believe are the foundational, "light bulb" notes that will help Silvie take in, and then digest, this book. I hope the notes to her and my markings will be the sugar that helps the medicine go down. I write "here" in the book with arrows pointing where she should pay attention. I write "learn this," and "here too is the answer." I write "Look" with eyes drawn in the double "o"s. I write "Here lies the heart of the book," with arrows showing the way. I want to help her—after I'm dead and gone—to catch what this book has to say about real Christianity and how it goes against the herd (you'll have to read the whole book, especially pp. 125 and 233-35, to get that one)! I would also love to have embroidered the three prayers on p. 215 so we could frame them and hang them in our house so we don't forget them!

One sentence that really encouraged me was on p. 324, where Kierkegaard says: "I myself manage to be only a very simple Christian." Pastor Marshall adds that this means Christians are "always on the road to becoming" Christians. In a nutshell, then, Christianity is about this "continuous striving" (see also p. 212). For me this is the ammunition we'll all need to stay warm in Christ Jesus through the many struggles of this life. So read your Bibles—for God's Word is your defense when things pile up against you. And may we all receive the Holy Spirit so that we'll be able to understand His Word when we finally pick it up and study it—which is what this book wants all of us to do (see pp. 150-53).[1]

---

[1] Dr. Robert L. Perkins, general editor of the 26 volume *International Kierkegaard Commentary* (1984–2010), was "very struck with this review" by Storbakken, and asked for an electronic version of it so he could send it to his own son and daughter (email, February 11, 2014). And poet, Jim Bodeen, called it "the best kind" of review—"one in a thousand" (letter, February 9, 2014).

APPENDIX THREE

On Postmodernism

When I was studying preaching at the seminary, we earned the best scores on our sermons if they were noteworthy for their novelty, creativity and imagination.[1] That was because we were told nobody would listen to us if we were predictable

---

[1] Luther would have been against this: "From [vainglory] stems the thought: 'I must preach something special and distinct, so that the people say, "This guy will become a fine man!"' He cannot preach the Word in harmony with the others. Instead, he brings something special and new, so that the people marvel and say: 'Truly this is a fine preacher who knows how to do it right. Never before have I heard anyone say it like that.' Then he gets all puffed up and is very proud of it and thinks he is an ox, though he is hardly a toad." Martin Luther, "Sermons on Matthew 21" (1537–40) *LW* 68:102. We might trace the American version of this back to Henry Ward Beecher (1813–1887): "The pulpit, or lack thereof, was the most innovative feature [of Plymouth Church in New York City]. When one of the trustees, a civil engineer, asked Henry how he wanted the audience located, the pastor's answer was emphatic: 'I want them to surround me, so that they will come up on every side, and behind me so that I shall be in the center of the crowd, and have the people surge all about me.' Instead of a traditional raised pulpit, Henry insisted on a wide stage that thrust out into the audience .... When the room was crowded, children often sat on stairs at the foot of the stage, close enough for the preacher to tousle their hair." Debby Applegate, *The Most Famous Man in America: The Biography of Henry Ward Beecher* (New York: Doubleday, 2006) 237. This Pulitzer Prize winning book is worth pondering.

and conventional.[2] On this account, all confidence in the startling, ancient and holy words faded, such as—few are chosen (Mt 22:14); friends of the world are enemies of God (Jas 4:4); Christians are hated (Jn 15:19); everyone gets the same (Mt 20:10); shun fornication (1 Cor 6:18); God hates sinners (Ps 5:5); Jesus came to blind those who see (Jn 9:39); faith comes by hearing Christ preached (Rom 10:17); hate yourself (Lk 14:26); the first covenant is obsolete (Heb 8:13); only Christ is needed (Lk 10:42); you are the man(2 Sam 12:7); it is finished (Jn 19:30); only one name can save you (Acts 4:12); those in hell wish they could escape by dying but they cannot (Rv 9:6); you did not choose me, but I chose you (Jn 15:16); not all sins are forgiven (Mt 12:31); you cannot serve Jesus by catering to others (Gal 1:10); give up trying to please others (1 Thes 2:2); and only the blood of Jesus saves us from the wrath of God (Rom 5:9).

Even so, over these last forty years, preaching still continues to hanker after updating and being reinvented over and over again—eschewing these ancient and troubling holy words of old. Therefore many, no doubt, will find the sermons collected in *Kierkegaard in the Pulpit* to be hidebound and

---

2 This view feeds into Edward O. Wilson's new book, *The Meaning of Human Existence* (New York: Liveright, 2014). In it he argues that "we are not predestined to reach any goal, nor are we answerable to any power but our own" (15). However we are "at once . . . . champions of truth and hypocrites" (28), "forever conflicted" (33),"independent, alone, and fragile" (26), and "sensory cripples" (90). But if we were to evolve out of our hypocrisy—being at present only a "work in progress" (178), and so technically open to improvement—that development would surely blunt our "creativity" (34), and so would inconsistently be undesirable. For without our foibles we would be "angelic robots—the outsized equivalents of ants" (33). For ants are supposedly "totally altruistic" (94)—even though they "eat their injured" (96), which is another one of Wilson's inconsistencies.

beside the point—if not hostile to the current temperament and bordering on the less than moral.

Because of that some will wonder if I have not misunderstood Kierkegaard as well. They might be like Professor Kyle Roberts of Bethel Seminary, Saint Paul, Minnesota, who has written *The Emergent Prophet: Kierkegaard and the Postmodern People of God*. In his book he struggles "to bring Kierkegaard's religious thought into dialogue with postmodern[3] expressions of Christianity (i.e., the emergent or

---

3 On the "prominent features of postmodernism," see Kyle Roberts, *The Emergent Prophet: Kierkegaard and the Postmodern People of God* (Eugene: Oregon: Cascade Books, 2013) 4-5: "tolerance of ambiguity, embrace of plurality, recognition of the indeterminacy (or at least incompleteness) of meaning, respect for individuality, suspicion of authority ('metanarratives'), to cite just a few examples." For a more hostile view of postmodernism, see *Postmodern Philosophy and Christian Thought*, ed. Merold Westphal (Bloomington and Indianapolis: Indiana University Press, 1999) 1: "[It] is all too easy for those with postmodern sympathies to see Christianity as the embodiment of everything to which it is quintessentially (however anti-essentialist it may be) opposed. Is Christianity not a prime example of the logocentric, totalizing, onto-theological, meta-narrative that, on the basis of exaggerated knowledge claims, seeks to impose an illegitimate hegemony on human thought and practice? . . . . Is this hegemony not allergic to alterity, reducing all others to the same by means of violence, intellectual, cultural, and all too often, physical?" Note also "the three central concepts" of postmodernism in David Ray Griffin, *Whitehead's Radically Different Postmodern Philosophy: An Argument for Its Contemporary Relevance* (Albany: State University of New York Press, 2007) vii: "anti-realism, opposition to transcendental arguments and transcendental standpoints, and rejection of truth as correspondence to reality." And for a more positive view of postmodernism, see James K. A. Smith, *Who's Afraid of Postmodernism? Taking Derrida, Lyotard, and Foucault to Church* (Grand Rapids, Michigan: Baker Academic, 2006) 21-24, 57-58, 76-79, 105-107. Smith takes three French, postmodern slogans: nothing outside of the text (Derrida); incredulity toward metanarratives (Lyotard), and power is knowledge (Foucault) and applies them to the church. The first then becomes "the centrality

emerging church)"⁴—something I have assiduously avoided doing. Roberts undertakes this arduous task because he believes that Kierkegaard's "prophetic voice is relevant to and should be welcomed by postmodern Christians in our present age, who sense an opportunity to revitalize our theology and practice of Christianity," since Kierkegaard "shares some important elements in common with . . . [the] postmodern-oriented renewal movement taking place [today] within (and beyond) both evangelicalism and mainline Protestantism."⁵ That movement he describes as the creative search for "fresh, vibrant, authentic forms of Christian faith and church that resonate with postmodern sensibilities concerning the nature of (and access to) truth; the value of dialogue; the nature of religious authority

> of Scripture" and the church in interpreting it; the second becomes the centrality of the narrative of the Bible (as opposed to its ideas) as a means for standing against competing narratives; and the third becomes "the necessity of the church to enact counterformation by counterdisciplines." All three of these adaptations are based on "a postcritical dogmatics of second naiveté" (117).

4   *The Emergent Prophet*, x. For another account on this same trend, see also Brett McCracken, *Hipster Christianity: When Church and Cool Collide* (Grand Rapids, Michigan: Baker Books, 2010) 76–77: "As with the history of secular hip, the 1960s looms very large in the history of Christian hip. A lot of things changed in the 1960s, but one of the biggest things that happened was that 'youth culture' exploded onto the scene and became the dominant force in American society . . . . This shift was felt strongly in the Christian church . . . . The idea of 'youth ministry' as a function of the local church that went beyond Sunday school-type Bible teaching was born . . . . The power had shifted from the establishment to the fickle young consumer, which meant that, no matter what they did, the youth had their parents' generation in their pocket." Against this development, McCracken concludes that this desire "to be cool, hip, fashionable, and recognized, . . . [is nothing but] a vain pursuit and a waste of time. It comes from a very human place, but it's a distraction and a self-destructing futility" (247). I would agree.

5   *The Emergent Prophet*, 2.

and sacred texts; skepticism of received interpretations and established (authoritarian) doctrine; preference for organic, egalitarian structures; openness to otherness and embrace of plurality; and an approach to the Christian life as a *quest*, or journey, rather than a fixed identity with a closed destination."[6]

In so far as Roberts' construal centers on the personal "appropriation" of the Christian faith,[7] he succeeds admirably well.[8] But when it comes to the weightier matters of how Kierkegaard and emergent Christianity match one another, he drops the ball—forgetting how "orthodox" he knows Kierkegaard really is.[9]

---

6   *The Emergent Prophet*, 6.
7   *The Emergent Prophet*, 21, 36, 84, 149.
8   This is one of Kierkegaard's great concerns: "[Let us] dare to carry out on Monday a little bit of what on Sunday . . . one sheds tears over" (PV 60)—and "God's Word is given in order that you shall act according to it, not that you shall practice interpreting obscure passages" (FSE 29).
9   *The Emergent Prophet*, 8, 75. For another recent Christian voice against Christian Orthodoxy, see David E. Fitch and Geoff Holsclaw, *Prodigal Christianity: Ten Signposts Into the Missional Frontier* (San Francisco: Jossey-Bass, 2013) 160–61: "God scattered all the peoples into multiple languages at Babel, preventing them from consolidating and becoming sufficient in themselves. Instead they now had to be dependent on God as he works through and among other people. The scattering was not a curse. It was God redirecting the sin of the people toward God's purposes. And the pluralism that resulted was actually a divinely intended 'gracious act' of God. And so we learn from Babel that God works to clarify, not obscure, the gospel through pluralism, through our vulnerable interactions with and being challenged by other people in other religions . . . . Pluralism then is not a bad thing for the church . . . . The prodigal God crosses all boundaries between . . . religion and religion." While this may look like nothing more than gracious, humble witnessing, it verges on syncretism. The trouble begins with denying the curse and ends with crossing religious boundaries. This book needs a good dose of 1 Thessalonians 2:4: "We speak, not to please men, but to please God who tests our hearts." And so Kierkegaard concludes that this world is "the time of testing related to an accounting and

Regarding the Bible (chapters 1 and 3), Kierkegaard would not go along with lessening submission to the authority

> judgment," and not "a lovely idyll with procreation and waltzing" (TM 178–79). Regarding that image of Babel, it apparently still plagues us: "No American painting or sculpture between World Wars I and II was able to accumulate, at least in the ordinary public's eye, the kind of cultural power that skyscrapers had . . . . Big buildings were always before you; mere paintings were not." Robert Hughes, *American Visions: The Epic History of Art in America* (New York: Knopf, 1997) 419. Note also how American art was turning away from the Church at the beginning of the twentieth century: "Tiffany and La Farge . . . . [produced] a large body of stained-glass work [which] could never have been tolerated in the churches of an earlier America. It signaled that religion could be voluptuous; that ritual could provide relief from the austerities of doctrine" (247–48).

of the Bible,[10] or exceeding its original meaning.[11] This is because Kierkegaard believed, as he says in *For Self-Examination*, that the Bible is a dangerous, "imperious book[12]—if one gives it a finger, it takes the whole hand; if one gives it the whole hand, it takes the whole man and may suddenly and radically change my whole life on a prodigious scale" (FSE 31). This resounding affirmation of Biblical force is completely missing in Roberts' book.[13]

10 *The Emergent Prophet*, 32. On this reduction, see also Terence E. Fretheim, *The Bible as Word of God in a Postmodern Age* (Minneapolis: Augsburg Fortress, 1998) 63: "[It] must be said clearly that God is actively engaged in that worldly experience, and God may work in and through that experience in such a way as to bring a critical word to bear on the Bible." This is because "the Bible at times fails us, even regarding matters of life and faith" (62). But Fretheim never says what the source is that is more reliable than the Bible—over against which it can be judged—and what it is that makes it a more reliable source. See also James K. A. Smith, *The Fall of Interpretation: Philosophical Foundations for a Creational Hermeneutic*, Second Edition (Grand Rapids, Michigan: Baker Academic, 2012) 53: "[The] New Testament writings are themselves interpretations of a person and an event. As a result we never have the Scriptures themselves . . . in any pure, unadorned sense; rather, every appeal to Scripture is always an appeal to an interpretation of Scripture." But that last interpretation is actually Scripture itself and not an interpretation of it—which undercuts Smith's hermeneutical proposal.

11 *The Emergent Prophet*, 79, 82.

12 If God's Word is truly this obtrusive, then it would seem to follow: "If it isn't scary, it isn't God." Merold Westphal, *Kierkegaard's Concept of Faith* (Grand Rapids, Michigan: Eerdmans, 2014) 86n10.

13 The acclaimed Biblical scholar, Brevard S. Childs (1923–2007), discusses this fact under the rubric of "coercion," in his book, *Isaiah* (Louisville, Kentucky: Westminster John Knox Press, 2001) 18, 21, 54, 58, 63, 68, 102, 263, 274, 421, 422, 437. See also pages 200, 204, and 405 on how the Bible "forces" its way on the reader. In this regard note also Robert W. Jenson's seminal essay, "Can a Text Defend Itself? An Essay *De Inspiratione Scripturae*," *dialog* 28 (Autumn1989): 251–56. Luther also thought the Biblical word could "jab the soul"

On the matter of doubt (chapter 2), Kierkegaard would not agree with Roberts that proofs "will get you nowhere."[14] He may have thought that about the certainty that supposedly is lodged in proofs based in logical syllogisms, but not when it comes to the "absolutely certain" Christian witness—or proofs—parents bequeath their children (JP 2:1170). Insofar

---

when preached. Martin Luther, "Commentary on Psalm 45" (1532), *LW* 12:225. On Luther as a postmodernist, see Kathryn A. Kleinhans, "Why Now? The Relevance of Luther in a Post-modern Age," *Currents in Theology and Mission* 24 (December 1997): 487–95. Kleinhans thinks of postmodernism as the critique of human autonomy and the hegemony of reason. In those regards she finds Luther to be quite postmodern. I would agree, but I am not as sanguine as she is that this is what postmodernism is. On Luther's critique of reason, see *The Devil's Whore: Reason and Philosophy in the Lutheran Tradition*, ed. Jennifer Hockenbery Dragseth (Minneapolis: Fortress, 2011) 49–50: "How can these positive statements on reason [by Luther] be reconciled with the negative [ones]? Reason is a marvelous gift of God, but it has its limitations. What is disastrous, according to Luther, is when reason oversteps its bounds and attempts to be the supreme judge in matters of faith. It cannot play this role because it is in various ways defective. First, it is insufficient; it fails to give humans what they need to know [*LW* 19:54] . . . . Its second defect is that when reason attempts to specify what God is like, it inevitably falls into error [*LW* 19:55–56] . . . . The third defect of reason is that it can give us no sure guidance in the human quest for salvation [*LW* 76:55] . . . . What reason tells us to do, gets us nowhere. On all these properly theological issues—the path to salvation, the true nature of God, God's attitude toward us—reason is blind. This kind of knowledge can come to us only through revelation. And what comes to us through revelation cannot be made subject to reason. When reason sets itself up as the final arbiter of truth in such matters, it trespasses onto foreign territory. . . . [However, by] submitting to revelation, granting revealed truth a privileged epistemic primacy, reason becomes 'enlightened reason.' Faith, in this sense, 'elevates reason.' Enlightened reason, for its part, 'serves' faith" [*LW* 1:124, 63, 112, 34:137; 76:55, 41:60, 52:84, 22:150–51, 19:53, 26:399, 19:54, 44:336, 32:112].
14   *The Emergent Prophet*, 43.

as "contemporary postmodern deconstructors ....[make] a virtual cult of the method of doubt, [they] unwittingly [subvert] doubt by refusing to doubt doubt itself,"[15] and consequently they miss the certainty in parental witnessing. So if we doubt the truth of Christianity out of humility and awareness of our inadequate perception, then we defame God, Kierkegaard would say, by not being able to "fasten down anything," by leaving "everything in abeyance," and by failing to "tie the knot at the end" (JFY 196).[16] Therefore all doubt concerning Christianity,[17] is nothing but "disobedience to God" (PV 123). It is "that gloomy darkness" and the "source of all excuses, ... that turns the relation around and doubts about God" (UDVS 279).[18]

---

15 Stephen N. Dunning "The Illusory Grandeur of Doubt," IKC 7:222.
16 This uncertainty goes against the preaching task itself: "[Preaching is right, according to Kierkegaard] only if it carries with it everything that will make fear of [God], in Him, something to be realized in one's life." Paul L. Holmer, *Communicating the Faith Indirectly*, ed. David J. Gouwens and Lee C. Barrett, Foreword by William H. Willimon, Afterward by David Cain (Eugene, Oregon: Cascade, 2013) 19.
17 See Mt 14:31, 21:21; Jn 20:27; Jas 1:6.
18 Kierkegaard further writes: "Without introducing *imitation*, it is impossible to gain mastery over doubts. Therefore, the state of things in Christendom is such that doubt has replaced faith. And then they want to stop doubt with—reasons; and they still are moving in that direction. They still have not learned that it is wasted effort—indeed, that it feeds doubt, gives it a basis for continuing. They are still not aware that *imitation* is the only force that, like a police force, can break up the mob of doubts and clear the area and compel one, if one does not want to be an *imitator*, at least to go home and hold one's tongue" (JFY 190–91). Merold Westphal misses this tie-in between certainty and discipleship in his book, *Whose Community? Which Interpretation? Philosophical Hermeneutics for the Church* (Grand Rapids, Michigan: Baker Academic, 2009). While he holds that all Christian claims to certainty are based on a false absolutism that fails to take into account human sin and perceptual limitations (15), he fails to include his own book in the mix with its own absolute claims against absolutism. As

Regarding Christ's atonement for the sins of the world (chapter 4), Kierkegaard would never favor reducing the crucifixion to a diaphanous mystery—free of all theories and doctrinal assertions.[19] Our Good Friday proclamation cannot be: "Swallow the red pill, taste and see the Pascal reality"![20] No, the significance of Christ's death for Kierkegaard is rather built on "the divine combat[21] of divine passion with itself, so that in a sense we human beings disappear like ants (although it still is infinite love for us)—this is forgotten" (JP 1:532). Roberts not only forgets it—but he also inveighs against it.

And Kierkegaard could never strip Christian love (chapter 5) of its "universal moral code."[22] It would then be nothing but "a hidden, private, mysterious feeling behind the lattice of the inexplicable," as Kierkegaard warns in *Works of Love* (WL 99)—a book which has precious little presence in Roberts' book. Only with a universal code in place can we "remove from love everything that is inflamed, everything that

---

a result he undercuts Christian discipleship which goes nowhere if its boldness is taken away (Acts 9:27, 19:8). For if there is no sure "faith in providence," then there is no venturing out into discipleship—following the Crucified One (UDVS 85). There is no "being put to death" (BA 234) due to the stringency of following the Lord Jesus (Mt 7:13–14, 10:16; Lk 6:22–23, 16:15; Jn 15:18–19). Westphal's mistake is reminiscent of the famous book, *Language, Truth, and Logic* (1936, 1946) by A. J. Ayer (1910–1989). In it Ayer argued that the only meaningful sentences were those that could be empirically verified—but it was later shown that the verification principle itself could not be empirically verified and so the book fell on its own sword. See W. V. O. Quine, *From a Logical Point of View* (Cambridge: Harvard University Press, 1953).

19 This is something that Luther knew kept Christianity alive and forceful (*LW* 33:21).
20 *The Emergent Prophet*, 101.
21 On that divine combat, see Jack Miles, *Christ: A Crisis in the Life of God* (New York: Knopf, 2001) 97, 99, 109.
22 *The Emergent Prophet*, 106, 115, 118.

is momentary, everything that is giddy" (WL 188).²³

Kierkegaard's attack on the church (chapter 6) excluded the possibility of an alternative church "in which judgment of the other is suspended,"²⁴ according to Roberts. Kierkegaard instead favored a church as a band of criminals. In such a church "each Christian . . . by staking his life on the absurd . . . has broken with the world [and] . . . is all the more intimate precisely because each one individually feels isolated . . . . This means that the Christian congregation is a society consisting of qualitative individuals and that the intimacy of the society is also conditioned by this polemical stance against the great human society" (JP 4:4175). Roberts skips this passage and by so doing seriously weakens his book.²⁵

---

23 This view of love may well contribute to the poor success rate of Christian sermons: "We preach that the Gospel should make truthful people who live before the world according to how they would like to answer before God, and that their life should resemble the preaching. But what happens is the opposite." Martin Luther, "Sermons on Matthew 23" (1537–40), *LW* 68:206. On this correlation of Luther and Kierkegaard, see Martin J. Heinecken, *The Moment Before God: An Interpretation of Kierkegaard* (Philadelphia: Muhlenberg, 1955) 379: "Kierkegaard and Luther stand exactly at the same point and do not differ basically in their understanding of the gospel and the church." See also Thomas Cahill, *Heretics and Heroes: How Renaissance Artists and Reformation Priests Created Our World* (New York: Doubleday, 2013) 173: "It is not so very surprising that Luther was often misunderstood in his time. He might have been better appreciated in the nineteenth century by Kierkegaard . . ."
24 *The Emergent Prophet*, 138.
25 So does Sylvia Walsh in her review of this book: "Although Kierkegaard finally gave up on the established church as a viable institution in Christendom, he did not give up on Christianity itself nor did he lack a positive conception of what the true church should be in the realm of temporality. As Roberts has pointed out, that is always a church militant, namely a church that is continually in the process of becoming victorious in the world through struggle in a hostile environment that is opposite of the essentially Christian . . . . Still, I think Kierkegaard

Finally Roberts should have spent much more time on *The Book on Adler*, wherein Kierkegaard attacks the subjectivism of the berserk vicar of Bornholm (BA 155) for brushing aside that the "essentially Christian exists before any Christian exists," in order to maintain the "objective continuance outside all believers" of the Christian faith (BA 117–18).[26]

Even though this book leaves much to be desired, it still is must reading for anyone who cares about Kierkegaard's interface with postmodernism—and his motto that we should not be "on good terms with the present moment" (JP 6:6184).[27]

---

had no idea what concrete shape a reformation of the Christian church and society should take. He was equally opposed to both communism and pietism as ways of achieving social equality in the world. Given his antipathy toward the numerical and the crowd, I suspect that he would also strongly disapprove of American mega-churches as the way to go." "Kierkegaard as Emerging Prophet," *Søren Kierkegaard Newsletter*, Number 62 (June 2014) 10.

26 Science even suffers from this lack of objectivity. On this weakness, see the amazing case of the University of Chicago Professor of Geology, J. Harlan Bretz (1882–1981), winner of the Penrose Medal (1979): "After European geologists dismissed a central role for a catastrophic flood in earth history, the idea became geological heresy. Although J. Harlan Bretz uncovered evidence of giant floods in eastern Washington in the 1920s, it took most of the twentieth century for other geologists to believe him. Geologists had so thoroughly denied the existence of great floods that they could not believe it when somebody actually found evidence for one . . . . A classic field geologist, Bretz figured out the story of the region's giant glacial floods, seeing what others at first could not and then would not see to sort out the pieces of a landscape-scale jigsaw puzzle." David R. Montgomery, *The Rocks Don't Lie: A Geologist Investigates Noah's Flood* (New York: Norton, 2012) 203, 210. Professor Bretz is featured in the documentary, "Megafloods of the Ice Age," NOVA (September 20, 2005).

27 In agreement with Roberts—and in opposition to Kierkegaard's motto—would be the book *Mediating Faith* (Minneapolis: Fortress, 2014) by Clint Schnekloth. Of this book Andrew Root writes: "[It is] a must-read for all pastors . . . [who] are brave enough to leave

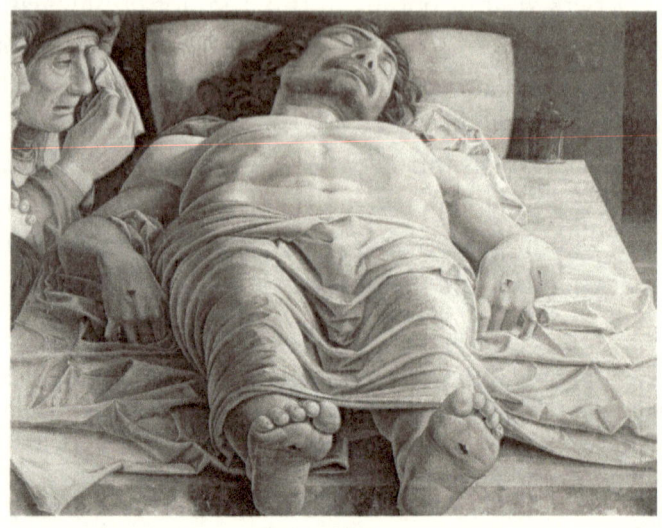

Andrea Mantegna, The Lamentation of Christ (1480).

the antiquated and enter into the depth and possibilities of our time." "Review," *Word & World* 35 (Winter 2015): 97.

APPENDIX FOUR

On Mary & Martha

Luke 10:38–42—with its story of the encounter of Jesus with the sisters, Mary and Martha, in their home in Bethany—has been called one of "the most famous" stories in the Bible,[1] and also one of the most misunderstood.[2] That is because Martha seems to have been unnecessarily denigrated in it.[3]

---

1   Paul Tillich, *The New Being* (New York: Scribner's, 1955) 152.
2   Warren Carter, "Getting Martha Out of the Kitchen: Luke 10:38–42 Again," *The Catholic Biblical Quarterly* 58 (April 1996): 266: "The nature and significance of Martha's action in [Luke 10:38] have received little investigation. Conventional analyses see Martha as the harried performer of kitchen duties without help from Mary. Several indicators in the context and in the presentation of the scene indicate this to be an unlikely reading which misconstrues the whole pericope." See also Blake R. Hefner, "Meister Eckhart and a Millennium with Mary and Martha," *Lutheran Quarterly* 5 (Summer 1991): 172: "[By] the late Middle Ages, Martha is cast, . . . not Mary, as the more mature and fruitful disciple. Quite contrary to the literal sense of the text, [she is depicted] as the happier, freer, and more fulfilled of the two sisters!"
3   This criticism starts in the early church with Ephrem the Syrian: "Martha's love was more fervent than Mary's, for before [Jesus] had arrived there, she was ready to serve him." *Luke*, ed. Arthur A. Just, Jr., Ancient Christian Commentary on Scripture: New Testament III (Downer

Kierkegaard also favored this story even though he stressed the active life over the studious, contemplative one, as represented by Mary.[4] Nevertheless he sides with Luther against Martha,[5] agreeing with him that she was "concerned about

> Grove, Illinois, InterVarsity, 2003) 183. See also the end of the sonnet by Giuseppe Gioacchino Belli (1719–1863), "Martha and Magdalene": "And Martha [said to the Savior]: 'So says you, but I know better. Listen, if I sat around on my salvation the way [Mary] does, who'd keep this house together?'" *Divine Inspiration: The Life of Jesus in World Poetry*, ed. Robert Atwan, George Dardess, Peggy Rosenthal (New York: Oxford, 1998) 209. See also Joanna Weaver, *Having a Mary Heart in a Martha World: Finding Intimacy With God in the Busyness of Life* (Colorado Springs, Colorado: WaterBrook Press, 2002) 3: "Martha . . . . appeals more to my perfectionist tendencies. What a woman! . . . . She is the original Martha Stewart, the New Testament's Proverbs 31 woman, and Israel's answer to Betty Crocker . . . . She's the Queen of the Kitchen—and the rest of the house as well." This criticism has also led to an equalization of the two sisters—as witnessed in the classic iconic depictions of them (see FIGURE). I would prefer more of an asymmetry between Mary and Martha—as I think both Luther and Kierkegaard would—and as is in the recent painting by Eileen Kennedy (see page 351).

4   On the importance of action for Kierkegaard, see Sermon Five above, "Be Doers of the Word." See also his regard for Saint Bernard (1090–1153) of Clairvaux's point: "'Let us not forget that Martha and Mary still were sisters' (meaning the other side of life should also be included)" (JP 4:5015). Bernard is known as "the difficult saint"—no wonder Kierkegaard liked him. Bernard McGinn, *The Doctors of the Church: Thirty-Three Men and Women Who Shaped Christianity* (New York: Crossroads, 1999) 107. See also footnote 27 in the appendix.

5   Kierkegaard writes that Martha's mistake was that she insisted "on learning much from life" (EUD 42). That is because by so doing she violates Col 3:2; Phil 3:20; 2 Cor 4:18. And that is significant because viewed "from eternity, to enjoy is the same as to squander, to dissipate; to suffer is like accumulating savings" (JP 4:4614). Even so, the Christian is not "to withdraw from life, from an honorable occupation, from a happy domestic life—on the contrary, [your eternal responsibility before God] will support and transfigure and illuminate your conduct in the relationships of life . . . . You will find more and more time for your

many things [and] believed that temporal, not spiritual things should be sought."[6] Kierkegaard goes on to use this story as the backbone[7] of his famous[8] *An Occasional Discourse* (1847)—popularly known as *Purity of Heart is to Will One Thing*.[9] In it he lifts up the saying about only "one thing is needful."[10] He does not, however, mention Mary and Martha who are integral to these famous words. But he does take from these sisters the categories of temporality and eternality—having Martha in effect stand for temporality and Mary for the eternal—

> duties and your tasks, while concern for your eternal responsibility will keep you from being busy and from busily taking part in everything possible—an activity that can best be called a waste of time" (UDVS 137).

6 Martin Luther, "First Psalm Lectures" (1513), LW 10:127. See also LW 78:135 from his 1532 sermon on Luke 15:1–10. And Joanna Weaver is right that "Martha's internal disabilities [were rooted in] the dark corners of pride and prejudice, the spiritual handicap of busyness that left her unable to enjoy the intimacy of [Christ's] presence." *Having a Mary Heart in a Martha World*, 60.

7 See UDVS 7, 23–25, 29–35, 60, 66, 75–77, 80, 107, 110, 116, 122, 128, 136–37, 144, 146, 148, 153–54.

8 George E. Arbaugh and George B. Arbaugh, *Kierkegaard's Authorship: A Guide to the Writings of Kierkegaard* (Rock Island, Illinois: Augustana College Library, 1967) 241: "[This] book is a classic of devotional literature [and] the best book with which to begin an acquaintance with Kierkegaard."

9 *An Occasional Discourse* (1847) was given this nickname by D. V. Steere in his 1938 publication of Søren Kierkegaard, *Purity of Heart is to Will One Thing: Spiritual Preparation for the Office of Confession*, ed. and trans. Douglas V. Steere (New York: Harper Torchbooks, 1938, 1948, 1956).

10 Biblical critics dispute this line, saying that there are textual warrants for it to read instead that "a few things are necessary," and not just one. See Frederick W. Danker, *Jesus and the New Age According to St. Luke* (Saint Louis: Clayton, 1972) 133; I. Howard Marshall, *Commentary on Luke* (Grand Rapids, Michigan, 1978) 453; and François Bovon, *Luke 2: A Commentary on the Gospel of Luke 9:51–19:27*, trans. Donald S. Deer (Minneapolis: Fortress, 2013) 73–74.

and then goes on to make those categories the center of his discourse.¹¹ Those categories matter to Kierkegaard because he believed that "temporality and eternity cannot be reconciled" in the double-minded person (UDVS 62). Indeed, temporality will always prevail over against the eternal whenever they clash in such a person.¹² And so if they ever are to be resolved, considerable "disturbance" and "shock" will be needed to move the double-minded person to purity of heart and the willing of one thing (UDVS 135, 142)—a turbulence which is also central to Kierkegaard's authorship.¹³

---

11 They are also central to his entire authorship. See Ronald F. Marshall, *Kierkegaard for the Church: Essays and Sermons* (Eugene, Oregon: Wipf & Stock, 2013) 201n77.

12 "It is easier, for example, to make a casserole for a grieving family than it is to offer a word of hope in Christ, easier to welcome a new neighbor with a fresh loaf of bread than to invite her to worship." Stephanie Frey, "Living With Martha," *The Christian Century* 121 (July 13, 2004): 16. See also Martin Luther, "Sermons on John 6–8" (1530), LW 23:12, 13: "God does not have His Gospel proclaimed for the sake of the belly, but for the . . . salvation of our souls . . . . The Christian adheres to such a foolish message and believes in [such a] stupid God." Therefore, as Kierkegaard writes: "The temporal and the eternal stand opposed to each other in this way. In time it holds true that if you want to succeed and become somebody and [have] all that [is] in this world, then you simply must manage to serve two masters, for you do not get very far in this world by willing one thing—precisely this is the road to failure in this world. But in eternity, willing to serve two masters is the road to perdition" (JP 4:4801).

13 On this militancy in Kierkegaard's view of Christianity, see Ronald F. Marshall, *Kierkegaard for the Church*, 62, 113–14, 124, 231–35, 295, 341, and the passage referred to in footnote 31 below. On the opposition of American culture to this militancy, note Perlstein's point: "A certain sort of bland religiosity had expanded enormously in the 1950s . . . . President Eisenhower [1890–1969] said, 'A system of government like ours makes no sense unless founded on a firm faith in religion—and I don't care what it is.' Blandness was supposed to be a good thing; it attenuated cultural conflict, smoothed edges, made a diverse nation

Martha falls short, according to Luke's Gospel, because she is too busy, distracted and anxious over her domestic duties.[14] Kierkegaard takes this brief description of Martha's problem and enlarges upon it in his *An Occasional Discourse*. In it he helps us understand what holds Martha back from following the example of her sister. He says, in effect,[15] that Martha was held back because of a "spell"[16] that overtook her, turning her into a double-minded person,[17] as warned against

> united and strong." Rick Perlstein, *The Invisible Bridge: The Fall of Nixon and the Rise of Reagan* (New York: Simon & Schuster, 2014) 447.

14 Some believe that there were more than three people for dinner, since Luke 10:23 and 38 imply that the disciples of Jesus also attended. That would bring the number for dinner to sixteen—including Lazarus, the brother of Martha and Mary. Mitzi J. Smith, "A Tale of Two Sisters: Am I My Sister's Keeper?" *Journal of Religious Thought* 52/53 (Winter 1995/ Spring1996): 70.

15 Kierkegaard, as I have already noted, never mentions Mary and Martha in this discourse, which I think is actually about them and the saying about only one thing being needed at the end of Luke 10:38–42. So in my exposition of this discourse, I insert the names of Mary and Martha (and their pronouns) where appropriate, with brackets, even though Kierkegaard never does so, in order to make the point that *An Occasional Discourse* is really about them—via the categories of temporality and eternity.

16 If we are caught up in a spell like this, then it is questionable that we are entirely free before God. Niels Jørgen Cappelørn veers off track in this regard: "In relation to God there is a dialectic that may not be surrendered; if it is surrendered, we end up either in deterministic necessity or in relativistic arbitrariness. God has a place for me, and I am entirely free to decide whether I will accept it and occupy it. But if I want to know in advance with certainty where it is, I can be certain of not encountering it." Søren Kierkegaard, *The Lily of the Field and the Bird of the Air: Three Godly Discourses*, Monotypes by Maja Lisa Engelhardt. Postscript by Niels Jørgen Cappelørn. Translation by Bruce H. Kirmmse (New York: Elizabeth Harris Gallery, 2013) 79.

17 For a helpful description of the double-minded, see again Cappelørn's "Postscript," 85: "[Double-mindedness], which is divided into two, riven, and split, expresses itself in hesitancy, vacillation, evasion. The

in James 4:8 (UDVS 24). How sad for Martha to have the power of this spell grow "with the increasing buzzing [and then spread] to trap [her] so that childhood or youth are scarcely granted the stillness, the remoteness, in which the eternal attains a divine growth" (UDVS 66). This growing spell catches her "in the thicket of deliberation, ... in the multifariously compounded complexity of interaction" (UDVS 131). This web of interactions becomes a "brilliant escape into that rubbish that [she is] many" (UDVS 133). Once under that spell, Martha goes the way of "corruptive strife and comparison that condescends and insults, that sighs and envies" (UDVS 81). That is why Mary's witness to the eternal sounds to Martha in her "busyness [like] nothing but flabby words" (UDVS 70). In this "busyness—in which one continually goes further and further, and noise, in which the true is continually forgotten more and more, and the multitude of circumstances, incentives, and hindrances—[it] continually makes it more impossible for [her] to gain any deeper knowledge of [herself]" (UDVS 67). Without that depth Martha cannot refrain from

---

double-minded person never wills only one thing, but always at least two things, preferably at the same time, and he wishes to arrive at the same endpoint by taking two different routes simultaneously. There will always be a difference between what he says and what he does. . . . [He] is fundamentally disobedient . . . . And, says Kierkegaard, where there is ambivalence, there the temptation *is*, and it is captivating; but where there is nothing ambivalent—namely, in the simple person—temptation is powerless, for there is nothing to take captive." For a cinematic depiction of this double-mindedness, see *Locke* (2013), directed by Steven Knight, where the lead character, Ivan Locke (played by Tom Hardy), juggles at least eight balls in the air for the entire movie: his paramour; his estranged wife; his needy son; his insecure co-worker; his irate boss; and an emergency room doctor—all on the telephone while racing down the freeway in the rain, wiping his dripping nose from a head cold.

wearying herself[18] with "makeshift, temporary palliatives; [and from grieving her] spirit with temporal consolations; [which] suicidally kill the wish; through hope, through faith, through love [to] win the highest that the most powerful is capable of" (UDVS 101). And so Martha "in temporality, in restlessness, in the noise, in the crush, in the crowd, in the jungle of evasions, alas, yes, here [she] completely deafens [her] conscience" (UDVS 128–29).[19] No wonder Kierkegaard thought that in such a person "temporality and eternity cannot be reconciled" (UDVS 62). Indeed, "Mary and Martha never enter a dialogue with each other."[20] For Martha is trapped "in the swarming

---

18   Indeed, the "melancholy law of transitoriness governs even our most passionate concerns." Paul Tillich, *The New Being*, 157. Apparently this gave out "in the nineteenth century, with the development of charitable organizations, [where] the person of Martha underwent a [positive] rehabilitation. In any case, Martha was a popular first name in that century." François Bovon, *Luke 2*, 77.

19   And so Martha joins "the majority of people . . . . They are like the well-fed person who works for the next day's food, but not like the hungry person who must use immediately what he can get. Basically they have lives in other categories, which gives them a deceptive security while they busy themselves with and concern themselves about the religious. They do not grasp that the religious is the *one thing needful*; they consider it *also to be needful*, especially for difficult times. They understand very well that a person can die of hunger when he does not have anything to live on, but they do not grasp that a human being lives on the Word that proceeds from the mouth of God [for] a human being absolutely needs God at every moment" (BA 105, 106). The self-esteem movement, with its commitment to self-reliance, also blunts this realization. For a critique, see Laura L. Smith and Charles H. Elliott, *Hollow Kids: Recapturing the Soul of a Generation Lost to the Self-Esteem Myth* (Roseville, California: Prima Publishing, Forum, 2001) 107: "Knowing that self-absorption poses a risk for most forms of mental disorders, how can we justify the continued drive to promote self-esteem? Although we can't say so with certainty, this promotion very well may exacerbate the very problems it's trying to solve."

20   Mitzi J. Smith, "A Tale of Two Sisters," 74. From the same year, in

multitude of excuses"—

> just like poisonous fumes over the fields, like the hosts of grasshoppers over Egypt, so excuses and the host of them become a general plague that nibbles off the sprout of the eternal, become a corrupting infection among the people—[with there always being] one more excuse available for the next person. (UDVS 68)

And what exactly are these insidious excuses? Martha does not want to be involved with the eternal because

> in the motley, teeming crowd, in the noise of the world, little attention is paid from day to day and year to year to whether a person completely wills the good if only he has influence and power, is in a big enterprise, is somebody to himself and to others.
> (UDVS 65)

This is all that matters—making your big enterprises successful in the world as it is right now. Because eternity, that "higher view of life" (UDVS 67), is of no help with such undertakings, there is little reason to pay any attention to it. So Martha

---

another set of discourses called, *The Gospel of Sufferings* (1847), Kierkegaard would say they were not talking to each other because Martha had been beguiled: "[The] more fortunate, the more favored person is only all too easily persuaded and beguiled by temporality, until it seems to him that things go so well for him that he does not need anything more; or if it nevertheless seems to him that things do not go so well for him, then he is still beguiled by temporality in such a way that it never occurs to him to look in the right place for the reason." (UDVS 309).

thinks she can do it all by herself, since "the world is more allied with the mediocre than with the truly good" (UDVS 98). But contrary to Martha, this higher way of life would ask of her "in quiet patience [to] leave everything up to the good itself" (UDVS 97). Martha will never do this, however, for in her "the ill nature of cowardly, fearful self-love meets the presumptuousness of the proud, defiant mind . . . in equal powerlessness" (UDVS 31).[21] This combination holds her back, and the times sweep her away:

> Nowadays it is not as it was in the days of old, when the opinion of the many was like foam on water, meaningless yet clamorous, blind yet crucial, impossible to follow because it changes faster than a woman changes color. Nowadays the outcome is no longer doubtful; the good is immediately victorious. Nowadays no sacrifice is demanded, no self-denial, because the world wills the good. Nowadays the opinion of the many is the opinion of the wise; the single individuals are fools. Nowadays the earth is the kingdom of God; the kingdom in heaven is only a reflection. Nowadays the world is the

---

21   This powerlessness wreaks havoc upon our volition—as Kierkegaard says when seizing up his entire authorship: "[It] is simply not the case [that our] ability to receive is entirely in order" (PV 54). (See also footnote 16 above.) And even though Martha may be serious about her defiance, not all "that is called earnestness is earnestness; there is much that is only a gloomy frame of mind, the ill humor of a worldly worried heart, a bitterness of mind that does not sigh to God but against God and denounces its fate, a foolish and fatuous busyness that busies itself with everything else but the one thing needful, that throughout a long life finds time for everything else but not one single moment for the only thing needful" (CD 365). Sounds like Martha to me, down to the last detail.

> most trustworthy thing we have, the only thing one can build upon, the only thing one can swear by. (UDVS 56-57)

But Mary will have nothing to do with this cynicism about the single individual, sacrifice, self-denial, and the kingdom of heaven or the eternal.[22] She instead hears the eternal word differently:

> "Oh, what would it profit a person if he won the whole world but lost himself;[23] what would it profit him if he won time and what belongs to time if he broke with the eternal; what would it profit him if he *swept through* the world at full sail with the fair winds of applause and admiration when he runs aground on eternity"? (UDVS 86)

Because of such worldly vacuity and danger, Mary goes the way of "the most important thing: in the service of the truth to uphold right and justice with self-sacrifice; . . . . [to] become intimate with God; . . . . to fear God . . . quite actually and

---

22 For the good of this world is illusory according to God: "Therefore every person is to test himself. Perhaps there has been someone in this world who was admired by men, extolled in his lifetime, missed in death, honored as a benefactor, commemorated with memorials, to whom God nevertheless was obliged to say: Unhappy man, you did not choose the better part" (EUD 368). And, alas, such a one was Martha. So I see Joanna Weaver veering off course when she notes: "I find it interesting that when Jesus corrected Martha, he didn't say: 'Why can't you be more like your sister, Mary?'" *Having a Mary Heart in a Martha World*, 5.

23 Mk 8:36.

literally; .... [and] to will as a single individual to be allied with God" (UDVS 71, 107, 137, 144).[24] This good way[25] firmly places her 'in the trustworthiness of the eternal" (EUD 259)—as charted out by the eternal itself, contrary to temporal ways. This higher life renounces all,[26] gives up being inquisitive,[27]

24 "This is what Mary was .... Beyond this, not much ... could be said about [her], and it is less than what [was] said about Martha." Paul Tillich, *The New Being*, 159. Such a one as Mary "has time to consider the one thing needful, the heart to wish for heaven's salvation, the earnestness to reject the flirting of light-minded ideas, the fear and trembling [Phil 2:12] in [her] soul to be terrified at the thought of breaking with heaven or of taking it in vain [2 Cor 6:1]" (EUD 258). In our day, however, Mary's convictions are anything but compelling. On the alleged stupidity of belief in God, see George Carlin, *Napalm & Silly Putty* (New York: Hyperion, 2001) 28: "Religion—easily—has the Greatest Bullshit Story Ever Told! Think about it: religion has actually convinced people—many of them adults—that there's an invisible man who lives in the sky and watches everything you do [Ps 139:2], every minute of every day. And who has a special list of ten things he does not want you to do [Ex 20:1–17; Mt 22:36–40]. And if you do any of these ten things, he has a special place, full of fire and smoke and burning and torture and anguish [Lk 16:23, 28; Rv 9:5], where he will send you to remain and suffer and burn and choke and scream and cry [Mk 9:48], forever and ever, till the end of time [Mt 25:46]. But he loves you! [Rv 3:19]. He loves you, and he needs money [Dt 14:22; Mal 3:10]! He always needs money. He's all-powerful, all-perfect, all-knowing, and all-wise [Rv 1:8], but somehow ... he just can't handle money. Religion takes in billions of dollars, pays no taxes, and somehow always needs a little more. Now, you talk about a good bullshit story. Holy shit!"
25 "Tersteegen's observation is very penetrating, ... that Mary has [not] chosen the best part—but the good part, that is, the best part beyond all comparison. That is to say, the positive is more than the superlative [for] the superlative subtracts, [for] 'reasons' in connection with faith are a subtraction" (JP 4:4752).
26 These refined efforts have been called the work of "productive solitude." Clancy Martin, "Distraction and Self-Deception," IKC 15:66.
27 Pope Francis (b. 1936) sides with Friedrich Wilhelm Nietzsche (1844–1900) against Kierkegaard on this prohibition of inquisitiveness. *Lu-*

and takes up the narrow way of the single individual[28] (UDVS 141, 142, 152). It sees the suffering from adversity to be good (UDVS 140),[29] since only through it can any of us be "weaned"

> *men Fidei* (The Light of Faith: Encyclical Letter) (Frederick, Maryland: The Word Among Us Press, 2013) 4, 44–45: "[Faith] encourages the scientist to remain constantly open to reality in all its inexhaustible richness." Kierkegaard is against inquisitiveness, not because he is closed-minded, but because of its prolixity: "[Can human wisdom] produce in . . . any person what the simplest person is able to do just as well as the very wise—action! Would not human wisdom rather make everything more difficult! Would not eloquence, which despite all its gloriousness never once manages to articulate simultaneously the variety that simultaneously dwells in a person's heart, rather anesthetize the energy of the act and let it fall asleep in protracted deliberation!" (EUD 113). This comes from his 1843 discourse on Job—which indeed is another greatly edifying exposition.
>
> 28   Kierkegaard's *An Occasional Discourse* is written for just such a single person, "who willingly reads slowly, reads repeatedly, and who reads aloud—for his own sake" (UDVS 5).
>
> 29   Making adversity positive is especially distressing to the double-minded. On this point see Kierkegaard's comments from 1855 on making life easy: "Sagacious as the human race is, it has spied out the secret of life, has got wind of the secret that if one wants to have life made easy (and this is just what people want), then this is easily done. One merely needs more and more to trivialize oneself, . . . then life becomes easier and easier . . . . Then the beloved's death, [for instance], or his unfaithfulness becomes at most a little pause, something like sitting out a dance at a ball; half an hour later you are dancing with a new partner—indeed, it would be boring to dance all night with one partner . . . . So, you see, all difficulties vanish; life becomes enjoyable, cheerful, jolly, easy—in short, it is a glorious world in which to live . . . . [And so] have one viewpoint today, tomorrow another, then one you had yesterday again, and then in turn a new one on Friday . . . . [Make] yourself into several persons, or parcel out yourself, have one viewpoint anonymously, another in one's name, one orally, another in writing, one as a public official, one as a private individual, one as your wife's husband, another at the club—and you will see all difficulties vanish" (TM 318–19). And contrary to this escape into triviality, Christianity says: "Get into the thick of it!" (JP 1:372). That is precisely what Mary

away from temporality.³⁰ And this life cannot come upon any of us without significant disturbance—"a blow" that seems to "crush" us, "like a sunstroke directly on the brain," "the infinite concentrated intensively in one single . . . moment," "like the deadliest danger, something every man must shrink from as more horrible than death," "a concentration of sin or past sins in one single blow," which, because it "can give momentum, compared to which any movement in reflection is a remaining-on-the-spot," it also is "the greatest favor which can be shown" a person (JP 4:4903).³¹ And all of this is because of the calm that follows upon those catastrophic but salutary disruptions:

> [And so] we compare the heart to the ocean, because its purity is this constancy in being deep and in being transparent. No storm may agitate it, no sudden gust of wind may move its surface; no drowsy fog may spread over it; there must be no dubious movement within it; no fleeting cloud may darken it; but it must lie still, deeply transparent, ... like the heart of someone who wills only one thing . . . . Just as the ocean reflects the height of heaven in its pure depth, so the heart, when it is still and deeply transparent, reflects in its pure depth the heavenly sublimity of the good.
> (UDVS 121)

---

did—and will you look at the row she kicked up all these many years later?!
30 This idea of being weaned away also comes from *The Gospel of Sufferings* (UDVS 257).
31 See also footnote 13 above.

This is Mary as she sits in her home in Bethany, at the feet of Jesus, being transformed by his "words of eternal life."[32] There she is "on the other side of the boundary within the bastion of eternity" (UDVS 60). And there is no hurry with her like there was with Martha. No, for "it is definitely so that eternally the good has always been victorious, but in time it is different. In time it takes a long time, the victory is slow, its uncertainty a slow linear measuring," and so "at the end it [seems as if she] had accomplished nothing for the good," like "a fish is pulled out of the water and cast onto the beach" (UDVS 61, 62). Martha would never tolerate such shenanigans, and so she counterfeits the eternal, making it into "the bluish deceptive illusion of time, . . . the dazzling jugglery of the moment" (UDVS 63). By so doing, however, she forfeits genuine Biblical eternity "and thereby makes time empty" (UDVS 64).[33] But Mary digs in and is stalwart.[34] She

---

32 See Jn 6:68, 17:3.
33 On the emptying of time, see UDVS 137 on the wasting of time, and footnote 5 above.
34 And so is Jesus. He never says to Martha: "You are absolutely right. Mary is violating the household codes and social norms; I'll send her back into the kitchen with you." Mitzi J. Smith, "A Tale of Two Sisters," 72. And neither do we have anywhere in the New Testament an episode where, say, Jesus visits a Judith and Joanna in Capernaum, and Judith comes to him in the kitchen while he is helping Joanna prepare the meal, and says to him, "Lord, tell Joanna to help me meditate on your words that I've written down." And Jesus responds, "Judith, Judith, you are worried about many words and trying to remember, and do, all that I have taught you and the whole world. Joanna has chosen the one thing needful, which shall not be taken away from her." Therefore I do not agree with those many interpreters who see Martha as a female version of the Good Samaritan (Lk 10:29–37), thereby exonerating her by appealing to the larger Biblical context. See, for example, Frederick W. Danker, *Luke* (Philadelphia: Fortress, 1976) 68–69; Fred B. Craddock, *Luke* (Louisville, Kentucky: John Knox, 1990) 149–52; and Luke Timothy Johnson, *The Gospel of Luke* (Collegeville, Minne-

chooses the good[35]—and thereby testifies to the fact that it "must be chosen" (JP 2:1356). Earnestness is required by the divine, eternal way of life, and so this life must be chosen. You cannot slide into it willy-nilly. But it does not thereby follow that Mary freely and easily chooses it either—like "pulling on one's socks" (PC 35, 95). That would be to have a will that "is not mature" (UDVS 76). No, this choice is different since it aims at eternity—and so it must have the "momentum of eternity" as its "moving force" which steers the person of pure heart "toward a better world" (UDVS 75). Mary knows that if she in honesty were to venture out and "risk everything" for the eternal God, she would "surely acquire the strength" needed to do it—a "superhuman strength" (UDVS 84). And so as Kierkegaard urged in a discourse from 1844, we are able to choose the one thing needful, the better part, when God gives us the "spirit of power, of love, and of self-control":

> [Therefore do] what you can for God, and God will do for you what you cannot do .... [The] only thing and the greatest ... [a person is] capable of doing for God—is to give oneself completely, consequently one's weakness also .... [So venture] it, you who threw off the chain of resolution and now may be boasting

---

sota: The Liturgical Press, 1991) 175. So Martha is no female Good Samaritan—for she is serving her *friends*, whereas the Good Samaritan helps out a *stranger*—an enemy (Lk 17:16–18)—who had been beaten up and left for dead along a remote road. A much closer case of comparable hospitality would be the one in Luke 14:7–14 about inviting over the poor, the maimed, the lame, and the blind who "cannot repay you." So I disagree again with Joanna Weaver that you can combine the two sisters by "doing the Martha Mary-ly." *Having a Mary Heart in a Martha World*, 204.

35 Lk 10:42.

of your freedom like a released prisoner. Venture to understand that this pride of yours is cowardliness; turn yourself in again so that justice may again bind you in the service of the resolution; venture it in trust in God, who will give a spirit of power and of love and of self-control! Venture it, you who once humbled yourself under God in the good resolution but made a mistake and in your own eyes and in the eyes of others became so very important to the good; venture it again in order to become nothing before God—he will surely give you a spirit of power, of love, and of self-control! (EUD 368–69)

This venturing is precisely what Kierkegaard wanted to make "vivid" in his 1847 discourse on willing the one thing needful (UDVS 122).[36] This was vivid to Mary—that she was both nothing and yet powerful in the extreme—and he wanted to make sure it was also vivid to the rest of us, so that we, like her, might venture out into this higher life of the eternal. And that is because in this new life everything is "reversed," because our minds have become "intimate with eternity's true thought," that the "purely momentary seems a gain, which . . . in the very next moment proves to be a deception [as] with everything momentary [like] the opinion of the crowd and going along with the crowd" (UDVS 135). With this salutary rearrangement, we will finally become exempt "from all foolish questions" like

whether I have won people (on the contrary,

---

36 See also UDVS 17, 123, 125, 127, 135, 139, 145, 148.

the question would probably be whether I dared to do the least thing to win them), . . . whether I had earthly advantage from it (on the contrary, the question would probably be whether I dared to do the least thing to gain it), . . . about what results I have produced, or whether I produced no results whatever, or whether loss and the ridicule of others were the only results I have produced. (UDVS 149)

But none of this matters to eternity because gaining ground in this world has been replaced with obeying God in this world and the next (UDVS 61)[37]—an obedience which is the one thing needful. And this replacement is powerful because it trumps eleven phony but intransigent fears: "financial loss, loss of reputation, lack of appreciation, disregard, the opinion of the world,[38] the mockery of fools, the laughter of light-

---

37 See also UDVS 43, 137. Even so, Martha still has a role to play, albeit a diminished one: " If that's really the case, [that Martha doesn't have a role to play in the church, then] let people all give up ministering to the needy; let them all choose the better part. . . . Let them devote their time to the work, let them pant for the sweetness of doctrine [Psalm 42], let them busy themselves with theology;. . . . don't let them bother at all about what stranger there may be in the neighborhood. . . . And yet it's not like that. . . . [Martha] didn't choose a bad one, but [Mary] chose a better [one]. What makes it better? Because you are concerned with many things, she with one" *Essential Sermons* (The Works of Saint Augustine, Part III—Homilies), trans. Edmunds Hill, O.P., ed. Boniface Ramsey (Hyde Park, New York: New City Press, 2007) 160—61.

38 On this hostility, see Edward O. Wilson, *The Meaning of Human Existence* (New York: Liveright, 2014) 153: "Obviously [all creation stories] invented by the many known thousands of religions and sects in fact have certainly been false. A great many educated citizens have realized that their own faiths are indeed false, or at least questionable in details. But they understand the rule attributed to the Roman stoic philosopher Seneca the Younger that religion is regarded by the common peo-

mindedness, the cowardly whining of deference, the inflated insignificance of the moment, the delusive, misty apparitions of miasma[39]" (UBVS 52). Free of those fears, you, with Mary,

---

ple as true, by the wise as false, and by rulers as useful." Wilson believes that if prosperous intellectuals speak out in America against religion, that is then unfairly taken as religious bigotry and "the equivalent of a personal threat" (155). Under this construal, Harvard University professors who are celebrated authors are the persecuted ones. Under this construal saying that religious faith "is the one thing that makes otherwise good people do bad things," is a neutral claim (154, 151). So Wilson regards statements like this as even-handed criticisms: "Intellectual compromisers one and all, they include liberal theologians of the Niebuhr school, philosophers battening on learned ambiguity, literary admirers of C. S. Lewis, and others persuaded, after deep thought [sic], that there must be Something Out There. They tend to be unconscious of prehistory and the biological evolution of human instinct, both of which beg to shed light on this very important subject" (156–57). In the end he hopes that one day such mistakes will finally be "outgrown" (158), even though he also knows that science itself teaches that the brain is "made for religion and religion for the human brain" (149). For a scientist who is religious and not a compromiser, see Leon R. Kass, *The Beginning of Wisdom: Reading Genesis* (New York: Free Press, 2003) 36n10: "Evolutionary theorists . . . . resist entering into the argument about hierarchy altogether. In his notebook, Darwin wrote an exhortatory note to himself, 'Never use higher or lower,' but he could not help himself from doing so; the terms are all over *Origin of Species*. Insofar as evolutionary theory offers any standard for higher and lower, that standard could only be a standard of success, namely, most surviving offspring—in which case, at least in Chicago, the cockroach would be the highest being. Because evolutionary theory does not deal with the *beings* and the *character* of their *lives*, but only with their coming into being, it can in principle never fully appreciate theoretically the different degrees and grades of *being present* that are manifestly here on earth . . . . This ought to make us wonder about the hierarchy-blind character of present evolutionary theory."

39 Miasma is a noxious, poisonous vapor. This could be about Kierkegaard's disdain for crowds and the herd mentality (UDVS 127–39, FSE 19, BA 161, PV 107–108, JP 3:2994). On a similar point, see Thomas E. Bergler, *The Juvenilization of American Christianity* (Grand Rapids,

are finally brought into "harmony with the dead and with the people you never saw, with strange[40] people whose language and customs you do not know, with all the people on the whole earth who are blood relatives and eternally related to divinity by eternity's task to will one thing" (UDVS 144).[41] So with Mary we will not worry over getting through difficult times. With company like that, it is of no concern. For the "person who merely asks how to get through does not really want to go further. But the one who asks about what lasts has already come through; he has already passed over[42] from temporality

---

Michigan: Eerdmans, 2012) 211: "The desire to gather a crowd can easily push leaders to compromise the message of the gospel and downplay spiritual maturity."

40 On another feature of this strangeness, see Martin Luther, "The Seven Penitential Psalms" (1525), LW 14:181: "[To wake in Psalm 102:7] is to hold fast and to look to, and long for, the eternal good. But in this he is alone, and no one is with him; for the others are sleeping. And he says 'on the housetop' as if he meant: The World is a house in which all men are enclosed and are sleeping. I alone am outside the house, on the roof, not yet in heaven and still not in the world. The world is below me, and heaven is above me. I hover between the life of the world and eternal life, lonely in the faith."

41 And so I agree with Richard John Neuhaus (1936–2009) that "Kierkegaard was eccentric in the precise meaning of the word—off center, even out of the center. He believed that the center of his time and place, and of any time and place, is where the easy lies are told . . . . Many have read him to experience the frisson of youthful dissent from establishment ways of thinking and being, and have then set him aside upon assuming what are taken to be the responsibilities of adulthood. That, I believe, is a grave mistake. Kierkegaard is for the young, but he is also for grownups who have attained the wisdom of knowing how fragile and partial is our knowing in the face of the absolute, who are prepared to begin ever anew the life-long discipline that is . . . Christianity." "Kierkegaard for Grownups," *First Things* 146 (October 2004): 33.

42 A good gauge for knowing whether you have passed over into eternity or not— that is, passed over to "the other side of the boundary within the bastion of eternity" (UDVS 60)—would be that list of eleven

into eternity, although he is still living" (UDVS 77). That was clearly Mary's question, at the feet of Jesus—What lasts? When that is finally asked of Jesus in earnestness, then eternity no longer is "a riddle;" then it is no longer a "desperate standby" (UDVS 114). This realization is what decisively "halts" us, so that we can finally "go on" in purity of heart to will one thing (UDVS 153)—contrary to Martha, but in the company of those "strange people" of eternity (UDVS 144), especially Mary.

---

fears (UDVS 52). If they sound foolish to you, then you have probably moved into the eternal realm—but if they still scare the bejeebers out of you, then you are probably dwelling in temporality. No doubt there will be some dialectical, back-and-forth here. On a contemporary denial of the eternal—for those who do not want to go further (UDVS 77) —see *The Good Book: A Humanist Bible*, ed. A. C. Grayling (New York: Walker, 2011) 74: "[There] are no eternities other than grief while it lasts, no certainties other than that grief must come, no escape other than from life itself and what it asks us to endure" (5:3.8). In the place of those disregarded eternities, we have on p. 393: "Time is the wisest of all counselors" (10:140.17).

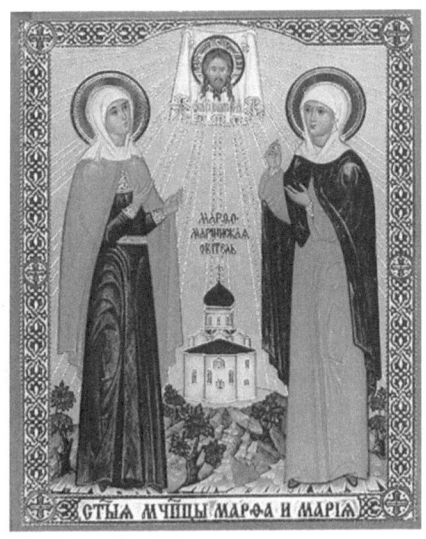

In the House of Martha and Mary

Appendix Five

On Daphne Hampson

Hampson

Thomte

In Daphne Hampson's new book on Kierkegaard,[1] she goes against Reidar Thomte's advice: "No student who is sympathetic to [Kierkegaard's] great inward struggle to arrive at the Truth upon which he could live and die,[2] who has a measure of appreciation for his tremendous dialectic powers and brilliant literary talents, could desire to furnish a critical

---

1   Daphne Hampson, *Kierkegaard: Exposition & Critique* (Oxford: Oxford University Press, 2013). Throughout I will be making heavy use of footnotes. On their importance for America, and my writing, note the famous "Footnote Four" from the 1938 United States Supreme Court case, *Carolene Products*, wherein Justice Harlan Fiske Stone argued, for the first time in American history, that "the Supreme Court need not . . . commit itself to the practice of judicial restraint in all cases"—something which "the burgeoning civil rights movement" especially rejoiced over. Damon Root, *Overruled: The Long War for Control of the U. S. Supreme Court* (New York: Palgrave MacMillan, 2014) 83. So thank God for footnotes—even in matters Kierkegaardian! See also Ronald F. Marshall, *Kierkegaard for the Church*, 7n21.

2   See JP 5:5100, p. 34.

estimate of his philosophy, for he finds himself standing under judgment."[3]

Hampson does not agree with Thomte and so she goes on to criticize Kierkegaard in spite of his warning not to[4]—

3   Reidar Thomte (1902–1994), *Kierkegaard's Philosophy of Religion* (London and Princeton: Oxford University Press and Princeton University Press, 1948) 204. According to Thomte, there is "only one objective in Kierkegaard's philosophy of religion, and it is expressed in the words of [his pseudonym] Johannes Climacus: 'I assume that there awaits me a highest good, an eternal happiness . . . . I have heard that Christianity proposes itself as a condition for the acquirement of this good. Now I ask how I am to become a Christian' [CUP 1:15–17, 617]. The pathos behind these words overpowered Kierkegaard's whole life. It was the burden of his whole work as an author. He who is not vitally interested at this point can never fully understand Kierkegaard. In all his works religiosity is expressed in terms of striving. Like Luther he held that faith is restless and perturbing. Christianity is not a comfort or an escape mechanism. It means to follow and imitate the Pattern [which is Christ Jesus], to accept the judgment of God upon one's life, and to seek the forgiveness of sins as one who is altogether unworthy of receiving it. 'The infinite humiliation and grace, then a striving grounded in gratitude, this is Christianity' [JP 1:993]. Kierkegaard had no sympathy with religious speculation or passive contemplation . . . . There is no religiosity and no ethical life apart from this principle; it is fundamental in all that Kierkegaard has written" (218–19). Thomte goes on to show how this principle is "repellent" (106), risky (109), based on "other-worldliness" (85, 138), offends (159), leads to a "leap" of faith (171), brings about "constant collisions" (172), promotes "dying to oneself" (173, 58), includes within it "cruelty" (180) and "self-denial" (185), and aims toward "maturity" (208). This vital interest is far more important to Thomte than any of our criticisms of Kierkegaard could ever be. On the back cover of the 2009 reprint (Wipf & Stock) of Thomte's classic, Robert L. Perkins writes: "Thomte is a master of incisive summary; his presentations of crucial distinctions are level-headed and to the point . . . . Not only is this book a good 'starter,' it is also a comprehensive review of the principal issues in Kierkegaard's philosophy of religion."

4   "[One] has to say . . . that it was Hegel who stood on the side of the future and Kierkegaard who belonged to the past." Hampson, *Kierke-*

risking Kierkegaard's judgment cascading down upon her. But when she criticizes Kierkegaard, she does it in such a way as to keep open the possibility of also admiring him. And she does that with gusto,[5] even though she rejects his Christian faith. What she likes about him is that he makes it crystal clear to her why she should not "wish to be Christian"—setting before her, as he does, "the implications of Christian claims," which end up discrediting for her those very claims. No wonder she believes that her life "would have been subtly different had [she never] encountered Kierkegaard."[6] So she goes down that road less traveled—knowing that most Kierkegaard scholars do not criticize him, or even letting the possibility of that "register on their radar" screens.[7] She takes this route because she believes his writings "invite" us to.[8] But this does not mean we can take cheap shots at him, since "[casting] aspersions without thinking through the complexity of Kierkegaard's position,"

---

gaard, 309. For contemporary excitement over Kierkegaard—against Hampson's judgment—see Dana Gioia, "Homage to Søren Kierkegaard," *First Things* 236 (October 2013) 46, and Gordon Marino, "Kierkegaard at 200," *The New York Times* (online), May 3, 2013.

5 "In what respects . . . has Kierkegaard made a lasting contribution, undimmed by time? I believe that what above all remains prescient today are his theological paradigm for the structure of the self, his astute pastoral insights, and not least (though least recognized) his conceptualization of the nature of God." Hampson, *Kierkegaard*, 311–12. Regarding God, Hampson thinks Kierkegaard believes that "God becomes for us what we are for others" (313). This, however, misses the asymmetry between God and neighbor: "There is only one whom a person can with the truth of eternity love more than himself—that is God . . . . A person should love God unconditionally *in obedience* and love him *in adoration*. It is ungodliness if any human being dares to love himself in this way, or dares to love another person in this way, or dares to allow another person to love him in this way" (WL 19).

6 Hampson, *Kierkegaard*, viii.
7 Hampson, *Kierkegaard*, 311.
8 Hampson, *Kierkegaard*, 7.

does no good for anyone.[9] Hampson therefore welcomes debate and is ready to "enter into" sharp exchanges over Kierkegaard's writings.[10]

Here then are my criticisms of her criticisms of Kierkegaard. First, consider how Hampson misconstrues Kierkegaard on universalism—quoting from his journals "that we all will be saved."[11] To her credit, she says that this endorsement of universalism conflicts with much of what he says elsewhere. Unfortunately she attempts to reconcile the two views by judging Kierkegaard's denials as disingenuous, while his private journal entries in favor of universalism tell what he really believed. Elsewhere Kierkegaard offers a better, more straightforward solution to our problem than the one Hampson gives. In another journal entry he writes:

---

9   Hampson, *Kierkegaard*, 213. Note also her qualification that "if Kierkegaard is to be understood, let alone justly evaluated, account must needs be taken of his context. One must surely think in concert with Kierkegaard, cognizant of the strengths and insights of the tradition to which he belonged and aware of the limitations in outlook of his surrounding society. It is for lack of these things that much critique seems irrelevant" (216). Furthermore she says that it is "too simplistic to judge Kierkegaard through the lens of socialist ideals (Adorno), or indeed feminist ideals (Walsh)" (218). In as much as Hampson adheres to these restrictions, she is following Thomte—where in general she goes the critical way.
10 Hampson, *Kierkegaard*, 3. But she also warns her readers that she will be a formidable opponent in as much as she has been working on Kierkegaard's writings for some forty years! (320).
11 Hampson, *Kierkegaard*, 315. See also JP 6:6947—as well as JP 6:6934, which she leaves out. In this last passage Kierkegaard attributes universalism to childishness: "This is the result of having gotten the very opposite, so-called Christianity, as a child."

> The [New Testament] clearly rests on the assumption that there is an eternal damnation and—perhaps not one in a million is saved. We who are brought up in Christianity live on the assumption that all of us surely will be saved. . . . O, but the [New Testament] is a terrifying book; for it takes into account this kind of a collision with true Christianity.
>
> (JP 6:6843, p. 484)

On this account, universalism is the false, official view of Christianity that we have been sold as a bill-of-goods, and eternal damnation is the truth that we need to substitute for this widespread counterfeit version of the Christian faith which we find all around us. Chasing down counterfeits—exposing them and exchanging them for the truth—is at the heart of Kierkegaard's writing project.[12] One would have thought that Hampson would have picked up on this basic strategy.[13]

Then there is Hampson's charge that Kierkegaard has no idea of the reform which he calls the church to—opposing, as he did, all reforms based on the changing of "external conditions."[14] But that is only half of the story. Kierkegaard also believed that reformation could begin with the self and then extend to the externalities by way of the self participating in them. In this way the externalities would not displace

---

12 See TM 166; JP 6:6921, 6:6967. And note his self-understanding: "I am the one who, so to speak, has to discover Christianity himself, work it out of the bewitchment into which it has been hexed" (JP 6:6934).

13 John Updike (1932–2009) made the same mistake in a famous essay from 1966 on Kierkegaard, which may have also misled Hampson. See Ronald F. Marshall, *Kierkegaard for the Church: Essays & Sermons*, Foreword by Carl E. Braaten and the Epilogue by Robert L. Perkins (Eugene, Oregon: Wipf and Stock, 2013) 64n40.

14 Hampson, *Kierkegaard*, 295.

individual, inner transformation, but arise out of them. He believed that "a reformation has to begin with each person's reformation of himself," even though we rarely settle for this and "the essentiality of the religious life before God" (TA 88–89). But when we do, there is an earthquake and Christianity is finally released and set "in motion" (JP 1:378). This happens when a shift takes place from the "conjunctive" to the "disjunctive"—that is, from what "sanctifies all our cherished relationships and our earthly fortune and striving,"[15] to a letting "go of everything, to [hating] one's father and mother and oneself" (JP 1:401).[16] Because this shift is so difficult, "shabby" preachers (JP 1:481), not "flabby" ones,[17] are what we need. These shabby preachers are the "poor men who walk about in poor clothing, despised men whom all ridicule, mock, and spit upon." This is because they preach that Christians are not supposed to be happy[18]—and so "if you desire, humanly

---

15 This conjunction is possible because God does not prevent us from taking Christianity "in vain" (JP 1:471). And so this whole life is a test (JP 1:1052) to see whether or not we will abide by genuine New Testament Christianity (TM 3–4, 26, 28–40, 42, 46–49, 51–53, 64, 74, 95–97, 123–24, 131–37, 160, 168, 185–86, 214–16, 498–505). We are tempted not to do so in order to spread Christianity to as many people as possible—"alas, it is all too easily the wrong way, which in the name of spreading, Christianity abolishes Christianity . . . . just as when a person increases his wine supply by diluting it with water and probably gets a far greater number of flasks of—wine and water—and finally a countless number of flasks—of water [only]" (JP 1:552).
16 See Lk 14:26, 33.
17 JP 1:512. When these shabby preachers settle in, they will scare the regular church-goers. And so they will cry out: "How can [we] get away from this man? His sermon catches up with [us] in every hiding place, and how can [we] get rid of him, since he is over [us] at every moment?" (BA 105).
18 And so Kierkegaard adds that "Christianity [as commonly practiced] is really all too joyous, and therefore really to stick to Christianity a man must be brought to madness by suffering. Most men, therefore, will

speaking, pleasant and happy days, then [you should] never get involved in *earnest* with Christianity" (JP 1:496). These tough-minded preachers refuse to peddle the "sloppy optimism" that states that everyone is going to heaven regardless of what they believe and do (JP 1:510).[19] Instead of saying that, these faithful preachers put back what has been cut out of genuine, true Christianity: "conversion, rebirth, imitation, dying away from this world, renunciation, [and] self-denial" (JP 1:397).[20] No wonder then that Christianity's missing, true form, looks, "humanly speaking," like pure and simple cruelty—even though this is "not the fault of Christianity," but is "due to the fact that it has to . . . manifest itself and expand in a sinful world" (JP 1:489). Furthermore Kierkegaard knows that no such reform is ever set in motion by our own doing. For he believed that a truly "godly view of life" is one where everything is "ascribed to

> be able to get a real impression of Christianity only in the moment of their death, because death actually takes away from them what must be surrendered in order to get an impression of Christianity" (JP 1:491). Therefore Kierkegaard believed that "in *Christendom* Christianity has been employed as a stimulant oriented toward enjoying life, as a new, intensified stimulation of life-enjoyment. Therefore Christendom is: refined life-enjoyment, dreadfully refined, for in paganism's enjoyment there is always a bad conscience. But in Christendom an attempt has been made to eliminate conscience by introducing atonement in the following manner: You have a God who has atoned—now you may really enjoy life. This is the greatest possible relapse" (JP 1:534).
>
> 19 No such optimism is possible because "the grief of sin must be very deep within a person, and therefore Christianity must be presented as the difficult thing it is, so that it may become entirely clear that Christianity only is related to the consciousness of sin" (JP 1:493).
>
> 20 The Scriptural references for these six elements are Rom 12:2; Jn 3:7; 1 Pt 2:21; Gal 6:14; Lk 14:33; Lk 9:23. These missing elements are designed to see to it, that, when properly put back into Christianity, "the true Christian fears God absolutely" (JP 1:492). They pretty well knock the wind out of phony Christianity—that "gentle, life-beautifying, and ennobling ground of comfort" (JP 1:496).

God" (EUD 386). We cannot therefore practice Christianity by ourselves. We must wait on God for his blessings, knowing full well that we cannot be "bearers of Christianity. And so I propose," he writes, "that we . . . confess that we are able to manifest only an approximation of Christianity" (JP 1:536).[21] This admission is the reformation that the church needs. So while Kierkegaard had no plans on how to socially engineer such a reformation all by himself, he did know what he was looking for—something which Hampson should have given him credit for, but does not do.

She also criticizes Kierkegaard for refusing to critically investigate the Bible.[22] On this matter she says he is stubborn and "obtuse," and closed-minded to the point of not even owning the books of the prominent Biblical critics of his time. But this complaint misses two subtleties in Kierkegaard. The first has to do with self-protection and the second with the nature of the Bible. Regarding self-protection, Kierkegaard argues that Biblical critics are disingenuous—they are not searching for the truth, as they say they are. No, they instead are trying to defend themselves against what the Bible says that attacks them and their deeply cherished opinions (FSE 33–35).[23] And on

---

21 See 2 Cor 4:7: "But we have this treasure in earthen vessels, to show that the transcendent power belongs to God and not to us" (RSV). Elsewhere I call this approximation a "Pythagorean Christianity." Ronald F. Marshall, *Kierkegaard for the Church*, 43–50.
22 Hampson, *Kierkegaard*, 86–87.
23 So Kierkegaard writes: "It seems as if all this research and pondering and scrutinizing would draw God's Word very close to me; the truth is that this is the very way, this is the most cunning way, to remove God's Word as far as possible from me, infinitely further than it is from one who never saw God's Word, infinitely further than it is from one who became so anxious and afraid of God's Word that he cast it as far away as possible" (FSE 35). A clever example of this "casting away," is Walter Brueggemann. Cameron B. R. Howard says of his book, *Ice Axes for Frozen Seas: A Biblical Theology of Provocation* (Waco, Texas:

the nature of the Bible, Kierkegaard sees it as anything but an inert text. Rather it is the very voice of God (FSE 39) spoken straight "to *us* human beings" (WL 14), and reads like a love letter to the forlorn lover (FSE 26). In this case we do not scrutinize and study the text, but read it deeply, passionately, and with earnestness—holding it close with heartfelt longing

---

Baylor University, 2014): "The [Biblical] text always has pride of place, even if—or because—the text will never yield a determinant portrait of God." "Review,*" Word & World* 35 (Winter 2015): 80. In this way Brueggemann takes away with one hand, what he gives with the other: The Biblical text is central but only until our interpretations usurp it in order to make sense out of what is obscure in it. And by so doing, anything that might be holy about it, is drained from it. The Bible becomes just another text for us to manhandle. Therefore, as Brueggemann says elsewhere, "[The] Bible will have its . . . way with us if we but attend with educated alertness . . . . [So the] hard work of [the] critical study [of the Bible is for us] to consider [which parts of it bear] truthful and faithful witness." "A Personal Reflection: Biblical Authority," *The Christian Century* 118 (January 3–10, 2001): 14, 15. On this disingenuousness, see Ronald F. Marshall, *Kierkegaard for the Church*, 42, 59, 64, 110, 150–53.

and affection.[24] Because of this love letter genre,[25] dictionaries and grammar books, doubts and parsing, are all out of place. Our goal instead is simply to have "uninhibited obedience that is much more afraid of showing reluctance than inaccuracy."[26]

---

24   For an example of this affection for the Bible, note the words of Kierkegaard's Constantin Constantius on the Book of Job: "If I did not have Job! It is impossible to describe all the shades of meaning and how manifold the meaning is that he has for me. I do not read him as one reads another book, with the eyes, but I lay the book, as it were, on my heart and read it with the eyes of the heart, in a *clairvoyance* interpreting the specific points in the most diverse ways. Just as the child puts his schoolbook under his pillow to make sure he has not forgotten his lesson when he wakes up in the morning, so I take the book to bed with me at night. Every word by him is food and clothing and healing for my wretched soul. Now a word by him arouses me from my lethargy and awakens new restlessness; now it calms the sterile raging within me, stops the dreadfulness in the mute nausea of my passion. Have you really read Job? Read him, read him again and again" (R 204). Hampson, like most Biblical scholars, knows nothing of this irreplaceable passion—for Kierkegaard's contention that the Bible is the inspired voice of God "is a castle built on insecure foundations" (90). See as well Hector Avalos, *The End of Biblical Studies* (Amherst, New York: Prometheus, 2007) 22: "Our argument is that there is really nothing in the entire book Christians call 'the Bible' that is any more relevant than anything else written in the ancient world." Two examples of the passé teachings of the Bible are the respectability of genocide and the divine origin of illness (17). On playing fast-and-loose with the Bible in popular culture, see Megan Amram's satirical piece, "Bible Systems Updates," *The New Yorker*, November 24, 2014: 66: "1.6 'Sodom and Gomorrah' N.S.F.W. glitch identified and removed. Bible now free of 'Homosexuality' virus . . . . 6.2 'Original Sin' glitch fixed; basic human goodness implied . . . . 6.12 'God' feature removed entirely. Replaced with 'The Cloud.'"

25   Unfortunately Hampson misidentifies and lessens this difference in genre—that the Bible is unlike other books: "Scholars now take for granted this difference in genre [that the] gospels are not straight historical reportage." Hampson, *Kierkegaard*, 89.

26   Vernard Eller, *Kierkegaard and Radical Discipleship: A New Perspective* (Princeton, New Jersey, Princeton University Press, 1968) 418. Note

Because both of these points go begging in Hampson's critical remarks, they miss the mark altogether.

She also criticizes Kierkegaard for attacking human autonomy and integrity.[27] Kierkegaard's negative view of people is defended in Ernest Becker's Pulitzer Prize winning study on death[28]—something Hampson leaves out. Furthermore

---

however this qualification: "Christian revelation presents itself as a judgment upon human standards. But even though we are not in a position to judge revelation, we can and must be able to determine the conditions under which the term *revelation* has a coherent use in the Christian context; how the doctrine of revelation functions as a regulative principle for the Christian form of life." Steven M. Emmanuel, *Kierkegaard and the Concept of Revelation* (Albany, New York: State University of New York Press, 1996) 146.

27 Hampson, *Kierkegaard*, 96, 311. According to Kierkegaard, the Bible also dwells on such somber reminders: "[Suffering] is close enough to us, even if light-mindedness and sensuality, even if worldly wisdom and impiety wish to remain ignorant of it, wish to remove such unfortunates and to remove these somber reminders not merely from the carefreeness of art but also from the Church and from the upbuilding contemplation that is bound to know that Holy Scripture has almost a preference for the lame and the crippled, for the blind and the lepers" (UDVS 110, 146).

28 Ernest Becker, *The Denial of Death* (New York: Free Press, 1973) 85: "[We] have seen a defiant Prometheanism that is basically innocuous: the confident power than can catapult man to the moon and free him somewhat of his complete dependence and confinement on earth—at least in his imagination. The ugly side of this Prometheanism is that it, too, is thoughtless, an empty-headed immersion in the delights of technics with no thought to goals or meaning; so man performs on the moon by hitting golf balls that do not swerve in the lack of atmosphere. The technical triumph of a versatile ape, as the makers of the film *2001* so chillingly conveyed to us. On more ominous levels, . . . modern man's defiance of accident, evil, and death takes the form of sky-rocketing production of consumer and military goods. Carried to its demonic extreme this defiance gave us Hitler and Vietnam: a rage against our impotence, a defiance of our animal condition, our pathetic creature limitations. If we don't have the omnipotence of gods, we at

she charges Kierkegaard with subjectivism and fascism for stressing the will over rational analysis.[29] However Kierkegaard also establishes "criteria to help us distinguish the genuine . . . from the fanatic, ... [noting] that a genuine person of faith will rely on the power of his or her moral example, and would never try to impose any views on others in a doctrinaire or manipulative way, much less employ violence to force others to conform to his or her way of thinking."[30] And she also criticizes Kierkegaard for being phony—not living up to the strict view

---

least can destroy like gods."

29 Hampson, *Kierkegaard*, 166–70, 173, 176. She also charges him with being anti-democratic (208–14). On this question in Kierkegaard research, see Dorothy M. Emmet, "Kierkegaard and the 'Existential' Philosophy," *Philosophy* 16 (July 1941): 262: "[Kierkegaard's thought runs the serious risk of being used as a] call to the sacred nation to realize its existence by its own absolute decision, a right on which no objective criticism can be brought to bear. Also the deep inner impulse which decides this choice can be made to depend on the blood, on realization of one's destiny in race and *Volk*." Against this likelihood, Kierkegaard's Anti-Climacus writes on the question of paying taxes to Caesar, in Luke 20:20–26: "O worldly passion, even if you are called holy and national, no, you do not extend so far that you can trap [Jesus'] indifference! . . . . What infinite indifference! . . . . In a worldly way they wanted to make it into a God-question, whether it was permissible to pay tax to the emperor; this is the way worldly mentality is so fond of prinking itself up into godliness, and this is the way they had also mixed God and the emperor together in the question, as if the two straightforwardly and directly had something to do with each other, as if they perhaps were rivals of each other and as if God were a kind of emperor. In other words, in the question they actually had covertly taken God in vain, had secularized him. [But as the greatest indifference] one must . . . not waste one word or one moment on talking about it—in order, then, to have more time to give to God what is God's. And he is the one they [ironically] want to proclaim king! [Jn 18:33–37; Acts 17:7]" (PC 169–70).

30 C. Stephen Evans, "Introduction," Kierkegaard, *Fear and Trembling*, trans. Sylvia Walsh (Cambridge: Cambridge University Press, 2006) xxv–xxvi.

of Christianity that he espouses.³¹ But this charge misses his "admission" (JFY 102) that the only Christianity we can live with is a "mitigation" of the true form (JFY 142), which must nevertheless be maintained as the ideal, even if we are not able to practice it perfectly (JFY 102, 207).

After considering Hampson's criticisms,³² I still feel no compunction to give up Thomte's admonition against such critical undertakings. And that is because criticisms of Kierkegaard are too narrowly conceived—leaving out too much of what he wrote in order to make them float. Therefore Kierkegaard's writings are much too rich and vast to be sufficiently mastered by any critic. No wonder, then, that the critics always seem to leave out the mitigating counter-examples and qualifications. That problem may well be the very judgment Thomte warned about befalling those who criticize Kierkegaard.³³

---

31   Hampson, *Kierkegaard*, 284, 287, 292.
32   I also question some of her expositions. Take, for example, her description of subpart III in the last section of *Practice in Christianity*. Hampson, *Kierkegaard*, 274. In it she skips over the lowliness and abasement in the opening prayer (PC 167) that leads to "the halt" that shows us how wrong we are (we "know nothing") and how "right" the revelation is (PC 177–78). With these words under her belt she might have been less inclined to mount the high horse of criticism, find Kierkegaard's resistance to modernity less puzzling (310), and appreciate Thomte more.
33   The more robust view of Kierkegaard—being impervious to criticism—also makes him better suited for countering a global culture that celebrates the likes of Kurt Cobain (1967–1994), whose wild rock music was nothing but "a pure expression of what it is to be young and angry and unsure, [all the while] selling some 75 million records worldwide." Bill Donahue, "Here We Are Now," *Sunset* 234 (January 2015): 26. And see also the National Book Award Winner, *Redeployment* (New York: Penguin, 2014), by the Marine veteran, Phil Klay. In his book a Marine Chaplain writes in his journal: "I have this sense that [Iraq] is holier than [the USA]. Gluttonous, fat, oversexed, over-consuming, materialistic home, where we're too lazy to see our own

faults" (151). This sounds like an earlier book, also in a Kierkegaardian vein: "You live in a deranged age—more deranged than usual, because despite great scientific and technological advances, man has not the faintest idea of who he is or what he is doing." Walker Percy, *Lost in the Cosmos: The Last Self-Help Book* (New York: Picador, 1983) 76.

Appendix Six

On the Lilies and the Birds

Over a period of three years, Kierkegaard wrote down three sets of discourses on Matthew 6[1] about the lilies of the field and the birds of the air.[2] He knew that this material could be taken in various ways:

---

1. On these verses see Frederick Dale Bruner, *Matthew: A Commentary, Volume 1: The Christbook – Matthew 1–12*, Revised & Expanded Edition (Grand Rapids, Michigan: Eerdmans, 2004) 335: "Paul wrote that 'to those who by simple steadiness in well-doing seek glory and honor and integrity from God, theirs is eternal life' (Rom 2:7) . . . . Jesus is asking his disciples through a series of illustrations [including the lilies and birds] to make only God God, to value only God's emoluments, and to stop flirting with the world's religion of obsessive ostentation." Kierkegaard's discourses on the lilies and the birds are an elaboration of this conviction.
2. In 1847, "What We Can Learn From the Lilies in the Field and From the Birds of the Air: Three Discourses" (UDVS 155–212); in 1848, "The Cares of the Pagans: Christian Discourses" (CD 3–91); and in 1849, "The Lily in the Field and the Bird of the Air: Three Devotional Discourses" (WA 1–45). See also the new translation of the 1849 set of discourses by Bruce Kirmmse, with a postscript by Niels Jørgen Cappelørn and monotypes by Maja Lisa Englehardt. Søren Kierkegaard, *The Lily of the Field and the Bird of the Air: Three Godly Discourses* (New York: Elizabeth Harris Gallery, 2013). Christopher A. P. Nelson has also suggested that some eight pages in Kierkegaard's book *Judge For Yourself!* (JFY 179–87), written in 1851, can help explain Kierkegaard's "enduring fascination" with the lilies and the birds in Matthew 6. Christopher A. P. Nelson, "The Joy of It," IKC 17:134.

> One can speak in many ways about the lilies and the birds; one can speak gently, movingly, ingratiatingly, fondly, almost as a poet speaks, and a human being also may speak this way, may coax the worried one. (UDVS 204)

But in the end, Kierkegaard sides with Martin Luther's darker view, seeing in the contrast that Jesus draws between us and the lilies and the birds, a massive offense against us.[3] But those verses hit us so hard not because of the way they are in and of themselves—but because of the way we take them.[4] They, after all, only sit there benignly, beckoning us calmly.[5] And that is so even though they are also "a witness against us," as Luther notes, "to condemn our unbelief before God." For in spite of the fact that we are God's "highest creatures," we still see in them that we are not wise "enough . . . to imitate the birds"[6]—

---

3   See the humiliation in UDVS 164; the slap in the mouth in CD 65; and the sadness and cruelty in WA 8. Nevertheless, in at least the 1847 set of discourses, Sylvia Walsh sees humor in the "reversal of the normal relation between the teacher and the learner." Sylvia Walsh, "If the Lily Could Speak: On the Contentment and Glory of Being a Human," IKC 15:150.
4   So Kierkegaard writes: "For the Gospel the most important thing is not to rebuke and scold; for the Gospel the most important thing is to bring people to be guided by it" (WA 20). Even so, it is still "not simply a joyful message [since] it addresses itself to those who are worried" (UDVS 160).
5   In 1851 Kierkegaard makes this exact point: "Their instruction . . . is always plain, uniform, reliable, not vacillating in mood, . . . always following the season and pertinent to the moment" (JFY 181).
6   Martin Luther, "The Sermon on the Mount" (1532), LW 21:200, 198. Luther goes on to say that the example of the lilies and birds shows us that "no greedy belly can be a Christian" (201). The Christian's motto then should be: "Not by seeking, but by His generosity; not by finding, but by chance" (208). Because this motto is so difficult to live by, all

which is "humiliating" (UDVS 164; CD 65). Kierkegaard therefore concludes that if we do not learn from them we have only ourselves to blame (WA 43).[7]

Due to this unintended offense, we have a very difficult time learning from the lilies and the birds—"indeed, it is a difficult walk, almost like walking on water" (CD 21). For we only "come to know with difficulty," Kierkegaard points out, "what religiously is the requirement for being a human being" (WA 3). The "majority of human beings miss and mistake" this requirement, or if they know about it and practice it at all, they do so only in "half-measures" (WA 26). In his three sets of discourses, Kierkegaard carefully and meticulously lays out these difficulties. I want to show how his writings on the lilies and the birds build upon Luther's dark view. I will not do this chronologically, taking up each treatise one after another, in order of their publications, explicating them page by page, noting differences here and there. Instead, I will treat them

---

that we feel, according to Luther, is shame, disgrace, and embarrassment when we look at the lilies and the birds (196–200).

7   Even so, Kierkegaard initially avoids adding this insult to injury: "[Our failure] cannot be a question of a lack of ability. It must be something else, perhaps only a little indisposition, which one does not immediately deal with too severely and treat as if it were unwillingness or perhaps even obstinacy" (WA 40). His sharper indictment comes a few pages later (and for different reasons): "If you do not become unconditionally joyful in this relationship, then the fault lies unconditionally in you, in your ineptitude in casting all your sorrow upon him, in your unwillingness to do so, in your conceitedness, in your self-willfulness, in short, it lies in your not being like the lily and the bird. There is only one sorrow concerning which the lily and the bird cannot be your teacher and which we therefore will not discuss here: the sorrow of sin" (WA 43). For that the Lamb of God is needed, who alone takes away the sin of the world (Jn 1:29; WA 158–59; CD 280). And so he concluded in 1851: "[In] the strictest sense this is still not Christianity; it is really Jewish piety. What is crucial in Christianity is not manifested here at all: to suffer because one adheres to God" (JFY 187).

all as one set, dwelling on the three themes of fear, Christ's lowliness as contrasted with the pagan, and how simple joy is found amid contention.[8] My goal in all of this is to provide a short introduction[9] to Kierkegaard's couple hundred pages worth of reflections on the lilies and the birds in order to help the reader become "gripped" (WA 35) by worldly destruction and the eternal—as was Noah:

> Just as Noah,[10] rescued, saw the destruction of a world, so also sadness sees the destruction of the visible world, sees all that decline whose life is fused with the visible, whereas faith, rescued, sees the eternal and the invisible.
> (UDVS 208)

---

8   In counter-distinction to my set of three themes, Sylvia Walsh notes the matter of gender inequality which she thinks mars the 1847 set of discourses. Sylvia Walsh, "If the Lily Could Speak," 138. And for a chronological approach to these three sets of discourses, see Bruce Kirmmse's preface to his new translation of the 1849 set published by Princeton University Press (2016).

9   I also want to highlight some of Kierkegaard's more arresting images—such as the row boat (CD 73), the deluded pagan (CD 45–46), plugged ears (CD 56), God and gravity (UDVS 182), the greedy (CD 34), the sleepwalker (CD 35), and the troll (CD 71). On Kierkegaard's use of images, metaphors, and analogies, see Ronald F. Marshall, *Kierkegaard for the Church: Essays and Sermons*, Foreword by Carl E. Braaten, and Epilogue by Robert L. Perkins (Eugene, Oregon: Wipf and Stock, 2013) 21–23, 97, 103, 148, 184.

10 On the story of Noah in Genesis 6–9, see Leon R. Kass, *The Beginning of Wisdom: Reading Genesis* (New York: Free Press, 2003) 164: "The sympathetic and thoughtful reader understands that the Flood is necessary and fitting. Identifying with Noah, he allows his aspirations to climb aboard onto Noah's ark, dreaming of a new world order." I would think that Kierkegaard would buy into this view.

Scared Off

In exploring the lilies and the birds, Kierkegaard points out how we are "scared off" by them (WA 32).[11] This happens when we get trapped in "the wretched sensibleness that inhumanly [has made us] so small-minded" (UDVS 173).[12] As a result we are "fused with the visible," and spellbound with delusions and lulled to sleep "with monotonous uniformity" (UDVS 208–209)—just like the pagan is:

> Without the prospect of eternity, never strengthened by the hope of heaven, never himself, abandoned by God, [the pagan] lives in despair, as if for punishment he were condemned to live these seventy years tortured by the thought of being nothing, tortured by the futility of his efforts to become something. For him the bird has nothing consoling, heaven no consolation—and it goes without saying that earthly life has no consolation for him either. Of him it cannot be said that he remains enslaved on the earth, persuaded by the enchantment of earthly life that led him to forget heaven—no, instead it is as if temporality did everything to push him away from itself by making him nothing. And yet he wants to belong to temporality on the most wretched conditions; he does not want to escape it. He clings tightly to being nothing, more and more tightly, because in a worldly way, and futilely, he tries to become something; with despair he clings more and more tightly to that—which

---

11 For a cinematic depiction of this fear, you can do no better than watching Alfred Hitchcock's *The Birds* (1963). See also *Alfred Hitchcock: Interviews*, ed. Sidney Gottlieb (Jackson, Mississippi: The University Press of Mississippi, 2003) 44–57, 100–102, 163–65.

12 And so we "desoul" ourselves (CD 47, 79).

to the point of despair he does not want to be. In this way he lives, not on earth, but as if he were hurled down into the underworld. . . . . It is not the fruits that withdraw themselves from him; it is he himself who withdraws himself even from being what he is. For he is not a human being—and he cannot become a Christian! (CD 45–46)

If we are not human when mired down in temporality and the visible, it is because we would rather be God (UDVS 178). But when we look to the lilies and the birds we are disabused of that fool's errand.[13] At that moment we see that being human is like being a bird (CD 25; WA 9).[14] Like the birds, we know "only one thing," that whatever happens is of no concern to us, and that being "unconditionally obedient to God" is all that matters (WA 29)—for all things come from him, and so we are to esteem the "giver . . . infinitely more than the gift" (CD 32). This is no doubt very disturbing to us (WA 28)—that we must submit[15] to God rather than share

---

13 Or as Kierkegaard puts it in 1851: "That is foolish aping" (JFY 184).
14 This emphasis on imitation is a virtue of Kierkegaard's treatment. For a recent analysis that could have benefited from Kierkegaard's discourses, see C. Christopher Smith and John Pattison, *Slow Church: Cultivating Community in the Patient Way of Jesus* (Downers Grove, Illinois: IVP Books, 2014) 105: "God wants us to go through life with eyes wide open. Not only will we walk more gently on the earth, we'll be more available to experience the wonder of a God who stoops low to feed the birds and clothe the lilies (Mt 6:25–34)." There is nothing here, however, of us imitating the birds and lilies in our lives. That is too bad, because Kierkegaard would have liked the critique in this book about reducing the church to "programs upon programs upon programs" (15).
15 Kierkegaard also believes that this submitting has to be done with dispatch: "God is not like something one buys in a shop, or like a piece of property that one, after having sagaciously and circumspectly exam-

in his glory to the point of usurping him. Therefore the only way we can realize our true humanity is to forget ourselves and even our own names—whether they are famous, wretched or insignificant, "in order to pray to God: 'Hallowed be *your* name!'" (WA 19). At that point we see that we are here to "simply and solely" seek God's kingdom (WA 20).[16] By so doing we are content "to speak just as tersely, just as solemnly, and just as inspiringly about being a human being as the Gospel speaks tersely about the lilies" (UDVS 170). For "out there in the field with the lilies, where every human being is what God has made him to be, is the wonder of creation; indeed, out there no one wants to be a prodigy!" (UDVS 189).[17] There,

---

ined, measured, and calculated for a long time, decides is worth buying. With regard to God, it is the ungodly calmness with which the indecisive person wants to begin (indeed, he wants to begin with doubt), precisely this that is the insubordination, because in this way God is thrust down from the throne, from being *the master*" (CD 88–89).

16 Here Kierkegaard capitalizes on "God, the great supplier or provider, or, as we indeed call him: providence" (JFY 184).

17 One, however, will still put in a good day's work—unlike the birds (UDVS 196–200)—for they are not calling us to be "inactive and lazy" (JFY 186). Even so, "at times the adult does his work but has no joy in it, yes, perhaps is even annoyed—ah, then he is eager to be put at ease by the child [and also by the lilies and the birds], eager to learn from it, is eager in his secret, grateful mind to call the child a teacher. But if necessary he would not hesitate to reprimand the teacher, and the adult would justifiably do that. Why? Because in an earnest sense the adult is the child's teacher, and the child is the adult's teacher only in the beautiful sense of jesting earnestness" (UDVS 198). This is because "by working, human beings resemble God" (UDVA 198–99). Earlier Kierkegaard adds: "It is certainly praiseworthy and pleasing to God that a person sows and reaps and gathers into barns, that he works in order to obtain food; but if he wants to forget God and thinks he supports himself by his labors, then he has worry about making a living" and needs correcting (UDVS 177). Knowing that God is working through us is not designed to shut us down, but to make us all the "more industrious" (JFY 186). The point, after all, is to understand in the right way

in the wonders of creation, we, with the lilies and the birds, "humbly feel like a superfluity" (CD 81; WA 77).[18] And the stakes are high, because "no eminent person" can be saved, but only "a lowly person"—for the eminent person's "ears are plugged" (CD 53, 56).[19]

Christ vs The Pagan

This redefinition of being human takes its glory from Christ Jesus—who shows us "what significance a lowly person has" (CD 42)—something that is also there in the lilies and birds.[20] Once "absorbed in" this lowly picture of Christ—as a believer and follower of him—we come to see God not only as our creator, as he is for all creatures, but also as our "brother" (CD 43). Along with this connection to God, as our brother in Christ Jesus, comes a life-giving dependence on God. For in this connection we see that "God is the only independence, because God has no gravity; only the things of the earth, especially earthly treasure, have that—therefore the person who is completely dependent on him is light" (UDVS 182).[21]

"what it means to work" (JFY 184).

18 Attached as he was to the lilies and the birds, Kierkegaard also thought of himself, and his writings, as a "superfluity" (JP 6:6709a).

19 For a modern dance piece on refusing to listen to revelation, see "The Envelope" (1986) by David Parsons. *The Parsons Dance Company* (1992) DVD Arthaus Musik NTSC: 100-265. In this dance the envelope is ignored, fussed over, danced around, and feared—but never opened and read.

20 Even so, Kierkegaard still thought of the lilies and birds as "unrivaled [professors] in the art of living" (JFY 181).

21 And so, leaning on 1 Corinthians 7:29-31, Kierkegaard notes that the Christian, "when he has abundance, is one who does not have abundance, so, then he is ignorant, and thus he indeed does not have abundance. But originally the Christian is a human being, and as such he is not like this; he becomes this as a Christian, and the more he becomes a

This lightness rescues us from the "dreadful disintegration" that brings about "decay while living," because of being "insanely busy with all sorts of things." As such, the decaying person "slaves from morning to night, accumulates money, [and then] hoards" what he has (CD 90). But the Christian, even the rich Christian, does not decay in this way. No, "he himself is a traveler—that is how ignorant the rich Christian is of his earthly wealth, yes, just like an absent-minded person" (CD 31).[22] As such, the Christian—"rising on the wings of faith" (UDVS 194), and then in the very "fortress of faith" (CD 87)[23]—is free from the devastating care for wealth, which marks the rich pagan:

> Indeed, you can see it on him when you look at him: him, the sallow money-grubber who accumulates and accumulates for himself—care—him, the starved glutton who starves in abundance, who also says: What will I eat? What will I drink? How will it be possible tomorrow (today it is still tolerable) to find a repast so delectable that it could please me?—him, the sleepless skinflint whom money, more cruel than the

---

Christian, the more he who has is as one who does not have" (CD 26).

[22] Kierkegaard therefore adds: "The ignorant bird lives like a sleepwalker in the power of sleep; it sees nothing. The rich Christian who became ignorant of his earthly wealth can, as in blindman's bluff, see nothing—because eternity blinds him, he cannot see by this earthly daylight" (CD 35).

[23] In that fortress, Kierkegaard goes on to say, the Christian is "cut off from all supplies from the surrounding world (the supplies of indecisiveness, vacillation, disconsolateness—indeed, there is nothing else equivalent to what supplies a fortress's needs from the outside), the more secure is the fortress . . . . Cut faith off from all connections with the surrounding world, starve it out—it becomes all the more impregnable, its life all the richer. And with faith in this fortress lives obedience" (CD 87).

cruelest executioner, keeps more sleepless than the most abominable criminal—him, the squint-eyed miser who never looks up from his money except to see enviously that someone else owns more—him, this dried-up, stingy wretch who is starving himself to death for money (something ordinarily unheard of, that anyone has done this for money). Look at them—and listen to what they say; they all say it, and this is the only thing they talk about; basically they are all saying: What will we eat and what will we drink? The more wealth and abundance they acquire, the more knowledge they also acquire; and this knowledge, which is the care, does not satisfy the hunger, does not quench the thirst—no, it stimulates the hunger and intensifies the thirst.

(CD 34)

Without these pagan cares, the Christian lives like one rowing a boat backwards—"absorbed in today," neither worried about yesterday nor tomorrow (CD 73).[24] As such a one has one's "back to the goal"—as one is turned "when one rows a boat, but so also is one positioned when one believes .... [For faith] turns its back to the eternal expressly in order to have it entirely present with it today .... To be totally contemporary with oneself today with the help of the eternal is also the most formative and generative; it is the gaining of the eternal" (CD 74–75).

---

24 And so the next day "is like a troll, which can assume all forms; it can look so enormously different, but for all that it is still—the next day" (CD 71). Note too that Jesus lived "without care about the next day" (CD 76).

Simple Joy Amidst Contention

Deprived of the worry that pagans think makes life rich,[25] the Christian, modeled after the lilies and the birds,[26] finds joy elsewhere. Even if the Christian, when taxes are due, pulls from the water "a fish in whose mouth is a coin that one uses to make payment [Mt 17:27]," that only looks to most like "a very meaningless answer" (CD 19)—albeit to the Christian it is nothing but miraculous (CD 19; WA 41). Against this derision, the Christian, like the birds, endures the harshness all the same, and goes on to find joy in the simple life (WA 29, 32):

---

25 See Lk 12:19: "And I will say to my soul, Soul, you have ample goods laid up for many years; take your ease, eat, drink, be merry" (RSV). From this point of view, being told to pay attention to the lilies and the birds is "pompous, impractical nonsense" (JFY 184).

26 In elaborating this point, Kierkegaard adds: "When you obey as the creation obeys, tomorrow does not exist, that unblessed day invented by garrulousness and disobedience. But when, because of silence and obedience, tomorrow does not exist, then in the silence and obedience today is, it *is*—and then the joy is as it is in the lily and the bird" (WA 38-39). On the similarities between Kierkegaard and Buddhism, see Jack Mulder, Jr., *Mystical and Buddhist Elements in Kierkegaard's Religious Thought* (Lewiston, New York: The Edwin Mellen Press, 2005) 262: "Kierkegaard and . . . the Buddhist traditions . . . . share some version of the view . . . that all finite attachments, insofar as they are even the smallest obstacles on the way to liberation, must be renounced. This purgative element is strong for these . . . traditions, and in some sense results in the death of the self." This also resembles Buddhist mindfulness. On that concept, see Paul E. Knitter, *Without Buddha I Could Not be a Christian* (Oxford: Oneworld, 2009) 181: "[Embrace] the moment as mindfully as you can, respond to it with the wisdom of feeling your connectedness with everyone and everything, and then respond with the compassion that naturally results when you feel so connected—and the moment will both teach you and guide you. That, essentially, is all you need to do."

Therefore, that you came into existence, that you exist, that *today* you receive what is necessary for life; that you came into existence, that you became a human being; that you can see, bear in mind that you can see, that you can hear, that you can smell, that you can taste, that you can feel; that the sun shines for you and for your sake, that when it becomes weary the moon begins to shine and the stars are lit; that winter comes, that all nature disguises itself, plays the game of stranger, and in order to delight you; that spring comes, that the birds return in great flocks, and in order to give you joy; that the leaves bud, the forest adorns itself and stands like a bride, and in order to give you joy; that autumn comes, that the bird flies away, not to make itself scarce and valuable, oh, no, but so that you will not become bored with it; that the forest hides its adornment for the sake of next time, that is, so that it can give you joy next time—and all this is supposed to be nothing to rejoice over! Oh, if I dared to chide, but out of respect for the lily and the bird I dare not, and therefore, instead of saying that this is nothing to rejoice over, I will say instead: If this does not give joy, then there is nothing to rejoice over. (WA 39–40)

Becoming aware of our many forgotten benefits, we in large part let the visible, tangible, temporal "world perish" (UDVS 209). For this to happen, we must enter into "the most colossal point of contention" with the world. This "most terrible struggle . . . . over the highest" matter takes place in our "innermost being [where] everything is at stake." And that is precisely because we are fighting within ourselves over "loving and preferring [wealth] to God" (UDVS 205).[27] It is this battle into which we are hurled when we look intently and properly upon the lilies of the field and the birds of the air.[28]

---

27 Even though wealth is a temptation—which always must be used properly to avoid harm (CD 32)—it does not follow "that there is a direct and inevitable transition from literally being a lowly person to becoming a Christian; neither has [Christianity] taught that if the worldly eminent person relinquished all his power he therefore was a Christian." That being said, being "a lowly person is no unfortunate introduction to becoming a Christian; to be in possession of external advantages is a detour that makes a double introduction necessary for the more apprehensive" (CD 54–55).

28 For a recent study on birds as a source of inspiration, see Chris Chester, *Providence of a Sparrow: Lessons from a Life Gone to the Birds* (Salt Lake City: The University of Utah Press, 2002). After having a house sparrow and other birds live with him in his home for many years, Chester concludes that the biggest lesson learned from it all was that "many things aren't as they appear" in life (270). So he notes that while his pet sparrow could not speak English at all, it could comprehend "a good bit of it" (59). Most intriguing is the comparison he draws between his bright little sparrow and the church: "[It's] difficult to dismiss the fact that [Baptist church] people base their creed on a so-called literal interpretation of Scripture. I'm concerned, therefore, about the implications of a Supreme Being so jaded by his customary pursuits that he's been reduced to searching for novelty at a church in southeast Portland. I would respectfully remind the sloganeer that the Bible states pointedly, 'There is no new thing under the sun.' In a larger sense, I wonder what happens to . . . a culture in which marketing departments trade on language as the means of invoking the demons of transient desire . . . . Signs become commands; directions become assurances—the antithesis of omen, suggestion, and the merely possible. Thus, we are pointed away from any number of instructive wrong turns that eventually bring us home. To the tranquility of having a tame house sparrow nap in your hand, you might say. It would appear that institutions charged with maintaining the intangibles of spirit and morality feel they can no longer rely on either the depth or the beauty of their core beliefs in order to remain competitive, resort instead to the expedient of vacuous catch phrases tarting up their parking lots. Frankly, I don't know which is more troubling, that they've got the *cajones* to post this drivel or that

These three themes regarding the lilies and the birds—being frightened by them, the lowly Christ going against the pagan, and simple joy being found in contention—all help[29] fill us "with the thought of the Eternal," by freeing us from "sheer flightiness" (JP 1:169) and then putting an end to "our mediocre Christianity" (CD 12).[30]

---

people's souls are impoverished enough to be moved by it" (83–84). Kierkegaard, I think, would like most of this harangue.

29 Kierkegaard is clear that while there is certainly help here, that does not mean that there are any guarantees of fully successful accomplishment: "Moreover, if a person, with the lily and the bird as prototypes, lived in such a way . . . that he thought the thought of God in everything, this is indeed piety, and a piety, entirely pure, that surely is never seen among men" (JFY 187). On this humble view of Christianity, see Ronald F. Marshall, *Kierkegaard for the Church*, 43–50.

30 In contrast to this mediocre Christianity, Kierkegaard writes: "God's idea with Christianity was, if I may put it this way, to get really tough with us human beings. To that end, he . . . introduced the category of discord, ... of 'the single individual' . . . with family, with father and mother, etc. God did it this way [because he did not want] to have anything to do with the rascality of being loved by battalions . . . . ordered to the church parade. No, the formula continues to be: the single individual in contrast to the others . . . . This was his thought, even though in one sense we human beings must, if we dared, say that it was the most mischievous whim God could have—to put us together in this way, or in this way to deter us from . . . running with the herd" (TM 188). Any book on Kierkegaard's Christian thought then would have to strive to cancel our personal "moorings" and replace them with better ones. John B. Hench, *Books as Weapons: Propaganda, Publishing, and the Battle for Global Markets in the Era of World War II* (Ithaca, New York: Cornell University Press, 2010) 227.

Conclusion

Old Christianity

You have now finished going over this book and its opposition to theological innovation. As you noticed, it does not hanker after a new Christian creed. The reason for this is that it has looked to Kierkegaard's writings for guidance, and he was deeply committed to "old" Christianity. He describes old Christianity by imagining a modern preacher, of all things:

> I can imagine a person [who] has grasped the essence of Christianity and [knows] that it can be proclaimed in truth only when it is served in self-denial and renunciation . . . . but cannot bring himself to such a life . . . . [He] cannot let go of the things of this world . . . . [And he knows that he could not] get anyone to accept [it] . . . . So he accommodates and takes the things of this world *also*—but of course he does not declare the true situation publicly, for then he perhaps would lose the things of this world, and in case, in such a situation they would probably lose their fascination for him. He pretends that his proclamation of Christianity is entirely as

it should be, that it is true Christianity. . . .
[Then with] a rare zeal and competence and
endurance he proclaims Christianity . . . and
wins many, many for Christianity . . . . [So
has] the man benefited Christianity? No, no,
no. He has damaged it incalculably . . . . His
false proclamation has given men a taste of
Christianity without renunciation and as being
just as true Christianity as the old—therefore
one must be mad to want to get involved with
the old Christianity. (JP 3:3764)

This old Christianity knows about and believes in the desperateness of sin (WA 35), the centrality and uniqueness of the blood sacrifice of Jesus to overcome God's wrath for our salvation (CD 280), the struggles of faith (PC 35), the pressing need for and difficulty in denying ourselves on a daily basis (FSE 77), and the fear of everlasting judgment (TM 29, 278; UDVS 223). Kierkegaard called all of this the "rigorousness" of Christianity—and without it Christianity loses its way (JP 3:3770). He knew that this rigorous view was a "radical characterization" of the one true faith (JP 6:6698).[1] He also

---

1   This does not make it "toxic," however. See Stephen Arterburn & Jack Felton, *Toxic Faith: Understanding and Overcoming Religious Addiction* (Nashville: Thomas Nelson, 1991); and Paul DeBlassie III, *Toxic Christianity: Healing the Religious Neurosis* (New York: Crossroad, 1992). Many, however, reject Christianity today because of its "association with tea-party extremists, Quran-burning ministers, and child-molesting priests." Greg Burk, "'Maleficent': Romancing the Devil." *The Seattle Times*, June 17, 2014. Also, there is never any resorting to physical violence in Kierkegaard's writings or life. On this ramping-up in the early church, see Philip Jenkins, *Jesus Wars* (New York: HarperCollins, 2010) 146: "As is common in such pamphlet wars, each side presumably thought it had carried the day, but Cyril was not content with

knew that when it is opposed in the church, as it inevitably will be, it is usually done surreptitiously.

In our day, however, its opponents are much more forthright. But for all their confidence and *savoir faire*, they still fail to make a good case for their new Christianity. And so when we, for instance, are told that in old Christianity the "antithesis of divine and human is altogether illusory,"[2] we demur and continue to hold on to this fundamental contrast. We do the same when we hear that Jesus did not indicate the "mode of the afterlife—whether embodied or disembodied."[3] And we also are not convinced when it is said that just as "Christ was incarnate in Jesus," so is he also incarnate in Buddha and Gandhi.[4] And the same can be said when we hear that God does not have the power "to compel or to force" anyone to do anything.[5] We also

---

out-arguing his opponent. Instead, Cyril now took positive steps to depose and destroy him, and entered crusading mode." Kierkegaard never enters into attacks at this level.

2   Ludwig Feuerbach, *The Essence of Christianity* (1843), trans. George Elliot (New York: Harper Torchbooks, 1957) 13.

3   John Hick, *The Second Christianity* (London: SCM, 1983) 118. Note also that Christians should change their view that other religions are "inferior" to it (78).

4   Matthew Fox, *The Coming of the Cosmic Christ: The Healing of Mother Earth and the Birth of a Global Renaissance* (San Francisco: HarpersSanFrancisco, 1988) 235.

5   John B. Cobb, Jr., *Can Christ Become Good News Again?* (Saint Louis, Missouri: Chalice Press, 1991) 23. For a critique of this view, see Bruce R. Reichenbach, "Reviews of Hasker & Keller," *Faith and Philosophy* 27 (April 2012): 217–18: "Since God cannot bring about unilateral change, he is unable to affect the process besides providing periodic luring impulses to do the good. As such, God is not a guilty bystander nor does God make others victims. But, one might ask, why isn't God more effective in luring actual entities to do the good? . . . . Why cannot orderliness be merely a result of efficient causation (viewed according to so-called natural laws) and novelty be the product of random mutation causing variation at times sustained by the environment? . . . . [And] if

cannot abide by the revision to Christianity which says that there is no Judgment Day.[6] And the same goes for saying that the Bible is "not the definitive Word of God for all time."[7]

No, this book of sermons is far closer to the books of Carroll and Oden[8] on the modern discovery of Christian orthodoxy, or old Christianity, as Kierkegaard put it. For he believed that it was obedience that was needed the most in the church. And so nothing new is to be introduced, according to him, but "everywhere the springs will be repaired in such a way again that the old, nothing but the old, will be like new again" (JP 5:6075). And so "the rule is quite simply this: the new is not a new *what* but a new *how* of the old *what*" (JP 4:4558). What is new, then, is practicing the old teachings in our new day. This will take place by resetting "the trigger springs for the essentially Christian so that it may stand its ground [since] Christianity remains the same, altered in no way; not an iota has changed"

---

actual occasions can be efficient causes and unilaterally effect changes [e.g. billiard balls], why cannot God be such a cause? . . . . Why must divine causal order differ from that exercised by other causes?"

6   John Shelby Spong, *Why Christianity Must Change or Die: A Bishop Speaks to Believers in Exile* (San Francisco: HarpersSanFrancisco, 1998) 210. Luther thought such changes were "newfangled rubbish" (LW 44:276).

7   Jim Burklo, *Open Christianity: Home by Another Road* (Scotts Valley, California: Rising Star Press, 2002) 61. See also Robert M. Price, *Preaching Deconstruction*, forward by Thomas J. J. Altizer (Raleigh, North Carolina: Mindvendor, 2014) 36: "We will find ourselves sent out by the risen Christ, not with a party line to which we must convert the nations, but rather like searchers in a scavenger hunt, chasers after meaning in the winding lanes of the world that is the Bible. It is a great huge world of many ideas and obstacles, not so different from the world outside the Bible."

8   Colleen Carroll, *The New Faithful: Why Young Adults are Embracing Christian Orthodoxy* (Chicago: Loyola Press, 2002); and Thomas C. Oden, *The Rebirth of Orthodoxy: Signs of New Life in Christianity* (San Francisco: HarperSanFrancisco, 2003).

(JP 3:3704). Kierkegaard therefore is instead doing what he can to make us change—not Christianity:

> It is not "doctrine" which ought to be revised, and it is not "the Church" which ought to be reformed, and so on—. No, it is existences which should be revised.[9] Our whole way of life is stuff and nonsense and lack of character;[10] the point is that all of us ought to make a fearful admission to Christianity.[11] But we shrink from this existential way—and thus there are all these

---

9 See 2 Cor 3:18: "And we all ... are being changed into his likeness from one degree of glory to another; for this comes from the Lord who is the Spirit" (RSV).

10 "Forget genius, talent, scholarship, and all that—Christianity is the existential, a character-task" (JP 6:6780).

11 Here is that fearful admission: "I myself feel all too deeply how miserable and mediocre my achievement is, but there is still some meaning to it. I will, if by that time I have not gone further, I will say in eternity: What we called Christianity was not really Christianity at all; it was a very toned-down conception, something distantly related to Christianity. But this I have confessed, I have loudly and clearly admitted that it is not really Christianity—so do what you will with me, O God, do with me according to your mercy! I am well aware that in every generation and also in mine there have lived people who have put forth the requirement to be Christian in a more rigorous sense, but I have been unable to join them. No, for me it has seemed truer to accept a more lenient form, a mitigation—but then to admit that this is not really Christianity. That is how I come" (JFY 142). And along with this admission also goes this hope: "O my God, make it stand firm!—that just as Christianity detests adultery, murder, theft, and everything else that can defile a person, it knows yet another defilement—cowardly sagacity and flabby sensibleness, despicable thralldom in probability, Christianly understood, is perhaps the most dangerous defilement.... In truth, Christianity detests and detests as a defilement what the world esteems and esteems as supreme" (JFY 102).

> escapes and inventions—that it is "doctrine" which ought to be revised, the Church and the state, etc. (JP 3:3731)

In our time this is just what we need—given the fact that we live in "an historical context marked by violence, indifference and egoism, [where] many men and women . . . feel that they have lost their bearings."[12] Kierkegaard believed that we will find our way again through the forgiveness of sins and the life of the spirit. When we do, we will both become very old and young again—at the same time:

> Anyone who in truth has experienced and experiences what it is to believe the forgiveness of one's sins has indeed become another person. Everything is forgotten—but still it is not with him as with the child who, after having received pardon, becomes essentially the same child again. No, he has become an eternity older, for he has now become spirit. All spontaneity and its selfishness, its selfish attachment to the world and to himself, have been lost. Now he is, humanly speaking, old, very old, but eternally he is young. (JP 1:67)

---

12 "Common Declaration of Pope Francis and Ecumenical Patriarch Bartholomew I," Jerusalem, May 25, 2014. On the violence, see especially John L. Allen Jr., *The Global War on Christians: Dispatches from the Frontlines of Anti-Christian Persecution* (New York: Image, 2013) 1: "However counterintuitive it may seem in light of popular stereotypes of Christianity as a powerful and sometimes oppressive social force, Christians today indisputably are the most persecuted religious body on the planet, and too often their new martyrs suffer [from a rising tide of legal oppression, social harassment, and direct physical violence] in silence."

This transformation comes about only by appropriating old Christianity.[13] That is because in old Christianity there is "a grace which hurts," which comes from this old version being "so high up" (JP 4:4483). As a result, when it is preached, an "uproar breaks out," and rightly so (JP 1:667).[14] Because of this uproar, preachers cower and end up preaching "how the wind blows," so that his congregation will "not deny him his career, offerings, and incidentals" (JP 4:4904). Nevertheless the struggle must be waged to transform us godless sinners into disciples of Jesus Christ. And this will take some doing—and these sermons of mine offer themselves to that end. For they are addressed to all of us who are taken up into the "fleeting pleasures of sin" (Heb 11:25). So these sermons will have their work cut out for them because we are

> just as the child [who] cannot stand quietly but hops up and down to get permission as quickly as possible to go out to the hill, over to the

---

13 And so a Christian sermon must do more than "shed light on the oddness of the everyday"—interesting though that may be. Stanley Hauerwas, *Without Apology: Sermons for Christ's Church* (New York: Seabury Books, 2013) xviii.

14 See, for instance, *Your Vigor for Life Appalls Me: Robert Crumb Letters 1958–1977*, ed. Ilse Thompson (Seattle, Washington: Fantagraphics Books, 1998) 167: "[The Church holds] men back from developing and exploring their full potential, it's a mental block, which holds unnecessary fears and limits on man, confines his thinking, tries to kill all imaginative and natural thinking, all universal questioning, I know this from experience." For a cinematic moment in this spiritual battle, see Woody Allen's movie, *Irrational Man*, released on July 9, 2015. Its lead character, the cynical philosophy professor, Abe Lucas, forgoes Kierkegaard's help in escaping the doldrums of despair by quipping that "Kierkegaard, in the end, was a Christian," which disqualifies him.

playground, . . . utterly impatient to get into the sensate hustle and bustle of this life.

(JP 6:6967)

Albrecht Dürer, *The Flagellation of Christ*, 1500.

Postscript

The Hotel Kierkegaard

The sermons in this book are neither intellectual exercises nor my theological investigations into thorny conceptual issues. Nowhere in this book can you find a sentence like this one on Kierkegaard's thought: "If temporality is a process, a continuum, and pure Being is a point whose unity transcends componentiality, then how can the point that is pure Being enter temporality without being dissolved in its opposite and thereby losing its essential, unified indissolubility?"[1] No, what

---

1 Michael Wyschogord, *Kierkegaard and Heidegger: The Ontology of Existence* (London: Routledge & Kegan Paul, 1954) 123–24. On Heidegger's relation to Kierkegaard, see also the more recent study, Vincent McCarthy, "Martin Heidegger: Kierkegaard's Influence Hidden and In Full View," *Kierkegaard and Existentialism*, ed. Jon Stewart, Kierkegaard Research: Sources, Reception and Resources, Volume 9 (Burlington, Vermont: Ashgate, 2011). Note particularly: "[Heidegger's path] is so similar to Kierkegaard's and so dependent on it that it appears at times to be a re-working of Kierkegaard's pioneering existentiell descriptions . . . . But for those reading both Kierkegaard and Heidegger still from within the categories of traditional Christian theology, this estimation would appear too generous insofar as Heidegger's secular phenomenology would constitute a form of contemporary Pelagianism in which

you instead have in these sermons are proclamations of the faith by which I struggle to live on a daily basis. And so they make up my religious hotel[2]—the place for lamentation and praise in my earthly sojourn. That is what Luther thought Christian preaching creates—a place or a church. "For where Christ is not preached, there is no Holy Spirit to create, call, and gather the Christian church, and outside it no one can come to the Lord Christ" (BC 416):

> For the churches are nothing else than lodging places . . . in which . . . people who feel sin, death, and the terrors and vexations of an afflicted and wounded conscience are healed.
> (LW 8:54)

In this place, this church, this lodge, this hotel—marked off by these sermons—I find relief for the sadness I suffer, as well as a place to rejoice in the goodness of God in Christ Jesus, our

---

humans seem to have it in their own power to recover from their Fallenness vis-à-vis Kierkegaard's more classic Augustinian position of the need for a divine supplement" (114). For Kierkegaard's connection to Augustine, see Lee C. Barrett, *Eros and Self-Emptying: The Intersections of Augustine and Kierkegaard* (Eugene, Oregon: Wipf & Stock, 2013).

2   On this image, see John Green, *The Fault in Our Stars* (New York: Penguin, 2012) 157: "All the rooms in the Hotel Filosoof were named after filosoofers: Mom and I were on the ground floor in the Kierkegaard . . . . Our room was small [with] a dusty old paisley chair with a sagging seat, a desk, and a bookshelf above the bed containing the collected works of Søren Kierkegaard." This book is a novel about a young couple dealing with cancer. A couple pages later we read: "One might marvel at the insanity of the situation: A mother sends her sixteen-year-old daughter alone with a seventeen-year-old boy out into [the city of Amsterdam] famous for its permissiveness. But this, too, was a side effect of dying: I could not run or dance or eat foods rich in nitrogen, but in the city of freedom, I was among the most liberated of its residents" (159).

Lord. (May this book draw you in—dear reader—to live here as well.)

Kierkegaard cared deeply about Christianity being a faith by which we live—and not just something over which we bicker and speculate:

> A thinker erects a huge building, a system, a system embracing the whole of existence, world history, etc., and if his personal life is considered, to our amazement the appalling and ludicrous discovery is made that he himself does not personally live in this huge, domed palace but in a shed alongside it, or in a doghouse, or at best in the janitor's quarters. Were he to be reminded of this by a single word,[3] he would be insulted. For he does not fear to be in error if he can only complete the system—with the help of being in error.
>
> (SUD 43–44)

So this collection of sermons is very dear to me and is where I live—not because of the compositions themselves, but because of the wonderful passages[4] from Holy Scriptures, Martin Luther,

---

3   And that word would be this short epithet: "You hypocrite!" (Mt 7:5, 15:7, 23:15).

4   "Language is the nest human beings make." *Airmail: The Letters of Robert Bly and Tomas Tranströmer*, ed. Thomas R. Smith (Minneapolis: Graywolf Press, 2013) 317. For a rare Biblical moment on the power of Scripture, see the last episode of the first season of the HBO drama, *The Leftovers*. This is the scene at the grave of a woman who killed herself. Before the preacher, Matt Jamison, will help the Police Chief, Kevin Garvey, Jr., bury her, he has to read Job 23:8-17. The police chief is a cynic and you would think he would have thrown down the Bible once

and Søren Kierkegaard scattered[5] throughout them. Those words not only lift me in times of praise and thanksgiving, but also comfort me and challenge me when I am in the darkness of loss and fear. And this is as it should be, because as Kierkegaard taught, "nonresidence is and remains a decisive objection. [For spiritually] understood, a man's thoughts must be the building in which he lives—otherwise the whole thing is deranged" (JP 3:3308).

That is because for Kierkegaard the faith drives toward action and righteous behavior. We believe so we can do good works (Mt 7:17; Eph 2:10). Kierkegaard is therefore appalled that the "secret of life if one wants a good standing is: clever rubbish about what one wants to do and how one is frustrated—and then no action" (JP 5:5897). So good deeds are a major part of the passion of the Christian life. Each individual Christian has responsibilities to bear. That is why throughout Kierkegaard's writings he struggles to help his readers "enter into the compression chamber of individuality" (JP 2:1998)—

---

he realized the reading was about the goodness of God's wrath. But he's instead strangely moved by the text and finishes the reading with the preacher smiling and saying Amen at the end.

5 So I agree that "Kierkegaard well understood that like a Zen koan, the truth expressed in a line or three can glister as a legitimate object of reflection and appropriation." *The Quotable Kierkegaard*, ed. Gordon Marino (Princeton, New Jersey: Princeton University Press, 2014) xix. All my sermons in this book build on such glistering passages. For a similar perspective, see Bob Dylan's MusiCares Person of the Year acceptance speech, given at the Los Angeles Convention Center, February 6, 2015: "My songs didn't come out of thin air. I didn't just make them up out of whole cloth . . . . I learned lyrics and how to write them from listening to folk songs . . . . For three or four years, all I listened to were folk standards. I went to sleep singing folk songs . . . . If you sang 'John Henry' as many times as me, ... you'd have written 'How many roads must a man walk down?' too."

in order to become "that strenuous being" (JP 2:2047).⁶ This strenuousness and compression build up the passion of the individual, Christian life. This does not mean, however, that Christians should give up on sociality and the congregation of believers in Christ (JP 5:5972). No, it is just that there can be no "escape into sociality"—because of our indolence and longing for indulgence (JP 2:2010). No, the "Christian stress is: *I* need Christianity" (JP 2:2028). And so our passion is "the pathos of gratitude for [our] salvation" (JP 2:2054). True Christian zeal, then, does not mean "to form an association." That would be a "swindle" (JP 2:2062). It instead means to passionately take up our discipleship and follow Christ wherever he may lead us.⁷

This passionate life is required because "before God the whole world is submerged in evil, it is lost—ergo, mercy can manifest itself only in his being very hard and rigorous with an individual. This gives such individuals an advantage over the others, who go on living securely—in damnation. There is nothing, nothing as consistent as Christianity. O, but how a man resists getting this consistency drummed into his head"

---

6   And so the category of individuality is far "too crucial to risk being bungled . . . . [It] is the category of eternity, and therefore within temporality it is altogether the most strenuous and the most sacrificing. It will be a long time before it gets any power in temporality, where cowardice flourishes" (JP 5:6006). Just think of it, we devote our time and money to doing research on "homosexual necrophilia in mallards"! David B. Williams, "How Birds, Bees and All the Rest Do It," *The Seattle Times*, June 29, 2014.

7   For example: love your enemies, and receive the Lord's Supper (Mt 5:44, 26:26); condemn the uncooperative, and preach the Gospel everywhere (Mk 6:11, 16:15); bind up the wounded, and hate yourself (Lk 10:37, 14:26); judge rightly, and receive the Holy Spirit (Jn 7:24, 20:22). See also Thaddée Matura, *Gospel Radicalism: The Hard Sayings of Jesus*, trans. Maggi Despot and Paul Lachance (Maryknoll, New York: Orbis, 1984); and A. E. Harvey, *Strenuous Commands: The Ethic of Jesus* (Philadelphia: Trinity Press International, 1990).

(JP 3:3770).[8] And so we have the reason for these sermons: to consistently drum into our hard heads the severe mercy of God in Christ Jesus. So read them out loud to yourself and see whether or not they live up to their design—"to place upon us . . . the pressure of the unconditioned, of God's will for us." (JP 4:4939)

---

[8] "Most men . . . fear external opposition and do not know the dreadful suffering of interior opposition . . . . The majority of people live far too securely in life and therefore get to know God so little. They have permanent positions, never strain themselves to the limit, have the comfort of wife and children—I shall never disparage this happiness, but I believe it my task to dispense with all this" (JP 5:5913, 5962). So I too give thanks to God for Kierkegaard's faithful witness: "O Lord, ... we thank you not for the genius of Kierkegaard but for what he did with it. He used the blessing and curse of genius to open the way to faith and to true life for those not so blessed—and cursed . . . . We thank you for his honesty. He called the risk of faith 'risk' and the offense of faith 'offense,' in this daring creation of yours filled with horror and outrage as well as with magnificence and marvel and mystery and humble goodness. We thank you that Kierkegaard's own suffering and anguish defeated neither him nor his faith in you. We thank you, as he did, that he held together in your grace . . . . May we live a little better because of his witness and have a little more life to bring into . . . your promise that you are not God of the dead but God of the living. In Jesus' name we pray. Amen." David Cain, "A Prayer of Thanksgiving for the Witness of Kierkegaard," *Søren Kierkegaard Newsletter*, Number 62 (June 2014): 24.

About the Author

Photo credit: Ty Swenson

The Rev. Ronald F. Marshall has been the pastor at First Lutheran Church of West Seattle since he was ordained there in 1979. Prior to that, he served congregations in Pullman, Naselle and Chinook, Washington; and in Compton, Santa Monica and Pasadena, California. He has been married to Dr. Jane L. Harty since 1972 and they have three grown children: Susannah, Ruth and Anders.

He received a Bachelor of Arts in Philosophy from Washington State University in 1971, magnum cum laude, and was elected to Phi Beta Kappa. He also received a Master of Divinity from Luther Seminary, in St. Paul, Minnesota, in 1975; and a Master in Religion from Claremont Graduate School in 1978.

Pastor Marshall has published over fifty articles, specializing in the thought of Martin Luther and Søren Kierkegaard. Two of his better known essays are "Deathly Evangelism," which has been republished twice—the last time in the online journal, *Semper Reformandum*; and "Eaten Alive," a critique of the way The Book of Jonah has been retold in children's books. He's also published eight sermons. He's a student of Bob Dylan's songs, writings, paintings and movies. In 1989 Pastor Marshall published *Deo Gloria—a History of First Lutheran Church of West Seattle* from 1918–1988; and in 2003, *Wittgenstein Reading the Comics*—a book on philosophical humor. He's also known for publishing, from 1990 to 2002, *CERTUS SERMO: An Independent Monthly Review of the Northwest Washington Synod of the Evangelical Lutheran Church in America*. In 2013 he published *Hunger Immortal: The First Thirty Years of the West Seattle Food Bank*, and *Kierkegaard for the Church*, which was hailed as a high water mark in Kierkegaard research.

Since 2003 he has been teaching a four-week class, open to the public, on "Reading the Koran in Four Weeks"—which he offers four times a year. Hundreds up and down the West Coast have taken this class. For more details on Pastor Marshall, go to flcws.org.

Index

Adler, Adolph 13n18
alcohol 17
Allen, Arthur 135n4
Allen, Thomas B. 268n3
Allen, Woody 385n14
Allhoff, Fritz 194n16
Amram, Megan 361n24
Amazing Grace (hymn) 183
analogies
    ants xxiv, 213
    baseball 45
    bees 126
    bird, terrified xlivn22
    birds, wild xiv
    bottleneck xxxv
    brothel 267
    child, hopping 385–86
    clock xln18
    closed doors 71
    clown xxxvin6
    club 343n29
    criminals, band 328
    dance hall 167, 219
    dirty glass 235–36
    dish 160
    dog dung 161
    dog, frenzied 69
    dog, hunting xliv
    doors 219
    falcon 20n31
    fire xxxix
    fish 46
    fortress 373
    fruit, wormy 140
    ghost towns 171
    goose, floating 78
    grasshoppers 178, 338
    halt 59, 350

Index

hotel 388–93
hover 349n40
hungry animal xxv
hungry monster 57
knot, tie it 57, 326
monster, righteous 90, 103
mountain 215
mouth, shut it 57
nest 389n4
ocean 343
pain in the leg 60
pan 236
peanut-brittle 212
penitentiary xxviii
poker 18n27
pulling plant 71
razors 172
record book 9
reptiles 40
rowing backward 374
scavenger hunt 382n7
serpents xxxiii, 173
ship xln18
shop 370n15
sickbed 188
skull 219–20
socks 345
soldiers 40
sparrow 377n28
straightjacket 195, 290n3
stretcher 238
swimming pool 52
tea leaves xxn2
thorn 266
toad 318n1
troll 374n24
velvet cushions 173
whip xliv
whiskey barrels 205
whore 141

widow 172
yeast, devil's 57

Anderson, G. H. 214n4
anger 63–65, 67
Applegate, Debby 318n1
Arbaugh, George E, George B 333n8
atonement xx–xxxiii, 132, 162–63, 181, 191, 205, 212, 235–36, 240–46
Atwan, Robert 332n3
Auden, W. H. 49
Augustine, Saint 2n3, 99, 199, 347n37, 388n1
Avalos, Hector 361n24
Ayer, A. J. 327n18

Balch, David L. 298n26
Barrett, Lee C. 388n1
Barth, Hans-Martin 299n30
Bartholomew I 384n12
Bartlett, M. Y. 129n12
Bass, Ellen 205
Becker, Ernest 362n28
Beecher, Henry Ward 318n1
Beilby, James 192n12
Bellin, Andy 18n27
Berenbaum, Michael 297 n19
Berg, Peter M. 192n15
Berger, Fred 114n5
Berger, Peter L. 265n1
Bergler, Thomas E. 349n39
Bernard of Clairvaux 62, 272, 332n4
Bible (passages)
    Gn 2:15 227
    Gn 7:21–22 133
    Gn 18:20–32 31
    Gn 22 xxin5, 27–38
    Ex 12:13 131n1, 255
    Lv 14:1–9 63
    Nm 21:4–9 131–41
    Jgs 7:2, 12 159
    Jgs 14:14 58n14

Index

Ruth 1:3–5 30
1 Sam 16:7 11n16, 157
1 Kgs 19:4–15 64–66
Neh 4:20 263
Job 1–2 30
Job 10:16–17 116
Job 13:15 147–48
Job 23:8–17
Job 24:12 178
Job 40:4–5 277
Job 41:8 90
Ps 34:5 73
Ps 49:7–9 260
Ps 51:17 190
Ps 88:18 43
Ps 104:29 232
Ps 119:37 276
Prv 13:24 306
Prv 16:32 242n2
Prv 24:17 274
Is 1:6 98
Is 49:6 165–76
Is 53:4–5 xxi, 254, 256
Is 53:6 267
Is 53:11 70
Jer 12:5 266
Jer 17:9 115
Ez 5:13 133
Ecc 9:18 xxviiin21
Hos 9:7–17 305
Hos 11:9 138, 221
Am 5:19 273
Dn 6:22 134
Mal 4:2 135
Mt 2:16 142
Mt 4:10 88
Mt 5:16 73
Mt 6:12 82–84
Mt 6:21 79
Mt 6:25–33 365–78
Mt 7:1 1n2, 7–8, 15

Index

Mt 7:14 88, 172, 282
Mt 7:17 140
Mt 7:21 76
Mt 8:26 113
Mt 9:38 154–64
Mt 10:16 5
Mt 10:24–25 246
Mt 10:28 219
Mt 10:37–38 33
Mt 13:55 197
Mt 22:37–39 35, 100, 102, 112, 170, 178, 227
Mt 24:13 39–49
Mt 25:10 277
Mt 26:39 100
Mt 26:41 260
Mk 1:15 36
Mk 7:21–22 115, 209
Mk 8:34 222–27
Mk 8:38 181, 270
Mk 9:35 86–96
Mk 10:45 36
Mk 13:32 285
Mk 14:16 228
Mk 16:8 247–53
Lk 6:32 95
Lk 9:62 54
Lk 10:16 161
Lk 10:37 207–208
Lk 10:38–42 331–51, 345n35
Lk 11:28 31, 54
Lk 12:16–21 17, 113
Lk 12:51 216
Lk 14:7–14 345n34
Lk 14:18–20 178, 190
Lk 14:26 97–107, 293n9, 319
Lk 14:33 172
Lk 15 184–94
Lk 16:16 304
Lk 16:23 37, 273
Lk 16:26 277
Lk 17:9 129

Lk 17:11–19 119–30
Lk 18:3–8 164
Lk 19:1–10 17
Lk 20:20–26 363n29
Jn 1:29 255
Jn 3:14–15 131
Jn 3:16 212
Jn 3:19 223
Jn 3:30 74, 108
Jn 3:36 243
Jn 5:22, 27 249, 273
Jn 6:27 145
Jn 6:53 73
Jn 7:24 16–22
Jn 9:6–7 63
Jn 10:29 185
Jn 12:25 108–18
Jn 12:32 71, 110
Jn 12:37 55
Jn 14:19 252
Jn 15:2 261
Jn 15:5 74, 85, 118, 239
Jn 15:12 202
Jn 16:33 213, 268
Jn 20:27 51
Jn 20:29 55, 138
Acts 1:11 283–89
Acts 2:23 xxiin8, 60, 244
Acts 2:37 188
Acts 4:12 214–15, 255, 319
Acts 7:51–58 216–21
Acts 8:35 254–65
Acts 10:34 301
Acts 17:6 265–71
Acts 20:27 281
Rom 1:22–25 224
Rom 5:2 244
Rom 5:3 218
Rom 5:9 162, 220, 226, 255, 319
Rom 7:13 102
Rom 7:18 42, 123, 209, 260

Rom 7:24 106, 180, 232, 250, 286
Rom 8:18 252
Rom 10:9 xliiin21
Rom 10:17 81, 163, 319
Rom 11:22 282
Rom 12:2 208
1 Cor 1:30 45
1 Cor 4:6 195–201
1 Cor 5:7 255
1 Cor 7:29–31 372n21
1 Cor 10:12 177, 279
1 Cor 10:31 122
1 Cor 11:26 235
1 Cor 11:29 228
1 Cor 12:26 174–75
2 Cor 1:4–5 152–53, 251–53
2 Cor 4:8–9 144
2 Cor 4:12–18 219
2 Cor 4:14 253
2 Cor 5:15 107, 108
2 Cor 8:9 37, 116, 139, 192, 234
Gal 1:6 39
Gal 2:20 116
Gal 3:13 44
Gal 5:1 250
Gal 5:16–24 187
Gal 5:17 111
Gal 5:23 12n17
Gal 6:9 81
Gal 6:14 193, 241
Eph 2:8 75, 80, 91, 163
Eph 2:10 174, 227, 251
Eph 4:14 112
Eph 5:2 70, 234
Eph 5:20 120–23
Eph 6:12 177
Phil 2:3 117, 226
Phil 2:10 277
Phil 2:12 39, 174
Phil 2:13 101
Phil 2:15 267

Phil 3:8 128, 280
Phil 3:13–14 280
Phil 3:18 240–41
Phil 4:10 218
Phil 4:13 45, 93, 117
Col 1:13 220
Col 1:20 244
Col 2:14 220, 233, 280
Col 3:2 31, 42
Col 3:16 60, 81, 85
Col 3:17 117, 140, 182, 227
1 Thes 1:3 202–208
1 Thes 2:4 323n9
1 Thes 5:17 164
2 Thes 2:15 177–82, 262
2 Thes 3:5 179
1 Tm 1:19–20 40, 177, 185
1 Tm 4:8 45, 61, 163
1 Tm 6:12 62, 101, 170, 202, 241
2 Tm 3:2–4 106
Titus 2:14 214
Heb 2:14 135
Heb 5:9 115
Heb 8:13 3012n39, 319
Heb 9:14 234
Heb 9:22 280
Heb 9:26 261
Heb 9:28 288
Heb 11:1 31
Heb 11:6 116
Heb 11:16 289
Heb 11:25 232
Heb 11:35–38 217, 246
Heb 12:2–12 65
Jas 1:17 xix
Jas 1:22 75–85
Jas 1:27 85, 174, 236, 239
Jas 2:8 206
Jas 2:21 80
Jas 2:24 80
Jas 2:26 227, 236, 281

Jas 3:16–17 94–95
Jas 4:6 90
1 Pt 2:24 281
1 Pt 4:13 151–52, 246
2 Pt 2:1 257
2 Pt 3:12 288
1 Jn 2:15 205
1 Jn 4:10 244

Bible
    affection for 360n24
    critics disingenuous 359
    eternal 201
    intellectuals 198
    manhandle 360n23
    memorize 201
    prefers blind 362n27
    reading 195–201, 342n28
    voice of God 220, 360
    wax nose 198
    whole 192, 281

Biles, Daniel V. 171n9
The Birds (movie) 369n11
Bly, Robert xvin1, 101n7, 144n2, 389n4
Bodeen, Jim 317n1
Books as Weapons 378n30
Bonhoeffer, Dietrich 87
Bovon, François 333n10, 337n18
Braaten, Carl E. 302n41
Braunstein, P. 187n9
Brecht, Martin 82n3, 300n33
Bretz, J. Harlan 329n26
Brokering, H. F. 124n7
Brown, John W. 54n10
Browning, Christopher R. 298n27
Brueggemann, Walter 360n23
Bruner, Frederick Dale 365n1
Bunyan, John 54n11
Burk, Greg 380n1
Burklo, Jim 382n7
Burr, William Henry 197

Index

Cahill, Thomas 328n23
Cannon, Lou 56n12
Cappelørn, Niels Jørgen 335n16, 336n17
Carlin, George 341n24
Carlson, Edgar M. 247n1
Carroll, Colleen 382n8
Carter, Warren 331n2
Catcher in the Rye, The 96
Chester, Chris 377n28
Childs, Brevard S. 256nn2–3, 324n13
Christianity, Christians
    admission 383n11
    admonition 165
    actions, required 80
    anguish xxv, 290
    assassinated 266
    atonement xx–xxxiii
    battle xxvi, 169, 187
    building 390
    certain 56, 70
    changed 78, 383
    childhood xxxixn13
    childlike xxx, xlv
    comfort 152–53
    commands 43
    condemnation 165
    corrupted xlv
    cross 240–46, 270
    crowds 165–76
    dangerous 172
    death xxx, 37, 125, 136, 168, 220
    defined 262
    devil 143–44, 269
    dialectic xxxii, xxxvi, 34, 141
    difficult xxxvi, 172
    disgust xl, 294–95
    dismaying 4n6
    dotage 203
    doubt 51–62
    earth, clean 227
    eternal 4n6

Index

existential 383
faith 59, 163–64, 174, 237, 241–42, 373
false teachers 257–59, 284
fast 117–18, 140–41, 194
fear of God 244
feelings 59, 107
fight 241, 376–77, 385
gentle xlvi
grace xxxi, 56, 210
happiness xxxviiin8, 205, 358
hell 272–82
heterogeneity xxix, xxxix
hexed xlv
hip 321n4
hope 383n11
hypocrisy 96
ideal xxxi, xli, xliv
inclusive xliiin21
intensity xxxv–xxxvi
inversion 204, 346
jest xxxn22
joy 211, 237, 332n5, 375
Judaism obsolete 245
judging 9
law, royal 206–208
light of heart 245
little 166
losers 154–56
love 202–208, 221
man's interest xxx
mediocre 14, 378, 383n11
miracles 55
motto 366n6
mythology 213
negative pedagogy 274
new 382–83
nice 290n4
nonsense 375n25
objective 329
obey 347
offense 366

old 112, 319, 330n27, 377n28, 379–86
orthodoxy 322n9
passion xxn2
peace 143–44, 216–17
Pentecost xxxv
personal 230
phony 358n20
prayer 124, 154–64
preaching xx–xxxiii
prosperity xxx
punishment xxix
rare 291n5
razors 173
real 69
rebellion, verbal 268
rebels 265
reform 356–59
remnant 165–76
repentance 71, 183–94
revealed 89
reverse 346
satisfaction xxxi
self-accusation xxvi, 190
self-denial xxix, xxxviiin12, 86, 100, 222
self-hatred 97–107, 108–18, 222
self-important xxxi
signs 284–86
simple 375–76
size 166
slogan, bad 218
spirit xxxviii
spreading thin 357n15
stagnant xxxvn2
striving xxx, 241
substitutes xxix
suffering xxx, xxxi, 123, 152
Sunday 211, 322n8
temptations 40
terror xxxixn13
test 27, 55, 145–47, 323n9
thanksgiving 119–30

    thick, into the 343n29
    thin 173
    tomorrow 375n26
    torment 149
    tough 378n30
    toxic 380n1
    troublers 268
    understanding 229
    watered-down 79
    Word, eternal 89
    Word, implanted 80
    Word, powerful 205
    Word rules 162
    world, new 268–69
    world, upset 265
    world, off track 267
    wretched life 173, 218
Christmas 142–53, 209–15, 216–21
church 259, 385n14, 388–89
Clemente, Sonja xviii
Clines, D. J. A 147n4
Cobain, Kurt 364n33
Cobb, John B. Jr. 52n3, 381n5
cogito xxxvn1
cognitive dissonance 75
cognitive therapy 63n2
Collins, John J. 199n12
Cooper, Terry D. 5n9, 9n13
Cosby, Bill 190n11
Costin, Carolyn 194n16
Couture, Suzette 114n5
Craddock, Fred B. 345n34
Crenshaw, James L. 27n1
Crowell, E. F. 151
Crumb, Robert 385n14

Danker, Frederick W. 333n10, 345n34
David 155
Davies, Pete 134n3

Dawn, Marva J. 164n4
Deardorff, Daniel xivn1
Deedat, Ahmed 241n5
DeHaven 172n16
depression 63–74, 101, 115
Dershowitz, Alan M. 190n11
Descartes, 52, 64n2
DeSteno, D. 129n12
Dever, Mark xxvn17
DeYong, Kevin xxxviiin8
Diamond, Jared 186n6
Dongell, J. 39n1
Dostoyevsky, Fyodor 119
Doyle, Michale W. 187n9
Dragseth, Jennifer Hockenbery 325n13
Dunning, Stephen N. 326n15
Dylan, Bob 8n12, 390n5
Dyson, Michael Eric 10n15
Dyson, Rosemary 296n17

Easter 247–53
Eddy, Paul R. 192n12
Edwards, Jonathan 279
Edwards, Jr., Mark U. 298n25, 300n36, 309n60, 310n68
Eller, Vernard 361n26
Elliott, Charles H. 337n19
Ellul, Jacques 60n18
Emmanuel, Steven M. 361n26
Emerson, Ralph Waldo 73
Emmet, Dorothy E. 362n29
enjoyment xl, 211, 332n5, 358n18
The Envelope (dance) 372n19
Epicurus 53n9, 111
eternal 334–51, 373n22
Evans, C. Stephen 363n30

Fatoohi, Louay 241n5
fear 40–41
feminism xxviin19
Feuerbach, Ludwig 381n2
Fingarette, Herbert 17n23
finitude xxxvii, 330, 332n5, 369
Fitch, David E. 322n9
Flew, Antony 305n46
Fogelin, Robert 53n7
footnotes 352n1
Forde, Gerhard 71n5, 79n2, 98n2, 306n49, 313n75
Forell, George Wolfgang 297
forgiveness 82–84
Foster, Pastor R. L. 232
Fox, Matthew 60n16, 381n4
Francis, Pope 342n27, 383n12
Frei, Hans 60n18
Fretheim, Terence E. 324n10
Frey, Stephanie 334n12

Gilmore, Mikal 8n12
Gitlin, Todd 187n9
God
    alternates 123
    beats us xlvn26
    combat within xxiv, 138, 220
    common sense 158
    damns sinners 272–73
    depend on 128, 232
    divine child abuse 257
    does all 242
    enmity 158
    feared 272–73
    fight for us 263–64
    fool 66
    help, swift 220
    knocks around xlv
    love 162
    Master 370n15
    need of 231

pressed to his heart 70
provider 371n16
pulls us 91, 182, 191, 243
reckless 154
reconciled 44, 92–93, 287
rock 264
silence before 243–44
speaks 196, 220
stupid 147
sublimity 212–13
target 264
tortures xlvn26
twofold 282
usurp 34
Word, as 59, 88, 196
worsens life 294
wrath 37, 71, 91, 133, 138, 140, 174, 189, 212, 243, 259

Gopnik, Adam xxiiin16
Grayling, A. C. 350n42
Green, John 388n2
Grimm, Harold J. 137n7
Griffin, David Ray 320n3
Gritsch, Eric W. 297, 306n48
Grundtvig, Nikolai 13n18
Guthrie Jr., Shirley C. 236n1

Habakus, Louise Kuo 137n6
Haecker, Theodor 114n6
Hafenreffer, Matthew 274–78
Hagen, Kenneth ln29
A Humanist Bible 350n42
Hampson, Daphne 352–64
Handey, Jack 278
Hanson, Pastor Rolf 232
Harrington, Anne 115
Harrowitz, Nancy A. 307n54

Hart, Johnny 302n39
Harty, Jane L. xix
Harvey, A. E. 391n7
Hauerwas, Stanley xxxvn1, 1n1, 201n15, 257n4
Haughey, John C. 17n24
Haugk, Kenneth C. 10n15
Hawks, Annie Sherwood xxxiin23
Haynes, Stephen R. 298n25
Hefling, Charles xxii–xxix
Hefner, Blake R. 331n2
Heidegger, Martin 387n1
Heinecken, Martin J. 328n23
Hench, John B. 378n30
Hick, John 214n3, 381n3
Holland, Julie 49n3
Holland, Mary 137n6
Holmer, Paul L. 326n16
Holmio, Armas K. E. 299n29, 310n67
Holsclaw, Geoff 322n9
Horney, Karen 93n6
Howard, Cameron B. R. 360n23
Hudson, Heather xix
Hughes, Robert 323n9
humans
    adulterous 233
    aliens 288
    animality xxvin18, xxxviii, 251, 362n28
    better off 239n4
    buoyant 38
    busyness 112–13
    capricious 223
    certitude 55
    comparison, bad 224
    corrupt 194
    crucified 242
    damnable knaves 103
    deranged 364n33
    desoul 369n12
    despise Gospel 147
    disability 104
    disobedience 179

Index

disordered 43, 180, 339n21, 367n7
dullness 103
easy life 342n29, 392n8
excuses 190
faithless 185
fear of God 244
fight least 242
fight self 101, 184, 242
foolish 127, 145
forgetful 123
fragile 126
heavy-minded 114–15
horrible times 268
illusions xlii
impenitent 267
imperfect 245
individually 167
ingratitude 119, 133
jealousy 175–76
laziness 104
light-minded 113–14
light weight 225, 372–73
lovability 191
love 202–208
lowly 372
multiplicity 111–12
natural xxvi, xxviii, xl, 56, 212, 218, 287
needing God 231
new 93, 251, 288, 383
new drives 251
obese 117–70
obey 347
off-scourging 217
ostentation 365n2
perfection 11n16, 157
personal 230
pleasures 111
poison 230
positive image 89, 99
pride 105
Promethean 362n28

Index

    provoke God 273
    read people 18n27
    reckless 104
    repeat Supper 245
    scared straight 133
    self-absorbed 175
    self-control 12n17, 111, 346
    self-defense 199
    self-judging 13n19
    self, old 251
    sexual filth 185–88
    shine 73
    sinful xxviin19, 104, 196, 231
    strange 349
    stress 49n3
    suffering 220, 246
    tested 259
    traveler 373
    unable 191
    upside-down 200
    vipers 286
    whirlpool xln18
    wretched 180
Hybels, Pastor Bill 170

Irrational Man (movie) 385n14

Jenkins, Philip 380n1
Jenson, Matt xxviin19
Jenson, Robert W. 44n2, 324n13
Jesus Christ
    anger at us 249
    cross unattractive 270
    death–death 221, 226, 234
    disarm torment 234
    eternal 252
    exalt him 128

    follow him 75, 108
    friend 227
    greatest 287
    half of 37
    hiding place 214
    humiliated 106
    light-hearted 114n5
    mad 205
    mediates two 205, 235, 255
    moves to mercy 263
    need of xxxii, xxxiin23
    offense 203–205
    our righteousness 45
    price 193
    Priest against God 61, 162
    prodigal son 193n15
    ram 38
    ransom 36–37, 241
    refuge 45, 180
    return 283–89
    sacrifice xxvii, 61, 70, 91, 116, 174, 192, 212, 220, 241
    satisfaction 37, 138, 163, 180–81
    steadfast 179–81
    stranger 210
    substitute 44, 92, 163, 181, 254–55
Job 178–79, 360n24
John the Baptist 155
Johnson, Ben xix
Johnson, Doug xix
Johnson, Luke T. 174n19, 345n34
Johnson, Samuel 141n11
Jonah 167
Judaism 290–313
    anti-Semitism 301, 311n73
    The Corsair 291n6
    family 293
    God's bad news 309n62
    God's warning 311
    harsh mercy 308
    humanism 294
    Jesus rebukes Jews 307

Jewish piety 367n7
Mary, Jewish 300
obsolete 245
pastoral 312
rigorousness 310
stubborn 308
supersession 302n39
wrath, God's 309
welfare of the Jew 307n55, 309
judgment 1–22
    cautious 11–12
    cold 2
    collaborative 21
    consequences 15
    constructive 19
    double standard 16
    indirect 15
    Jesus judged 3–4
    precipitous 13
    religious 14
    revenge 8
    slow 21
    tentative 19
    wisdom 5–6
Judith and Joanna story 344n34
Just, Arthur A. 331n3

Karp, Jonathan 313n75
Kass, Leon R. 348n38, 368n10
Keillor, Garrison 183
Keillor, Steven 239n4
Kennedy, Eileen xix, 332n3
Kenny, Anthony 105n8
Kierkegaard
    alone 167
    amen 243
    anguish xxv
    atonement xx, xxxii
    authorship 334, 353n3
    bewitchment 356n12

Bible 200, 305n45
Buddhism 375n26
busy, bad 77–78, 333n5
Christmas 210
Christ's return 286
church 370n14
comparison, bad 224
counterfeits 356
criticism of 352–64
crowds 349n39
dialectician 10
double-minded 335–36
easy life 58, 342n29
eccentric 203, 349n41
effervesce 41
enemies xliv
eternal 219
explosion 293
faith 137, 148–51
fanaticism xiv, xlv, 218
fat 169
father xlin19
grace 210
heaven opens 219
hell xxviin20
Holy Spirit xxxixn14
inquisitiveness 342n27
inverted dialectic 218
joy 114, 205, 211
Judaism 290–313
leap 181
life, my xlv
Lord's Supper 48
love as duty 130, 202–208
Lutheran ln29, 110, 137n7, 210, 217, 266, 295, 328n23, 366
madness 3n5, 6
missionary xxviin20, xxxvn2
natural man 288
praise 2n3
prayer xix, xlivn22, 110–15, 156, 243, 392n8
preaching 24–26, 188, 218

reasons bad 57
restlessness 179, 182
rigorousness xiv, xxxvin6, xln19, 203, 250, 310, 380
self, collect 112
self-denial 59, 95–96
self-doubt 59
self-hatred xli, xliiin22, 102
self-will, bad 232
showdown 170n7
sickbed 188
slog in bog 217
slogan, bad 218
society, against 170
speak to self 26
squander 332n5
strive 82
suicide 155
suffering 220
Sunday 211, 322n8
superfluity 372
thanksgiving 121
Tersteegen 341n25
testing 323n9, 340n22
universalism 355–56
vale of tears 267
venture 346
violence, physical 380n1
weaned 343n30
will crushed 59
works 371n17, 390–91
world seems good 267
wrath of God xxivn17
writings
  An Occasional Discourse 333–51
  Fear and Trembling 28–31, 97
  Judge For Yourself! 210–12
  Practice in Christianity 110–15
  Upbuilding Discourses in Various Spirits 222–27
  Works of Love 95–96, 130, 202–208
  Kierkegaard for the Church (review) 314–17

419

King, Rodney 56n12
King, Stephen 57
Kinnaman, David 1n2
Kirmmse, Bruce xix, 335n16, 365n2, 368n8
Kittelson, James M. 297
Kleinhans, Kathryn A. 325n13
Klinghoffer, David 294n11, 311n71
Kluck, Ted xxxviiin8
Knitter, P. 214n3, 292 n8
Koenig, Richard E. 173n17
Korsmo, Dale xix
Krugman, Paul 65n3

Lambiase, Jacqueline 186n4
The Leftovers (HBO) 389n4
Levenson, Jon D. 293n11
Levy, Bernard 168n4
Lien, Harry J. 158
Lincoln, President 119
Lindberg, Carter 296n17, 307n54j
Linehard, Marc xxiin6
Locke (movie) 336n17
Loeschen, John R. 299n30
Longgood, William F. 126n10
　love
　　faith, opposed 34
　　judging 5n7
　　madness 6n10
Luckmann, Thomas 265n1
Lüdemann, Gerd 197
Lusterman, Don-David 186n7
Luther, Martin
　agitatur ad Christum 43, 60, 127, 189, 260, 279
　anfechtung 66
　anti-Semitism 311n73
　aspra veritas 65, 90
　assertions 89
　babblers 20n31
　bum, lazy 68

Index

Catechism, Large 47, 82, 87, 117, 143, 186, 217, 229
certainty 57
chastening 122–23
Christianissima saeveritas 304
Christ's return 286
comparison, bad 225
conversion 20n33
crazy beggars 53
cross, praise to utmost 240
cross sweetens 72
crude 155
deus placatus 287
doubt as plague 53, 55
ecclesiola 169
effrontery 54
expiation xxin6
extra nos 36, 107, 179
faith 237
feelings 60, 107
fists 68
forgiveness 47
ghost town churches 171
Gott mit Christum bezahlen 255
hell 20n32, 275
hotheads 18
Ich trit an deine stat 44
incurvatus in se 36, 180
ingratitude 120
ivory palaces 169
James: straw 75–76
The Jews and Their Lies 297–304
joy 237
Judaism 245, 290–313
judgment 8n12, 238–39
knight of faith 59
love 221
nudam vocem 30, 60
opposites 217, 218
prayer 47, 61, 69, 124–28, 164
preaching 23, 25n4, 67, 137, 146
prophet 266

    quottidie converti 185
    razors 173
    reason 141, 159, 325n13
    rebels 265
    repentance 183
    rubbish 382n6
    self-hatred 100
    serpent of salvation 139
    simul iustus et peccator 261–62
    sinful 231
    size 166
    softies 65
    soldiers 40
    suffering 221
    thanksgiving 124–28
    trial 28
    truth, hard 65, 90
    universities xxxivn1
    vexation of life 144, 217
    will evil 58
    Word, regulates 125
    works 46, 79–80, 94, 140, 207, 270–71
    world, unlike it 61, 237
    wrath of God xxin6
Luther, Martin Franz Julius 298
Lutheran Campus Ministry xxiin8

Machado, Antonio 103
Marino, Gordon 100n6, 390n5
Marius, Richard 307n54
marriage 204
Marsden, George M. xxxvn1
Marshall, I. Howard 333n10
Marshall, Ronald F. xxn1, xxin4, xlviiin28,
    23, 72n6, 92n3, 107n12, 111n1, 140n10,
    258n5, 278n3, 334nn11, 13, 352n1, 356n13,
    359n21, 360n23, 368n9, 378n29
Martensen, Hans 13n18
Martin, Clancy 342n26
Martin, H. V. 114n6

Marty, Martin 297
Matheson, George 186
Matura, Thaddée 391n7
May, Rollo 37n1
McCracken, Brett 321n4
McGinn, Bernard 332n4
McGinn, Colin 53n8, 105n9
McLeod-Harrison, Mark S. xliiin21
McMillan, Margaret 113n7
medicines 63
Merton, Thomas 200n14
Meyer, Carl Stamm 295n15
Miles, Jack 327n21
Miller, William 285
Milton, John 278
Missourians 54
Mollenkott, Virginia R. 1n2
Møller, Peder 13n18
money 207–208
Monroe, Dave 194n16
Montgomery, David R. 329n26
Moonies 173
Morris, Desmond 112n2
Moses 154–55
Mowinkel, Sigmund 209n1
Mulder, Jr., Jack 375n26
Munk, Kaj 216n1
Mynster, Jacob 13n18

Nehushtan 136
Nelson, Christopher A. P. 365n2
Nelson, Jon and Alice xix
neophilia 112
Nesvig, Philip M. xix
Neuhaus, Richard John 112n2, 349n41
Neusner, Jacob 294n11
New Testament therapy 65
Nixon, President 112
Ngien, Dennis 312n74
Niebuhr, H. Richard 193n14

Noah 167, 170, 368

Oberman, Heiko A. 66n4, 297
objectless anxiety 36–37
O'Connor, Richard 64n2
Oden, Thomas C. 382n8

Packer, J. I. xxvn17
pastors
    add nothing 160
    ears 161
    flabby 357
    lament 172
    losers 162
    modern 379–80
    pretty people 159
    shabby 357
    slowly formed 252
    talkers, empty 232
    toad 318n1
    uncouth bumpkins 158
    zealous in the Word 20
Pattison, John 370n14
Paul, Saint 155
Paulson, Steven D. 206n6
Pelikan, Jaroslav li–lii, 197n4, 254n1
Percy, Walker 364n33
Perkins, Robert L. 317n1, 353n3
Perlstein, Rick 335n13
Peterson, Eugene 98n1, 171
Pfatteicher, P. H. 142n1
Pious XII, Pope 197n8
Pitt, Brad 113
Porter, T. M. 166n2
Poussaint, Alvin F. 190n11
Price, Reynolds 60n17
process theology 381n5
Promise Keepers 166
prophets 48

Quash, Ben 257n6
Quine, W. V. O. 327n18
Qur'an 35, 241, 277, 380n1

Rasmussen, Joel D. S. 295n14
Ray, Inna Jane xxiin8
Reichenbach, Bruce R. 381n5
Reichert, Tom 186n4
repentance 46
revelation xxvi
Richburg, Keith B. 186n8
Roberts, Kyle 320–30
Robinson, Anthony B. xxxiiin24
Root, Andrew 330n27
Root, Damon 352n1
Rosemond, John 306n50
Rudelbach, Andreas xli, 13n18
Rupp, Gordon 299
Russell, Bertrand 52n4
Rutledge, Fleming xxxiiin24

Sacrament of the Altar 48, 73, 84, 94, 117, 128–29, 152, 181, 193, 201, 205, 214, 221, 226–27, 228–39, 245, 251, 263, 270
Sagmoen, Jeff xix
Salinger, J. D. 96
Santayana, George 53n9
Sawyer, J. F. A. 256n1
Scanzoni, Letha 1n1
Schaller, Lyle E. 169n5
Schmid, Heinrich 276n2
Schnekloth, Clint 330n27
Schoeman, Roy H. 302n40
Schramm, Brooks 308n58
Schuller, Robert H. 99n3n5
science 348n38
self-esteem movement 337n19
self-reliance 73
sermons xxxiv–liii, 23–26

enrage 25
   living voice 24
   slaughter 25n4
   unpopular 26n5
   upsetting 24
Shakespeare, William 202–203
Sherman, Franklin 296n17
sickness 63
Simemon-Netto, Uwe 297n20
Smith, C. Christopher 370n14
Smith, James K. A. 320n3, 324n10
Smith, Laura L. 337n19
Smith, Mitzi J. 335n14, 338n20, 344n34
Socrates 15n22, 141
Solomon, Andrew 63n1
Solomon, King 225–26
Sontag, F. 173n18
Spanish flu 134
Spinoza 117
Spong, John Shelby 197, 278n4, 283, 382n6
Sponheim, Paul R. 194n17
Stark, Rodney 310n65
Steere, D. V. 333n9
Steitz, Christopher R. 199n10
Stephen, Saint 216–21
Stjerna, Kirsi I. 308n58
Storbakken, Rollie 314–17
Stransky, T. F. 214n4
Strawson, Peter 52n6
sub specie aeternitatis 117
success 63
Summer of Love (1967) 187
Super Size Me (movie) 167
Sutcliffe, Adam 311n71
Swanson, David F. 10n14

Taylor, Robert 105n10
temporality xxxvii, xln18, xlii, 42–43,
   46, 149, 178, 181, 210, 218, 223, 288, 330, 332n5,
   334–51, 370

Index

Thielicke, Helmut 183
Thomte, Reidar 352–53, 355n9
Tillich, Paul 26n5, 52n22, 331n1, 337n18, 341n24
Tudvad, Peter 295n13

uncertainty 55
Ufer, Karl A. 158
Ungar, Debi & Irwin 187n9
Updike, John 356n13
United States of America 66n3, 364n33

viaticum 238
Vidu, Adonis xxiin8
von Rad, Gerhard 32n2
Walls, J. 39n1
Walsh, Sylvia xxn1, xxiin7, 328n25, 363n30, 366n3
Ward, Michael 257n4
Warner, Michael 279n6
Washington, Dinah 216
Watkin, Julia xlin20
Watson, Richard 64n2
Watts, Isaac 246
Weaver, Joanna 332n3, 333n6, 340n22, 345n34
Webb, Val 51n1
Wessel, the Rev. James H. 88
Westberg, G. E. 172n15
Westphal, Merold 292n8, 320n3, 324n12, 326n18
Wiener, Peter F. 299
Wilken, Robert Louis lin30
Williams, David B. 390n6
Willow Creek Church 170
Wilson, Edward O. 319n2, 348n38
Wilson, Derek 301n38
Winter, Michael 191n12
Witten, Marsha G. xxviin19, 184
Wolff, Hans Walter 138n8
Wolterstorff, Nicholas 194n16

Yoon-Jung, David 295n14

Zacchaeus 174

www.ingramcontent.com/pod-product-compliance
Lightning Source LLC
Chambersburg PA
CBHW030515230426
43665CB00010B/615